JAPANESE STUDIES
IN THE UNITED STATES:
THE 1990S

Japanese Studies Series XXVI

JAPANESE STUDIES
IN THE UNITED STATES:
THE 1990s

Japanese Studies Series XXVI

1996

THE JAPAN FOUNDATION

Association for Asian Studies, Inc.
1 Lane Hall, University of Michigan
Ann Arbor, MI 48109

Printed by Braun-Brumfield, Inc., Ann Arbor.

© 1996 by   The Japan Foundation
Ark Mori Building
1-12-32 Akasaka
Minato-ku
Tokyo 107
JAPAN

Published 1996
Printed in the United States of America

Library of Congress Cataloging in Publication Data

Japanese Studies in the United States: The 1990s.

  p. cm. — (Japanese studies series ; 26)
  Includes bibliographical references and index.

  ISBN 0-924304-27-8

  1. Japan—Study and teaching—United States. I. Kokusai Kōryū Kikin.
II. Association for Asian Studies. III. Series.
DS834.95.J356 1996
952'.007'073—dc20   96-22246
                                          CIP

Contents

List of Tables

CHAPTER TWO

CHAPTER THREE

CHAPTER FOUR

CHAPTER FIVE

CHAPTER SIX

CHAPTER SEVEN

CHAPTER EIGHT

CHAPTER NINE

CHAPTER TEN

APPENDIX B

APPENDIX C

Preface

In 1992, the Japan Foundation initiated a survey of recent trends in Japanese studies in North America in cooperation with the Association for Asian Studies. The information provided by the survey was compiled in January 1995 as the *Directory of Japan Specialists and Japanese Studies Institutions in the United States and Canada*, and is also used to analyze research trends presented in two volumes: *Japanese Studies in Canada, the 1990s*, and this volume, *Japanese Studies in the United States, the 1990s*, which succeeds the *Japanese Studies in the United States, the 1980s*, published in 1984.

Now in the 1990s, the age of interdependency and globalization, the field of Japanese studies in the United States seems to have undergone considerable changes in terms of both quality and quantity.

We believe this volume provides a vivid picture of the current state of Japanese studies in the United States, and hope that it will be useful in promoting collaborative efforts and networking among the people who are engaged in activities related to Japan.

We wish to express our deep appreciation and thanks to Professor Patricia G. Steinhoff of the University of Hawaii, who devotedly directed and concluded this total directory project, and the Association for Asian Studies, which undertook not only the planning and data-gathering for the survey but also the compilation and publication.

Kusaba Muneharu
Executive Vice President
Japan Foundation
December 1995

Introduction

This analytical study of the state of Japanese Studies in the United States in the 1990s culminates a project that combined the preparation of a new edition of the *Directory of Japan Specialists and Japanese Studies Institutions in the United States and Canada* with a three-part questionnaire survey of Japan specialists, Japanese Studies institutions, and the librarians who manage Japanese collections. When we began discussing the project with The Japan Foundation, the Ann Arbor staff and I thought that updating the directory would be a relatively simple task, so we readily agreed when the Foundation asked that we also carry out a survey of the field. By combining the directory entry forms with the survey, we hoped to reduce the burden on respondents by gathering basic information once rather than twice, to raise the survey response rate through the incentive of a directory listing, and to make the project more efficient and cost-effective by combining the data collection, tracking, and data entry processes. The jury is still out on whether we achieved any of these lofty goals, because the combined task turned out to be much more complex than we had imagined.

The basic intent of the survey was to replicate one The Japan Foundation had commissioned in the early 1980s through the Social Science Research Council-American Council of Learned Societies Joint Committee on Japanese Studies. While making sure that all the old questions were included, the Foundation was very receptive to adding new questions that would help us explore the central issues that seemed to be emerging in Japanese Studies in the 1990s. In particular, we added both a separate questionnaire for the librarians who manage Japanese collections and an extensive set of questions about research materials and the research process to help us understand the library needs of Japan specialists in the United States.

I have approached the data analysis as I would any social science investigation, using the data available to explore issues and pursue ideas. My strategy is always to try to see the traces of larger social processes that enable us to make sense of small bits of evidence, and to reconstruct a clearer picture of what is happening. The processes that define Japanese Studies in the 1990s are described in Chapter One, and traced throughout the data analysis in subsequent chapters. The result is thus rather different from a simple survey report.

I have used several analytic strategies to place the survey data into a larger context. The availability of data on many of the same questions, reported in surveys of Japanese Studies completed in the 1970s and 1980s, has made it possible to put the current situation in historical perspective.[1] Whenever possible, I have tried to incorporate survey data reported in earlier studies into the tables presented in this study. In addition to showing quite clearly how specific aspects of the field have changed, this practice also serves to make the older data more readily available. All of the earlier surveys prior to the directory projects were published only as limited edition reports distributed to participating institutions and other interested parties, and they can now be found only in a few libraries and personal collections. To standardize our references to these studies, I consistently cite them by the date of publication of the survey report, even though the data were obviously collected a year or two earlier and the table headings in the original report may give a different date.

I have not tried to incorporate the discussion or conclusions of previous survey reports into the present study. I have simply reproduced the numbers they reported (usually in simple percentages) in order to make quantitative comparisons. Mindful of how useful these earlier survey reports have been both for this assessment of the field and for all the occasions when statistics about Japanese Studies can help to make a persuasive case for the support of particular programs, I have also tried to present full tables of data from the present study whenever possible. However, this volume does not contain many of the appendices and lists that characterized earlier survey reports, because such information is now contained in the three volumes of the directory. One very clear indicator of the growth of Japanese Studies is that it now requires four fat volumes to cover what fit into one thin one just twenty-five years ago.

An unusual feature of the whole series of surveys of Japanese Studies in the United States is that they have attempted to produce a census of all Japan specialists and all Japanese Studies institutions, rather than following the usual survey research practice of surveying only a selected sample. This approach has made the task bigger and the cost greater as the number of specialists and institutions has increased, but it offers much more opportunity to see just how the field has developed and changed. Of course none of the surveys achieved the impossible goal of getting a usable survey form back from every single potential respondent, but they all achieved response rates that represent a very high proportion of the known or estimated total, thanks to the excellent cooperation of Japan specialists and Japanese Studies institutions with each study. I therefore will treat the absolute number of cases in each survey as a reasonably comparable estimate of the actual total at the time of that study, even though they all undercount the elusive perfect total.

For the present study, these figures correspond to the total number of Japan specialists and Japanese Studies institutions in the United States that were included in the 1995 edition of the *Directory of Japan Specialists and Japanese Studies Institutions in the United States and Canada*. A somewhat

---

[1] These studies are discussed and cited fully in Chapter 1.

smaller but still substantial number responded to the survey questions that were attached to the directory questionnaires. Because I have used a variety of devices to expand the analysis beyond the basic survey numbers for particular parts of the analysis, and also because not everyone responds to every question even when they do turn in a survey, I report the relevant sample size in the discussion and on the tables for each part of the analysis. A basic description of the data collection procedures is included in the introduction to the directory, and a more detailed technical description of the data collection and survey sample appears as Appendix A of this volume.

I have tried to keep the statistical basis for the analysis at the level of percentage comparisons and an occasional comparison of means or averages, but sometimes the reader will be asked to suffer through an explanation of how the data were collected or transformed, in order to get to that simple comparison. I found it impossible to relegate such methodological detail to the appendix, or even to hide it in footnotes, because the logic of the data manipulation is often essential to understanding the interpretation. In some cases, it is the key point of the analysis. I am also using so many different kinds of data, from so many different questionnaires, that it seemed safer to explain the data as they were being used for a particular analysis. The reader with no tolerance for such matters, who is willing to trust my interpretations without following the logic and seeing the evidence, can simply read Chapters One and Eleven.

Acknowledgments

In the course of this analysis I have developed a deep appreciation for the Japan specialists and research staff who carried out the earlier surveys of Japanese Studies in the United States. Their genuine concern for the development of Japanese Studies was an inspiration, and their careful documentation of methodological details made it possible for me to match their data and make more appropriate comparisons. I hope that I have provided enough detail for the next person who takes up this task in the new century.

I want to thank The Japan Foundation for their generous support of this project and for the intellectual freedom they gave me to pursue it as I thought best. The Foundation staff in both Tokyo and New York have been unfailingly helpful and understanding, despite many delays in completing the task. I want to thank the officers and staff of The Japan Foundation in Tokyo (Mr. Takashi Ueda, Mr. Munehiro Waketa, Ms. Sanae Tada and Mr. Jun Wada, all at various times with the Japanese Studies section) and the two heads of the New York office with whom I have worked—Mr. Masahiko Noro and Mr. Natsuo Amemiya. Particularly warm thanks are due to Mr. Satoshi Yura and Mr.

Michael Paschal of the New York office, who have managed all of the communications for the project between Tokyo, Ann Arbor, and Honolulu.

The Association for Asian Studies has provided excellent support. Current AAS Secretary-Treasurer John Campbell, former Secretary-Treasurer Peter Gosling, administrator Carol Hansen, comptroller Carol Kelingos and former comptroller Carol Hackett have been a real pleasure to work with. The Association's Northeast Asia Council has solidly supported the project over the years, for which I am grateful. The AAS staff members who have worked directly on the project have been absolutely wonderful even when the work dragged on far longer than it should have. Donna Ashton supervised all the details of data collection, processing, printing, and project administration with great efficiency and equally great charm; Ronald Peterson used his wizardry to keep everybody's equipment running and meet every one of my impossible programming requirements, while Jennifer Hastings and Birgit Villeminey entered and checked the data. We are all aware that the project was only possible because of the fine cooperation we received from Japan specialists and Japanese Studies staff who filled out very long questionnaires and responded to follow-up queries from the AAS staff.

While the superb staff in Ann Arbor handled the data collection and production of the directories with occasional on-site visits from me, I did the data analysis and writing of this volume in Honolulu. University of Hawaii graduate students Ida Yoshinaga, Kimberly Scott, and Heather Pelant helped with data cleaning and data management chores, and John Hirano provided essential computer support and figured out how to move the data smoothly between two database management systems and a statistical analysis package. Suzanne Culter read an early draft of the manuscript and provided valuable feedback. Back in Ann Arbor, Joanne Heald copyedited the manuscript and saved me from many minor embarrassments, and Jon Wilson did the book design, final formatting, and production of the volume for printing. The wonders of computer technology have made all of this possible, but I am responsible for any errors that cannot be blamed on the computer.

Finally, my husband William Steinhoff has watched over my welfare during this long project, gently prodding me to change plans, extend deadlines, and catch up on my sleep when my ambitions outran my physical capacities. My deep thanks to everyone.

Patricia G. Steinhoff
Honolulu, June, 1996

PART I:

OVERVIEW

1

Themes of Change

This assessment of Japanese Studies in the United States in the 1990s is the latest in a long series of reports on the state of the field that have been produced under various auspices since the 1930s. Such a record of systematic research is apparently unique among area studies fields in the United States, some of which have never been studied at all. Although each study differed in purpose, scope, and scale, the existence of this tradition of periodic assessment makes it possible not only to offer a snapshot of the state of Japanese Studies in the United States in the mid-1990s, but to examine how the field has been changing over time.

The first known study specifically on Japan[1] was a survey carried out in 1933 by Yasaka Takagi of Tokyo Imperial University, covering individuals who were engaged in or "interested in" Japanese Studies, and academic institutions offering courses related to Japan. It was commissioned by the American Council of the Institute of Pacific Relations, which published it in 1935.[2] Conducted by a sympathetic and knowledgeable observer who hoped to increase American understanding of Japan, the survey revealed starkly how limited the resources for the study of Japan were in the United States prior to the war. While the U.S. government may have carried out some surveys in conjunction with the creation of Japanese language training programs during the war, none are known to be in the public record. There also do not seem to be any surveys from the first two postwar decades, when returning veterans went to graduate school on the G.I. Bill as the first cohort of American-trained Japan specialists.

The first postwar study of the field was carried out in 1968–69 by the newly formed Social Science Research Council-American Council of Learned Societies Joint Committee on Japanese Studies and published in 1970. It

---

[1] Jansen discusses a 1928 survey of all accredited academic institutions in the United States by the Institute for Pacific Relations, which asked about any course coverage of China and Japan, but the Takagi survey seems to be the first devoted entirely to Japan. Marius B. Jansen, "History: General Survey," in The Japan Foundation, *Japanese Studies in the United States: Part I, History and Present Condition,* Japanese Studies Series XVII, ed. by Marius B. Jansen (Ann Arbor: Association for Asian Studies, 1988), pp. 11–13.

[2] Yasaka Takagi, *Japanese Studies in the Universities and Colleges of the United States* (Institute of Pacific Relations, 1935), pamphlet, 50 pp.

included a survey of Japan specialists, a compilation of data on Japanese Studies resources from various sources, and a series of narrative reports on the state of Japanese Studies in particular disciplines.[3] This assessment was intended to assist the Japanese Studies community in finding new funding sources after the major supporters of the field in the immediate postwar period had begun to turn their attention elsewhere. It is the first study whose findings we will use for comparative purposes in this report, and we will refer to it subsequently as the 1970 SSRC-ACLS report.

The second postwar study, carried out by Elizabeth T. Massey and Joseph A. Massey for the Subcommittee on Japanese Studies of the U.S.-Japan Conference on Cultural and Educational Interchange (CULCON) and published in 1977, supplemented the 1970 report with a survey of Japanese Studies programs at academic institutions.[4] This study was carried out as part of a binational effort to assess the institutional base for Japanese Studies in the United States and American Studies in Japan, through the newly created institution of CULCON, a joint creation of the two governments whose mission was to improve cultural and educational interchange. We will use this study for some comparisons of institutional strength, and will refer to it subsequently as the 1977 CULCON report

By the 1980s The Japan Foundation had become a major source of support for Japanese Studies in the United States. As part of an initiative to survey the state of Japanese Studies throughout the world, the Foundation commissioned several different kinds of research on Japanese Studies in the United States. In other countries and regions these various kinds of research were combined into a single package because the scale of Japanese Studies was so small, but by that time Japanese Studies in the United States had become sufficiently large and complex that each component became a separate study. The Japan Foundation first commissioned a survey of both specialists and academic institutions through the SSRC-ACLS Joint Committee, which was carried out by a commercial survey firm in 1982 and published by The Japan Foundation in 1984.[5] We will refer subsequently to this study as the 1984 Japan Foundation report. In the late 1980s The Japan Foundation commissioned a series of essays on the history and present state of Japanese Studies in the United States in various disciplines, which was edited by Marius

[3] SSRC-ACLS Joint Committee on Japanese Studies, *Japanese Studies in the United States: A Report on the State of the Field, Current Resources and Future Needs,* (New York, February, 1970, mimeographed), 369 pp.

[4] Elizabeth T. Massey and Joseph A. Massy, *CULCON Report on Japanese Studies at Colleges and Universities in the United States in the Mid-70s,* prepared for the Subcommittee on Japanese Studies, U.S.-Japan Conference on Cultural and Educational Interchange, New York: The Japan Society, Inc., March, 1977).

[5] The Japan Foundation, *Japanese Studies in the United States: The 1980's,* (Tokyo: The Japan Foundation, 1984).

Jansen and published in 1988.[6] The Japan Foundation also generously underwrote the cost of producing a comprehensive directory of Japan specialists and Japanese Studies institutions in the United States and Canada, which was carried out in cooperation with the Association for Asian Studies under the editorship of Patricia Steinhoff and published in 1989.[7] When comparisons are made to data collected for this project, we will refer to it as the 1989 directory study.

In conjunction with a major update of that directory for the 1990s, The Japan Foundation commissioned another survey of Japan specialists and Japanese Studies institutions, which was carried out in 1993–94, again in cooperation with the Association for Asian Studies and under the editorship of Patricia Steinhoff. The updated directory was published in 1995,[8] and the present volume constitutes the survey report for the United States.[9] Data from the present study are cited as 1995, which is the publication date of the directory in conjunction with which they were collected.

Since this report is primarily an analysis of survey data, we have not made use of the two sets of essays on the state of Japanese Studies in various disciplines that were noted above as part of the series of previous studies of the field. They are narrative accounts of areas of research activity that acknowledge the seminal contributions of particular scholars and trace changes in the focus and quality of research.

We have tried very hard to make this volume not simply a mechanical report of survey results, but a more interpretive analysis of the underlying processes of change that will continue to shape Japanese Studies into the next century. The current situation and these processes of change can better be understood if we first review very briefly the history of Japanese Studies in the United States.

[6] The Japan Foundation, *Japanese Studies in the United States: Part I, History and Present Condition.* Japanese Studies Series XVII, ed. by Marius B. Jansen, (Ann Arbor: Association for Asian Studies, 1988).

[7] The Japan Foundation, *Directory of Japan Specialists and Japanese Studies Institutions in the United States and Canada, Japanese Studies in the United States, Part II,* Japanese Studies Series XVIII. ed. by Patricia G. Steinhoff, 2 vols. (Ann Arbor: Association for Asian Studies, 1989). A follow-up study of Japan Foundation grantees in the United States was also carried out at the same time and under the same auspices. It was published as The Japan Foundation, *Japan Foundation Grantees from the United States, 1972-1986, A Follow-up Study,* (Ann Arbor: Association for Japan Studies, Inc., 1989).

[8] The Japan Foundation, *Directory of Japan Specialists and Japanese Studies Institutions in the United States and Canada, Japanese Studies in the United States,* Japanese Studies Series XXIV, ed. by Patricia G. Steinhoff, 3 vols., (Ann Arbor: Association for Asian Studies, 1995).

[9] A separate survey analysis of the Canadian data was prepared by Professor Suzanne Culter of McGill University and published as Suzanne Culter, "Survey Results: Japan Specialists and Japanese Studies Programs in Canada," in The Japan Foundation, *Japanese Studies in Canada: The 1990s,* Japanese Studies Series XXV, ed. by Suzanne Culter, (Ann Arbor: Association for Asian Studies, 1995).

BACKGROUND OF JAPANESE STUDIES IN THE UNITED STATES

Marius Jansen has carefully documented the history of Japanese Studies in the United States in two chapters in the 1988 volume of essays commissioned by The Japan Foundation.[10] He summarizes the early stages of this development as follows:

> The first [stage] was entirely derivative, . . . drawn from the writings produced by Europeans. A second stage was based upon residence in Japan by Americans who had found temporary or permanent employment in Meiji Japan. Around the turn of the century, a few institutions and individuals tried to introduce treatment of Japan into the curricula of leading academic institutions on the East and West coasts. The crisis of World War II brought a decisive fourth stage in which young Americans were trained in Japanese language for service in war and Occupation duties. After the guns were stilled and the Occupation of Japan became routinized, United States graduate programs began to produce specialists able to man the "area" programs that proliferated throughout the United States.[11]

In quantitative terms, Japanese Studies in the United States is overwhelmingly a postwar phenomenon, traceable directly to the American experience in World War II. The 1970 SSRC-ACLS report made this point by contrasting its findings with the 1935 Takagi survey that listed 101 persons involved or interested in the study of Japan, observing that

> Obviously the list was grossly inflated. Only about sixty of those named were actually involved in college or university instruction, and many of these only peripherally.[12]

Although the 1935 study found 25 academic institutions with some activity in Japanese Studies, only eight (Harvard, Yale, Columbia, Berkeley, Washington, Stanford, Hawaii, and Northwestern) offered any Japanese language training.

> This was uniformly the work of native instructors and, almost without exception, the responsibility of one man per institution. There were no proper teaching materials. Training was available only to advanced graduate students and only after they had persuasively demonstrated their need for it.[13]

The 1970 report's indictment of the prewar situation continues:

---

[10] Marius B. Jansen, "History: General Survey" and "Stages of Growth " in The Japan Foundation, *Japanese Studies in the United States: Part I, History and Present Condition*, Japanese Studies Series XVII, ed. by Marius B. Jansen, (Ann Arbor: The Association for Asian Studies, 1988).

[11] Jansen, "History: General Survey," p. 7.

[12] SSRC-ACLS 1970 report, p. 11.

[13] SSRC-ACLS 1970 report, p. 12.

Instruction in Japanese studies other than language was largely conducted by non-professionals: returned missionaries, specialists in international relations or men trained in other fields who had developed a Japanese interest late in their academic careers. Most were generalists who taught about both China and Japan. Few read or spoke Japanese. Among the 101 persons on the extended list eight were native Japanese and these comprised almost the entire corps of language training personnel in the United States. There were only thirteen Americans sufficiently trained in the language to be able to use Japanese materials in their research. Of these, five were still students....Such was the state of Japanese studies in 1934: a field dominated by part-time practitioners and amateurs who offered only the bare beginnings of serious professional training at the college and university level.[14]

The report also noted that the five American students who could use Japanese in their research were forced to obtain their advanced training in Japan and Europe.

By contrast, the 1970 SSRC-ACLS report counted 500 Japan specialists (including advanced graduate students) and 135 colleges and universities that offered some instruction on Japan. As Jansen notes,

Much of this development took place under the umbrella of "area" programs that tried to bring together teaching and research in a number of disciplines. History tended to come first, as history had always, or usually been taught in geographically discrete (usually country) units. Disciplines more insistent upon methodology—economics, sociology, anthropology, and to some extent political science—were slower to recognize the need of Japan specialists among their numbers. The inter-disciplinary area program offered a way around academic parochialism.[15]

This postwar critique of the prewar condition of Japanese studies reveals a number of themes that continue to reverberate in the field today. These include an emphasis on Japanese language competence and formal graduate training in Japanese Studies as the defining characteristics of the professional Japan specialist, the corresponding need for academic programs in Japanese Studies staffed by qualified professional Japan specialists in order to produce more such specialists, and the organization of the study of Japan under an interdisciplinary area studies model. This model "fit" the perspective of the core humanities disciplines (language and literature and history) first engaged in the study of Japan, and also offered a way to circumvent the lack of interest or active resistance to Japanese Studies found in other disciplines. Despite the growth that had been achieved by 1970, the underlying condition of Japanese Studies was still that of an exotic specialty based on mastery of a very difficult and obscure language. The subject was only available for advanced study at a

[14] SSRC-ACLS 1970 report, p. 12.
[15] Jansen, p. 22.

small number of elite academic institutions, and even there, it was set apart from the normal array of disciplines and existed in its own isolated compartment as a haven in which Japan specialists could talk essentially to each other.

By 1950 area studies programs for Japanese Studies had been established at six institutions (Yale University [1945], the University of Washington [1946], the University of Michigan [1947], Harvard University [1947], Columbia University [1948], and the University of California at Berkeley [1949]) and soon scholars with wartime language training and postwar graduate training began to expand academic offerings on Japan at these and many other institutions.[16] As the supply of returning veterans with prior experience in Japan began to dry up, they were followed by a new cohort of graduate students who were enticed into Japanese Studies by U.S. government fellowships under the National Defense Education Act, a federal program that supported academic programs in language and area studies in order to improve the national resource of persons who could speak and read less common languages. The area studies model was replicated at more institutions as the number of specialists expanded, but most institutions had only one or two Japan specialists on their faculty and thus could not hope to offer a full interdisciplinary program.

There were also some Japan specialists in the professional fields of business, law, and education by the 1970s, as the academic market tightened and persons with an interest in Japan looked to other ways of making a living with specialized skills for which there was little demand. The number of major Japanese Studies programs in the United States had grown to ten, a status reinforced by their receipt of endowment gifts of one million dollars each from the new-created Japan Foundation.

In the early 1980s the growth curve seemed to have flattened out, and the 1984 Japan Foundation report saw declining opportunities for academic employment in Japanese Studies, balanced only by the need to replace the impending retirements from the immediate postwar generation of specialists. Even then, they expected that only half of the positions vacated by a retiring Japan specialist would be filled by another Japan specialist. Yet within a few years, a boom in interest in Japan swept the country in the wake of the realization that Japan was an accessible and fascinating culture, a site of new economic opportunities, and a growing economic rival of the United States. A new cohort entered Japanese Studies with rather different motivations, interests, and expectations. This sudden "loss of irrelevance" of the study of

---

[16] Jansen, p. 21.

Japan had a major impact on the field, and the contours of those changes are only now becoming clear.[17]

PROCESSES OF CHANGE

The present study picks up the story at this point, and traces these new developments into the mid-1990s. Five major processes characterize the changes in Japanese Studies over the past decade: growth, differentiation, specialization, normalization, and internationalization. Each appears in many aspects of the field and will recur in our discussions in nearly every chapter. To set the stage for that analysis, we will here define and briefly describe each process.

Growth

The most basic theme of the postwar development of Japanese Studies is its sheer growth. Whether measured in absolute numbers or percentage increases, we will document growth in virtually every aspect of Japanese Studies, using a variety of baselines for comparison. Although it is obvious that Japanese Studies has been growing throughout the entire postwar period and that the earliest decades will show the greatest percentage increase because the prewar base was so low, it is also true that during the 1970s and early 1980s the growth of Japanese Studies was generally viewed as leveling off or reaching a saturation point that could not be overcome. The boom of the late 1980s thus came as something of a surprise. It constituted a new phenomenon based on a changed status for Japanese Studies that had not really been anticipated, even though by then there was ample evidence of how much Japan itself, and its status in the world, had changed.

Theoretically, growth could merely replicate existing patterns on a larger scale without any internal change, but that does not seem to have been the case in Japanese Studies. Instead, concomitant with growth in numbers we see the twin processes of differentiation and specialization, plus evidence of normalization and internationalization. Growth has been the engine driving these other processes of change, in large measure because this period of growth was fueled by new perceptions about the significance and utility of the study of Japan, and thus new demands for a more relevant Japanese Studies. The relationships between growth and the other four processes are also reciprocal. The pressures to differentiate and specialize lead to growth, just as the consequences of normalization and internationalization produce more growth.

[17] Patricia G. Steinhoff, "Japanese Studies in the Postwar United States: The Loss of Irrelevance," *IHJ Bulletin,* (Winter, 1993).

To understand the directions that future growth is likely to take, we must therefore look not only at the simple volume and trajectory of growth, but at how other processes precipitated by growth are shaping the field in new ways.

Differentiation

Differentiation refers to the development of new forms of Japanese Studies, as practiced by Japan specialists and represented in institutions. Differentiation simultaneously expands Japanese Studies into new areas of study, and makes Japan specialists less like one another in training, knowledge, and outlook. Some differentiation can be accommodated within the area studies model, but ultimately it is a force that pulls away from the common ground and the humanities-based standards that the interdisciplinary language and area studies model emphasizes. By studying what is new in Japanese Studies, and how segments of the field differ from each other, we can begin to see how the field is likely to be configured in the near future, and what its new needs will be.

Although we will examine many aspects of differentiation in Japanese Studies in the course of this analysis, the most fundamental one must be stated right at the outset: Japanese Studies in the United States is no longer simply about academic specialists working in academic institutions. While academics may still constitute the majority in our survey (perhaps in part because we are better equipped to find them), non-academic Japan specialists have become too large a component of the field to ignore. Much of our analysis therefore involves trying to determine how academic and non-academic Japan specialists are similar or different, and what other factors may divide or unify them.

Specialization

Specialization is closely related to differentiation, but highlights the phenomenon of deeper concentration on a narrower area that characterizes each of the different fields of study into which Japanese Studies has been dividing. If differentiation refers to the surface qualities of expansion and variety, specialization refers to the depth with which each specific variation of Japanese Studies is expressed. Specialization comes about as each discipline or profession makes its own demands on Japan specialists, forcing them to relate the study of Japan to the central concerns of their discipline, and to provide, create, and build upon knowledge about Japan that is specifically tailored to the needs and interests of that discipline. Because the disciplinary audience uses different criteria to evaluate the Japan specialist's knowledge and contributions than the interdisciplinary Japanese Studies audience, the specialist is increasingly forced to orient his training and research output to one audience at the cost of losing the other. This in turn enhances the sense of differentiation, because the contributions of Japan specialists are less easily shared across disciplinary and professional boundaries. These tensions affect many parts of the Japanese Studies community today, but are perhaps most visible and acute in the social sciences. We will pay particular attention to this phenomenon in our analysis.

Although specialization ultimately traces back to the training and professional requirements of individual Japan specialists, these processes can also be identified in the institutional forms of Japanese Studies, in the array of goods and services that Japan specialists produce, and in the networks that specialists create and maintain. Yet specialization is not an unchecked, unidirectional process, because many integrative forces help sustain a sense of common identity among Japan specialists in different disciplines and occupations. Variations in the extent of specialization can help us understand additional dimensions of the future of Japanese Studies in the United States, and suggest ways to cope with it.

Normalization

Normalization refers to the fact that the study of Japan has gradually been transformed from an exotic, elite enterprise completely removed from everyday American life into a more ordinary subject that is accessible to or incorporated into the non-elite mainstream. Unquestionably, the impetus for the normalization of Japanese Studies stems from the new relevance of Japan to American society. Normalization can only come about when the number of Japan specialists is large enough that they become accessible to non-specialists, but it is also very much a function of the external demand for knowledge about Japan. It is thus not simply a matter of growth, but of where that growth is located, and how it reaches new and different audiences.

Normalization fundamentally changes the purpose of Japanese Studies in the United States, and raises new questions about the meaning of specialization. It is therefore imperative that we understand the extent of normalization of Japanese Studies in different spheres of American society, in order to assess its impact on what Japan specialists and non-specialists will do in the future, and what kinds of training and resources they will need. Exploring this issue will also help academic Japan specialists redefine their role in a changing environment.

Internationalization

Japanese Studies in the United States is by definition "international," but during the past decade it has become more internationalized, in ways not previously contemplated. Although internationalization is a bit harder to tease out of our survey data than some of the other processes, it is clearly a development that will increase steadily in the future. There are two general dimensions to this new internationalization. The first concerns the much greater movement of people, products, and ideas between Japan and the United States, in directions and for purposes that would have been hard to imagine twenty-five years ago. This development has ramifications for the sense of proximity, familiarity, and equality between the two countries and their people, which in turn affects both Japan specialists and the role of Japanese Studies in the United States. In this sense it is closely related to normalization.

A second dimension of the internationalization of Japanese Studies concerns the introduction of third countries and their people into what had been largely conceived as a two-way relationship between the United States and Japan. As Japan itself has become more internationalized, both externally and internally, Japanese Studies in the United States has also become more internationalized. Parallel to the changes in Japan's position in the world that have made Japan itself a more international phenomenon for study, during the same period of time Japanese Studies in the United States has risen to international stature in its scale and quality. These simultaneous developments affect where people go in order to study Japan, and how they frame and contextualize their object of study, both of which in turn alter the content and aims of Japanese Studies in the United States. As with normalization, the extent and characteristics of internationalization must be grasped in order to understand what American-trained Japan specialists will do in the future, and what this implies for their training.

We have outlined these five processes in advance partly so that we may employ the terms as a convenient shorthand in the analysis that follows. Our descriptions of each process also constitute implied research questions and issues for careful reflection, to which we will return at the end of the survey analysis for a final assessment.

CHAPTER ORGANIZATION

Despite the centrality of these processes of change to the story this report has to tell, to organize the entire survey report in terms of the five processes as separate and sequential inquiries would distort its basic purpose and serve only to confuse the reader. It would also mask the important message that the processes are intertwined and interactive. We have therefore relied on the more traditional distinction between institutions and specialists that every study of the field has used as its basic data collection and presentation strategy. However, because of both the real changes in the field and the methodological complexity of this study, we have found it necessary to work back and forth between these two realms, first presenting a broad overview of each in Part I, and then taking a deeper look at their internal complexities in Parts II and III. In particular, we have postponed the discussion of academic institutions and their Japanese Studies programs until the larger context in which they now function has become absolutely clear.

Since overall growth is central to any understanding of Japanese Studies in the United States in the 1990s, we begin our analysis in Part I with two chapters that document the scale and scope of growth at the most general level. Chapter Two, "A Demographic Profile of Japan Specialists," examines growth in the overall number of Japan specialists, and then explores the demographic composition of the field in terms of age, gender, occupation, and discipline. We introduce another aspect of the growth of Japan specialists, and project the changes into the future, by examining most of these same variables among current doctoral candidates in Japanese Studies. In addition to using simple comparisons with the published data from previous surveys, we exploit the common framework of data collection used in the two Japan Foundation-sponsored directory studies to examine recent changes in the demographic characteristics of Japan specialists and doctoral candidates in Japanese Studies in greater detail.

Chapter Three, "The Spread of Japanese Studies" provides an overview of the institutional growth of Japanese Studies, beginning with overall changes in the geographic dispersion of Japan specialists. We then examine the expansion of Japanese Studies at academic institutions, followed by the movement of Japan specialists into new types of non-academic institutions. Although the focus of this chapter is on institutions, we use two devices to broaden its scope beyond the limits of the survey data we collected directly from institutions. The first device is to base this overview on the institutional affiliations reported by Japan specialists, which captures the full scope of the academic and non-academic institutions at which they are employed. The second device is to project the information about academic institutions at which Japan specialists are employed onto a national database of over 3,000 academic institutions in the United States, which enables us to examine in more detail the kinds of institutions to which Japanese Studies now extends.

The main theme of these two chapters is growth, but along the way we point to evidence of processes of differentiation, specialization, normalization, and internationalization. We take up these processes more directly in the next three chapters that comprise Part II, while documenting further evidence of growth in more specific areas.

Chapter Four, "Expertise and Credentials of Japan Specialists," traces out patterns of differentiation and specialization in the course of exploring Japan specialists' substantive areas of expertise, language competence, and academic credentials. This chapter relies both on the information specialists provided for their directory listings and on the survey questions that were completed by a slightly smaller sample.

Chapter Five, "Professional Activity of Japan Specialists," explores the themes of differentiation and specialization in the professional lives of Japan specialists. We look at how Japan specialists spend the time they devote to Japan, their access to Japan, their networks of professional relationships in Japan and the United States, and how those relationships are maintained across time and space. We also examine what Japan specialists must do in order to keep up with their fields. This chapter relies primarily on survey questions, as opposed to the directory information provided by Japan specialists. It pursues further the forms of differentiation and specialization that are appearing in Japanese Studies, and also points to the growing internationalization of the field.

Chapter Six, "Research and Publications of Japan Specialists," begins with a look at the broadening audience for Japanese Studies and an overview of the publication output of Japan specialists. We then look more closely at the different kinds of research Japan specialists pursue, as additional evidence of differentiation and specialization, as well as the normalization and internationalization of Japanese Studies. We summarize these findings with a categorization of six types of research on Japan, and explore the emerging relationships among the specialists who do them. We conclude with a look at where research on Japan appears in print, and how well the intended audience is able to find it through the resources for searching that are now widely available in American libraries.

The first four chapters of Part III look at various aspects of academic Japanese Studies and its institutional presence. Chapter Seven, "Academic Courses on Japan," looks at growth in the number and types of area and language courses on Japan, and the increase in enrollments, using data provided by institutions to point to evidence of both growth and normalization. The chapter then returns to the survey of Japan specialists for a look at their satisfaction with teaching and teaching materials.

Chapter Eight, "Academic Programs in Japanese Studies," examines the size and scope of Japanese Studies programs at the undergraduate and graduate levels, using classification schemes developed and applied in earlier studies. We look at turnover and growth in programs, and then trace changes in the range of institutions awarding doctoral degrees related to Japan. We carry this analysis forward to the institutions where current doctoral candidates are studying to find hints of normalization even in this most specialized level of training.

Chapter Nine, "Staffing of Japanese Studies Programs," examines the most critical resource for the academic study of Japan, the Japan specialists who staff the programs. By comparing staff listed by institutions with the Japan specialists listed in the specialists' directory, we are able to analyze some of the barriers to program expansion at institutions with small Japanese Studies programs, as well as gain new insight into the complexity and diversity now present at institutions with large Japanese Studies programs.

Chapter Ten, "Libraries, Other Activities, and Funding of Japanese Studies Programs," assesses the state of various resources for the study of Japan in the United States, from library resources to study abroad programs and outreach services, and concludes with an assessment of funding for Japanese Studies. This analysis, too, points to the differentiation, specialization, and normalization of Japanese Studies.

Chapter Eleven, "Japanese Studies in the 1990s and Beyond," returns to the five main themes of the analysis to present some general conclusions about the state of Japanese Studies in the United States at the mid-point of the 1990s and where it seems to be heading for the remainder of the twentieth century. In the course of this summary we identify several problem areas which will require creative attention and new resources to position the field for the new century.

2

A Demographic Profile of Japan Specialists

THE NUMBER OF JAPAN SPECIALISTS IN THE UNITED STATES

For at least the past twenty-five years, we have been trying to count the number of Japan specialists in the United States and find out more about them. Through the early 1960s we "knew" how many Japan specialists there were in the United States, because the overall number was so small and the professional networks were so close that something resembling a total could actually be counted. Since then we have had only estimates, based on various lists and surveys that documented growth but could no longer keep track of it. The problem has gotten bigger as the number of specialists has increased, but even the earliest study in 1970 agonized over who to include and how to estimate the missing segment. In order to understand what the numbers mean, and particularly if we want to compare the findings of the series of studies to see what has changed, we have to know how the data were collected.

In any survey, before definitions can be applied to individual cases there has to be a pool of potential cases and some way of locating them. In the United States there is no national association of Japan specialists to which everyone belongs. If there were, even though the boundaries of that fictional association would also be problematic, we could simply count its membership list. In the absence of such a comprehensive professional association, every study has had to find other ways to identify the constituents of that elusive category called Japan specialists. Each began with a list of known or possible Japan specialists to which a questionnaire was sent, but also tried to cross-check that list to some extent by counting the number of people teaching Japan-related courses at American colleges and universities. The core of each mailing list was generally the Association for Asian Studies membership list, which includes information on each member's country or geographic area of specialization. Each study also added to that list, based on other lists kept by

17

various organizations with an interest in Japan. For the 1989 and 1995 directories, only half of the final mailing list was derived from the AAS list.

One might think that finding a pool of people and sending them a questionnaire solves the problem, but that is only the beginning. The lists always include some cases that seem marginal, especially after the questionnaires come back. The more one tries to makes the initial list inclusive in order to get a "complete" count, the more decisions the study has to make later about where to draw the line.

There is considerable general agreement about who is or is not a Japan specialist, but as with most social phenomena, the edges are never as clear-cut as the center. There is high agreement about how to define the mainstream of Japanese Studies and how to apply that definition to individual cases, but problems arise about how far to stretch the definition to include cases that only marginally meet the established standards. Worse yet, the definition itself may be contested by cases that clearly do not fit the established criteria, but seem to have some other claim to inclusion. Those problematic cases at the margins often turn out to be harbingers of change in the field as a whole; they may be thrown out of one study, but they will come back to haunt the next one. If we understand the enterprise not simply as describing Japan specialists at one moment but as trying to understand the development and future of the field, then we have to pay particular attention to these changing boundaries.[1]

Table 2.1 shows how the four major postwar surveys of Japan specialists have defined their parameters, and the numbers they have reported. To avoid confusion, we refer to each of the studies by its publication date, rather than the year in which the data were collected, which is generally a year or two earlier. None of the numbers given can be taken at face value as a true measure of either the absolute size or the relative growth of the field, but they give us some useful estimates and also some hints about how the internal composition of the field has changed.

The 1970 and 1984 studies defined their range as academic Japanese Studies and basically limited their pool to Japan specialists at academic institutions, but found themselves sneaking in a few people outside of academics whose presence as Japan specialists could not be ignored. The widening discrepancy between institutional staff lists and questionnaire mailing lists also attests to the inappropriateness of limiting studies to academics by the mid-1980s. Consequently, the 1989 and 1995 directory studies widened the occupational boundary and purposely included Japan specialists outside of academics. Hence the mailing lists for the questionnaires

---

[1] I have discussed elsewhere the problem of how these selections help to define and redefine the field of Japanese Studies. See Patricia G. Steinhoff, "Defining Japanese Studies in the 1990s: Who Knows? Who Wants to Know?" The World of Japanese Studies Guest Column, *Japan Foundation Newsletter*, (January, 1995).

were much larger and "softer," forcing the studies to grapple with more boundary problems within the data. This shows up as a larger gap between the size of the mailing list and the size of the final survey sample. These differences must be accounted for when comparisons are made with the findings from the earlier studies.

Table 2.1. Procedures and Number of Japan Specialists Counted in Four Major Surveys of the Field, 1970–95*

Year	Range of Specialists Included	Mailing List	Academic Staff Lists**	Survey Sample
1970	Academics	597	416	332
1984	Academics	1,535	781	841
1989	Academics and non-academics	4,009	936	1,224
1995	Academics and non-academics	4,442	1,452	*1,638 1,552

* 1970 information from 1970 SSRC-ACLS Report, Appendix 3, p. 107; 1984 information from 1984 Japan Foundation Report, Appendix 1, pp. 89-93; 1989 information from 1989 Directory of Japan Specialists and Japanese Studies Institutions in the United States and Canada, vol. 1, pp. ix-xi.

**The 1970 SSRC-ACLS report contained a roster of individuals at specific institutions. The 1984 Japan Foundation report gave the number of positions at each institution, calculating part-time positions as 1/2. We assume that the half positions were mostly occupied by different individuals. Although we could not account for any half positions concealed in the whole numbers within one institution's total, we did compensate for 56 identified fractional totals by counting each as one additional person. The 1989 and 1995 figures are based on a count of names on staff lists reported for institutional directory entries. They undercount language instructors, who are not listed by some large institutions in their directory entries.

Since the 1989 and 1995 directory studies used essentially the same lists and methods, their figures can be compared directly. Ironically, since the 1995 study was able to follow up the 1989 sample quite effectively, it produced new boundary problems of age and occupation: a substantial sample of retired Japan specialists whose presence is significant in contemporary American Japanese Studies, but who must be treated carefully in the data analysis if we are to get an accurate picture of the present and future of the field.

The insertion in Table 2.1. of two different numbers for the survey sample of the 1995 study points to the boundary that is currently most problematic, and the only one where we have chosen to draw the line of exclusion for the survey analysis, rather than dealing with the issue within the analysis. That line concerns the geographic limits of "Japanese Studies in the United States." When we were first approached by The Japan Foundation in the mid-1980s to do a directory of Japan specialists in the United States, the Americans involved persuaded the Foundation that because of the overlapping networks it made more sense for the directory to encompass both the United States and Canada. For purposes of this study we have excluded the Canadian portion. However, the overlap in intellectual networks between the United States and Canada in the 1980s was simply a hint of problems to come.

In the 1989 directory, there were many Japanese nationals listed who were employed as Japan specialists in the United States, just as there have been in all previous studies. There was never any question about the inclusion of these individuals. Now, five years later, some of them have returned to Japan. On the surface they are no longer Japan specialists in the United States, although they may be publishing and participating in other U.S.-based intellectual activities. Similarly, the 1989 directory included a fair number of American Japan specialists with addresses in Japan. At that time, we presumed that they were in Japan temporarily. By 1995, however, a substantial number of American Japan specialists have taken regular employment positions in Japan. Some teach at Japanese universities, while others are employed by Japanese or foreign companies. Many of them remain very active in American intellectual networks concerned with Japan, and are likely to return to the United States in the future. The same kind of interchange is now taking place on a smaller scale between North America and Europe, and also with other countries of Asia. Of the 86 persons in the 1995 directory who were living and working outside the United States when the data were collected, 51 were in Japan, 25 in Canada, and 10 in other countries.

When five percent of American Japan specialists are living and working outside the country and the number is likely to increase in the future, the geographic boundaries of the United States no longer define the perimeter of Japan specialists' spheres of activity in a stable way. Our decision for the directory was to include such people unless they have left the United States permanently, so that we can continue to track them in the future and try to understand this aspect of globalization. Since the count of 1,224 American Japan specialists for 1989 also includes some people who were then living and working outside the United States, the comparable figure for 1995 is 1,638, even though it is a bit problematic to compare that figure with the 1970 and 1984 numbers. Although these expatriates remain members of the intellectual community of Japan specialists in the United States, they fall outside the geographic parameters necessary for the present study of what is happening inside the country, and we have therefore reluctantly excluded them from the survey analysis. Except where otherwise indicated, the sample we will use is the 1,552 Japan specialists who currently reside in the United States. Since the exclusion is based on the address reported for the directory, this number may include persons who are temporarily in Japan, but who have listed a permanent address in the United States.

Having made all the necessary protestations and qualifications, we can now take the leap of faith and compare these rather rubbery numbers. In very rough terms, the 1995 figures represent a one-fourth to one-third increase over the 1,224 U.S. participants in the 1989 directory study, depending upon which 1995 figure you use for the comparison. The 1995 numbers are also nearly double the 841 respondents in the 1984 Japan Foundation survey of Japan specialists, four and one-half to five times the 1970 SSRC-ACLS survey sample of 332, and nearly four times its roster of 416 names. These numbers are all solid counts of real people who received a questionnaire and returned it to the study, so they constitute minimal estimates of the actual number of Japan specialists in the United States at the time of each survey.

What we do not know is the percentage of those who did not return questionnaires that also should be counted. The mailing list numbers for 1970 and 1984 probably offer a reasonable basis for estimating the size of the missing component of the field. That certainly cannot be said for the 1989 and 1995 mailing lists, which contain many more people that no one, including the individuals themselves, would define as Japan specialists.[2] While we cannot estimate the missing component very accurately for 1989 and 1995, since the procedures were reasonably comparable for the two studies we can investigate the change in the actual directory sample. That is, we can ask who was retained in the 1995 directory, who was lost, and who was added. Of the 1,224 Japan specialists in the United States who appeared in the 1989 directory, nearly 89 percent also appear in the 1995 directory, but four percent are not currently residing the United States and thus have been excluded from the present study. Of the 136 persons who did not reappear in the 1995 directory, 39 are deceased, 4 have returned permanently to Japan, and 18 no longer consider themselves active Japan specialists. The project was unable to locate only 75 persons, or 6.1 percent of the 1989 total.

This is a remarkably high rate of follow-up for a national sample of such size after an interval of five years. It reflects both the strong social networks linking Japan specialists and the intensive follow-up measures taken to locate this group. Those follow-up efforts were much more effective for academic Japan specialists, because the concurrent survey of institutions provided independent information on their academic staff, and missing specialists often

---

[2] For the 1989 directory, the Canadian data were collected separately by a Canadian team so the mailing list figure represents just the American data collection, but it includes an unknown number of persons on the U.S. mailing list who were working in Canada. This number cannot be reconstructed, but some estimate can be derived from the report in the introduction to the 1989 directory that among the completed questionnaires from the U.S. study there were 70 persons working in Canada. For 1995 the figure of 4,442 represents actual mailings within the United States. It does not include either mailings to Canada (715) or mailings to addresses in other countries and therefore underrepresents the increase from the 1989 mailing list.

turned up on a different staff list.[3] Japan specialists who were not currently employed as academic faculty constituted only a quarter of the 1989 directory entrants, but we were 3.6 times as likely to lose track of them by 1995.

We can also utilize the internal composition of the growth over these last two studies to examine change, by comparing entries from individuals who are new to the 1995 directory sample with those who also appeared in the 1989 directory. While comparison of the overall demographic parameters of the two directories shows strong continuity because of the high proportion of carry-over entries, the strategy of internal comparison of new and carry-over entrants reveals some trends that will shape the future of the field for the coming decade.

The carry-over entrants from the 1989 directory comprised two-thirds of the Japan specialists listed in the 1995 directory. Nearly a quarter of the 513 new entrants were unquestionably new to the field: they completed their doctorates after the first edition of the directory was published in 1989. While some of the others also acquired their expertise on Japan too late for the earlier edition of the directory, most were missed in 1989 either because we did not reach them effectively, or because they chose not to complete the questionnaire.[4] In examining the demographic characteristics of Japan specialists we will utilize comparisons with previous studies whenever possible, and will use the strategy of internal comparison of the new and carry-over groups for further clarification of where the field is heading. We will look first at the basic demographic factors of age and gender, and then relate these to occupational and disciplinary factors.

AGE AND GENDER

Despite the steady infusion of new specialists, the Japanese Studies community of North America is graying rapidly. In 1970 about half of the Japan specialists were 40 or under, but today less than one in eight is that young, and Japan specialists who are over 60 now account for nearly a third of the total. As shown in Table 2.2, there is now hardly anyone in the 21-30 age cohort, which accounted for 11 percent of all Japan specialists in 1970, but had dropped to 2 percent in 1983. Twenty-five years ago it was not uncommon for Japan specialists to complete a doctorate and begin teaching while they were still in

---

[3] Although we had initially suggested that we would reprint the 1989 entry if we did not receive an update from the individual, in the end we were reluctant to do so until we had verified that the person remained alive and active as a Japan specialist. This was accomplished by direct telephone contact if the person did not appear on the updated staff lists provided by Japanese Studies institutions that had submitted entries for the 1995 edition. A national telephone directory on CD-ROM helped immensely in the tracking.

[4] About ten percent of the new entrants had submitted a questionnaire for the 1989 directory, but their entries were not included then, either because the questionnaire contained too little information, or because they did not yet meet the criteria for inclusion.

their twenties. Today, higher disciplinary and language training standards make that an extremely rare occurrence. In the expanding academic market of the 1960s there were also regular academic positions available for those who had not yet finished writing their dissertations, a less common occurrence today.

It must also be remembered that the age distribution of Japan specialists in 1970 was abnormal because of the newness of the field. In 1970 there simply were no "old" Japan specialists to speak of, since nearly everyone became a Japan specialist after the war. In fact, since Japanese Studies in the United States is so overwhelmingly a postwar phenomenon, nearly all the Japan specialists the country has ever had remain alive today. In that sense the age distribution of the field has been normalizing over time, as it takes on the characteristics of the overall U.S. population.

Table 2.2. Age Distribution of Japan Specialists in 1970, 1984, and 1995*

Age	1970	1984	In 1989**	New 1995	All 1995
	%	%	%	%	%
21–30	11	2	–	2.6	0.9
31–40	38	25	3.8	26.8	11.3
41–50	32	34	29.6	34.3	31.1
51–60	15	26	28.3	19.3	25.3
61–70	4	12	24.8	12.4	20.7
71+	–	–	13.6	4.7	10.7

*Data for 1970 from 1970 SSRC-ACLS Report, Appendix 3, p. 108; for 198 from 1984 Japan Foundation Report, Table 1, p. 13.

**The "In 1989" column represents those who were in the 1989 directory and also in the 1995 edition. New 1995 includes only those who appeared for the first time in the 1995 directory.

Although we have followed the rather unusual set of age categories divided at ages 21, 31, 41, 51, and 61 that was employed by the earlier studies (and added 71+) in order to present the comparative analysis in Table 2.2, for further analysis of the 1995 study data we prefer to use a different categorization, divided at ages 35, 45, 55, and 65. The latter set of age categories is more intuitive, since it corresponds to birth years in rounded decades of the twentieth century, and divides at the normal retirement age of 65. It also offers a more balanced picture of the actual age distribution of the 1995 sample, since there are relatively few people in the study under the age of 35.

The current age distribution of Japan specialists in the United States reflects both the general aging of the U.S. population due to longer lifespans, and the baby boom-bulge in the middle years, in addition to the long period of disciplinary and language training required to meet current standards. Only 3.3 percent of the 1,552 specialists in our sample are under 35, while 21.1 percent are 65 or older. The 45–54 baby-boom age group is the largest, with 30.6 percent of the total. The remainder are nearly equally distributed in the 35–44 (20.1 percent) and 55–64 (22.7 percent) age groups. Age was not reported, and could not be estimated, for 2.2 percent of the sample.[5] These figures are shown in Table 2.3, below.

The median age of the 1995 sample is 54, compared with a median age of about 40 in 1970. The mean age in 1995 is 54.9. Nineteen percent of the 1995 directory entrants were born before 1930, while only four percent were born after 1959. Comparison of the two segments of the 1995 directory sample helps to clarify why the field seems to be aging so rapidly despite such a large increment of "new" specialists in the past two decades. Two factors account for this phenomenon. First, two-thirds of the entrants in the 1995 directory were in the previous edition, in which the median age was 47. Not only are they all six years older, but the study's intensive follow-up procedures helped to retain older specialists in the database even after retirement. More than a quarter of those who appeared in both directories are now 65 or older, and virtually none are under 35.

Second, those who are new to the directory for this edition, while younger overall, are not simply a replacement cohort of youngsters. The mean age is 57.3 for those who were in the 1989 directory, and 48.8 for those who are new to the 1995 edition. Paralleling the overall age distribution in the 1989 directory, less than 10 percent of the new entrants are under 35, while another ten percent are 65 or older. Although some lateral movement of relatively older people into Japan specialization is likely to continue, it also seems probable that somewhat more of the new entrants over the next decade will be relatively younger persons making an initial career choice to specialize in Japan. However, they are unlikely to achieve full professional specialization until their thirties or even forties, so the under-35 age category is unlikely to expand in the future.

New entrants to the directory also reflect the increasing presence of women in American professional life. The 1970 study did not even bother to report the gender ratio, and consistently referred to Japan specialists as "men." There were some women in the field, however, and not all of them were MA-level language teachers, despite the impression created by the report. Although

---

[5] Date of birth was not reported by 208 respondents for their directory entries. The omissions were equally divided by sex, but since the sex distribution itself is quite uneven and the number of cases with missing data was substantial, any analyses by age would have been biased. We were able to estimate the decade of birth for 148 cases from the date of their first college degree, by assuming that they obtained a BA during their twenties. This estimate may be slightly biased downward if some persons received the BA in their thirties, but this was preferable to the larger distortion of omitting the cases entirely. The estimated cases fell into all age groups, but were more concentrated at the younger end of the spectrum.

we do not have access to their original survey data, using the roster of 416 Japan scholars that is included as a supplement in the 1970 report, we have calculated the gender ratio in 1970 as 88.7 percent male and 11.3 percent female. By 1984, this had increased to 19 percent female.

Table 2.3. Japan Specialists by Age and 1989 Directory Status

Age Category	In 1989 Sample		New in 1995		1995 Total	
	#	%	#	%	#	%
35 or less	1	0.1	50	9.7	51	3.3
35–44	141	13.6	171	33.3	312	20.1
45–54	333	32.1	142	27.7	475	30.6
55–64	270	26.0	82	16.0	352	22.7
65 or more	277	26.7	51	9.9	326	21.1
Not stated	17	1.6	17	3.3	34	2.2
Total	1,039	66.9	513	33.1	1,552	100.0

In 1989 we saw signs of a further shift in the gender ratio in Japanese Studies. While three-fourths of the specialists in the 1989 directory were male, we noted that nearly half of the doctoral candidates were women. That shift is now reflected within the 1995 directory. Three-fourths of the carry-over group from 1989 are men, but well over a third (37.6 percent) of the new entrants in 1995 are women.

Overall, the 1995 sample is 70.6 percent male and 29.4 percent female.[6] The lopsided gender distribution is largely due to the small number of female Japan specialists in the older age groups. As Table 2.4 shows, the gender balance has improved steadily with each new age cohort entering the field. While only 11.9 percent of those 65 or older (who were born before 1930) were female, one-third of those aged 45-54 and 43.9 percent of those 35–44 are female. The under-35 category, while too small to be reliable, has a majority of women.[7]

---

[6] Although a small number of specialists declined to report gender in their directory entries, for this analysis we were able to determine gender for all of them from other available information, including name, personal knowledge, and degrees from single-sex colleges.

[7] Since Japan specialists now seem to be completing doctorates in their mid-thirties, the gender distribution in this small category is skewed somewhat by female language instructors and other non-academic professionals without doctorates, who enter the field at an earlier age. By the next survey, this age cohort will have filled out with those who complete their doctorates after the age of 35, and the balance will probably still slightly favor males.

Table 2.4. Japan Specialists by Gender and Age

Gender Age	Female		Male		Total	
	#	%	#	%	#	%
35 or less	27	52.9	24	47.1	51	3.3
35–44	137	43.9	177	56.1	312	20.1
45–54	160	33.7	315	66.3	475	30.6
55–64	72	20.5	280	79.5	352	22.7
65 or more	39	11.9	289	88.1	328	21.1
Not stated	21	61.8	13	38.2	34	2.2
Total	456	29.4	1,096	70.6	1,552	100.0

To the extent that Japanese studies is "normalized" in the society and its specialists are drawn from the overall population rather than some special group such as returning veterans, the distribution of Japan specialists should reflect social changes in the larger society. Some evidence of normalization can be found in these statistics. The age composition of Japanese Studies mirrors the overall aging of the population as lifespans lengthen and the postwar baby boom generation reaches middle age. Likewise its gender composition reflects the great strides that have been made in gender equity in the United States over the past three decades. More significant than the simple increase in the proportion of women in the 1995 directory, however, is their occupational location, the factor we will examine next.

OCCUPATIONS AND DISCIPLINES

As noted earlier, the 1970 and 1984 studies were intended as surveys of academic Japan specialists, and only included a very small percentage who were not employed as academic faculty. The 1989 and 1995 directory samples are more diversified, although academics still dominate. In the 1995 sample, the most fundamental occupational distinction is whether or not respondents are employed as academic faculty. Slightly over seventy percent (71.4%) of the sample is classified as academic, but as the age distribution suggests, this includes a substantial number of emeritus and retired faculty. Based on the respondent's current primary occupation, 65.5 percent are currently working as faculty in higher education, 25.1 percent are currently employed but not as academic faculty, and the remaining 9.3 percent are retired or not employed. The latter category includes a small number who identify themselves as independent scholars.[8] Since these classifications are based on occupation rather than place of employment, academic administrators, academic librarians, and non-faculty researchers are included in the non-faculty or non-academic category. An additional 50 persons or 3.2 percent of the sample, with a variety of primary occupations ranging from librarian to lawyer, listed college or university faculty as their second occupation, but we have preserved the classification based on primary occupation.

While it is not surprising that a field based on acquired expertise would tend to retain the wisdom of its elders, the large number of retirees does complicate the analysis of where the field is headed in the future. Removing this group helps to clarify the emerging patterns. Among those currently working, three-quarters are academic faculty and one-quarter are not. Among new entrants to the 1995 directory who are currently employed, however, there is a shift toward non-faculty employment, with 29 percent not employed as faculty.

The gender distribution among faculty parallels the overall gender distribution with 28.9 percent female, but the non-faculty category is somewhat higher at 34.1 percent female. The retired group, by contrast, is 80 percent male. Among new entrants in the 1995 directory, the percentage of women is very similar for both faculty and non-faculty Japan specialists. In both categories, nearly 40 percent of the new entrants are women. This compares favorably with the gender ratios among those who were listed in the 1989 directory, where 24.2 percent of faculty and 30.9 percent of non-faculty are female. At this level of generality we find no indication that women are currently being excluded from academic faculty employment; nor do we see any indication that they seek academic employment because they are excluded from other areas. However, earlier patterns of exclusion will affect the overall distribution for at least another decade.

Although the overall age distributions for faculty and non-faculty are very similar, the place of new directory entrants in these two groups differs. The dominant pattern among those employed as faculty is generational replacement plus expansion, as the new directory entrants are primarily in the younger age cohorts. That is, newly trained younger scholars are both replacing retirees and taking positions that expand Japanese Studies to new departments and institutions. Among faculty, new entrants comprise well over half of the 35–44 age group and their proportion drops sharply in successive age groups.

The age pattern among non-academic specialists is quite different. They comprise less than half of the 35–44 age group, but are over a third of those aged 55–64 and a quarter of those over 65. Nearly a third of the new non-faculty entrants in the 1995 directory sample were born before 1940, compared to less than 20 percent of the new entrants who are employed as faculty. These

---

[8] Only 18 persons in the retired or independent scholar category are under the age of 60. However, the retirees are not entirely carryovers from the 1989 directory. Some new listings for 1995 are emeritus faculty and other retirees.

older non-faculty Japan specialists would have completed their education before the academic job crunch of the 1970s, which drove many new PhDs out of academics. This suggests that these new but older non-faculty Japan specialists in the directory are more likely to have acquired their expertise on Japan through an accumulation of experience over the course of their careers, rather than by formal academic preparation in Japanese Studies before beginning their careers, which is the standard pattern for new faculty.

The fact that new entrants in the 1995 directory comprise a larger proportion of the non-faculty category may be partly due to the study's greater difficulty in tracking 1989 respondents who were not faculty, but it also points to the more recent recognition and proliferation of non-academic specialists as a visible component of Japanese Studies. The reluctance of academic Japan specialists to recognize other bases of knowledge, and the directory project's own heavily academic orientation, may be partly responsible for the invisibility of such specialists in the past. However, non-faculty Japan specialists are unquestionably part of the present and future of Japanese Studies in the United States.

What is not yet clear from our experience in these two studies is whether non-faculty Japan specialists are inherently a less stable category, with more people moving in and out of self-identification as Japan specialists as their work and interests change, or whether their commitment to the study of Japan and the networks that bind them together will prove to be as enduring as those of academic Japan specialists. If the latter is true, we should be able to develop better ways to keep track of them in the future.

The non-faculty Japan specialists represent a wide range of occupations, some of which are closely related to academic faculty employment, such as librarian, researcher or educational administrator. While some academic administrators may be academics who have been promoted into administrative positions, this seems less likely for specialists who are new to the directory in 1995. More probably, they are persons trained as academics who have for various reasons taken administrative positions instead of faculty posts. Other common categories are business, research institution or foundation staff, and various forms of government and diplomatic service. Although their collective impact is unmistakable evidence of the expansion of the boundaries of Japanese Studies, the individual occupational categories produce numbers too small for detailed analysis, and no trends can be discerned. A more fruitful approach to examining this expansion of boundaries is to consider instead the general disciplinary background of Japan specialists.

Table 2.5 shows the change in disciplinary distribution of Japan specialists since 1970. The high percentage listed as "other" in 1970 suggests that there has been representation of a wide range of disciplines in Japanese Studies for some time, but the numbers were initially too small for separate analysis. By the 1984 study professions (business and library science) were recognized, and for the present study we have also distinguished interdisciplinary fields. The professions, with strong representation also from law and education, now represents one of the largest groupings.

Table 2.5. Disciplinary Distribution of Japan Specialists in 1970, 1984, and 1995*

Discipline	1970 %	1984 %	In 1989 %	New 1995 %	Total 1995 #	Total 1995 %
Anthropology	10	7	6.5	4.8	92	6.0
Art, Art History	5	10	6.7	5.4	97	6.3
Economics	4	5	6.0	5.2	89	5.8
History	33	24	17.0	15.0	252	16.3
Lang. & Literature	19	22	19.8	24.0	327	21.2
Political Science	10	13	8.1	8.6	128	8.3
Religion/ Philos.	-	6	5.9	5.8	91	5.9
Sociology	4	4	3.5	3.8	55	3.6
Interdisciplinary	-	-	3.9	3.4	58	3.8
Professions	-	4	13.8	12.2	205	13.3
Other	15	6	8.8	11.6	150	9.7
Total %	100	101	100.0	99.8		100.2
# of Specialists	332	841	1043	499	1544	

*1970 data from 1970 SSRC-ACLS Report, p.110; 1984 data from 1984 Japan Foundation Report, Table A-2, p. 95. In 1989 data includes persons in 1995 directory who also appeared in the 1989 edition; New 1995 includes only those persons who appeared first in the 1995 edition.

The changes in disciplinary distribution among the standard disciplines are also quite striking. History has declined steadily from a third of the specialists in 1970 to 15 percent of new directory entrants in 1995, and 16.3 percent overall in the 1995 study. The language and literature category has held its own at 21–22 percent, and even shows a slight advance to 24.0 percent among the new entrants to the 1995 directory. Economics has increased slightly, but anthropology, political science, and sociology have all decreased somewhat. Religion-philosophy holds about the same percentage as in earlier studies, while the art and art history category has dropped from a 1983 peak of 10 percent to about where it began in 1970. Our figures would be considerably lower for 1995 if we had not included art practitioners along with art historians.

In order to analyze patterns of disciplinary variation in the 1995 sample in relation to other variables, we will use somewhat broader disciplinary clusters, which unfortunately rearrange the discipline combinations that were used in the earlier studies. Thus for purposes of comparison with the earlier studies we have had to combine language and literature in Table 2.5, for subsequent analysis of the 1995 data we have separated literature from language and linguistics. We have also separated art and art history. The new discipline clusters are as follows: humanities (including history, art history, religion, philosophy, and literature); social sciences (including anthropology, economics, political science, sociology, and other social sciences with smaller representation); language and linguistics; interdisciplinary fields (Asian studies, women's studies, international studies, urban studies, etc.); arts (including performing and practicing arts); and professions (including business, law, library science, and education). These clusters are large enough to support more detailed analysis, and they appear to be relatively internally consistent but systematically different from each other.

There are also twelve scientists and engineers in the 1995 study. The group was too small to analyze and too distinctive to combine with another. We regard their presence as a strong indicator that more scientists and engineers will be found among Japan specialists in future surveys as a new form of differentiation in Japanese Studies. We present their distribution here as a baseline, but will drop them from subsequent analysis of disciplinary patterns because of the small number of cases.

Applying these new categories, overall about three-quarters of the 1995 directory entrants listed one of the traditional humanities and social sciences disciplines or languages and linguistics as their primary discipline. This is still substantial, but represents a sizable drop from the 85–90 percent in these disciplinary areas in the earlier studies. The remaining quarter of the 1995 sample listed a professional discipline, an interdisciplinary field, a natural science or an artistic field as their primary discipline, as shown in Table 2.6.

Table 2.6. Japan Specialists by Discipline Cluster and 1989 Directory Status

Discipline Group	In 1989 Sample		New in 1995		1995 Total	
	#	%	#	%	#	%
Humanities	412	40.0	167	33.7	579	37.9
Lang. & Ling.	50	4.8	50	10.1	100	6.5
Social Sciences	331	32.1	152	30.6	483	31.6
Arts	30	2.9	16	3.2	46	3.0
Interdisciplinary	43	4.2	38	7.7	81	5.3
Professions	158	15.3	68	13.7	226	14.8
Sciences	7	0.7	5	1.0	12	0.8
Total	1,031	67.5	496	32.5	1,527	99.9

Comparison of new 1995 directory entrants with those who carried over from the 1989 edition reveals a moderate shift away from humanities and social sciences and toward the less traditional fields, primarily through increased representation in interdisciplinary fields such as Asian studies, women's studies, international studies, and urban studies. This shift represents an expansion of the boundaries of Japanese Studies into new areas, or a differentiation of disciplines. To a considerable extent these are new interdisciplinary fields that barely existed before the 1980s. In that sense the differentiation of disciplines within Japanese Studies reflects the general disciplinary differentiation in American academics during this period, and may also be seen as evidence of the normalization of Japanese Studies in the academic world.

There is a further movement among new 1995 directory entrants who are classified within the traditional disciplines, away from the humanities and social sciences and into languages and linguistics. Despite these shifts in the distribution, the actual number of new entrants in every disciplinary group is well above the numbers needed to replace the retirees in the sample. In sum, there is general growth across the board plus a redistribution of some of the growth into new areas, notably into nontraditional interdisciplinary fields and professional disciplines. Such disciplinary differentiation is the luxury, or perhaps necessity, of an expanding field.

The picture becomes even more interesting when we ask what specialists do with their disciplinary training. Table 2.7 shows the percentage in a disciplinary group who are currently employed as faculty or non-faculty. This breakdown is given separately for those who were in the 1989 directory sample and those who are new to the study in 1995, so that we can distinguish clearly what the newest group of entrants into the field are doing with their disciplinary training. As the table shows, in the traditional academic disciplines of the humanities, social sciences, and language and linguistics, more than three-quarters of both 1989 entrants and those who were new entrants in the 1995 directory have become academic faculty. However, the pattern is quite different in the non-traditional disciplines. In professional disciplines and interdisciplinary fields at least half of the specialists who were in the 1989 directory are faculty, while among the new entrants in those same fields, well over half have gone into non-faculty careers. In short, whereas the majority of earlier specialists with non-traditional training have made careers out of teaching those subjects to others, the new entrants seem to have found a more direct market for their skills.

Table 2.7. Current Employment Distribution of Japan Specialists, by Disciplinary Group and 1989 Directory Status*

Discipline Group	In 1989 (% and #)		New 1995 (% and #)		Total* (% and #)	
	Faculty	Non-Fac	Faculty	Non-Fac	Faculty	Non-Fac
Humanities	80.9	19.1	86.1	13.9	82.5	17.5
(#)	(293)	(69)	(136)	(22)	(429)	(91)
Social Sci.	78.2	21.8	76.2	23.8	77.5	22.5
(#)	(226)	(63)	(109)	(34)	(335)	(97)
Lang. Ling.	84.8	15.2	83.0	17.0	83.9	16.1
(#)	(39)	(7)	(39)	(8)	(78)	(15)
Professions	50.0	50.0	33.8	66.2	45.1	54.9
(#)	(74)	(74)	(22)	(43)	(96)	(117)
Interdisc.	57.9	42.1	43.2	56.8	50.7	49.3
(#)	(22)	(16)	(16)	(21)	(38)	(37)
Arts	57.7	42.3	66.7	33.3	61.0	39.0
(#)	(15)	(11)	(10)	(5)	(25)	(16)
All Fields	73.6	26.4	71.4	28.6	72.9	27.1
(#)	(669)	(240)	(332)	(133)	(1,001)	(373)

*Table does not include retirees, scientists and engineers, or 25 cases missing essential data. N=1,374.

This new development is a strong indicator of the trend toward normalization of Japanese Studies, since it means that academic faculty are no longer simply reproducing themselves, but are training people who will use their skills in Japanese Studies for other purposes. In this context, it is noteworthy that almost ten percent of the academic faculty in the 1995 sample are specialists in a professional discipline such as business or law. However, the trend toward normalization of instruction is not restricted to faculty in the non-traditional disciplines. Faculty in the traditional humanities, language, and social science disciplines of Japanese Studies also contribute to the education of new specialists in interdisciplinary fields and to a lesser extent, the professions.

Although the growing representation of professional fields in Japanese Studies suggests that doctoral study is no longer the only route to becoming a Japan specialist, looking at the numbers and distribution of current doctoral candidates offers a way of projecting the current analysis into the near future.

DOCTORAL CANDIDATES IN JAPANESE STUDIES

The simplest statistics point to a striking increase in doctoral candidates in Japanese Studies in the United States since the late 1980s: the 1977

CULCON study reported 314 doctoral candidates; the 1989 directory listed 412 doctoral candidates; and the 1995 directory lists 803.[9] To understand this growth, we must first assess the reliability of such a comparison by examining how the numbers were collected.

The 1977 CULCON study relied on institutional reports of the number of doctoral candidates currently enrolled. The 1984 Japan Foundation study used the same method, but produced numbers sufficiently ambiguous that we could not use them for this comparison.[10] The two directory projects used a different method. They obtained lists of doctoral candidates, including the name, department, and dissertation topic, from both the institution and from individual Japan specialist faculty members, and the lists were cross-checked to eliminate duplicates. Contributions from faculty members substantially increased the number of doctoral candidates reported. Since the numbers both of doctoral programs and of candidates in those programs were considerably smaller in the 1970s, the reporting to the CULCON survey was probably fairly complete and reliable, even if the same method today would not produce equally reliable data. If we accept the earlier number as reasonably comparable despite the difference in collection method, the series suggests that the current period of growth began sometime in the 1980s and has proceeded at a faster pace in the 1990s.

There is some overlap between the numbers of doctoral candidates listed in the 1989 and 1995 directories, because 135 persons appear on both lists who are still engaged in doctoral work or had just completed their degrees when the 1995 directory was published. These cases are included because they are part of the total number of current doctoral candidates at the time the 1995 data were collected. Such overlap would occur in any series of counts of doctoral students within a decade or so. If only a number count of doctoral students is obtained from institutions there is no way to know about this overlap, but our method of obtaining actual names made it possible to calculate the overlap.[11]

---

[9] We have omitted from the actual number reported in the two directories the 15 in 1989 and 31 in 1995 who were studying at Canadian institutions, plus one person on each list who had slipped in by error and was not working on Japan. In addition, three entries on the published 1989 list were found to be duplicate entries with variant names and these also were cleaned.

[10] That survey reported 308 doctoral students currently enrolled and then added in a footnote that the number did not include 174 students at Columbia who were "concurrently enrolled in both master's and doctoral programs." That number far exceeds any subsequently reported by Columbia. The double counting of an unknown number of persons made these data unusable.

[11] Both directories retained in the doctoral candidate lists a small number of persons who were initially reported as doctoral candidates, but completed their degrees while the directory was in production. Since they did not have a full entry in the specialist directory, their doctoral candidate listings were kept, with an indication that they had recently completed their degrees. In 1989 the published list included six such persons, and in 1995 there were 55 from U.S. institutions. However, during our follow-up check for evidence of doctoral completion we found that a sizable number of those on the 1989 list as current candidates had official degree completion dates of 1987 and 1988. The proportion of listed candidates who had just completed their degrees is thus probably about the same in both years.

The design of the two directory studies permits us to follow what has happened to those persons who were identified as doctoral candidates in 1989, and then to interpret the 1995 data in light of that information. Since the 1995 study was conceived as an "update" of the 1989 directory, both institutions and individual faculty members who had participated in the 1989 directory project received a printout of the doctoral candidates they had previously reported, and were asked whether those individuals had completed their degrees or were still engaged in doctoral study. They were then asked to report both current doctoral candidates, and any others who had completed doctorates since 1988 but had not been reported in the earlier survey. Faculty members were able to provide much more follow-up information on their own students, as might be expected. Institutional respondents could report that students were no longer active doctoral candidates, but seldom knew if the candidate had completed the degree or dropped out. Since this information is often collected by student help calling department secretaries, the lack of institutional memory is understandable. In addition to this direct follow-up information from survey respondents, we utilized the 1995 directory information on specialists and the staff of academic programs to find persons on the 1989 doctoral candidates list. This information from multiple sources has been used in two ways.

First, to correct for any underreporting or oversights in the 1989 doctoral candidates list, we have added to the follow-up pool all the additional names that we could verify as belonging to the same cohort of 1989 doctoral candidates. Japan specialists with full entries in the 1995 directory who received their doctorates from an American institution after 1988 were included. Also added were the new names of persons who did not appear on the 1989 list but had completed their degrees before 1995, which were contributed by institutions and faculty members who participated in the 1995 survey. This may skew the pool slightly toward those who completed their degrees, but it seemed the most reasonable way to reconstitute the 1989 cohort. These additions produced a final follow-up sample of 445 names, 412 from the 1989 directory list and 33 as subsequent additions.

Second, this list was checked against all follow-up information provided by Japan specialists and institutions, as well as against the directory name index and entries, to determine whether the candidate had completed the doctorate and whether he or she was included in the 1995 directory in some capacity. As a final follow-up, Doctoral Dissertations on Asia and Dissertation Abstracts were checked for evidence of degree completion in unknown cases, and to provide the year of the degree whenever possible.[12]

---

[12] Frank J. Shulman, ed., *Doctoral Dissertations on Asia*, vol. 15, 1 & 2 (Ann Arbor: Association for Asian Studies, 1992) was searched for dissertations through 1990–91. *Comprehensive Dissertation Index Supplement, Author Index*, (Ann Arbor: UMI Company, 1991–94) were searched for subsequent years. 1994 was the latest issue available, but its content logs the point at which data collection was completed for the 1995 directory by at least a year.

By 1995, 61.1 percent of the 1989 cohort of 445 doctoral candidates had completed their degrees, 25.8 percent had not yet completed, and the completion status of 13.0 percent was unknown. The details of the follow-up are shown in Table 2.8. Just over half of those who had completed their degree were included in the 1995 directory, either as Japan specialists, as staff listed at academic institutions, or both.

Table 2.8. Follow-up of 1989 Doctoral Candidates to 1995

Directory Status	Ph.D. Completion			Total
	Yes	No	Unknown	
Specialist Directory Only	11.8% (32)	3.5% (4)	0 (0.0%)	8.1% (36)
Institution Staff List Only	12.5% (34)	6.1% (7)	3.4% (2)	9.7% (43)
In Both Directories	26.5% (72)	2.6% (3)	0 (0.0%)	16.8% (75)
In Neither Directory	49.3% (134)	87.8% (101)	96.6% (56)	65.4% (291)
Total	100.1% (272)	100.0% (115)	100.0% (58)	100.0% (445)
% Completion	61.1%	25.8	13.0	100.0
# Carried on 1995 Cands. List	30	105	–	135

This number is not as low as it might appear at first glance, for several reasons. First, a fair number of those who completed doctoral degrees in Japanese Studies at American academic institutions are foreign nationals who have since left the United States, and in most cases no longer fall within the purview of the study. Second, a substantial number of recent American PhDs are also working overseas. Most of them did not receive a directory questionnaire, and thus were not included in the directory. These cases are indications of the internationalization of Japanese Studies in the United States. Because such people are visible only in their absence from the follow-up, we do not know why they left the United States and whether they plan to return. Third, even among those who have remained in the United States, the directory's survey was far less likely to have reached them if they are not employed in an academic institution.

From the 1989 cohort of 445 doctoral candidates, 135 or 30.3 percent appear on the 1995 doctoral candidates list, but 30 of those completed their degree while the 1995 directory was in production. Hence 105 persons from the

1989 list were still active doctoral candidates in 1995. Another ten persons were reported not to have completed their degrees, but were no longer listed as active degree candidates in 1995. One of every eight of those who had not yet completed their degrees were already working as Japan specialists and were included in the 1995 directory as a result of that professional activity. This group included nine who were also on the 1995 doctoral candidates list and are still completing their degrees, and five who are no longer listed as active doctoral candidates. The 58 whose degree completion status remains "unknown" were not necessarily lost to follow-up. Two were identified on the staff lists of Japanese Studies programs, but it was not clear whether they had completed their degrees. Ultimately, only 12.5 percent of the cohort could not be traced at all, which is a very low figure for a national (actually international!) sample over a six-year period.

Looked at from another perspective, if we include the listings of current doctoral candidates, 61.9 percent of the 1989 cohort is represented in some way in the 1995 directory. Slightly over a third of the cohort (34.5 percent or 154 persons) is listed in the 1995 specialist or institutional directory entries. The doctoral candidates list in the 1995 directory contains 30.3 percent of the 1989 doctoral cohort, but some of them also appear in regular directory entries because they are already employed as Japan specialists, hence there is a slight overlap in these percentages.

The completion rates for all disciplines were above 50 percent except for art history (48.4 percent) and religion (45.0 percent). Performing arts was just at 50 percent, but the number of cases was quite small. There was no difference in completion rates by gender. Further analysis of the 1989 cohort will be presented in the context of comparison with the 1995 cohort of doctoral candidates, to which we now turn.

As noted earlier, 803 doctoral students at American institutions were reported to the 1995 study by institutions and Japan specialists. Of this total, 135 students had also appeared on the 1989 list and 668 were new students. While the directory was in production, 55 of these students completed their degrees. We have chosen to leave all of these students in the sample for analysis, in order to provide a clearer snapshot of the full cohort of doctoral students in Japanese Studies at the time the survey was conducted, thus making it comparable to other surveys. The group of 55 students who completed their degrees while the directory was in production is too small to evaluate for differences in distribution, but the distribution of carry-over students does differ on some dimensions. Leaving both groups in the sample enables us to use those differences to extend the analysis.

DEMOGRAPHIC DISTRIBUTION OF DOCTORAL CANDIDATES

The gender ratio in Japanese Studies will continue to equalize in the future, if the ratio among doctoral students is any indication. The gender ratio for the 1989 follow-up group was 43.8 percent female and 52.6 percent male, with 3.6 percent not reported to the study and not discernible from other evidence. In the 1995 doctoral cohort the ratio stands at 42.9 percent female and 46.6 percent male. Gender could not be determined for another 10.5 percent of the sample, because it was not reported and could not be deduced from the name. Even if all the undetermined cases turned out to be male, these ratios are closer to parity than the field has ever achieved before.

The main reason for this indeterminacy is the growing proportion of the doctoral candidate sample that have first names that are neither Japanese nor European, and from which we were unable to make any determination of gender. Although it is certainly a very crude measure, this also hints at the internationalization of American graduate education in Japanese Studies. We are more reluctant than the U.S. government to make ethnic assignments on the basis of name, but at a very informal level it appears that a substantial percentage of the doctoral candidates are either recent immigrants to the United States or foreign students. Many such students remain in the United States after graduation, but some fraction of them will undoubtedly return to their country of origin. Like the international mobility of Japan specialists that we briefly examined earlier, and the 1989 doctoral candidates who have since left the country, this is strong evidence of the internationalization of Japanese Studies in the United States. American doctoral programs in Japanese Studies are no longer just training Americans and a few Japanese who will remain in the country to teach; we are training students from all over the world, who will end up all over the world as well.

Due to the indirect nature of the collection of doctoral candidates' data, age is not available for analysis. The relatively high rates of carryover from the 1989 to the 1995 directory suggest that these candidates, like their recent predecessors, are likely to be in their mid- to late thirties before they complete their doctorates and begin professional employment as Japan specialists. Hence the age distribution of the field will probably continue to be heavily skewed toward the older age categories, despite the infusion of a large cohort of new PhDs.

DISCIPLINARY DISTRIBUTION OF DOCTORAL CANDIDATES

The disciplinary distribution of doctoral candidates has changed incrementally but not radically from 1989 to 1995. History and literature still dominate, with political science now reaching the same level as history (although this may change when dissertation topics are selected by those in language and culture programs). As shown in Table 2.9, since the sample size for 1995 is nearly double that for 1989, a stable or even slightly larger number of doctoral candidates in a discipline translates into a decline in percentage. The only discipline to experience a decrease in the actual number of students was economics. During the 1980s there were strong financial incentives for students to do doctoral work in Japanese economics, both in terms of student fellowship support and market demand for the specialists after graduation. Although the overall number of such students was small, many of them went into the private sector at salaries much higher than were available in academics, where there was also some resistance to hiring Japan specialists. The reason for the current drop is not clear, but the category is so small that it may be either a temporary decline or an artifact of the small numbers.

Table 2.9. Disciplines of Doctoral Candidates in Japanese Studies, 1989 and 1995

	1989		1995 Carryover		1995 New		1995 Total	
Discipline	#	%	#	%	#	%	#	%
Anthropology	35	7.9	11	8.3	74	11.1	85	10.6
Art History	32	7.2	16	12.1	21	3.1	37	4.6
Economics	21	4.7	5	3.8	15	2.2	20	2.5
Education	16	3.6	7	5.3	20	3.0	27	3.4
History	67	15.1	20	14.5	88	13.2	108	13.4
Linguistics	34	7.6	10	7.6	61	9.1	71	8.9
Literature	84	18.9	19	13.6	72	10.8	91	11.3
Performing Arts	13	2.9	4	3.0	22	3.3	26	3.3
Political Science	58	13.0	21	15.9	96	14.4	117	14.6
Religion-Philosophy	29	6.5	10	7.6	34	5.1	44	5.5
Sociology	25	5.6	6	4.5	28	4.2	34	4.3
Other	25	5.6	4	2.3	51	7.6	55	6.8
Asian, E. Asian Stud.	6	1.3	2	1.5	86	12.9	88	11.0
Total	445	99.9	135	100.0	668	100.0	803	100.2

Because of the change in sample size, the percentage distribution is a better measure of the current attractiveness of a discipline to doctoral candidates. That attractiveness may be a function of the availability of financial support, perceived market demand for the specialty, familiarity with the discipline, the intellectual excitement of current research in the field, or many other possibilities. Whatever the reasons for the individual's choice, the resulting distribution will shape Japanese Studies in the future. The biggest changes in the percentage distribution are an increase in the attractiveness of anthropology and to a lesser extent political science, and decreases in art history and economics. There are also modest declines in religion and sociology. The apparent drop in literature and history is due to the large number of 1995 doctoral candidates in language, literature, and culture departments for whom a dissertation topic was not reported. They were therefore placed in the generic category of Asian and East Asian Studies, which consequently comprises 11 percent of the 1995 sample as opposed to 1.3 percent of the 1989 sample. Most of the students in this category will subsequently be placed into literature or history on the basis of their research. There is also a notable increase in the "other" category, which consists of very small numbers of students in a wide range of disciplines. The increase is due not only to increases in the number of students in standard but underpopulated Japanese Studies disciplines such as psychology, but also to students doing work on Japan in disciplines that have rarely been represented at all in Japanese Studies, such as nursing, engineering, and information sciences.

Dividing the 1995 candidates into new students and carryovers from 1989 offers a way of assessing both the speed of doctoral completion and the current attractiveness of various disciplines. For art history, the drop in percentage of doctoral candidates is even more troubling when it becomes apparent that a rather high proportion of the 1995 doctoral candidates are carryovers from 1989. We have no way of knowing if this was a relatively new group of students in 1989, but we do know that only one of the 37 students listed in the 1995 directory had recently completed the doctorate. In the other disciplines with comparable numbers of students in 1989 (linguistics and anthropology), the number that carried over to the 1995 list was considerably smaller, and a far larger number of those completed the doctorate while the directory was in production. Religion-philosophy and education also have slightly elevated numbers of carry-over students, but for education the excess was attributable to students who completed their degrees while the directory was in production. Thus students in art history, and to a lesser degree religion and philosophy, seem to be taking longer to complete their doctorates.

For anthropology, removal of the carry-over students reveals an even greater influx of new students into the 1995 cohort. The number of new students alone is more than double the number of anthropology doctoral students in 1989, an increase not equaled in any other discipline, although language and linguistics came close. Since the market factors that affected economics are not present for anthropology, the most likely reason for the increase is the intellectual attraction of current research. Within contemporary Japanese Studies, anthropologists and sociologists study a very similar array of topics with an overlapping range of methodological approaches, and an undergraduate course on Japan in either discipline would have a very similar syllabus. However, within the American academic context the two disciplines differ considerably both in disciplinary receptivity to specialization on Japan and in the content of doctoral-level training requirements. Anthropology is a more attractive choice for students who do not want or need the quantitative methodological training required in sociology doctoral programs, even though much of the theoretical and substantive work on modern urban societies that would be relevant to the study of Japan comes from sociology.

The systematic diversion into anthropology of students who want to study contemporary Japanese urban society using qualitative methods serves to heighten the disciplinary differences between anthropology and sociology, and to reinforce the disciplinary resistance to area specialists within sociology departments. The effect will be most noticeable at larger institutions where the Japanese Studies program is expanding into a broader array of disciplines, and is likely to meet with less resistance to hiring a Japan specialist in the anthropology department. At smaller institutions, where more of Japanese Studies hiring is serendipitous and there may be a combined anthropology-sociology department anyway, the difference will be negligible. In the long run, the increased supply of Japan specialists in anthropology will mean that many more institutions can expand their Japanese Studies programs from the language, literature, and history core into the social sciences.

The overall number of doctoral students in political science has also doubled since 1989. This includes a relatively high rate of carry-over students, about a third of whom received their degrees while the directory was in production. In sheer numbers this retains the 1989 position of political science as the largest social science component of the doctoral student cohort, and puts it very close to history and literature even after the anticipated shift of students out of the generic East Asian Studies category into the latter two fields. Among the doctoral dissertation topics reported for political science students, many are comparative or multi-country studies with relatively limited Japan content. Such studies are highly regarded in political science departments, but their prevalence suggests that the reported numbers of doctoral candidates include many students who are unlikely either to continue to do research on Japan or even to teach courses wholly on Japan in the future. At the same time, there is also plenty of intellectual attraction in the contemporary study of Japanese politics, due to an unusual combination of high-quality research published over the past decade and political changes in Japan that call into question many older research findings and standard assumptions about how things work in Japan. Hence although the sheer number of doctoral candidates in political science probably inflates the actual supply of new Japan specialists who will continue to contribute to the field, we can expect a strong group of political scientists to emerge from this pool.

For purposes of comparability we have assigned doctoral candidates to disciplines based primarily on their departmental affiliation and when that was ambiguous, on the basis of their dissertation topic. In an initial coding based on dissertation topic, however, 37 persons were assigned to women's studies and another dozen to industrial relations. These areas of specialization coincide with the growth in interdisciplinary fields previously noted for Japan specialists. Even though nearly all of these students have been trained in traditional academic disciplines such as history and sociology, they may find job placements in interdisciplinary programs and thus in the future contribute to the shift away from the traditional disciplinary focus of Japanese Studies.

We are reluctant to make direct comparisons between the disciplinary distribution of current doctoral candidates and the disciplinary distributions of Japan specialists that were presented in Tables 2.4 and 2.5. Not all Japan specialists have doctorates, and even among those who do, many did not write a dissertation concerned with Japan. The doctoral candidates sample underrepresents the professional fields that require a different terminal degree, and disciplines in which relatively more specialists have entered Japanese Studies after doing doctoral work on an unrelated subject. Since these differences affect the whole percentage distribution, direct comparison of individual percentages would be ill-advised. What we can say is that among those who are currently doctoral candidates in Japanese Studies, there continues to be solid representation of the traditional academic disciplines in which such training is standard, and that the strong showing of anthropology and political science in particular bodes well for the future supply of trained specialists in the social sciences.

The growth in the number of doctoral students in Japanese Studies suggests that the overall growth in the field will continue for at least the next several years. Because Japanese Studies has already become sufficiently normalized in the United States that a quarter of those employed are not academic faculty, the production of new doctorates is no longer heavily constrained by demand in the academic market. In the next chapter we will look more closely at the growth of Japanese Studies in both academic and non-academic institutions, as we explore where Japan specialists are employed in the 1990s.

3

The Spread of Japanese Studies

This chapter examines the spread of Japanese Studies by asking where Japan specialists can be found in the 1990s. We look first at the general geographic distribution of Japan specialists, and then at the institutions with which they are affiliated. The two are closely related, since being a Japan specialist is closely bound up with professional work, and except for retirees it is generally the locus of work that determines one's geographic location. We will also look separately at academic institutions and non-academic institutions

GEOGRAPHIC AND REGIONAL DISTRIBUTION

Not surprisingly, the largest number of Japan specialists can be found in the two largest states: California has the highest number of Japan specialists, 291 or 18.8 percent of the sample, and New York is second with 142 or 9.1 percent. The rest of the distribution does not strictly follow population size. Massachusetts is third with 106, or 6.8 percent. Six states have between 50 and 100 specialists in the sample: Illinois (78 or 5.0 percent); Hawaii (75 or 4.8 percent); Pennsylvania (69 or 4.4 percent); The District of Columbia (58 or 3.7 percent); Ohio (51 or 3.3 percent) and Washington state (50 or 3.2 percent). Nine other states have more than 25 specialists in the sample: Virginia (47) Michigan (45); New Jersey (44); Indiana (41); Maryland (41); North Carolina (32); Connecticut and Oregon (31); and Wisconsin (30). At the other end of the spectrum, six states had none: Delaware, Mississippi, North Dakota, South Dakota, West Virginia, and Wyoming.

In order to pursue more detailed analyses, we have condensed the geographic location of Japan specialists into seven regions: Northeast (all of New England, including New York); Mid-Atlantic; South; Midwest; Southwest; Mountain; and Pacific (the West Coast states plus Alaska and Hawaii). For some analyses the number of cases in the Southwest and Mountain regions is too small for separate analysis, so they are combined. The first question to be considered is how the regional distribution of Japan specialists has changed over time.

For most of the short history of Japanese Studies in the United States the locus of work for recognized Japan specialists has been an academic institution, as we have already documented in Chapter Two. In fact, prior to the 1989 directory, studies did not report the geographic distribution of Japan specialists. The only way to reconstruct it is from the reported affiliations of Japan specialists with particular academic institutions. Using this method, we have reconstructed the geographic distribution of Japan specialists into six major regions of the United states from 1970 to 1995. This approach is inexact for two reasons. First, by the time of the 1984 Japan Foundation survey nine percent of the sample is reported not to be affiliated with an academic institution. We do not know where those specialists were, so the reconstruction is undercounted by nearly a tenth. Second, the 1977 and 1984 reconstructions are based on institutional faculty counts rendered as FTE (full-time equivalents of position counts), rather than on counts of real people. We have rounded up to the next whole number for every fractional total reported, but we have no way of knowing how many individuals may have been combined to produce the whole numbers reported.

Table 3.1. Change in Regional Distribution of Japan Specialists, 1970–1995*

Year	*1970*	*1977*	*1984*	*1989*	*1995*	*89–95*
Region	*% & #*	*% & #*	*% & #*	*% & #*	*% & #*	*increase*
Northeast	25.1 (103)	17.6 (155)	18.2 (142)	23.7 (282)	19.9 (307)	+8.9%
Mid- Atlantic	7.5 (31)	9.1 (80)	7.2 (56)	13.1 (156)	17.0 (263)	+68.6%
South	3.9 (16)	7.0 (62)	7.0 (55)	6.3 (75)	6.7 (104)	+42.7%
Midwest	23.6 (97)	24.4 (215)	21.1 (165)	21.2 (253)	20.9 (323)	+27.7%
Southwest- Mountain	6.1 (25)	9.1 (80)	7.9 (62)	5.5 (66)	6.3 (98)	+48.5%
Pacific	33.8 (139)	32.7 (288)	38.5 (301)	30.1 (359)	29.2 (451)	+25.6%
Total N	(411)	(880)	(781)	(1,191)	(1,546)	

* 1970 data based on roster of specialists at academic institutions included as a supplement to the 1970 SSRC-ACLS study. 1977 data based on count of faculty from the 1977 CULCON institutional survey. 1984 data from 1984 Japan Foundation study, based on faculty counts reported in institutional survey. 1989 data reported in "Introduction" to Directory of Japan Specialists and Japanese Studies in the United States and Canada, vol. 1, p. xiv and based on specialists in the directory. 1995 data based on specialists included in the 1995 study.

The results of these recalculations are shown in Table 3.1, above, where a few anomalies are immediately apparent. The actual counts of specialists were higher in 1977 than in 1984, in total and in every region except the Pacific. We suspect that this is due to a particularly energetic attempt to ferret out possible Japan specialists at academic institutions in the 1977 CULCON study, and a more laissez-faire approach relying on returned questionnaires in the 1984 Japan Foundation study, rather than to the disappearance of one-eighth of the nation's Japan specialists in the short interval between the two studies. Some Japan specialists did in fact leave academic employment during the late 1970s, but the 87 individuals without academic affiliation in the 1984 study who are missing from the table do not make up the difference entirely. We need to keep their absence in mind, however, in comparing the first three data points with the two more recent directory surveys, which include both academic and non-academic specialists.

Despite the drop in numbers between the 1977 and 1984 studies, the regional distributions are very similar. The biggest changes come in the 1989 and 1995 directory studies, in which the proportion of Japan specialists in the Northeast and Mid-Atlantic regions increases while the Pacific shows a corresponding percentage decline, even though the actual number of specialists in the Pacific region continued to grow. The proportional increase is sharpest in the Mid-Atlantic region. There is also a decline in the proportional representation of Japan specialists in the Midwest region beginning in the 1984 study although there, as in the Pacific region, the actual number of specialists continued to grow steadily.

Since the 1989 and 1995 studies used the same methods, we can also look at the increase in the number of Japan specialists in each region between these two dates, which further clarifies the distribution shifts between regions. These figures are shown in the far right column of Table 3.1. Every region experienced an increase in the absolute number of Japan specialists between 1989 and 1995; hence the shifts in the distribution between regions are due to differences in the size of that increase, rather than to loss of specialists in some regions to the gain of others. The Mid-Atlantic region experienced the largest increase, 68.6 percent, while the Northeast experienced the slowest growth with an increase of 8.9 percent. The South and Southwest-Mountain regions each experienced growth of over 40 percent, while the Midwest and Pacific regions grew by about 25 percent.

To a considerable extent these varying rates of increase in the number of Japan specialists reflect the combination of economic and demographic processes that have affected these regions very generally during the time period in question. As a result of overall industrial restructuring in the United States, the Northeast, Midwest, and Pacific regions have experienced both economic recession and outmigration, while the South and Southwest-Mountain regions have correspondingly experienced both healthy economic conditions and considerable population growth during these same years.

However, we should not rely too heavily on either the 1989–1995 increase or the recent economic and demographic conditions in trying to understand the changes in the Northeast and Mid-Atlantic regions, since in both regions the number of Japan specialists jumped sharply in the 1989 study, with a corresponding increase in their proportional representation. In effect, the relevant changes began earlier for these two regions, and they have to do with the changing market demand for Japan specialists. The growing number of Japan specialists who are not employed as faculty implies that the geographic distribution of the field is no longer tied as tightly to the location of colleges and universities that emphasize the study of Japan, and may be shifting toward other sorts of market centers.

As shown in Table 3.2, the regional distribution of Japan specialists is quite different for faculty, non-faculty, and retirees. In the Midwest, South, and Southwest-Mountain regions, about three-quarters of all Japan specialists are employed as academic faculty. That percentage drops to around 60 percent in the Northeast and Pacific regions, and is just above half in the Mid-Atlantic region. All three of the latter regions have correspondingly higher proportions of persons employed in non-faculty positions. The percentage with non-faculty employment is highest in the Mid-Atlantic region, which is also the area showing the fastest rate of growth since 1989 at 68.6 percent.

Table 3.2. Current Employment Status of Japan Specialists, by Region

Region	Faculty %	Non-Faculty %	Retired %	Total N
Northeast	60.6	30.6	8.8	307
Mid-Atlantic	53.2	37.3	9.5	263
South	76.9	17.3	5.8	104
Midwest	78.6	12.1	9.3	323
Southwest-Mountain	73.5	18.4	8.2	98
Pacific	62.3	26.8	10.9	451
Total N*	1,014	387	145	1,546

*Six persons with APO or Guam addresses are not included in the table.

However, once again a closer look at those Japan specialists who are new to the directory in 1995 provides a clearer glimpse of where the field is moving.

The employment distribution of Japan specialists who are new to the directory in 1995 differs rather sharply by region, as shown in Table 3.3. In the Northeast and particularly in the Mid-Atlantic region, very high proportions of the specialists who were in the 1989 study are not employed as academic faculty, and about a third of Japan specialists who are new to the 1995 study also have non-faculty employment. This confirms our earlier observation that the changes in these two regions began before 1989, and are related to the availability of non-faculty employment opportunities. In the Pacific region, Japan specialists who were included in the 1989 study still were most likely to be faculty, but the new specialists in the Pacific region have a very high rate of non-faculty employment (40.4 percent). In the South, Midwest, and Southwest-Mountain regions, the overwhelming majority of those new to the study in 1995 are employed as faculty.

Table 3.3. Percent Distribution of Current Employment Status of Japan Specialists, by Region and 1989 Directory Status

Region	In 1989 Study (N=1,036)			New in 1995 (N=510)		
	Faculty	Non fac.	Retired	Faculty	Non fac.	Retired
Northeast	60.8	29.9	9.3	60.2	32.0	7.8
Mid- Atlantic	49.7	39.3	11.0	60.0	33.3	6.7
South	72.1	20.6	7.4	86.1	11.1	2.8
Midwest	75.9	12.0	12.0	84.1	12.1	3.7
Southwest-Mountain	70.0	18.3	11.7	78.9	18.4	2.6
Pacific	66.3	21.0	12.7	52.9	40.4	6.6

Japan specialists operate in a national, if not international job market, so it seems more likely that job opportunities draw specialists to an area, rather than that the area has a fixed pool of available Japan specialists who shift their type of work depending on local market conditions. To the extent that this assumption holds, we can read the impact of new specialists on the employment distribution of each region as an indicator of the kinds of new employment opportunities the region offers. Understood in this way, the Northeast, Mid-Atlantic, and Pacific regions are drawing Japan specialists to non-academic employment opportunities, while the South, Midwest, and Southwest-Mountain regions are areas of relatively strong growth in academic employment.

These current forms of employment opportunity must also be understood in relation to each region's previous development in Japanese Studies. The South and Southwest-Mountain regions have traditionally had very little academic Japanese Studies. Hence the academic opportunities they now display reflect the general expansion and normalization of Japanese Studies in American colleges and universities, plus the favorable demographic and economic conditions in the region that support such growth. The Northeast and Pacific regions, on the other hand, already have strong academic Japanese Studies programs in place but are also centers of business and government activity generating a high demand for expertise on contemporary Japan. The remaining two regions represent the polar cases. The Midwest has a strong tradition of academic Japanese Studies, but does not presently offer much opportunity for non-faculty employment in Japanese Studies. By contrast, the Mid-Atlantic has not been particularly strong in academic Japanese Studies, but the new political and economic relevance of Japan makes this region a major source of non-faculty employment opportunities.

This analysis of the regional distribution of Japan specialists has led us back to the distinction between Japan specialists who are employed as academic faculty and those who are employed in other kinds of professional work related to Japan. If the question is where Japan specialists are located, however, the more basic distinction is whether or not they are affiliated with an academic institution, regardless of the specific nature of their work. In the following sections we will look more closely at the institutional affiliations of Japan specialists to see how they have expanded and differentiated, and what those patterns tell us about the current state of Japanese Studies in the United States.

JAPANESE STUDIES AT ACADEMIC INSTITUTIONS

There is no question that the number of academic institutions at which there are Japan specialists has grown steadily over the postwar period, and that the density of that presence as measured by the number of Japan specialists per institution has also increased. Table 3.4 shows this increase, using data either presented in or reconstructed from earlier studies to compare with the 1995 data.

It is possible to count the number of institutions and the number of specialists at each institution either from data collected directly from institutions, or from rosters of individuals that list their institutional affiliation. As usual, the methods of data collection have varied from study to study. The 1970 and 1977 figures we use are both taken from the 1977 CULCON study, which recalculated the 1970 SSRC-ACLS data for comparison. The 1970 data were based on a roster of individuals, whereas the 1977 data were based on a questionnaire sent to institutions, plus some rather intensive follow-up using other available sources of data. We have calculated the 1984 distribution from the same faculty FTE data used for the regional analysis reported above, and the same caveats apply. It is a rather incomplete count based on institutional questionnaires only.

The 1989 data were collected in much the same manner as the 1977 ands 1984 studies, except that questionnaire data provided by institutions was supplemented with information from individual Japan specialists whose institutions did not submit a questionnaire. This has the effect of increasing the count of institutions with only one or two specialists. For 1995 the institutional data were collected through a broader canvas of institutions, and again supplemented with information provided by individual specialists whose institutions did not submit a questionnaire.

In the earliest studies the counts from either source were roughly comparable, but in more recent studies they diverge, and neither is really complete. Although for 1989 and 1995 we are combining data from institutional and individual sources to obtain a more complete count, we have eliminated any duplication by only using the individual data when the institutional source was not available. In Chapter Nine we will look more closely at the extent of overlap and non-overlap between the two sources and consider its implications, but for this analysis we have simply excluded it.

All of these surveys purport to count the number of institutions at which some minimal level of Japanese Studies is available, and to indicate roughly the extent of that availability in terms of the number of specialists at the institution. The 1984 study probably undercounts to a greater degree than the others, but is still a useful addition to the series. Because of their cross-referencing procedures, the 1989 and 1995 studies probably offer a somewhat more complete count of institutions with only one or two Japan specialists, but even these studies have undoubtedly missed some institutions. With these caveats the data can be compared.

The overall pattern of growth is clear. The absolute number of academic institutions with some Japanese Studies has tripled in the past 25 years, from 139 in 1970 to 440 in 1995. Indeed, the number of institutions with a Japan specialist in 1995 is larger than the total number of Japan specialists in the United States in 1970!

The density of this Japanese Studies presence has also increased steadily over time. In 1970 over half the institutions had only one Japan specialist, and only six institutions had 12 or more specialists. Even if the 1977 and 1984 studies may have undercounted institutions with a lone Japan specialist, they both document the increase in the number of programs that had achieved some sort of critical mass in Japanese Studies, whether one defines that mass as four, eight, or twelve specialists. The 1989 and 1995 studies both show an increase in the number and percent of institutions with a minimal presence of one specialist, but they also show that many more institutions had developed a critical mass of Japan specialists and could offer a full program. We will explore the density and internal composition of academic programs in greater detail in Chapter Eight. Here we will look more closely at the

Chapter Three

remarkable increase in the number of institutions with some minimal Japanese Studies presence. This increase is so large that it has necessarily extended Japanese Studies to different kinds of academic institutions.

Table 3.4. Institutions with Japan Specialists, 1970–1995, by Number of Specialists

Year	1	2-3	4–7	8–11	12 or More	Total
1970	56.1 (78)	24.5 (34)	12.2 (17)	2.9 (4)	4.3 (6)	100% (139)
1977	35.7 (70)	29.1 (57)	21.9 (43)	5.6 (11)	7.7 (15)	100% (196)
1984	33.0 (61)	30.3 (56)	24.8 (46)	4.9 (9)	7.0 (13)	100% (185)
1989	43.5 (127)	23.3 (68)	17.8 (52)	6.2 (18)	9.2 (27)	100% (292)
1995	47.7 (185)	23.7 (92)	16.2 (63)	5.2 (20)	7.2 (28)	100% (388)*

*Percentages are based on 388 cases for which full staffing data were available. An additional 36 institutions did not have a Japan specialist on their regular instructional faculty but listed someone in another capacity; no staffing data were reported for 16 institutions that do have established Japanese Studies programs.

In order to examine current patterns of growth and institutional differentiation, we will confine this analysis to the increase in institutions from 1989 to 1995. This is also the comparison for which we can be most confident of the comparability of the data. We begin the analysis with a more detailed review of data collection procedures and results in 1989 and 1995, followed by an assessment of exactly which institutions are new in 1995.

The 1989 institutional data collection was based on the same procedure used for the 1977 and 1984 surveys, a mailing list of institutions with known or possible Japanese Studies programs. When the number of responses to the institutional questionnaire turned out to be lower than expected, we supplemented the count with a list of Japan specialists who were affiliated with academic institutions that had not returned an institutional questionnaire. For 1995, we attempted to circumvent this problem by purchasing a mailing list of 3,139 academic institutions in the United States, and sending the institutional questionnaire to all of them. The response rate was somewhat better, but we still found it necessary to supplement with a list of Japan specialists whose academic affiliations were not represented in the institutional questionnaire responses. We thus distinguish between institutions with full directory listings and those with a supplemental listing.

The 1995 sample includes 247 academic institutions in the United States with a full program listing in the directory. An additional 193 academic institutions had at least one Japan specialist listed in the specialists directory, but did not submit institutional data. These latter institutions received a secondary listing in the institutional directory as "Other Academic Institutions with Japan Specialist Staff."[1] Taken together, these two categories provide the broadest and simplest measure of the number of academic institutions in the United States at which there is some Japanese Studies. We are well aware that this is not a complete census, but it is the best and most comprehensive count we can produce with a voluntary survey.

The number of institutions identified by this measure in 1995 represents a substantial increase over the number included in the 1989 directory. When both full directory entries and secondary listings are combined, there is an increase of about 50 percent overall in the number of institutions represented. Most of the increase is in full directory entries, where there was a 129 percent increase, from 108 in 1989 to 247 in 1995. By contrast, the number of secondary listings increased only 2.7 percent, from 188 to 193. The basic numbers are shown in Table 3.5.

Table 3.5. Full and Secondary Directory Listings of Japanese Studies at American Academic Institutions, 1989 and 1995

1989 / 1995	Full Entry		Secondary Listing		No Listing		Total
	#	%	#	%	#	%	#
Full Entry	98	(39.7)	43	(17.4)	106	(42.9)	247
Secondary Listing	3	(1.6)	114	(59.1)	76	(39.4)	193
No Listing	7		31		–		38
Total	108		188		182		478

Figuring out how much of this is actually new growth in the presence of Japanese Studies is difficult. About 40 percent (98) of the 1995 full directory entries were institutions that had a full entry in 1989. Another 43 or 17.4 percent were institutions that had a secondary listing in 1989. Many of the

[1] In addition to these two categories, another 99 institutions submitted some data for the study, but do not currently have a Japanese studies program that could be listed in the directory. The information they provided will be incorporated into the analysis whenever possible.

latter programs had a substantial number of Japan specialists in 1989, but did not submit material for a full directory entry. It is this sort of slippage that led to the creation of the secondary list based on directory entries submitted by individual Japan specialists. The remaining full directory entries in 1995 (106 or 42.9 percent) were from institutions that were not represented at all in 1989, and may with some caution be considered "new."

While the total number of secondary listings did not change much from 1989 to 1995, there was substantial change in the composition of this category. Through intensive follow-up we were able to get a full directory entry for all but three institutions with more than five Japan specialists listed in the directory. The secondary listing for 1995 therefore represents academic institutions that have at least one to five faculty members with expertise on Japan, but we do not know whether they have an actual program in Japanese studies. About sixty percent (114) of these institutions were also represented on the secondary list in 1989, and just under 40 percent (76) were new to the directory in 1995.

In sum, there was some movement from secondary listing to full directory entries, but about 40 percent of the 1995 institutions in both categories were completely new. By contrast, there was 8.6 percent attrition overall. Only ten programs with full entries in 1989 did not have full entries in 1995. These were very small programs in 1989, and less than a third of them even appeared on the secondary list in 1995. Of the 188 institutions with secondary listings in 1989, only 31 (16.5 percent) do not appear in the 1995 directory. In two-thirds of these cases the listed individual has moved to a different institution; the remainder were deceased or lost to follow-up (and in most cases probably deceased or no longer active in the field). By this assessment, there has been a 40 percent increase in the number of academic institutions with some Japanese Studies presence, offset by attrition to produce about 30 percent net growth.

Next we need to determine where that growth occurred. For most of the analysis in this study we are limited to the 247 institutions that actually submitted data to the project. However, we can utilize the full set of 440 entries and secondary listings to examine the spread of Japanese Studies into American academic institutions as a whole. For this larger set of institutions we have no internal information except the fact that a Japan specialist is affiliated there. A second problem is that even if we had comparable information for all the cases in the expanded sample, we still would not know how all of these institutions with some Japanese Studies presence fit into the larger landscape of higher education in the United States.

The solution to both problems derives from the fact that the 1995 institutional sample was in fact drawn from the population of all institutions of higher education in the United States, since the questionnaire was sent to a mailing list representing that population. Although no such listing is ever perfect, the number of institutions on our list closely matches other published figures for the total number of two-year and four-year degree granting institutions in the United States. We could therefore collect additional data on this population of academic institutions from available secondary sources, and then compare the institutions that have some Japanese Studies presence with those that do not.

LEVEL AND SELECTIVITY OF INSTITUTIONS WITH JAPAN SPECIALISTS

Data on student enrollment, number of faculty, and several other characteristics of academic institutions were collected from the Peterson series of guides to colleges and universities[2] for the entire mailing list of 3,139 U.S. academic institutions that received the study's survey. Not all data were available for every institution, but at least 2,500 cases were available for each analysis. These data permit us to assess the degree to which Japanese Studies is available at least minimally at institutions of various sizes and types in the United States. For this analysis Japanese Studies is present if there is either a documented program (full directory entry) or at least one Japan specialist faculty member (secondary listing) at the institution.

By this measure, Japanese Studies can now be found at 7.7 percent of U.S. academic institutions offering associate degrees, a quarter (23.7 percent) of institutions offering the bachelor's degree, nearly a third (30.2 percent) of institutions offering MA degrees and over half (53.8 percent) of all institutions offering doctoral degrees. We can apply the same analysis retrospectively to the 1989 sample to assess where the extension of Japanese Studies to new institutions has taken place in the past five years.

The picture is considerably easier to evaluate if we use the same Peterson data as the base for both years. This requires only a minor leap of faith on the reader's part. Even though they do not represent the precise conditions of each institution in 1989, the figures do represent the institution's status four years later and thus capture the direction of any change. The results are shown in Table 3.6, along with the rate of increase. Note that the table combines separate analyses of each level at which degrees are offered by institutions, so there is considerable overlap in institutions

[2] *Peterson's Guide to Four-Year Colleges*,1995 ed., (Princeton, N.J.: Peterson's Guides, Inc., 1995), and *Peterson's Guide to Two-Year Colleges*, 1995 ed., (Princeton, N.J.: Peterson's Guides, Inc., 1995). Although the publication date is 1995, the data were colllected from institutions for the 1993-94 academic year, and thus correspond closely to the data collection for our study.

between the categories.[3] The results also cannot be interpreted to mean there is a Japanese Studies program at the level specified, which will be examined in a later chapter. It simply means that there is some Japanese Studies available at an institution that offers academic degrees at that level.

Table 3.6. Availability of Japanese Studies at American Academic Institutions in 1989 and 1995, by Level of Degree

Degree	1989		1995		Institutions		Increase	
Level*	#	%	#	%	#	%	#	%
AA	63	3.8	129	7.7	1670	53.2	+66	+105.0
BA	269	16.5	383	23.5	1627	51.8	+114	+42.4
MA	224	21.6	314	30.2	1039	33.1	+90	+40.3
PhD	153	45.5	181	53.8	336	10.7	+28	+18.3
All Inst.	296	9.4	440	14.0	3139	100.0	+144	+48.6

* This table combines separate analyses of institutions for each level at which degrees are offered, so there is considerable overlap between categories and the numbers cannot be summed vertically.

While Japanese Studies has achieved the greatest presence at institutions offering doctoral degrees, the rate of increase since 1989 has been greater at institutions offering less advanced degrees. And although the spread of Japanese Studies is highest for institutions offering the doctorate, we also have to take into consideration the actual number of institutions offering degrees at each level. That is, the absolute number of institutions offering the BA that have some Japanese Studies is substantially larger than the number offering PhD degrees that have some Japanese Studies. Thus even after we account for the nesting effect between degree levels, this is significant evidence of the increasing normalization of Japanese Studies from an obscure and elite graduate specialization to an accessible form of knowledge that is more widely available to undergraduates.

Given the nature of the data collection and follow-up procedures, we are more likely to have missed programs at two-year and four-year

---

[3] Virtually all of the institutions with doctoral programs also offered MA and BA programs. There was of course less overlap in the opposite direction: nearly two-thirds of the institutions offering bachelor's degrees also offered MAs, but only a fifth offered doctoral programs. Institutions offering associate degrees (largely two-year community colleges) were the least "nested" with higher degree programs. There was about a 40 percent overlap between associate and bachelors degree programs in both directions, but only 6 percent of institutions offering associate degrees also offered doctorates. These appear to be comprehensive state institutions offering a full range of degrees in specialized fields.

institutions, and more likely to have missed them in 1989 than in 1995. Therefore, the penetration rate reported here could be somewhat underestimated, and the rate of growth from 1989 to 1995 may be slightly overestimated. We must also caution that the issue here is not the scale of Japanese Studies activity at an institution, which will be taken up later, but its simple presence or absence. The figures suggest that there is still plenty of room for extension of Japanese Studies into new institutions, but relatively more room at institutions that do not offer advanced degrees.

It is well known from previous studies and confirmed in these data that Japanese Studies began in the United States primarily as a graduate-level specialization, and has slowly filtered down to undergraduate programs. Given the stature of the institutions with the original graduate-level programs in Japanese Studies, the field has also been associated from its inception with quite selective academic institutions. The Peterson data includes a measure of "difficulty of entrance," a five-point scale ranging from "none" to "most difficult to enter" that can be used to assess the academic selectivity of Japanese Studies in the 1990s. The results are shown in Table 3.7.

Table 3.7. Availability of Japanese Studies at American Academic Institutions in 1989 and 1995, by Difficulty of Entrance

Year	1989		1995		Institutions		Increase	
Entrance	#	%	#	%	#	%	#	%
none	13	1.3	43	4.3	990	39.0	+30	+230.8
minimal	7	2.0	16	4.5	354	13.9	+9	+128.6
moderate	163	16.0	233	22.9	1017	40.0	+70	+42.9
very diff.	66	46.5	84	59.2	142	5.6	+18	+27.3
most diff.	23	62.1	27	73.0	37	1.5	+4	17.4
Total*	272	10.8	403	15.9	2540	100.0	+131	+48.2

*Entrance difficulty coded from Peterson's Guide to Four-Year Colleges, 1995 ed. and Peterson's Guide to Two-Year Colleges, 1995 ed. Data were not available for 599 institutions, including 24 from the 1989 sample and 37 from the 1995 sample.

In 1995 there was some availability of Japanese Studies at nearly three-fourths of the institutions rated as "most difficult to enter" and at nearly sixty percent of those at the next level, "very difficult to enter." By contrast, Japanese Studies was present at less than a quarter of the institutions that were "moderately difficult to enter," and at less than five percent of those in the categories of "minimal" or "no difficulty of entrance." The pyramidal distribution of institutions across these five categories indicates that Japanese Studies remains heavily concentrated at the highly selective institutions that comprise barely seven percent of all higher education institutions in the United States, with a much smaller impact on the other 97 percent.

The percentage increases in availability of Japanese Studies at the lowest two categories of selectivity are remarkable, but they are based on very small numbers in a huge potential pool. In fact, the greatest growth in the actual number of institutions with Japanese Studies has been in the middle category, institutions that are moderately difficult to enter, which comprise most of the top half of the pyramid. In this large category the availability of Japanese Studies has increased over 40 percent since 1989, from 16 percent of all institutions in 1989 to almost 23 percent in 1995. It is here that real growth is likely to continue to concentrate for the remainder of the 1990s.

Placing too much emphasis on the selectivity of institutions distorts the overall picture, and also goes against the egalitarian American grain. The table also shows that in actual numbers, the bulk of Japanese Studies is now at institutions in the middle category of "moderately difficult to enter." Indeed, there are nearly ten times as many institutions in this category with some Japanese Studies available as the number of such institutions in the most selective category. There are even more institutions with no entrance restrictions at all that have some Japanese Studies (43) than the number of institutions with Japanese Studies at the most selective level (27). Again, the measure used here is a very basic assessment of whether Japanese Studies is present or absent at each institution. It is not a measure of the size or impact of the programs themselves, which we will consider in Chapter Eight.

Another important corrective to the notion of selectivity is institutional size. While "very selective" and "most selective" may convey an image of exclusivity and smallness, in fact the evidence shows that Japanese Studies is concentrated at large academic institutions, and thus may be accessible to greater numbers of students than the sheer number of institutions would suggest. Table 3.8 shows the availability of Japanese Studies at academic institutions by size of total enrollment, again applying the Peterson data as the standard base for comparing both 1989 and 1995 study data. There is a very direct relationship between institution size and presence of Japanese Studies for both 1989 and 1995.

Table 3.8. Availability of Japanese Studies at American Academic Institutions in 1989 and 1995, by Total Enrollment

Year	1989		1995		Institutions		Increase	
Total Enrolled	#	%	#	%	#	%	#	%
<1,000	16	2.2	29	3.0	713	26.5	+13	+81.2
1,000–<2,000	35	6.3	64	11.4	561	20.8	+29	+82.9
2,000–5,000	43	6.5	69	10.5	657	24.4	+26	+60.5
5,000–<10,000	39	10.1	75	19.3	388	14.4	+36	+92.3
10,000–<15,000	42	23.0	67	36.6	183	6.8	+25	+59.5
15,000–<20,000	36	45.0	40	50.0	80	3.0	+4	+11.1
20,000+	65	58.5	73	65.7	111	4.1	+8	+12.3
Total*	276	10.2	417	15.5	2693	100.0	+141	+51.1

*Enrollment category assignments from Peterson's Guide to Four-Year Colleges, 1995 ed. and Peterson's Guide to Two-Year Colleges, 1995 ed. Data were not available for 446 institutions, including 20 with Japanese Studies in 1989 and 23 with Japanese Studies in 1995.

SIZE OF INSTITUTIONS WITH JAPAN SPECIALISTS

In 1995, Japanese Studies was available at two-thirds of institutions with total enrollment of 20,000 or more, at half of the institutions with total enrollment between 15,000 and 20,000, and at more than a third of those enrolling between 10,000 and 15,000 students. Because 70 percent of all higher educational institutions in the United States have total enrollments of less than 5,000 students, this category has been divided more finely. Growth has been high at these small institutions, but highest at those in the middle range, with enrollments between 5,000 and 10,000.

Larger institutions are more likely to be comprehensive research institutions offering a wide range of graduate programs. Hence the high availability of Japanese Studies at the largest institutions reflects the long-standing association of Japanese Studies with institutions offering graduate education. The growing presence of Japanese Studies at smaller institutions also underscores its deeper extension into undergraduate environments. To look at this phenomenon more closely we can ask what is the likelihood of some

Japanese Studies being available at institutions with undergraduate enrollments of various sizes.

As shown in Table 3.9, the likelihood remains greater at institutions with larger undergraduate enrollments. However, the actual number of institutions at which some Japanese Studies is available is remarkably similar in every size category except for the smallest institutions, those with less than 1,000 undergraduate students. The faster growth since 1989 of Japanese Studies at institutions with less than 10,000 undergraduates has caused the leveling out of the number of institutions with Japanese Studies across all the enrollment categories.[4]

Table 3.9. Availability of Japanese Studies at American Academic Institutions in 1989 and 1995, by Undergraduate Enrollment

Year	1989		1995		Institutions		Increase	
Undergrad. Enrollment	#	%	#	%	#	%	#	%
<1,000	19	2.7	35	5.0	709	27.6	+16	+84.2
1,000–<2,000	42	7.4	70	12.4	566	22.0	+28	+66.7
2,000–<5,000	53	8.4	86	13.5	637	24.8	+33	+62.3
5,000–<10,000	46	12.5	76	20.7	367	14.3	+30	+65.2
10,000–<15,000	47	30.3	64	41.3	155	6.0	+17	+36.2
15,000+	64	46.7	74	54.0	137	5.3	+10	+15.6
Total*	271	10.5	405	15.7	2571	100.0	+134	+49.4

*Enrollment category assignments from Peterson's Guide to Four-Year Colleges, 1995 ed. and Peterson's Guide to Two-Year Colleges, 1995 ed. Data were not available for 568 institutions, including 25 with Japanese Studies in 1989 and 35 with Japanese Studies in 1995.

In short, even though Japanese Studies is not yet available at smaller undergraduate institutions to the same extent as at larger institutions with graduate programs, the extension into new institutions and thus the development of new Japanese Studies programs in the 1990s is overwhelmingly at these

---

[4] Although not shown in the table, the numbers in each size category except the smallest and the largest are about equally divided between institutions with a full directory entry and those with a secondary listing. Surprisingly, in both the smallest and largest enrollment categories, substantially more of the institutions had full directory entries: three-fifths in the under-1,000 undergraduate enrollment category and two-thirds in the 15,000 and over category.

smaller undergraduate institutions. The implications of this new distribution are substantial. They point to an increased demand for program and faculty support at a much greater number and broader range of smaller undergraduate institutions than heretofore.

Put another way, eighty percent (107) of the 134 new programs and faculty institutional affiliations identified in 1995 are located at institutions with undergraduate enrollments of less than 10,000, and 88.8 percent of all bachelor's-degree institutions serve less than 10,000 undergraduate students each. Nearly half the institutions at which there is some Japanese Studies available fall below the 5,000 undergraduate student enrollment level, where three-fourths of all institutions offering the bachelor's degree can also be found. These institutions place greater emphasis on undergraduate teaching than on research and graduate education, and less than one in twenty offers the doctorate. This is a fundamentally different academic environment from the large research institutions where most Japan specialists are trained. The need in the future will not be simply for more faculty and program support at small institutions quantitatively, but for qualitatively different kinds of support. As this demand increases, it will have strong ramifications for instructional, research, and service programs in Japanese Studies at the major research institutions as well.

One further analysis using the Peterson data will help to clarify the major obstacle to extension of Japanese Studies into smaller institutions. Table 3.10 shows the availability of Japanese Studies at U.S. academic institutions by faculty size. Although both the total number of faculty and the number of faculty expressed as full-time equivalents (FTE) were available in the Peterson data, the latter measure provides a clearer picture of institutional resources that is not artificially inflated by large numbers of part-time lecturers.

Table 3.10. Availability of Japanese Studies at American Academic Institutions in 1989 and 1995, by Faculty Size in FTE

Year	1989		1995		Institutions		Increase	
Faculty FTE	#	%	#	%	#	%	#	%
Under 50	6	0.7	18	2.1	845	33.0	+12	+200.0
50–99	34	5.1	57	8.5	669	26.2	+23	+67.6
100–499	103	12.2	187	22.0	849	33.2	+84	+81.6
500–999	55	45.5	72	59.5	121	4.7	+17	+30.9
1,000 +	63	85.2	64	86.5	74	2.9	+1	+1.6
Total*	261	10.2	398	15.6	2,558	100.0	+137	+52.5

*Faculty FTE assignments from Peterson's Guide to Four-Year Colleges, 1995 ed. and Peterson's Guide to Two-Year Colleges, 1995 ed. Data were unavailable for 581 cases, including 35 with Japanese Studies in 1989 and 42 with Japanese Studies in 1995.

As might be expected from the earlier findings about institutional size in terms of enrollment, institutions with 1,000 or more faculty FTE are most likely to have a Japanese Studies program. Fully 86.5 percent of such institutions have some availability of Japanese Studies, the highest rate of any variable examined. The fact that this number has barely changed since 1989 also suggests that it is close to the saturation point. Although it is not shown in the table, more than 70 percent of these institutions have a full directory entry.

About sixty percent of institutions with 500–999 faculty FTE now have some Japanese Studies, and this category has expanded 30.9 percent since 1989. The greatest numerical growth since 1989 has been at institutions with 100-499 faculty, where 84 new institutions have been added since 1989, a growth rate above eighty percent. While the growth rates have been high at institutions with less than 100 faculty FTE, the actual numbers are small and the rate of availability remains low.

An institution with a thousand or more faculty FTE, or even 500, can readily accommodate at least one Japan specialist, and is most likely to feel that it ought to have a Japanese Studies program as part of its full complement of academic offerings. An institution with only a few hundred faculty has much less latitude to accommodate an unusual academic specialty unless there is considerable student interest. The substantial number of institutions with 100-499 faculty FTE that do have some Japanese Studies presence, and the strong growth in this category since 1989, provides further evidence of the normalization of Japanese Studies in American academics, and the growing demand for Japanese Studies at the undergraduate level. By the same token, it seems unrealistic to expect that institutions with less than 100 faculty FTE, even more so those with less than 50, will be able to find room for a Japan specialist on their faculty unless there is strong student demand, some special circumstance, or sheer serendipity involved.

GEOGRAPHIC DISTRIBUTION OF INSTITUTIONS WITH JAPAN SPECIALISTS

Previous analyses have identified geographic patterns in the availability of Japanese Studies in various regions of the United States. Using our broad measure of presence or absence, by 1995 Japanese Studies was available in every state except three: Mississippi, North Dakota, and Wyoming. Regionally, the largest numbers of institutions with Japanese Studies were in the Midwest (113) and Pacific (92) regions. However, the overall number of academic institutions also varies by region, so a clearer picture can be obtained by examining the spread of Japanese Studies against the national mailing list of 3,139 institutions. The results for 1989 and 1995 are shown in Table 3.11, below.

Table 3.11. Geographic Distribution of Japanese Studies at American Academic Institutions in 1989 and 1995, by Region

Year	1989		1995		Institutions		Increase	
Region	#	%	#	%	#	%	#	%
Northeast	61	14.5	76	18.0	422	13.4	+15	+24.5
Mid-Atlantic	40	8.8	69	15.1	457	14.6	+29	+72.5
South	30	4.5	48	7.1	673	21.4	+18	+66.7
Midwest	72	9.3	113	14.7	771	24.6	+41	+56.9
Southwest	14	5.2	24	9.0	268	8.5	+10	+71.4
Mountain	8	5.3	18	12.0	150	4.8	+10	+125.0
Pacific	71	17.8	92	23.1	398	12.7	+21	+29.6
Total	296	9.4	440	14.0	3,139	100.0	+144	+48.6

The Pacific region has the highest overall availability rate, with some Japanese Studies available at nearly one out of four academic institutions in the region. Next is the Northeast, where almost one of every five institutions has some Japanese Studies. The lowest availability rate is in the South, where despite a 66.7 percent growth rate since 1989, Japanese Studies is still only present at 7.1 percent of academic institutions. The greatest increase in number of institutions came in the Midwest and the Mid-Atlantic regions, both of which have seen over 50 percent growth since 1989. The Southwest and Mountain regions also showed very rapid growth. The small Mountain region has now almost caught up to the Mid-Atlantic and Midwest in its overall rate of availability of Japanese Studies, but the South and Southwest still lag behind.

While regional variations remain, the growth of Japanese Studies since 1989 has served to narrow the differences between regions rather than exacerbate them. There is plenty of room for further growth of Japanese Studies in all parts of the United States, but as we have already seen, that will come about mostly through extension to additional undergraduate institutions. By 1995, Japanese Studies was already available at over two-thirds of the institutions with doctoral programs in the Pacific region, and at half or more of the doctoral-level institutions in the Northeast, Mid-Atlantic, and Midwest regions. Even in the South and Southwest-Mountain regions, Japanese Studies is already available at more than 40 percent of doctoral-level institutions. As shown in Table 3.12, there is considerably more room for growth at other levels.

The table reveals more clearly the high rate of availability of Japanese Studies at Pacific region institutions, where two-thirds of doctoral institutions, nearly half of MA-granting institutions and 40 percent of BA-granting institutions have some Japanese Studies. About a quarter of institutions offering bachelor's degrees in the Northeast, Mid-Atlantic, and Midwest have some Japanese Studies available.

Table 3.12. Rate of Availability (in percent) of Japanese Studies at American Institutions in 1995, by Region and Level of Degree Offered*

Degree Region	Associate	Bachelor's	Master's	Doctorate
Northeast	7.4 (15)	27.8 (74)	34.1 (62)	55.6 (30)
Mid-Atlantic	9.4 (21)	24.4 (61)	29.3 (46)	59.2 (29)
South	5.2 (19)	14.0 (46)	22.3 (43)	44.6 (29)
Midwest	8.6 (38)	23.5 (100)	29.2 (70)	60.0 (42)
Southwest-Mountain	4.8 (12)	19.2 (38)	24.5 (35)	42.9 (27)
Pacific	12.6 (24)	40.5 (64)	46.8 (58)	68.6 (24)
All Regions	7.7 (129)	23.5 (383)	30.2 (314)	53.9 (181)

*This table combines separate analyses for each level at which degrees are offered. There is considerable overlap between categories, and the numbers cannot be summed horizontally.

Assuming that advanced degree programs are "nested" at institutions that also offer bachelors degrees, a little mental arithmetic reveals that to date it is primarily in the Midwest and Mid-Atlantic regions that Japanese Studies is available at undergraduate institutions that do not offer advanced degrees. Interestingly, this pattern has emerged even though the penetration of Japanese Studies into institutions offering master's degrees is not particularly high in these two regions, apparently because these two regions have a relatively higher percentage of four-year colleges that do not offer advanced degrees. By contrast, in the Pacific and Southwest-Mountain regions, roughly three-quarters of institutions offering bachelor's degrees also offer master's degrees.

Growth, as we have been analyzing it up to this point, means the introduction of some amount of Japanese Studies at an institution that previously had none, which we have been careful to call "presence," "availability," or "extension." In terms of employment opportunity and the overall quality of Japanese Studies, one might well argue that every institution that already has some Japanese Studies is a potential candidate for internal expansion of its program into new disciplines and through greater depth of coverage. To assess the scope of existing Japanese Studies programs and their pattern of internal growth we must leave behind the secondary list of institutions with Japan specialist faculty and look more closely at the data contributed by the 247 academic institutions with full entries in the 1995 institutional directory, which we will do in Chapter Eight.

We can conclude this general analysis of the spread of Japanese Studies into American academic institutions by asking whether there is evidence of saturation, and if so, whether the rise in non-academic employment of Japan specialists should be read as a consequence of the lack of opportunity for academic employment. The answer to both questions is clearly negative. While there may well be years with a poor academic job market for Japan specialists, and in any particular year there might appear to be too many candidates competing for scarce slots in one discipline, there have been just as many years when academic positions in Japanese Studies remained unfilled because of a shortage of qualified candidates.

The results of this careful analysis of the extension of Japanese Studies into American academic institutions of various types suggest that the subject is now quite commonly available at larger and moderately selective institutions, and not simply at those offering graduate degrees. Having broken through the barrier of being treated as an exotic field suitable only for elite graduate institutions, Japanese Studies still has plenty of room to expand into the mainstream of undergraduate institutions. Moreover, the large proportion of institutions that have only one or two Japan specialists on their faculty suggests that there also remains plenty of room to increase the density of Japanese Studies at institutions that already have a minimal presence.

There are, however, two potential limitations to this continued expansion. The first is that as Japanese Studies reaches the ranks of smaller institutions, the institutional opportunities to make a new appointment shrink, and the probability that the institution could commit a scarce position to a Japan specialist also shrinks. More appointments of Japan specialists at small institutions are likely to be serendipitous, rather than deliberate institutional commitments that are explicitly advertised as positions for a Japan or East Asian specialist. Job seekers in Japanese Studies will need to search more broadly and present themselves more creatively in order to fill these unmarked disciplinary slots.

The second potential limitation is that as Japanese Studies spreads more widely into the American academic mainstream, there will be less of a fit between the elite academic preparation and qualifications of trained Japan specialists and the institutions settings at which jobs become available. For the next decade much of the expansion will remain at institutions that are moderately selective, and this will be matched by the continued expansion of doctoral training in Japanese Studies into public institutions that are somewhat more accessible as well. Over time, normalization of both doctoral training and job opportunities should begin to even out the fit between the two. In the interim, however, there may be some status gaps to overcome. Some new PhDs who feel that there are no academic positions available in the United States that suit their qualifications may choose either non-academic employment or academic employment in another country as a preferable alternative. We will take up these issues again in Chapter Nine, in the context of a more detailed analysis of the actual academic job market in Japanese Studies.

NON-ACADEMIC EMPLOYMENT IN JAPANESE STUDIES

Another approach to the question of possible saturation of academic employment as the reason for non-academic employment is to look more closely at the types of non-academic institutions that currently employ Japan specialists, to see if they seem to draw from the same pool of specialists that would otherwise go into academics. The 1989 and 1995 directory data on non-academic institutions do not lend themselves readily to comparative analysis, but we can offer some circumstantial evidence of the direction of development, and some baseline data on non-academic employment in 1995 that may prove to be useful in the future.

The 1977 CULCON study reported some institutional data on library holdings from eight museums and seven libraries not affiliated with academic institutions, but no staff counts were reported.[5] The 1984 Japan Foundation study reported that its institutional questionnaire was sent to seven non-academic institutions, but only the Library of Congress responded.[6] For the 1989 directory study, non-academic institutions were defined as museums, freestanding libraries, research institutes, and other organizations engaged in the study of Japan that had professional Japan specialists on their staff. Institutional questionnaires were sent to a mailing list of such organizations that were known or thought to have sufficient connection to the study of Japan that they might want to be listed in the directory. This procedure resulted in a set of 51 institutional directory entries with varying degrees of involvement in Japanese Studies.

The 1995 directory initially used the same definition and procedures, which resulted in a slightly smaller but very similar list of 45 entries for the institutional directory. However, our improved data linkage procedures in 1995 suddenly brought to light an extensive pool of Japan specialists who were employed at non-academic institutions that fell outside that list of non-academic

---

[5] 1977 CULCON Report, Appendix V, Table 33 p. 138.
[6] 1984 Japan Foundation Report, Appendix 2, p. 110-11.

institutional entries. Because of the growing significance of non-academic employment in Japanese Studies, we printed a supplemental list of 167 American Japan specialists who work at 149 "Other non-academic institutions with Japan specialist staff" in the 1995 directory, analogous to the supplemental list of Japan specialists at "other academic institutions."

Table 3.13 gives the combined tally from these two sources by type of institution. It shows the number of institutions and the number of Japan specialists employed by each type of institution. Libraries and museums have been combined because many of the museums also have libraries and library staff, and the categories were difficult to separate. This category does not include Japan-specialist librarians at academic institutions, who for purposes of this chapter have been considered as employees of academic institutions.

Table 3.13. Non-Academic Institutions with Japan Specialist Staff

Type of Institution	Institutions		Specialists	
	#	%	#	%
Museums, Libraries	35	18.3	66	24.4
Research Institutes	22	11.5	32	11.9
Consulting Firms	31	16.2	32	11.9
Corporations, Financial Institutions	21	11.0	22	8.1
Government Agencies	21	11.0	34	12.6
Law Offices	17	8.9	18	6.7
Foundations, Societies	19	9.9	39	14.4
Media Organizations	11	5.8	13	4.8
Schools, Educ. Orgs.	10	5.2	10	3.7
Other	4	2.1	4	1.5
Total	191	99.9	270	100.0

At most, forty percent of these institutions fit our earlier definition of non-academic Japanese Studies institutions. In addition to federal, state, and local governments, they include law firms, consulting firms, brokerage houses, media companies, large corporations, and small businesses. Although there have always been some Japan specialists in government agencies, their higher visibility now reflects the increased demand for specialists with doctoral-level training in Japanese Studies to handle high priority economic and political aspects of the U.S.-Japan relationship. The relatively high percentage of consulting firms, corporations, financial institutions, and law offices with Japan specialists on staff attests to the strong market demand for such expertise in the U.S. economy. Similarly, the presence of media organizations and schools (secondary and commercial) in the list reflects general public demand for knowledge about Japan. While some of these positions require doctoral training in Japanese Studies, many require either experiential training or other academic credentials such as advanced professional degrees. They clearly reflect the differentiation of Japanese Studies rather than simply a saturation of the academic market for Japan specialists.

The number of Japan specialists we have counted at these non-academic institutions is still modest, but we predict that future studies will report rapid growth from these baseline numbers. Our 1995 study undoubtedly undercounts the actual number of Japan specialists working in these environments, because heretofore we have not known how to find them except through the earlier definition of non-academic institutions as libraries, museums, and research institutes. Now that we know more clearly what kinds of non-academic institutions employ Japan specialists, it may be easier to locate these individuals in the future.

Although the list was generated largely from the directory entries of Japan specialists and thus in one sense is simply another specification of what non-faculty Japan specialists do, putting it into institutional perspective reveals more clearly the two major trends in contemporary Japanese Studies. First, these institutional affiliations shed more light on the kinds of highly specialized knowledge of Japan that now have market value, and many of them require decidedly non-traditional expertise. Second, most of these institutions are not special institutions devoted to the study of Japan; they are the normal institutions of American society, which now require the expertise of professional Japan specialists in order to function. They represent, therefore, the normalization and integration of the study of Japan not just into the American academic mainstream, but into the mainstream of American society itself.

With this broader understanding of the range of institutions settings in which Japan specialists now work, we next direct our inquiry into the kinds of expertise Japan specialists possess, and what they do with it.

PART II:

JAPAN SPECIALISTS
IN THE 1990S

4

Expertise and Credentials of Japan Specialists

In this chapter we will examine the nature of the expertise that the term "Japan specialist" embodies, by looking at the areas of specialization reported by Japan specialists and the professional qualifications that underlie their expertise.

VARIETIES OF EXPERTISE

Chapter Three pointed in very general terms to the differentiation of Japan specialists into academic and non-academic employment. However, each of those institutional categories includes persons with a variety of specific occupations or positions that require differing kinds of expertise. Table 4.1 shows the occupational distribution of Japan specialists within different institutional settings, including those with no reported institutional affiliation. At academic institutions, over three-fourths of the Japan specialists are current faculty. The addition of emeritus faculty (some of whom still teach or participate in academic affairs) raises this to about 85 percent. The remainder are mostly librarians and educational administrators. No other occupation accounts for as much as one percent of those employed at academic institutions.

The population is much more diverse in the category of non-academic institutions, with persons in business (16.3 percent) or some form of government service (13.9 percent) the most numerous. These two categories constitute close to a third of the total. Foundation staff, lawyers, research staff, and museum curators each comprise about eight percent of the total, and together make up another third of the distribution. Pre-collegiate teachers, librarians, mass media professionals, faculty, and other professionals account for another five percent each. Among the relatively small group of Japan specialists without institutional affiliations, the distribution again differs. The largest working categories with no institutional affiliation are translators and interpreters (14.1 percent), independent business persons (11.5 percent), and writers (10.3 percent).

One anomaly of Table 4.1 is the number of persons with no listed affiliation or a non-academic affiliation who report their occupation as college or university faculty. In some cases these may be persons who currently teach but do not have a regular affiliation with an academic institution, while in other cases the person may have reported the primary occupation with which they define themselves, even though they are not currently employed in that capacity. And in a few cases, our data management was simply unable to keep up with the specialist's changing affiliations.

Table 4.1. Occupational Distribution of Japan Specialists by Institutional Affiliation

Occupation	Academic Institution		Non-Academic Institution		No Affiliation	
	#	%	#	%	#	%
Faculty	994	80.9	11	4.5	12	15.4
Educ. Administration	25	2.0	5	2.0	0	0.0
Librarian	42	3.4	12	4.9	1	1.3
Research Staff	11	0.9	20	8.2	3	3.8
Foundation Staff	5	0.4	21	8.6	1	1.3
Government Service	4	0.3	34	13.9	4	5.1
Mass Media	1	0.1	12	4.9	3	3.8
Business	8	0.7	40	16.3	9	11.5
Translator, Interp.	4	0.3	4	1.6	11	14.1
Writer	9	0.7	5	2.0	8	10.3
Lawyer	3	0.2	21	8.6	6	7.7
Museum Curator	2	0.2	20	8.2	1	1.3
Teacher (pre-collegiate)	0	0.0	13	5.3	1	1.3
Other Occupations	7	0.6	12	4.9	4	5.1
Emeritus Faculty	95	7.7	3	1.2	0	0.0
Independent, Retired	19	1.5	12	4.9	14	17.9
Total	1,229	99.9	245	100.0	78	99.9

We have also left all emeritus faculty, independent scholars, and retirees in the table so the count is complete. Their distribution across all three institutional categories makes clear the imprecision of the various distinctions we use to divide the sample into occupational, institutional, or employment groupings. At the same time, the table reveals the underlying structure of the main variable we have created to classify Japan specialists by their employment status. The faculty category in the top row of the table is largely but not completely composed of persons currently affiliated with academic institutions. The retiree-independent scholar category includes persons listed in the bottom two rows of the table, which again spans various institutional affiliations. Everyone else is classified as non-faculty.

This diversity of occupations hints at the wide range of expertise American Japan specialists now offer in various institutional settings. And even though academic faculty still dominate the pool, we must remember that they also represent quite a wide variety of academic disciplines. What makes all of these people Japan specialists? Let us begin with what it is they know.

In both the 1989 and 1995 directory questionnaires, Japan specialists were offered the opportunity to define their areas of expertise along three dimensions: historical period, geographic area, and subject matter. Respondents were permitted to select as many categories as they wished in each dimension, and their selections were used to construct the indexes that appeared in both editions of the directory to help identify individuals with particular kinds of expertise. We can now use the same information to assess the overall range of expertise on Japan that is available in the United States.

SPECIALIZATION IN A HISTORICAL PERIOD

Respondents were offered a list of sixteen periods of Japanese history, including three subdivisions of the Tokugawa era and two of the Showa era. A total of 4,516 historical-period selections were made by 1,347 respondents, or an average of 3.35 responses per person. For the Tokugawa and Showa eras some persons selected subperiods but not the whole era, and vice versa, so we were unable to eliminate the overlap by reducing categories.

As shown in Table 4.2, there is much greater emphasis on modern and contemporary Japan than on the study of earlier periods in Japanese history. Only five percent of specialists have expertise on Japan's prehistory, and only slightly more specialize in the Nara period. About 10–12 percent have expertise in each period from Heian to Tokugawa, but roughly a fifth claim specialization on Tokugawa Japan. About half that many claim expertise on any one part of the Tokugawa period: early, late, or Bakumatsu. The extent of specialists' expertise rises sharply for Meiji and Taisho Japan, and peaks on the Showa era. Over half of all Japan specialists claim to specialize in the postwar portion of Showa, but only a quarter listed the first two decades of Showa (to 1945).

Table 4.2. Historical Periods of Specialization

Historical Period	# of Responses	% of Respondents
Prehistory	69	5.1
Nara	103	7.6
Heian	174	12.9
Kamakura	172	12.8
Ashikaga	135	10.0
Sengoku	131	9.7
Tokugawa	261	19.4
Early Tokugawa	112	8.3
Late Tokugawa	127	9.4
Bakumatsu	149	11.1
Meiji	514	38.2
Taisho	458	34.0
Showa	567	42.1
Early Showa	324	24.1
Postwar Showa	741	55.0
Heisei	479	35.6

There was little variation by employment category for periods prior to the Meiji era. Retirees were more likely to claim specialization on the Meiji era, and least likely to have expertise on the postwar Showa or Heisei periods. As might be expected, there were strong differences in emphasis between disciplinary groups. Only in the humanities and arts, and to a lesser extent in language and linguistics, was there any appreciable interest in premodern Japan. Even so, about half of all humanists claimed expertise on Meiji, Taisho, and Showa Japan. By contrast, about three-quarters of the social scientists and professionals report specialization in postwar Showa Japan, while less than five percent claim expertise in any period prior to the Tokugawa. As the field differentiates away from the core disciplines of the humanities, this tendency to focus on modern and contemporary Japan will undoubtedly accelerate.

SPECIALIZATION ON A GEOGRAPHIC AREA

The impact of the social sciences and professions can also be seen in the pattern of specialization by geographic area. The geographic specialization data are a bit more complex than the historical periods, however, since respondents were asked both about areas of geographic specialization within Japan, and about whether they study Japan in relation to other countries or regions. On the domestic side, the overwhelming majority of respondents (88.6 percent) reported that they study Japan as a whole, as shown in Table 4.3. Relatively small numbers of respondents reported specializing on a particular prefecture or region of Japan. Not surprisingly, the most frequently selected regions were those encompassing the Tokyo metropolitan area (Kanto) and the Kansai region (Kinki), each of which was selected by about 13 percent of the sample. The low level of regional specialization is particularly noteworthy. Of the 1,372 persons who responded to the overall question, only 393 reported any regional expertise, and the average number of regions reported was 1.39.

Considerably more respondents (643) reported that they study Japan in relation to some other country or region. Within this group there was an average of 2.39 responses per person. About half report that they relate Japan to China, and half report studying Japan in relation to some non-Asian country.

Next most frequently selected were Korea (41.5 percent), Southeast Asia (27.2 percent), and Taiwan (25.5 percent). This pattern of responses suggests a contemporary social science interest in comparing Japan to countries with similar economic or political circumstances.

There is virtually no difference by employment category in interest in China versus non-Asian world areas. However, among non-faculty Japan specialists there is substantially greater interest in relating Japan to East Asia. The picture becomes even clearer when we look for disciplinary variations. Humanists are nearly twice as likely to study Japan in relation to China as social scientists. The latter were also much more interested in studying Japan in relation to Korea, Southeast Asia, Taiwan, or other world areas.

Taken together, the various aspects of this pattern reveal quite a bit about the nature of specialization on Japan in the contemporary United States. First, it is clear that Japan specialists take a holistic view of Japan, since the overwhelming majority make no regional choices at all, and relatively few specialize in any particular region. Second, Japan specialists tend to focus rather exclusively on Japan, as evidenced by the low level of response to the international part of the question. This single-minded focus on Japan tends to set Japan specialists apart from specialists on other parts of Asia, with whom they may feel little sense of community. And finally, among those who do look beyond Japan, there is a sharp split between humanists with historical and cultural interests in Japan's ties to China, on the one hand, and social scientists and professionals who compare Japan with economically and politically relevant cases regardless of differences in history and culture, on the other. This sharp divergence in outlook underscores the significance of disciplinary differences as signs of differentiation and specialization within Japanese Studies in the 1990s.

Table 4.3. Geographic Areas of Specialization, Domestic and International

Geographic Region	# of Responses	% of Respondents
DOMESTIC		
All Japan	1,215	88.6
Chubu	76	5.5
Chugoku	62	4.5
Hokkaido	36	2.6
Kanto	174	12.7
Kinki	178	13.0
Kyushu	105	7.7
Shikoku	21	1.5
Tohoku	44	3.2
Total N	1,911	1,372
INTERNATIONAL		
Other Countries (general)	63	9.8
China	323	50.2
Hong Kong	86	13.4
Taiwan	164	25.5
Korea	267	41.5
Southeast Asia	175	27.2
Pacific Islands	60	9.3
Former Soviet Union	71	11.0
Other World Areas	330	51.3
TOTAL N	1,539	643

SUBJECT MATTER SPECIALIZATION

If geographic focus and historical period are relatively straightforward and stable aspects of a specialist's expertise, subject matter specialization is far more volatile and complex. It is the area that reflects a specialist's changing interests and development over time, and thus on a larger scale it also reflects such changes in Japanese Studies as a whole. It is correspondingly very difficult to measure, and there were no attempts to do so prior to the 1989 directory study, except by using academic discipline. Discipline measures a specialist's original training rather than the current uses to which that training is applied. What is required is a much more fine-grained measure of the specific domains of knowledge and topics of interest in which the specialist claims expertise.

One way to collect such information is simply to ask each specialist to write a brief statement of current research interests. Both the 1989 and 1995 directory studies did so, and the directories published the statements in each specialist's directory entry. Such material is extremely difficult to analyze, let alone to index. To cope with the indexing problem, the 1989 directory study also developed an extensive list of subject matter specialization categories in fifteen broad domains of knowledge, from which respondents could select the areas of their own expertise. The scheme was based on a coding system originally developed for classifying publications in the Bibliography of Asian Studies. It was therefore oriented to professional research on Asia, but not specifically Japan. We modified the coding system through consultation with Japan specialists in various disciplines to make the categories as relevant to Japan as possible. However, the scheme is intended to reflect domains of knowledge rather than disciplinary organization, so a particular subject matter specialization may well turn up under a different domain than the one most closely identified with the specialist's discipline. In fact, this should happen frequently because of the interdisciplinary area studies approach that has characterized the training of many Japan specialists.

Since the coding scheme for subject matter specialization was designed to be used in conjunction with the separate coding systems for historical period and geographic area, we tried to keep these dimensions out of the subject matter codes. For example, the codes in the domains of history and literature generally refer to types of history or genres of literature rather than time periods, but in some cases the disciplinary specialists argued vehemently that some time period references were essential to make the category comprehensible to respondents. There were also unavoidable differences between domains in the degree of generality or specificity of the categories. This in turn affects the number of categories respondents choose within a domain.

The 1989 directory published a subject matter specialization index using the categories that had been presented to respondents in the directory entry questionnaires. However, respondents also wrote in a number of new categories in each domain, which appeared in the individual entry but not in the index. These additions were subsequently edited and used to expand the categories for the 1995 directory questionnaire. Respondents again wrote in a number of new categories in 1995, which we were able to edit and incorporate into the index published in Volume III of the 1995 directory. Table 4.4 shows how the subcategories have expanded in each domain through this process.

Table 4.4. Growth in Subject Matter Sub-categories, 1989–1995

Domain	1989	1995 Questionnaire	1995 Directory
Anthropology, Psychology, Sociology	24	32	35
Art and Art History	8	22	24
Business and Economics	14	18	22
Communications, Library Science	8	13	14
Education	7	13	14
Geography and Environment	8	16	17
History	9	11	14
Language and Linguistics	9	13	14
Law	9	20	23
Literature	11	27	30
Performing Arts	15	22	22
Philosophy	8	8	8
Politics	8	15	18
Religion	12	15	16
Science and Technology	8	10	10
Total*	158	255	281

* Figures do not include the general domain, which was also available as a category.

Overall, the number of subcategories in the fifteen subject domains expanded 61.4 percent from the 1989 questionnaire to the 1995 questionnaire, or 77.8 percent from 1989 to the final index entries in the 1995 directory. The expansion does not seem to correlate with the overall number of specialists working in a particular subject matter domain, but it does seem to be related to the specificity of current areas of interest in some domains, which respondents find they can no longer express satisfactorily through general categories.

In domains with relatively stable categories, specialists seem to accept the generic scheme offered, but define their interest more precisely through the substantive categories in other domains. A historian, for example, might select "social history" in the history domain but then define the specific topic through the anthropology-psychology-sociology domain's more substantive categories. Because of this variability in the nature of subcategories within each domain, the overall increase across all domains is probably a reliable indicator of the general trend toward specialization, while any comparison of the size of the increase between domains would be suspect.

Subject matter specialization subcategories clearly reflect the current research and professional interests of respondents. After changes of address, changes and additions of subject matter subcategories were probably the most common way that respondents updated their 1989 directory entries for the 1995 edition of the directory. They did not necessarily delete old subcategory listings, unless they felt they no longer had any interest or expertise in those areas. There was some tendency for persons with the least evidence of any specialization on Japan to report expertise on vast numbers of subcategories, but generally those specialists who were accepted for directory listing, and thus are included in this sample, selected specializations consonant with the other material in their questionnaires.

The actual content of the subcategories that were added for 1995 offers a good indicator of the new directions of research interest in Japanese Studies. In many cases the added categories specify more precisely an area previously included in a more generic way, as when the general category of "minority and ethnic groups" was specified by popular demand into four additional categories: Burakumin, Ainu, refugees and foreign workers, and Korean residents in Japan. Table 4.5. lists the new categories added to each domain for 1995. Categories with an asterisk were derived from write-in responses to the 1995 questionnaires and added to the index. All other categories were included in the 1995 questionnaire.

The list reveals four general trends: the proliferation of specific economic and legal categories related to the increased economic interest in Japan within the United States; greater attention to issues related to women, which appear in several domains; greater and more focused interest in a wide range of social and environmental problems in Japan; and an increase in categories reflecting various aspects of internationalization. The new categories can thus be understood as a complex combination of changes in the relationship between the United States and Japan that have generated demand for new types of expertise; changes in the population of Japan Specialists in the United States, which has brought new interests and forms of expertise into the field; and a greater intimacy and familiarity with Japan that has led to more willingness to explore sensitive issues and social problems.

Table 4.5. New Subject Matter Subcategories in 1995

Anthropology, Psychology, Sociology

Burakumin

Ainu

Refugees, Foreign Workers

Korean Residents in Japan

Modernization and Development

Mental Illness, Psychoanalysis, Psychotherapy

Occupations and Professions

Suicide

Migration, International Migration*

Cross-cultural and Intercultural Communication*

Art and Art History

Ink painting, Calligraphy

Illustrated Texts

Woodblock Prints

Cartoons, Popular Graphics

Buddhist Art

Swords, Armor

Papermaking, bookbinding

Ethnic Costume

Basketry

Folk Art

Flower Arranging

Tea Ceremony

Performance Art

Artistic Patronage, Collecting*

Business and Economics

Comparative Economics

Capital Markets, Investment

Industrial Policy

Consumer Behavior

Women & Work; Women in Business*

Small Entrepreneurship*

Multinational Corporations; Japanese Companies Abroad*

Business History*

Communications, Information, Library Science

Film and Film Studies

Print Media

Machine Translation

Artificial Intelligence

Museums

Education

Teaching Methods, Pedagogy

Early Childhood Education

Adult Education

Corporate Education

Informal Education

Teaching of Traditional Skills, Apprenticeship

International/Intercultural Education*

Geography and Environment

Water Resources

Environmental Pollution

Conservation

Fishing and Fishery Management

Political Geography

Historical Cartography

Transportation

Pilgrimage

History

Military History

Historiography

History of Science*

Local and Regional History*

Women's History*

Language, Linguistics

Rhetoric, Discourse Analysis

Language Learning and Acquisition

Language Testing and Evaluation

Translation, Scientific Translation

Interpretation, Simultaneous
Interpretation*

Law

Human Rights Law

Labor Law

Mental Health Law

Environmental Law

Taxation and Finance Law

Trademark and Copyright Law

Land Use Law

Property Law

Securities Law

Maritime Law

International Trade Law

Contracts, International Contracts*

Anti-Trust and Anti-Monopoly Law*

Corporate Law*

Literature

Classical Poetry

Tokugawa Poetry

Modern Poetry

Diaries

Kanbun Writings

Historical Fiction

Myths

Literary Translation

Literary Themes

Literary Theory

Literary Criticism

Hermeneutics, Semiotics, Discourse
Analysis

Women's Literature

Folk Tales, Folk Literature

Popular Fiction*

Feminist Theory and Criticism*

Oral Narrative, Oral Performance*

Music, Dance, and Theatre Arts

Kyogen

Taiko

Popular Music

Folk Storytelling, Street Performances

Martial Arts

Ritual Performances

Folk and Popular Festivals

Politics and Government

Japanese Marxism

Political Economy

Political Violence, Terrorism

Environmental Problems

Health Policy

Industrial Policy

Public Administration

Political Parties and Electoral Politics*

Women and Politics

Educational Policy

Religion

Monastic Institutions

State Shinto, Religion and Politics

Shamanism

Jishu Buddhism*

Science and Technology

Science Policy

Research Management

*Not included in questionnaire, but added to index because of write-in responses.

It should also be noted that while the 1995 write-in categories necessarily have only a few individual specialists listed under them in the directory index, virtually all of the new categories that were added to the 1995 questionnaire have substantial numbers of specialists listed. They therefore reflect significant new areas of interest and expertise in Japanese Studies, which should be reflected in additional research output over the next few years.

The overall pattern of subject matter specializations, new and old, offers another strategy for assessing the general areas of expertise and interest in Japanese Studies in the United States during the 1990s that is more specific than discipline. Table 4.6 offers several different measures through which we can tease out such a pattern. They include the total number of selections in each domain, the number of respondents making selections in that domain, the mean number of selections made by each respondent in the domain, and the percentage of all respondents who selected one or more subcategories in that domain. Each offers a slightly different rank order, but by combining them we can identify the most popular domains and evaluate the significance of their relative rankings.

Table 4.6. Domains of Subject Matter Specialization, by Number of Responses and Number and Percent of Respondents

Domain	Responses		Respondents	
	#	Mean	#	%
Anthropology, Psychology, Sociology	2,444	3.97	615	40.8
Art and Art History	846	3.14	269	17.9
Business and Economics	1,518	3.42	444	29.5
Communications, Library Science	434	1.90	229	15.2
Education	579	2.15	269	17.9
Geography and Environment	226	1.81	125	8.3
History	1,546	2.42	638	42.3
Language and Linguistics	829	2.74	303	20.1
Law	464	2.71	171	11.3
Literature	1,627	4.51	361	24.0
Music, Dance, Theatre Arts	625	3.08	203	13.5
Philosophy	407	2.05	199	13.2
Politics	1,404	3.15	446	29.6
Religion	1,094	3.27	335	22.2
Science and Technology	416	2.14	194	12.9
Total*	14,459	9.59	1,507	

*Selections are independent, so percentages exceed 100.0. Data were not available for 45 respondents.

The 1,507 respondents who reported subject matter specializations made 14,459 selections, or a mean of 9.59 per person. Each respondent selected from an average of 3.19 of the fifteen subject domains. The anthropology-psychology-sociology domain was selected most often. It had not only the second largest percentage of respondents making selections (40.8 percent) but also the second highest mean number of selections per person (3.97). The domain covers three related social sciences, and it also has quite specific topical categories, but in addition, it was selected by an unusually broad range of respondents, a point we will pursue in greater detail.

The second most frequently selected domain was literature. However, in this case the domain was only selected by a quarter of the respondents, but they chose an average of 4.51 subcategories in the domain, which contained a relatively high number of quite specific subcategories. By contrast, categories in the domain of history were selected by the greatest number of respondents (42.3 percent) but they only chose an average of 2.42 subcategories each, because the categories offered were quite general. The business-economics domain ranked fourth in total number of selections, with 29.5 percent of respondents making an average of 3.42 selections each. Subcategories in politics were selected fifth most frequently, by 29.6 percent of respondents at a rate of 3.15 subcategory selections per person. Religion was sixth in number of selections, with 22.2 percent of respondents making an average of 3.27 choices each.

In sum, the anthropology-psychology-sociology domain and history were the most broadly selected domains, and the large disparity in the number of selections within each domain appears to be due primarily to the difference in the number and type of subcategories available for selection. The domains of business and economics and politics and government were selected by the same proportion of respondents, but the intensity of selection within the domain was slightly higher in the former. Literature ranks exceptionally high in number of selections, but only because a relatively small number of respondents picked a large number of finely distinguished subcategories, while the domain of religion falls comfortably into sixth place on all counts.

Since respondents selected specializations from an average of slightly more than three domains, we should also examine the patterns of domain selection in more detail. Table 4.7. shows the mean number of subject matter subcategories selected in each domain, by the respondent's disciplinary group. We have underlined all cells with a mean of 1.0 or higher as a simple measure of high intensity of selection.

Table 4.7. Mean Number of Subject Matter Specialization Subcategories Selected, by Subject Matter Domain and Discipline Group

DOMAIN	Human	Soc. Sci.	Lang.	Profess	Interdisc.	Arts
Anthro-Psych-Sociolgy	1.02	2.62	1.49	1.21	1.51	1.02
Art History	0.98	0.13	0.36	0.15	0.26	2.72
Business/ Economics	0.28	1.70	0.24	1.81	1.26	0.12
Communications	0.19	0.15	0.33	0.63	0.60	0.23
Education	0.21	0.34	0.68	0.89	0.33	0.21
Geography	0.13	0.22	0.43	0.08	0.21	0.70
History	1.90	0.47	0.34	0.42	1.11	0.14
Language	0.26	0.67	2.83	0.24	0.26	0.07
Law	0.07	0.19	0.10	1.38	0.29	0.02
Literature	2.26	0.11	1.05	0.30	0.8	1.02
Performing Arts	0.46	0.25	0.35	0.06	0.43	3.30
Philosophy	0.48	0.13	0.24	0.09	0.19	0.14
Politics	0.53	1.60	0.19	0.40	2.83	0.00
Religion	1.33	0.33	0.53	0.16	0.53	0.95
Science, Tech.	0.15	0.33	0.24	0.38	0.50	0.07
# Respondents*	570	478	94	213	80	43

*Omits 12 in natural sciences plus 62 for whom relevant data were not available.

The most striking finding in the table is that while most domains are selected heavily only by specialists in one or two disciplinary groups, respondents from all six disciplinary groups selected an average of at least one subcategory per person from the anthropology-psychology-sociology domain. This result could be interpreted in rather different ways, some of which are probably wishful thinking. One possibility is that Japan specialists in all disciplinary groups acknowledge the importance of expertise in the subject matter in this domain, which could translate into a broader demand for Japan specialists in these three disciplines to be included in academic Japanese Studies programs. Or conversely, the finding could imply that Japan specialists regardless of their disciplinary background consider themselves to have sufficient expertise in this domain that trained disciplinary specialists are not necessary. Since the domain is quite broad, with a large number of subcategories, and the average number of selections is much higher for social scientists, it seems likely that persons in all disciplinary groups have identified some specific topics in this domain on which they have expertise, and it is the cumulative effect of such narrow selections that has made the domain so widely chosen.

Read vertically, the table shows the cluster of domains in which persons in each disciplinary group are most likely to have expertise. Each disciplinary group's expertise is clustered fairly heavily in three or four domains, but there is some modest degree of specialization in every other domain as well. This pattern underscores the fact that the subject matter specializations of Japan specialists are not narrowly defined within particular disciplines or even domains of knowledge, but rather reflect the holistic interdisciplinary area studies model that has played such a central role in the field's development. In the present situation of growing specialization and separation between disciplinary groups, this overlap constitutes an important force that links specialists across disciplinary lines and makes it possible for them to communicate about subjects of common interest despite differences of approach. A careful look at the table reveals some points at which the overlap is close to zero. An absence of interest or expertise in a few domains should not be catastrophic, but the wholesale withdrawal of one disciplinary group from involvement in other domains would not be a healthy development for Japanese Studies. Since this is the first time such an analysis of subject matter specializations has been done, we will be able to learn much more from reading the equivalent table when the next study is carried out.

We may also ask whether the subject matter expertise of non-faculty differs from that of faculty. As shown in Table 4.8, there are some important differences, although the general pattern of high selection of specializations within the anthropology-psychology-sociology domain holds across all employment status categories. Aside from this domain, faculty Japan specialists only show means above 1.0 for the domains of history and literature, while non-faculty Japan specialists only have mean selection rates above 1.0 for the domains of business-economics and politics. In the domain of politics, faculty report nearly as much specialization as non-faculty although it does not reach the mean of 1.0, and retirees have an even higher mean level of expertise at 1.14. The same cannot be said for the domain of business and economics, as non-faculty have twice the mean selection rates as specialists in the other two employment status categories.

In short, non-faculty Japan specialists appear to be substantially better equipped than academic faculty to meet the market demand for expertise in the domain of business and economics, even though there are undoubtedly individual Japan specialists within the large category of faculty who possess equivalent levels of expertise. Non-faculty Japan specialists do indeed know something that is quite different from what academic Japan specialists can offer.

Table 4.8. Mean Number of Subject Matter Specialization Subcategories Selected, by
Subject Matter Domain and Employment Status

Domain	Faculty	Non-Faculty	Retired
Anthro-Psychology-Sociology	1.74	1.38	1.43
Art History	0.51	0.67	0.66
Business-Economics	0.80	1.64	0.79
Communications	0.19	0.63	0.11
Education	0.40	0.41	0.23
Geography, Environment	0.16	0.13	0.11
History	1.08	0.81	1.20
Language, Linguistics	0.65	0.36	0.36
Law	0.22	0.55	0.28
Literature	1.31	0.52	0.87
Performing Arts	0.46	0.32	0.35
Philosophy	0.31	0.19	0.20
Politics	0.85	1.08	1.14
Religion	0.82	0.39	0.90
Science, Technology	0.21	0.50	0.19
# Respondents*	998	367	142

*Subject matter specializations not available for 45 respondents.

Having identified the general content of Japan specialists' expertise, we may now ask how they have acquired it, and how they maintain and expand it. This inquiry will take us beyond the basic information published in the 1995 directory, to the survey items that were included in the same instrument. Unfortunately, some specialists either chose not to update their directory entries, or made such changes without completing the new survey questions. The sample for the survey questions is therefore somewhat smaller than the full directory sample of 1,552 that we have used up to this point in the analysis, but it is still a respectable 1,072 cases. Methodological details of the survey are provided in Appendix A.

In this chapter we will explore the foundations of Japan specialists' expertise in two general areas, Japanese language competence and academic credentials. A third foundation area, direct experience, is more elusive. We will try to explore it in the context of examining what Japan specialists do, in Chapter Five. Every Japan specialist should possess some combination of these three foundations, but the field is now too diversified to expect that everyone will need or possess the same qualifications in each area. Our task is to identify systematic patterns of qualification and in the process to highlight problems that need to be addressed.

JAPANESE LANGUAGE SKILLS OF SPECIALISTS

Needs and Competence

Although all of the postwar studies of the state of Japanese Studies in the United States have been concerned about Japanese language training for students, the 1984 Japan Foundation study was the first to try to assess the language competence of Japan specialists.[1] That survey asked respondents to report their own language competence in the four basic skills using a five-point scale, and also asked how they had learned the language. We have replicated these questions with some refinements, and added a new question on how language skills are maintained.

The poles of the continuum of language competence are those who do not know Japanese at all, on the one end, and native speakers, on the other end. In our 1995 survey, 998 persons responded to the language-learning question that included these two options. Less than five percent (4.6 percent) reported that they do not know any Japanese, and 17.1 percent reported that they were native speakers. This is a slightly lower percentage of native speakers than was reported in the 1984 Japan Foundation survey, but the percentage who did not know any Japanese was not reported in the 1984 study. Our 4.6 percent figure appears to be a slight underreport due to persons who did not answer the question at all, since the number reporting "no usable proficiency" on the questions concerning language skills is higher and the total number of respondents is slightly different. We cannot obtain a percentage of actual native speakers from the questions on language skills, because they ask only for "native fluency."

The 1984 self-report questions on language competence featured a five-point scale ranging from "no usable proficiency" to "native fluency." The points in between measured language competence "adequate for everyday usage," "sufficient for limited scholarly needs," and "can handle scholarly needs with ease." We felt that the gap between the latter two categories was too large, and added "meets scholarly needs adequately" in between, to cover the stage at which specialists do conduct research in Japanese, but with considerable strain.

---

[1] The 1970 SSRC-ACLS report discussed Japan specialists' length of study of Japanese language in Japan and the United States by age group, but did not assess individual competence or provide figures that could be used for comparison.

Chapter Four

Table 4.9. Specialists' Japanese Language Competence by Language Skill, 1984 and
1995

Language Skill and Competence Level	1984		1995	
	%	Cum %	%	Cum %
LISTENING				
No Usable Proficiency	10	10	8.9	8.9
Adequate for Daily Needs	14	24	15.4	24.4
Limited Scholarly Needs	19	43	12.2	36.5
Adequate for Scholarship	--	--	19.0	55.5
Scholarship with Ease	28	71	20.4	75.9
Native Proficiency	29	100	24.1	100.0
N	789		1,010	
SPEAKING				
No Usable Proficiency	9	9	9.5	9.5
Adequate for Daily Needs	16	25	15.6	25.1
Limited Scholarly Needs	21	46	13.5	38.6
Adequate for Scholarship	--	--	20.9	59.5
Scholarship with Ease	27	73	17.7	77.2
Native Proficiency	27	100	22.8	100.0
N	813		1,010	
READING				
No Usable Proficiency	12	12	16.4	16.4
Adequate for Daily Needs	6	18	7.8	24.2
Limited Scholarly Needs	19	37	9.8	34.1
Adequate for Scholarship	--	--	24.6	77.2
Scholarship with Ease	37	74	24.6	77.2
Native Proficiency	26	100	22.8	100.0
N	805		1,007	
WRITING				
No Usable Proficiency	22	22	24.6	24.6
Adequate for Daily Needs	22	44	18.7	43.3
Limited Scholarly Needs	20	64	16.6	59.9
Adequate for Scholarship	–	–	14.2	74.0
Scholarship with Ease	13	77	6.3	80.3
Native Proficiency	23	100	19.7	100.0
N	797		989	

*1984 data from 1984 Japan Foundation Report, Table 21, p. 40.

The distributions for 1989 and 1995 are shown in Table 4.9 above. The percentage reporting no usable language proficiency is roughly the same for speaking and listening, but a larger percentage than in 1984 report that they cannot read or write Japanese. A smaller percentage also now claim native proficiency in each of the four skills. The pattern at the extreme ends of the continuum might suggest an overall decline in language competence, but the cumulative percentages clarify the picture.

In fact the proportion of Japan specialists with research competence in Japanese has increased in all four skills; a smaller cumulative percentage of the sample has Japanese language skills that are not adequate for scholarly needs (the first three categories) than was true in 1984. Moreover, for every skill except writing in Japanese, nearly two-thirds of the sample reports competence that is adequate for research purposes. We may also speculate that the addition of another point in the scale has caused respondents to define their own research competence more precisely and perhaps more realistically.

The expansion of Japanese Studies into a broader range of academic disciplines, plus the increased number of Japan specialists who work outside of academia, suggests that there may be less consensus now on the importance of language skills. The survey asked how important respondents thought it was for their work to be able to understand Japanese, speak it fluently, read modern Japanese, read classical Japanese, and write Japanese. This question used a simple three-point scale. A solid majority thought it was indispensable to be able to understand spoken Japanese (57.5 percent), speak Japanese fluently (52.6 percent), and read modern Japanese (66.9 percent). However, around 10 percent of the sample said these skills were not necessary for their work. Only a quarter found it indispensable to read classical Japanese (26.9 percent) or to write in Japanese (27.5 percent).[2] Nearly half found classical Japanese unnecessary, while about a quarter thought the ability to write in Japanese was not necessary. The remainder found each of these skills to be useful but not indispensable.

Moreover, there was a very high correlation between one's personal competence in these skills and the perception of their utility. For each of the four basic skills, those who reported no usable competence generally felt the skill was "not necessary." The proportion who thought a skill was "useful" increased steadily with competence level, and persons with research-level competence overwhelmingly felt that these language skills were "indispensable." This finding may suggest that ignorance is bliss, or that those who have put tremendous effort into learning Japanese have to justify it somehow, but it may also reflect genuine differences in the types of work that Japan specialists do, and real variations in their need for Japanese language skills.

---

[2] Throughout this discussion we understand "write in Japanese" to mean composing written texts such as letters, reports, or essays, and not the simple act of writing Chinese characters. We trust that the survey respondents understood it the same way.

Table 4.10. Language Competence and Perception of its Importance, by Language
Skill and Age, 1995*

Competence Levels	Perception Mean	#	Ability Mean	#
LISTENING				
<35	1.71	38	3.83	36
35–44	1.66	211	3.47	210
45–54	1.51	314	2.94	323
55–64	1.38	217	2.84	224
>64	1.35	189	2.55	204
Total	1.49	969	2.99	997
SPEAKING				
<35	1.59	39	3.67	36
35–44	1.60	211	3.33	210
45–54	1.43	314	2.83	322
55–64	1.28	213	2.76	226
>64	1.29	189	2.53	204
Total	1.41	976	2.90	998
READING (Modern)				
<35	1.79	38	3.69	36
35–44	1.77	211	3.45	210
45–54	1.59	312	2.92	324
55–64	1.45	214	2.76	223
>64	1.41	192	2.57	202
Total	1.57	967	2.96	985
WRITING				
<35	1.29	38	2.18	36
35–44	1.20	209	2.62	209
45–54	0.99	311	2.07	324
55–64	0.87	207	2.05	218
>64	0.82	180	1.81	190
Total	1.00	945	2.18	977

* Perception is measured on a 3-point scale: 0 = not necessary; 1 = useful; 2 = indispensable.
The mean falls between 0 and 2.0. Language competence is measured on a 6-point scale: 0 =
no usable competence; 1 = adequate for daily needs but not for research; 2 = sufficient for
limited scholarly needs; 3 = meets research needs adequately; 4 = meets research needs with
ease; 5 = native proficiency. The mean falls between 0 and 5.0.

We can explore these possibilities by a close examination of three overlapping variables that could affect both language skills and the perception of the need for them. To make the analysis easier to evaluate, we will use the mean rank on each language competence scale, rather than showing the full distribution. Table 4.10 above shows the results for age. For each language skill, both actual language competence and the respondent's perception of the importance of the skill are highest among the youngest Japan specialists and decline steadily in each successive age cohort. These results reflect improved language training and rising expectations of language competence over the past several decades. The only category for which the results may be unreliable is the youngest, both because of its small size and because it contains a relatively higher proportion of native speaking language teachers. Yet the mean scores in this category are consistent with the overall pattern. The high correlation between language competence and perception is apparent despite the difference in scale between the two measures.

For the first three skills of listening comprehension, speaking, and reading, the mean for all age groups is above 1.0, meaning that there is a general perception that these skills are at least useful. In younger age groups the mean approaches 2.0, meaning that a higher proportion think the skill is indispensable. On the self-assessment of language competence, a mean of 3.0 reflects language competence that meets research needs adequately. For the two youngest age groups the means exceed this level, while for the 45-54 age group they fall just below it. Only in the two oldest age groups is the average level of Japanese language competence less than adequate for research needs. Of course the mean score is an average for individuals with widely varying language abilities, and there are certainly other factors at work besides age. One which captures part of the age effect but also makes an occupational distinction is the variable of current employment status, which we have previously found to be related to the specialization patterns of Japan specialists. The results for language perception and competence are shown in Table 4.11.

For all four language skills, in both language competence and perception of its importance, current faculty have the highest mean scores, retirees (who are predominantly emeritus faculty) have the next highest, and non-faculty have lower mean scores. The difference between current faculty and retirees reflects the age difference noted in the previous analysis, while the distinction between faculty and non-faculty adds the new dimension of type of work. For the three basic skills of listening, speaking and reading modern Japanese, current faculty have average self-reported competency scores above 3.0, which means that faculty in general possess research-level competence in Japanese. Both retirees and non-faculty have mean scores below that level. Retirees score higher than non-faculty, but the differences between them are not great.

Table 4.11. Language Competence and Perception of Its Importance, by Language
Skill and Current Employment Status, 1995

Employment Status and Four Language Skills	*Mean*	*Perception* #	*Mean*	*Ability* #
LISTENING				
Faculty	1.56	671	3.12	685
Retired	1.42	89	2.72	96
Not Faculty	1.33	223	2.70	229
Total	1.49	983	2.99	1,010
SPEAKING				
Faculty	1.48	667	3.03	685
Retired	1.34	90	2.67	97
Not Faculty	1.24	222	2.90	228
Total	1.41	979	2.90	1,010
READING				
Faculty	1.65	669	3.16	680
Retired	1.57	89	2.79	97
Not Faculty	1.32	222	2.43	230
Total	1.57	980	2.96	1,007
WRITING				
Faculty	1.05	655	2.34	670
Retired	0.98	82	2.09	94
Not Faculty	0.85	221	1.73	225
Total	1.00	958	2.18	989

These findings suggest that while academic Japan specialists need research level competence in Japanese for their work, other types of Japan specialists may not find these skills necessary. One way of investigating this possibility is through differences between disciplinary groups, which we already have found are related differentially to non-academic employment.

Disciplinary groups scale almost as perfectly as age and employment status for every language skill, on both actual competence and perception of its importance, as shown in Table 4.12. The only group too small to be reliable is the arts, which ranks lowest on perception of the importance of each skill, but registers mean scores above interdisciplinary fields on self-reported competence in all skills except listening comprehension.

Table 4.12. Language Competence and Perception of Its Importance, by Language Skill and Disciplinary Category, 1995

Disciplinary Categories and Four Language Skills	Mean	Perception (#)	Mean	Ability (#)
LISTENING				
Language & Linguistics	1.90	69	4.29	68
Humanities	1.53	395	3.20	399
Social Sciences	1.53	291	2.94	305
Professions	1.25	133	2.39	136
Interdisciplinary	1.30	50	2.21	53
Arts	1.19	26	2.18	28
Total	1.49	964	3.00	989
SPEAKING				
Language & Linguistics	1.87	70	4.25	68
Humanities	1.45	395	3.10	399
Social Sciences	1.45	285	2.85	307
Professions	1.18	50	2.04	52
Interdisciplinary	1.18	50	2.04	52
Arts	1.04	26	2.18	28
Total	1.41	960	2.91	989
READING				
Language & Linguistics	1.91	69	4.27	67
Humanities	1.76	395	3.37	403
Social Sciences	1.51	290	2.80	303
Professions	1.21	132	2.13	134
Interdisciplinary	1.14	49	1.77	53
Arts	1.07	26	2.07	27
Total	1.57	961	2.96	987
WRITING				
Language & Linguistics	1.71	68	3.90	67
Humanities	1.03	385	2.29	392
Social Sciences	0.95	280	2.12	298
Professions	0.83	130	1.66	134
Interdisciplinary	0.66	50	1.18	51
Arts	0.62	26	1.55	27
Total	0.99	939	2.18	969

The relatively small category of language and linguistics scores 4.25 or higher in competence on all skills except writing. These scores, near native fluency, clearly reflect the high proportion of native speakers of Japanese in this category. Specialists in the humanities have mean scores above 3.0 in listening, speaking, and reading, while the social sciences have mean scores just under 3.0. Interestingly, although their mean language competence scores are lower, the social scientists perceive listening and speaking skills to be just as important for their work as the humanists do, with mean scores midway between "useful" and "indispensable." The two groups diverge on the importance of reading skills, with humanists finding them nearly indispensable (mean = 1.76) and having mean competence of 3.37, while social scientists find reading skills midway between "useful" and "indispensable", and their own average competence falls a bit below the "adequate for research needs" level at 2.80.

Beyond the core academic disciplines, the mean scores indicate that listening, reading, and speaking Japanese are considered useful, and average language competence in listening, speaking, and reading is only sufficient for limited research needs. For all three of these disciplinary groups, listening and speaking competence levels are higher than reading competence, with corresponding perception of their relative importance. Only the largely native-speaking language and linguistics specialists think the ability to write Japanese is anywhere near indispensable, and even they do not generally have sufficient writing ability in Japanese to meet their research needs with ease.

Although we cannot combine these variables further without moving to multivariate statistical techniques that are beyond the scope of this report, the general pattern is now both clear and consistent. In sum, younger age cohorts of Japan specialists have both greater language competence and greater appreciation of the importance of Japanese language skills, but there are also differences in both language competence and perception of its importance between faculty and non-faculty, and between the central academic disciplines engaged in Japanese Studies and those farther removed from the traditional core fields.

It must be emphasized that this analysis is of mean scores, and every category has some specialists with very high language competence. On all three of these dimensions (age, employment status, and disciplinary group) the standard deviations on the competence measures scale in the reverse direction from the mean scores, implying that there is more internal variability among the categories that have lower mean scores.

In this sample, gender also had a systematic effect on both competence levels and perceptions of the importance of language skills. Most of the effect was due to the confounding of gender with native Japanese status, as measured by Japanese citizenship. While the native Japanese in the survey sample were almost equally divided by gender, only a quarter of the much larger population of non-Japanese were women. The result of this differential is that while nearly a quarter of the women in the survey sample were native Japanese, only 8.3 percent of the men were. Although this factor accounted for most of the gender gap, even when Japanese citizens were removed from the analysis, women who were not native Japanese had both higher mean language competence and higher mean perceptions of the importance of language skills than did men who were not native Japanese. However, as we noted earlier in the study, the women in this sample tend to be found in the younger age groups, and we have already found that Japanese language competence is higher in the younger age groups. The only two categories where the presence of native Japanese would have an appreciable effect on the overall means are the youngest age category (under 35) and the language and linguistics discipline category. We have noted this possibility in the discussion of each case.

In this analysis we have looked separately at each of the four language skills in order to see the variability in their importance for different groups of Japan specialists. However, to simplify the use of language competence as a variable in subsequent analyses, the respondents' self-reported competence in the three main Japanese language skills of listening comprehension, speaking fluency, and reading ability can be summed to produce a general measure of language competence. We have dropped writing because of the general consensus that it is less important, and because the lower levels of competence might also confound the meaning of the combined scores. The basic sum of the three scores produces a range from 0 for persons with no usable competence in any of the three language skills to 15, for native proficiency in all three.

Overall, 7.9 percent of the survey respondents reported no usable Japanese language skills at all, 12.2 percent had language skills at the level of meeting daily needs, while another 21.0 percent had scores indicating they could meet only minimal scholarly needs. The remainder had scores representing either language skill levels that were adequate for scholarly use (21.0 percent) or reported full scholarly language competence (37.9 percent with either native proficiency or the ability to meet scholarly needs with ease). We have simplified this configuration further by distinguishing between those with Japanese language competence suitable for scholarly use (54.7 percent) and those without that level of language competence (41.1 percent).

Language Learning and Maintenance

Japan specialists in the 1995 survey sample learned their Japanese in virtually the same way the 1984 Japan Foundation survey sample did. There was a very small drop in the proportion of respondents who were native speakers or learned Japanese as children, matched by equally small increases in respondents who had formal training in Japanese in Japan, and those who studied informally outside of Japan.

Respondents were also asked how they maintain their Japanese. The most common response was reading for research purposes, cited by just over half of the respondents. Watching TV and movies, and reading for non-research purposes, were each reported by a third of the respondents. More than a quarter (29.9 percent) said they use Japanese at work, or use it in Japan (27.1 percent). About 15 percent reported using Japanese in leisure activities, or at home. Very few reported taking formal language courses, using a tutor, or participating in a language circle. However, 18.4 percent of respondents reported that they do not have opportunities to maintain their Japanese, and 12.9 percent reported that they do not have time to make use of available opportunities.

When these responses were examined in light of language proficiency, it became apparent that those who have research-level competence in Japanese (the top three categories for listening, speaking, and reading) use their Japanese actively in research, at work, in non-research reading and TV and movie viewing, and on trips to Japan. Those who report that they do not have opportunities to maintain their Japanese, or do not have time to do so, have considerably lower language proficiency. It seems more likely that these respondents did not ever have sufficient language proficiency to read for research or pleasure or to use spoken Japanese at work or at leisure, rather than that their language levels have deteriorated from functional to non-functional levels because of lack of opportunity or time for language maintenance. Not only do those who have a greater investment in Japanese language learning have a greater incentive to maintain their skills, it is simply much easier to do so when the experience is productive and pleasurable rather than painful and difficult.

This suggests that it is doubly important to ensure that budding Japan specialists acquire a high level of language proficiency during their initial training and research. Those who do not achieve a threshold level of research competence in Japanese by the time they complete their dissertations will be less able to maintain their language skills in the United States, and thus less inclined and less able to continue doing research on Japan. Similarly, those who become interested in Japan in mid-career and learn just enough Japanese to do work on Japan with assistance from others are unlikely to be able to maintain and improve their language skills subsequently.

At the same time, the survey results clearly indicate that there are ways to work on Japan that do not require language competence, and that about a quarter of those now working professionally on Japan are able to do so either with no usable language skills or with language sufficient only for meeting everyday needs in Japan. For listening comprehension and spoken Japanese these percentages have remained stable since the 1984 survey, but the percentage of respondents who do not have at least limited research ability to read modern Japanese has increased from 18 to 24 percent in the past decade.

This change probably reflects the occupational and disciplinary shift away from traditional forms of academic research that require reading, rather than a decline in the skill level of persons attempting to do the same kind of work that was done a decade ago.

Academic Credentials

The highest academic degree of the Japan specialist is normally the doctorate (Ph.D.), but even this qualification is far from universal, as previous studies have shown. The 1970 SSRC-ACLS survey did not report academic degrees for the survey sample, but we have tabulated degrees from the roster of 417 Japan specialists that was included as a supplement to the report. The 1984 Japan Foundation survey asked for the respondent's highest degree. Both distributions are shown in Table 4.13, along with the 1995 figures, which we have had to derive in a different way.

Table 4.13. Percent Distribution of Highest Degree Earned by Japan Specialists, 1970, 1984, and 1995*

Highest Degree	1970	1984	1995**
Ph.D.	79.9	81	77.4
ABD	10.8	7	1.8
MA	7.0	9	11.1
JD or other Law Degree	0.7	--	6.5
MBA (Business)	0.0	--	2.9
MLS or Library Science	--	--	2.5
MD (Medical degree)	0.2	--	0.5
MFA (Master of Fine Arts)	--	--	1.3
BA, unknown, other	1.4	--	3.9

* 1970 data from 1970 SSRC-ACLS Report, calculated from supplemental roster of specialists. 1984 data from 1984 Japan Foundation Report, Table 2, p. 14.

** 1995 figure for MAs is for persons with no other advanced degree, but all other degrees are reported in total, and there is some overlap between them. Overlap not calculated for ABDs.

Since the 1989 and 1995 studies were designed to produce complete biographical directory entries, they asked respondents to list all of their academic degrees. In the United States sample for 1995, 1,528 people reported a total of 4,240 academic degrees, including 1,463 bachelor's degrees, 1,423 master's degrees, 1,143 doctoral degrees, and 211 graduate-level professional degrees. Since each person reported an average of 2.8 degrees, with a fair number reporting multiple bachelor's or master's degrees, we have only tried to sort out the overlap for graduate degrees. Within this range alone, 1,440 persons earned 2,777 higher degrees, a mean of 1.93. As might be expected, the overlap was greatest for master's degrees, with 73.6 percent of the sample earning an MA plus a doctorate or professional degree, and 7.8 percent earning multiple MAs, but 6.5 percent also earned both a doctorate and a professional degree or even a second doctorate.

There has been a slight drop in the proportion with a doctorate, and a major decrease in the representation of those who have completed all doctoral work except the dissertation (ABD). This is not due to a decrease in doctoral candidates, as demonstrated in Chapter Two, but rather to a greater reluctance to count them as professional Japan specialists unless they hold a regular professional post before completing their doctorate, which had become much less common by the 1990s. The proportion of MAs has increased slightly over time, reflecting the increased demand for MA level-language instructors. The major difference in the 1995 distribution, however, is the greatly increased representation of persons with other professional degrees. One in eight Japan specialists now holds a professional degree. Most notable are degrees in law (6.5 percent), business (2.9 percent), and library science (2.5 percent). However, more than a third of those who hold such professional credentials also have earned a doctorate. While doctorates remain central to the training of academic Japan specialists, these findings suggest that we need to be concerned about training for specialization on Japan in fields that use degrees other than the doctorate for professional certification.

There are so many varieties of MA-level degrees that we have not attempted to differentiate among them, except to separate out the Master's in Business Administration, Master's in Library Science, and Master of Fine Arts, which constitute recognized professional degrees that are regarded as terminal credentials in lieu of a doctorate in their respective professional fields. It is therefore particularly noteworthy that so many with professional degrees also hold doctorates. This probably reflects the reality that our sample is heavily composed of academics, who may need a doctorate in addition to a professional credential in order to teach that graduate-level professional field in a university.

A brief comparison of specialists with academic doctorates and those with professional degrees reveals systematic differences along the lines we have come to expect, as shown in the various decks of Table 4.14.[3] A

---

[3] To make the best use of a relatively small sample with professional degrees, we have ignored the overlap betwen the two groups, and we simply compare all those with a doctorate (1,133 in this analysis) with all who have a professional degree (234). Persons with an MA and no other degree are omitted from the comparison. However, persons with master's level professional degrees in public administration and international affairs that may serve as a formal credential for government service are included in the professional category for this analysis.

comparison of the employment status of the two groups shows that the proportion of retirees is about the same in both groups, but almost half (48.7 percent) of those with professional degrees have non-faculty employment, while more than three-quarters (77.2 percent) of those with doctorates are employed as faculty (Deck A). There is also a gender gap: the professional group is only 20.9 percent female, compared to 26.5 percent of the doctoral group (Deck B), although there is virtually no difference in the two age distributions that might account for it. The regional distribution of the two groups supports the institutional analysis of Chapter Three, as specialists with professional degrees are concentrated more heavily in the Mid-Atlantic and Pacific regions (not shown), where employment in non-academic institutions was found to be higher.

Table 4.14. Comparison of Specialists with Doctorates and Specialists with Professional Degrees, by Employment Status, Gender, and Language Competence

	Doctorate		*Professional*	
	#	%	#	%
A. Employment Status				
Faculty	875	77.2	97	41.5
Not Faculty	143	12.6	114	48.7
Retired	115	10.2	23	9.8
Total	1,133	100.0	234	100.0
B. Gender				
Male	833	73.5	185	79.1
Female	300	26.5	49	20.9
Total	1,133	100.0	234	100.0
C. Language Competence*				
Scholarly Use	455	60.9	71	47.7
Not Scholarly Use	237	31.7	55	36.9
None	55	7.4	23	15.4
Total	747	100.0	149	100.0

*Sample size is reduced for the language analysis because the scale is based on survey data that are available for a smaller number of respondents.

There is also a strong difference in language competence between the two groups. Among specialists with a doctorate, only seven percent had no usable Japanese language proficiency, and 60.9 percent had language skills suitable for scholarly use. By contrast, less than half (47.7 percent) of those with professional degrees had language competence suitable for scholarly use, and 15 percent had no usable Japanese language skills (Deck C).

The figure of 60 percent with doctorates having language competence suitable for scholarly use may seem rather low for Japan specialists, but the sample includes many persons who were not trained as Japan specialists in graduate school and became interested in the study of Japan at some later point, as well as some who because of the nature of their specialization are able to work without using Japanese. This is not a new phenomenon, but has been true of Japanese Studies in the United States during its entire history. We can explore this issue further through a survey question included in both the 1984 and 1995 studies, that asked whether the respondent wrote a doctoral dissertation that was wholly on Japan, partly on Japan, or not at all about Japan.

In our survey sample, even among those who have completed a doctorate, only about half wrote their dissertation wholly on Japan, with the remainder divided evenly between those who wrote partly about Japan and those who wrote on a topic unrelated to Japan. This is about the same distribution reported in the 1984 sample, as shown in Table 4.15. There has been a very slight shift in percentage away from dissertations wholly on Japan and toward those not at all about Japan, a shift most pronounced among social scientists. This undoubtedly reflects the recent awakening of interest in Japan among social scientists not originally trained as Japan specialists, but who now find Japan a relevant case for comparative study.

Table 4.15. Relation of Doctoral Dissertation to Japan, 1984 and 1995

	Wholly Japan	*Partly Japan*	*Not on Japan*	*N*
1984 Study				
History	70	20	10	(173)
Language & Literature	54	25	21	(178)
Arts	46	11	43	(56)
Social Sciences	54	24	22	(272)
Total Sample	58	22	21	(679)
1995 Study				
History	68.7	22.7	8.6	163
Language & Literature	62.3	27.3	10.4	20.9
Social Sciences	50.4	20.9	28.7	230
Other**	40.0	18.9	41.1	190
Total Sample	54.4	22.2	23.4	(737)

*1984 data from 1984 Japan Foundation Report, Table 5, p. 18.

**We are unable to reconstruct exactly the same categories used for the 1984 study, but categories except arts and other should be equivalent.

The tendency to do comparative dissertation work involving Japan is closely related to age. Relatively few Japan specialists aged 55 or older wrote a dissertation that was partly on Japan, but the percentage jumps to 22.6 percent in the 45–54 age category, and to 27.6 percent in the 35–44 age group, as shown in Deck A of Table 4.16. (The under 35 group is too small to be reliable, and the skewed distribution may simply mean that it is "faster" to do a dissertation only partly on Japan, especially if one uses systematic comparative data available in English.) The most important finding here is the steady increase among the younger age groups in those who have written a dissertation wholly on Japan. Even here, there may be sampling considerations that make certain groups less well represented in those age groups. For example, the shorter post-dissertation period during which one could develop an interest in Japan and acquire sufficient expertise to be selected into the study sample may mean that only the older age categories include Japan specialists who did not do their dissertation on Japan.

Table 4.16. Japan As Subject of Doctoral Dissertation, by Age, Gender, Academic Status and Language Competence

	Wholly Japan	Partly Japan	Not on Japan	Total # of Cases
A. Age				
35 or Under	44.4	50.0	5.6	18
35–44	58.6	27.8	13.6	169
45–54	57.9	22.6	19.6	235
55–64	49.4	16.5	34.1	222
65 or Older	49.3	18.1	32.6	144
B. Gender				
Male	52.9	21.8	25.3	541
Female	58.4	22.8	18.8	197
C. Academic Status				
Academic	53.9	22.7	23.4	638
Non-Academic	57.0	18.0	25.0	100
D. Language Competence				
None	1.9	16.7	81.5	54
Not Scholarly	42.4	19.6	37.9	224
Scholarly Use	66.8	24.3	8.9	440

There is also a gender gap, with female Japan specialists considerably more likely to have written a dissertation wholly on Japan and less likely to have written on an unrelated subject (Deck B).

It is not surprising that doctoral training and dissertation research on Japan are closely associated with academic occupations (Deck C). It is surprising that non-academics who do have doctorates are just as likely— even slightly more likely—to have written a dissertation exclusively on Japan. About a quarter on both groups wrote a dissertation that was not about Japan at all. In short, the non-academics with doctoral training are indistinguishable from academics; the difference lies in the larger proportion of non-academics who do not hold a doctorate at all.

Japanese language competence is also closely related to dissertation topic (Deck D). Among those with Japanese language competence that is suitable for scholarly use, two-thirds wrote a dissertation wholly on Japan, and less than ten percent wrote on an unrelated topic. Only one person with no Japanese language skills claimed to have written a dissertation wholly on Japan, and more than 80 percent of those without Japanese language wrote their dissertations on subjects unrelated to Japan. However, over 40 percent of those who reported that their Japanese is not adequate for scholarly use wrote dissertations that were wholly on Japan, a larger percentage than wrote on unrelated topics! Unless this group is being exceptionally modest about its language competence or those skills have deteriorated, this is a troubling finding. We need further exploration to discover whether these dissertations are in fields where language skills are less essential, or were simply inadequate to the task that was undertaken. While we cannot pursue such a detailed inquiry here, we will examine this question again in the context of the research that Japan specialists are currently conducting.

This assessment of the language competence and academic credentials of Japan specialists, combined with our earlier exploration of patterns of specialization, all point to a division within the field between those with traditional language, area, and disciplinary training acquired largely through formal academic study, versus those who have come to Japanese Studies through some other more experiential route. Persons in the latter category can no longer be dismissed as "not Japan specialists" because they clearly are doing Japanese Studies in a professional capacity, and are helping to meet a market demand for forms of expertise on Japan that the more traditionally trained specialists cannot fulfill.

In Chapter Five we will continue to press toward a fuller understanding of these less traditional Japan specialists, as we examine what Japan specialists actually do, and how they go about the study of Japan.

5

Professional Activity of Japan Specialists

Expertise on Japan is not a fixed body of knowledge and skills that can be acquired once through training and certification and then drawn upon for the remainder of one's professional life. The body of knowledge about Japan keeps expanding, actual conditions in Japan keep changing, and language skills deteriorate if they are not constantly renewed and reinforced. Maintaining one's expertise as a Japan specialist therefore requires regular, sustained effort. At the aggregate level, maintaining the overall level of expertise on Japan in the United States requires an infrastructure of support for the various activities that individual Japan specialists must do to retain and expand their knowledge and skills. In this chapter we will explore the professional activities of Japan specialists, seeking to understand what professional demands are made on Japan specialists' time, how they maintain their skills and keep abreast of developments in their fields of specialization, and what sorts of resources these activities require.

HOW JAPAN SPECIALISTS SPEND THEIR TIME

We begin with a basic assessment of how much time Japan specialists spend on Japan-related activities, and how that time is distributed. Japan specialists on average spend over half of their work time and about a quarter of their leisure time on activities related to Japan. The amounts of time spent on Japan vary, but less than one might expect, depending on whether the specialist is employed as a faculty member, employed primarily in a non-faculty capacity, or is retired. Current faculty spend an average of 58.2 percent of their work time on Japan, while those employed in non-faculty positions spend an average of 53.4 percent, and retirees spend 52.8 percent. The differences can be seen more sharply if the percent of work time devoted to Japan is divided into quartiles rather than expressed as a mean. In all three groups, 42.5 percent spend between 75 and 100 percent of their work time on Japan. The difference is that current faculty are about twice as likely to spend 50–75 percent of their time on Japan,

101

while non-faculty and retirees are nearly twice as likely to spend less than a quarter of their working time on Japan.[1] Those who are not employed as faculty devote somewhat less of their leisure time to Japan-related activities (23.8 percent) than do faculty (27.3 percent) or retirees (28.6 percent).

Table 5.1. Mean Percent of Time Devoted to Japan and Percent of Japan Specialists Engaged, by Activity and Current Employment Status, 1995

Activity	Faculty		Non-Faculty		Retired		N
	mean time %	% engaged	mean time %	% engaged	mean time %	% engaged	#
Teaching	38.9 (607)	89.7	27.6 (79)	34.0	33.4 (35)	43.8	721
Research	29.7 (580)	85.7	30.4 (135)	59.7	40.0 (71)	88.8	786
Student Advising	12.8 (496)	73.3	13.8 (56)	24.8	18.5 (24)	30.0	576
Writing & Lecturing	18.2 (473)	69.9	23.8 (114)	50.9	21.6 (22)	27.5	609
Admin.	10.6 (196)	29.0	33.4 (72)	31.9	14.6 (16)	20.2	284
Consulting	12.1 (214)	31.6	34.3 (115)	50.9	21.6 (22)	27.5	351
Service	8.5 (246)	36.3	15.5 (57)	25.2	8.0 (15)	18.8	318
Lang. Study & Maint.	12.4 (210)	31.0	18.1 (75)	33.2	19.0 (23)	28.8	308
Prof. Social Activities	8.6 (246)	27.0	9.5 (74)	32.7	9.8 (20)	25.0	340
Leisure Activities	10.3 (216)	32.7	13.2 (85)	37.6	20.0 (28)	35.0	329
Total N	677		226		80		983

The time that specialists spend on Japan is devoted to a wide variety of activities, the most common being research, teaching, and writing and lecturing. Table 5.1, above, shows the average percentage of Japan-related time respondents spent on each type of activity. Since each person's pattern of activity varies, the number of respondents for each question differs. To preserve the intensity level of each activity for those who engage in it, we have based the means on those who actually answered each question. The

---

[1] Based on questionnaire responses, N=983 for work time, 816 for leisure time.

number of respondents and percent engaged in the activity are also given to aid in interpreting the results.

About ninety percent of current faculty teach about Japan, and that activity takes up nearly 40 percent of all the time they devote to Japan. Only a third of non-faculty teach, and for those who do, teaching occupies just over a quarter of the time they spend on Japan. Eighty-six percent of faculty Japan specialists do research on Japan, and that takes up about 30 percent of the time they devote to Japan. A smaller percentage of non-faculty Japan specialists do research, but those who do spend about the same fraction of their time on it as faculty.

Three-quarters of faculty advise students, an activity that takes an average of 12.8 percent of their time spent on Japan. Non-faculty and retirees report even higher percentages of time spent on student advising, but relatively few of them do any advising at all. The numbers are probably skewed by a few non-faculty whose primary role is some form of student advising, plus librarians who advise students about available research materials.

Faculty are most likely of the three groups to engage in writing and lecturing on Japan (69.9 percent), but they spend the least amount of time on it (18.2 percent). Half of the non-faculty Japan specialists engage in Japan-related consulting, which takes on average a third of the time they devote to Japan. Consulting is less common among faculty, and occupies only a small percentage of the time they spend on Japan. Smaller numbers in all three categories participate in administration, service activities, professional social activity, and leisure activities related to Japan. These activities occupy a relatively small part of the time they devote to Japan.

Whether specialists have Japanese language competence that is suitable for scholarly use is also related to the amount of professional time the specialist spends on Japan. In general, the greater the language competence the higher the percentage of professional time devoted to Japan. Combining these two variables produces a measure of the intensity of one's involvement with Japan. To score high on intensity one would either have to have Japanese language competence adequate for scholarly use and spend more than 25 percent of their professional time on Japan-related activity, have less than adequate Japanese for scholarly use and spend more than half of their professional time on Japan, or, if they have no usable Japanese language, spend at least 75 percent of their professional time on Japan.

Overall, just over two-thirds of the survey sample has high intensity of specialization on Japan, but the percentage varies by occupational status. Nearly three-quarters (72.6 percent) of Japan specialists who are currently employed as faculty score high on the intensity measure. The scores for retirees and non-faculty Japan specialists are nearly identical, with slightly under 60 percent having high intensity of specialization on Japan. Although we will continue to use the summary language competence scores for some purposes, the intensity of specialization on Japan offers a useful summary measure for certain parts of the analysis.

In one sense, the professional demands made on Japan specialists' time are also part and parcel of the activities through which they renew and expand their knowledge and reinforce their language skills. Teaching, research, writing and lecturing, student advising, consulting—even administration, service, professional social activities and leisure activities—provide both the stimulus and the opportunity for the maintenance and development of Japan specialists' knowledge and skills.

This categorization of activities is not very useful, however, for analyzing just how that expertise is maintained and developed, and what infrastructure and resources are necessary to support such professional development. We can understand these development processes better by examining several different avenues through which they happen: travel to Japan, networking or contacts with other people, and individual study and research. Of course, these three avenues for professional development overlap and combine in actual practice, but by distinguishing them analytically we can see more clearly how important each one is for various types of Japan specialists, and what infrastructure and resources are necessary to support them. In the course of this inquiry, we will also note how these different avenues interconnect.

ACCESS TO JAPAN

One of the most basic ways that Japan specialists develop and maintain their expertise is through periods of immersion in Japan. Whatever the specific purpose of a trip to Japan, it also provides an opportunity for many other kinds of informal learning and skill-building to take place. And once the Japan specialist has acquired a certain level of expertise and familiarity, even very brief trips to Japan serve to reinforce and add to one's knowledge.

Every study of Japanese Studies in the United States has tried to evaluate the extent to which Japan specialists have experienced this important exposure to Japan in the past, and how accessible Japan is to them for research and other purposes. In the 1970 SSRC-ACLS study, the preoccupation was with exposure to Japan as a basic element of language training for students, and a necessity for research at both the doctoral and faculty levels, since Japan was relatively inaccessible for reasons of distance and cost. The 1970 study reported that only 55 percent of the Japan specialists surveyed had spent any language training time in Japan, and that nearly half of the sample had spent twelve months or less as students in Japan, almost always for dissertation research. A third had spent no research time at all in Japan as students.[2] Likewise, two-thirds had spent one year or less doing research in Japan as faculty members, and a third of the sample had spent no time at all doing research in Japan after they became faculty members. Fourteen percent of the specialists had never been to Japan for research, either as faculty or as students, and the median lifetime number of research trips to Japan was two. Even allowing for the fact that the sample was composed primarily of younger scholars, this is an extremely low level of access to the country of specialization.

By the time of the 1984 Japan Foundation study, only eight percent of the sample had not been to Japan in the previous decade, and 41 percent had spent more than a year in Japan during the previous ten years. The level of access to Japan had increased sufficiently that the study was asking about satisfaction with the frequency of visits to Japan and the reasons for those visits. In the 1995 survey we have replicated the questions asked in 1984, and the comparison documents a remarkable increase in Japan specialists' access to Japan during the past decade.

In 1995, nearly two-thirds of Japan specialists report that they are not able to visit Japan as often as they would like, while a third are satisfied with the frequency of their trips. Only a tiny fraction (1.4 percent) complained that they go to Japan more often than they would like. These differences in satisfaction corresponded to actual differences in frequency of travel: the few who complained of too frequent visits did indeed go to Japan much more frequently than the others, while those who were satisfied with the frequency of their travel to Japan went more often than those who were not satisfied. These figures represent a real but rather modest increase in satisfaction with access to Japan since 1983, when three-quarters of the sample went to Japan less often that they would have liked, and just a quarter were satisfied with their travel frequency.

This shift in attitude is also grounded in reality, although from the increase in number of trips one might have expected a greater increase in satisfaction levels. The average number of trips to Japan taken by Japan specialists has roughly tripled in the past decade, compared to the previous decade, as reported in the 1984 Japan Foundation study. The average number of trips in the past ten years for research has increased from 1.9 to 3.9, to attend conferences from 0.7 to 3.5, to maintain contacts from 0.7 to 4.1, to meet specific persons or organizations from 0.6 to 5.3, and trips for pleasure from 0.3 to 3.2.

[2] 1970 SSRC-ACLS Report, pp. 116 and 124.

There was little difference in satisfaction with their access to Japan between faculty, non-faculty, and retirees, except that faculty were more likely to wish they could get to Japan more often. The three employment groups did differ in their reasons for traveling to Japan, as shown in Table 5.2. The table shows the mean number of trips taken in the past ten years for each purpose. Since varying numbers of persons reported travel to Japan for each purpose, the number and percent in each category are provided to aid in interpreting the table.

Table 5.2. Mean Number of Trips to Japan in Past Ten Years, by Purpose of Trip and Current Employment Status, 1995

Purpose of Trip	Faculty Mean	%	Non-Faculty Mean	%	Retired Mean	%	Total N
Conduct Research	3.97	77.1	3.62	37.8	3.31	45.0	628
Attend Conference	2.76	32.0	5.49	32.4	3.63	32.0	330
Meet Org. or Person	3.36	22.5	8.45	48.7	2.88	25.0	296
Maintain Contacts	3.37	22.3	6.17	27.3	2.64	22.0	241
Personal Reasons	3.28	24.3	3.33	29.0	2.34	21.0	258
Total N		690		238		100	1,028

Three-quarters of faculty Japan specialists traveled to Japan during the past decade for research purposes, making an average of 3.97 trips during the decade. Fewer non-faculty Japan specialists and retirees traveled for research, and those who did took slightly fewer trips. About the same percentage in each of the three employment groups, a third, traveled to Japan to attend conferences. However, faculty had the lowest number of trips for this purposes (2.76) and non-faculty the highest (5.49). About half of the non-faculty Japan specialists traveled to Japan to meet specific organizations or persons, twice the percentage of faculty or retirees who traveled to Japan for this reason. Non-faculty who went to Japan to meet specific organizations or persons took an average of 8.45 trips for this purpose, compared to 3.36 for faculty and 2.88 for retirees. Non-faculty were also slightly more likely to visit Japan in order to maintain contacts, and took such trips twice as frequently as faculty, an average of 6.7 trips in the past ten years. More non-faculty Japan specialists traveled to Japan for personal reasons, but on average they did not make more trips than faculty did for personal reasons.

Consistent with the sharp increase in number of trips to Japan, Japan specialists have spent a substantial amount of time in Japan during the past decade. About thirty percent have spent two years or more in Japan, and their average length of time in Japan was 3.3 years. Nearly sixty percent of the sample reported that they had spent less than two years in Japan during the past decade. For this group the average length of time spent in Japan was 7.14 months. Among this group, faculty spent slightly longer (7.4 months) than non-faculty (6.7 months) or retirees (6.8 months). The contrast suggests that while some specialists are now spending quite extended periods of time living in Japan, others go relatively frequently on brief trips.

Despite the fact that the great majority of travel to Japan was for business purposes, nearly half the respondents (46.8 percent) reported that they had paid for their most recent trip with their own personal funds. About thirty percent traveled on money provided by their institution. Compared with the situation in 1984, this represents a slight decrease in the percentage using personal funds and a slight increase in those with support from their own institution, as shown in Table 5.3. For every other type of funding (government sources, private foundations, private institutions or private clients), slightly more respondents reported receiving funding from Japanese sources than reported funding from comparable US sources. This is a reversal of the situation in 1984, when funding from US sources exceeded that from Japanese sources.

Table 5.3. Sources of Funds for Most Recent Trip to Japan, 1984 and 1995*

Funding Source	*1984 %*	*1995 %*
Personal Funds	48	46.8
Own Institution	28	31.6
US Government	17	11.4
Japanese Government	13	13.2
Private US Foundation	14	8.8
Private Japanese Foundation	11	10.6
Private US Institution	-	7.9
Private Japanese Institution	-	10.2
Private US Client	-	2.7
Private Japanese Client	-	3.4
Other	10	-
Base Number of Respondents	785	952

*This is a multiple response variable, so percentages for each category are independently calculated from the base number of respondents. 1984 data from 1984 Japan Foundation Report, Table 45, p.73. 1984 percentages were reported as rounded whole numbers.

When we compare only those sources for which data are available for both 1984 and 1995, it becomes clear that the percentage of travel supported by Japanese government or foundation sources has remained at the same level, while the percent receiving US funding has dropped substantially. We have no way of estimating the yen or dollar value of this funding, and thus no way of determining how the actual amounts of funding have changed. However, during the decade between the two studies the value of the dollar dropped from ¥240 to less than ¥100, making yen support attractive not only because of its greater purchasing power but also as protection against sudden currency fluctuations. The number of US Japan specialists also increased during the decade, and the percentages reported represent a somewhat larger number of cases in 1995. Under these difficult circumstances it is perhaps most surprising that so many of the categories of funding are still reported by roughly the same percentage of respondents, and that the actual volume of travel has increased as much as the data indicate.

The four new sources of funding included in the 1995 study respond to two new features of the funding landscape: the increase in non-academic Japan specialists, many of whom received travel funding from private clients in Japan (9.1 percent) and the US (8.2 percent); and the greater involvement of American Japan specialists with private institutions on both sides of the Pacific, including corporations and private colleges as well as non-profit institutions of various types. While these sources of funding are still relatively small in the overall distribution, they are large enough to be noticeable, and to require that we establish baseline figures for comparison in future studies.

Another general reflection of the increased access to Japan is that a smaller percentage of respondents in 1995 answered the follow-up question about why they have not been to Japan in the past three years, since more of them have been to Japan during that time. The distribution of reasons among those who did reply is somewhat different from the 1984 results as well.

Respondents who have not been to Japan in the past three years cited insufficient funds as the single most important reason for not traveling, but at 71.8 percent this was down slightly from the 76 percent who offered it as a reason in 1984 (See Table 5.4). Compared with the 1984 study, more cited personal reasons, or that travel to Japan was not necessary for their research interests. Personal reasons were often elaborated as health problems, reflecting the aging of the survey sample. Only slightly more cited an inability to get sufficient released time from their institution. Fear of jeopardizing one's career by spending time in Japan was cited by only 5.1 percent, less than half the percentage that offered this reason in 1984. Clearly, travel to Japan is no longer a liability to one's career. About 17.6 percent of the respondents cited other reasons, most commonly that they had simply been too busy to go to Japan. This is triple the number giving such "other" reasons in 1984.

Table 5.4. Reasons Respondent Has Not Traveled to Japan in the Past Three Years, 1984 and 1995*

Reason	1984 %	1995 %
Not Necessary for Research	20	25.5
Insufficient Funds	76	71.8
Insufficient Released Time	10	11.8
Would Jeopardize US Career	11	5.1
Personal Reasons	23	29.0
Other	6	17.6
Base Number of Respondents	321	255
% of All Survey Respondents Answering	37.4	23.8

*1984 data from 1984 Japan Foundation Report, Table 44, p. 72. In both studies, responses are independent so percentages do not add to 100.0.

While it has become easier during the past decade for Japan specialists to get to Japan, the pattern of travel, the sources of funding, and the reasons for not going to Japan all point to the continuing factor of cost as a barrier to access. The costs of travel to Japan have reversed from the situation twenty-five years ago. Then, the real barrier was the cost of the airfare, since it was relatively inexpensive to survive in Japan at ¥360 to the dollar when Japan had a standard of living markedly lower than that in the United States. Now the airfare is a relatively minor consideration; the real expense is living in Japan now that the standard of living is as high if not higher than most parts of the United States, and the yen hovers around ¥100 to the dollar.

Under these circumstances, specialists who have spent long periods of time in Japan have primarily been employed there on a more or less full-time basis. For others, the solution is to take very short trips, preferably at someone else's expense. The high proportion reporting that their last trip was paid for with personal funds probably reflects a combination of the ease with which one can travel to Japan for a short period of time, plus the fact that even with grant support, a long stay will require that one supplement the funding by dipping into personal reserves or working. The fact that nearly three-fourths of those who have not gone to Japan recently were deterred by insufficient funds is compounded, as noted earlier, by the unfavorable rate of exchange and the risks involved in trying to finance a stay in Japan with dollars, whether one's own or someone else's.

The range of purposes given for trips to Japan is a clear reminder of the interrelationship among the various avenues that Japan specialists use for professional development. Basically, specialists go to Japan to do research and to meet people. The substantial numbers of Japan specialists who now go to Japan for conferences, to meet a specific person or organization, or more generally to "maintain contacts" highlights the importance of human relationships as an avenue for professional development. In the next section we will look more closely at the kinds of network ties Japan specialists maintain, and the purposes they serve.

NETWORKS OF JAPAN SPECIALISTS

Networking refers to all of the ways in which Japan specialists make contact with others for professional purposes, and the study of networks also helps us to understand how the field is organized. While many aspects of research on Japan are necessarily solitary pursuits, the professional lives of Japan specialists are enriched by a high degree of contact with others who have similar professional interests. For Japan specialists, network contacts can be divided into two basic categories: Japanese scholars in Japan and other Japan specialists who are primarily outside of Japan. The survey explored both of these types of networks.

Relations with Japanese Scholars

One simple measure of networks is the sheer number of persons in the field that one knows. Less than five percent of survey respondents reported that they do not know any Japanese scholars in Japan. Just under a quarter know less than five, and just over a quarter know between five and ten Japanese scholars in Japan. Over a third of the sample report that they know more than ten Japanese scholars. These network ties are widest for retirees (51 percent know more than ten) and current faculty (41.2 percent know more than ten). By contrast, only a third of non-faculty Japan specialists know more than ten Japanese scholars in Japan, and ten percent do not know any. In short, the acquaintance of Japanese scholars is far more important for academics, and older (retired) academics have accumulated more relations than younger ones. Equally unsurprising is the finding that those who have Japanese language competence suitable for scholarly purposes are twice as likely to know more than ten Japanese scholars.

American Japan specialists have a wide array of reasons for maintaining contact with Japanese scholars. The salience of these reasons increases with their Japanese language competence and also with the intensity of their involvement with Japan, but the pattern of responses remains basically the same. There are some clear differences between employment categories, however, in the reasons that Japan specialists give for seeking contact with Japanese scholars. Table 5.5 shows the reasons given by Japan specialists in the three employment categories in 1995, with the total responses from the largely academic 1984 sample for comparison. Several new response categories were added in 1995, but these do not affect the individual comparisons because each response is independent. The average number of responses was 4.71.

Table 5.5. Ways in which Contact with Japanese Scholars is Useful, by Employment Status, 1995, with 1984 Comparison*

Reasons for Contact	1995 Retired %	1995 Faculty %	1995 Non-Faculty %	1995 Total %	1984 Total %
No contact at all	7.1	4.9	12.7	6.8	9
Introductions	49.0	67.8	58.7	63.9	61
Keep up with Japan	51.0	65.0	57.3	61.9	--
Keep up w/Japan Scholarship	37.8	64.7	36.2	55.8	73
Research Materials	45.9	63.5	39.0	56.4	35
Critique Work	22.4	44.8	23.0	37.8	42
Res. Collaboration	25.5	40.1	19.2	34.1	34
Present Research	14.3	35.5	12.2	28.3	--
Opportunity for Students	13.3	37.4	5.6	28.1	--
Friendship	55.1	67.5	58.7	64.4	--
Provide Affiliation	15.3	42.7	14.6	33.8	--
Total Sample Size	98	668	213	979	827

*This is a multiple response variable. Figure given is the percent of respondents in an employment category who gave a particular response. 1984 data from 1984 Japan Foundation Report, Table 46, p. 74. 1984 figures were reported rounded to whole numbers.

The most common response in 1984 was to keep abreast of developments in Japanese scholarship. The overall selection of this response dropped considerably in 1995, but faculty selected it nearly twice as often as retirees or non-faculty. In 1995 the highest ranked category of response overall was "they are friends whose company I enjoy," which was not included in the 1984 list of responses, perhaps because the question was explicitly framed in terms of the utility of such contacts. This reason was selected by two-thirds of faculty and more than half of retirees and non-faculty. Friendship stands as an important counterbalance to the next most common reason for contact with Japanese scholars, to provide the introductions that are utterly essential to any professional work in Japan. Not surprisingly, faculty have the greatest need for introductions from scholars and retirees the least, with non-faculty in the middle position.

Keeping up with changing conditions in Japan ranks higher than keeping up with Japanese scholarship as a reason for contact with Japanese scholars, but this is not simply due to the larger percentage of non-faculty in the sample. Even academics ranked it very slightly higher. This shift reflects not only the greater number of both academic and non-academic Japan specialists who now deal with contemporary matters, but also the rapidity with which conditions in Japan have indeed been changing. No social scientist or businessperson can afford to wait for published Japanese scholarship to find out what is happening in Japan today.

Equally important in the list of reasons, particularly for academics, Japanese scholars help provide access to research materials. This response is chosen much more frequently in 1995 than in 1984 because of the steady increase in the proportion of American Japan specialists who conduct research on Japan using primary source materials. Such materials are often rare and difficult to obtain; they may be accessible only through Japanese colleagues. However, even materials that are commonly available in Japan may be difficult to obtain in the United States, and asking a Japanese colleague may be the most efficient way to get them. Reflecting the need scholars have for such material, this reason is also more important to retired academics than to non-faculty Japan specialists.

Lower on the list, but still important to faculty in particular, is the use of Japanese scholars to critique one's work, as research collaborators, and as significant audiences for the presentation of one's research. The final two new categories of response reflect the special needs of faculty Japan specialists: Japanese scholars as a source of academic affiliation for their own research visits to Japan, and also as academic mentors and sponsors for their graduate students.

Overall, the results reveal a complex set of bonds linking American Japan specialists to Japanese scholars. Those ties are strongest between American and Japanese academics, who share not only substantive intellectual interests, but a common culture of research activity, teaching, and mentoring of graduate students. Underlying all of the instrumental aspects of these relationships is friendship, often based on previous student-teacher or student-mentor relations, or past experiences of being students, research collaborators, or even teaching colleagues together. It is significant that nowadays these past common experiences may have occurred on either side of the Pacific, and that if a mentor relationship was involved, either the Japanese or the American scholar may have played that role. The central role of personal friendship and the reciprocality of roles in these relations are strong evidence that relations between American Japan specialists and Japanese scholars cannot be understood simply as unilateral or exploitive, as the colonial or orientalist models would suggest.

Relations with Other Japan Specialists

Relations with Japanese scholars are only one aspect of the professional networks of contemporary American Japan specialists. Relations with other Japan specialists in and outside of Japan constitute another important set of ties.

Virtually all American Japan specialists know at least one other Japan specialist, with less than one percent claiming not to know any others, and less than 10 percent knowing less than five others. Nearly two-thirds know more than ten other Japan specialists, and over a third know more than 25 others. In short, American Japan specialists have substantially wider professional networks among other Japan specialists than among Japanese scholars. Even though American Japan specialists are now dispersed quite broadly around the country, these relations stem from the high concentration of graduate training in Japanese Studies at a relatively small number of institutions, common periods of residence in Japan as students and researchers, and regular opportunities for Japan specialists to gather to present research results and discuss topics of mutual interest. While the breadth of networks among American Japan specialists does not seem to vary directly with Japanese language competence or employment status, it is not surprising that networks are substantially greater among those with high intensity of involvement with Japan.

We asked survey respondents their reasons for maintaining contact with other Japan specialists, offering virtually the same list of possible reasons as for contacts with Japanese scholars. The response level was nearly as high, with an average of 4.5 responses. As with relations with Japanese scholars, the most frequently reported reason for maintaining contact with other Japan specialists is personal friendship, which was cited by 71.7 percent of the respondents. The next most common reason is to keep up with what is happening in Japanese Studies, the largely American and English-language equivalent of keeping up with Japanese scholarship. Interestingly, the third most important reason for contact with other Japan specialists is for introductions. While formal introductions are much less critical in American society than in Japan, other Japan specialists with good connections can also be the necessary link for introductions in Japan.

More than half the respondents also cited the importance of other Japan specialists for critiquing their work. Only slightly less important were keeping up with Japanese scholarship and obtaining research materials through contacts with Japan specialists. The salience of every response was greater for those with high intensity of involvement in Japan, but the pattern was consistent throughout.

As with reasons for contact with Japanese scholars, the response patterns were somewhat different for faculty, non-faculty, and retired Japan specialists, as shown in Table 5.6. However, this set of questions was not asked on the 1984 survey, so no comparison over time is possible. While it remains the highest response category for all three groups, the fact that friendship is a somewhat lower response for retirees reflects their gradual withdrawal from the networks of active Japan specialists, rather than a lower degree of friendships among Japan specialists of an older generation. If anything those friendships were closer and more salient when the field was smaller and specialization on Japan was a more marginal activity in American academics.

Table 5.6. Ways in which Contact with Other Japan Specialists is Useful, by Employment Status, 1995*

Reasons for contact	Faculty %	Non-Faculty %	Retired %	Total %
No contact at all	2.0	4.0	7.4	3.0
Introductions	60.4	58.3	28.7	56.9
Keep up with J. Studies	70.4	62.3	50.0	66.6
Keep up with J. Scholarship	58.0	33.2	29.8	49.6
Obtain Research Materials	52.4	39.5	24.5	46.7
Critique One's Work	63.0	30.5	27.7	52.2
Research Collaboration	37.8	17.9	11.7	30.7
Present Own Research	49.0	16.6	18.1	38.6
Opportunities for Students	41.9	7.6	13.8	31.4
Friendship	73.9	70.4	59.6	71.7
Total Sample Size	659	223	94	976

*This is a multiple response variable. Figure given is the percent of respondents in an employment category who gave a particular response.

Non-faculty specialists as well as academics use their relations with other Japan specialists to keep up to date in the field. Faculty and non-faculty alike see their relations with other Japan specialists as an important source of introductions. Among faculty this may be largely for introductions in Japan, but it also includes introductions across generational lines, where even in the open United States there may be barriers to direct contact with strangers who differ greatly in age. Japan specialists who work outside of academics may also view these relations as a source of introductions to other academic Japan specialists to whom they might otherwise not feel they have direct access.

A cluster of reasons for contact are distinctive for faculty Japan specialists and less important to either non-faculty specialists or retirees. Faculty Japan specialists use their contact with other Japan specialists to keep abreast of developments in Japanese scholarship, as the major arena for critiques of their own work, as a source of opportunities to present their work, as leads to research materials, as opportunities for research collaboration, and as a reservoir of potential opportunities for their students.

All of these are critical resources for academic Japan specialists, which almost inevitably draw them beyond the bounds of their own institutions. Once again, the fact that friendship is the most frequently cited response makes it clear that what is being described here is not "keeping up with Japanese Studies" by reading books and book reviews, but active communication among large networks of friends who share a strong common academic culture reinforced by deeply shared intellectual and professional interests and layers of mutual interaction.

We have pointed to the structural features of American Japanese Studies that enable these friendships to develop through graduate education at the same institutions and periods of common residence in Japan for language study and research. To the extent that Japan specialists who are now working outside of academia have passed through the same formative experiences, they participate in these same networks. There are undoubtedly other rather distinct networks among non-academic Japan specialists, but unfortunately this study is less equipped to examine them. What we can explore are the mechanisms through which participants in the predominantly academic networks maintain contact across long spans of time and space, largely in the United States, but also increasingly encompassing Japan as well.

Attendance at Professional Meetings and Conferences

Attendance at professional meetings and conferences is one of the most common vehicles for professional networking among Japanese specialists, as among American academics in general. While only a minority of Japan specialists attend such meetings, those who do tend to be regular attendees and participants. Table 5.7 shows the percentage of Japan specialists who report that they have attended various types of professional meetings over the past five years, compared with the rates reported in the 1984 Japan Foundation report. Since the 1984 study sample was almost entirely academic while the 1995 sample has a substantial non-academic representation, we have also presented the 1995 results just for academics to facilitate comparison.

Table 5.7. Attendance at Professional Meetings and Conferences in the Past Five
Years, 1984 and 1995*

Meeting Type	Total for Partic. %	1984 Obs. %	Academics Partic. %	Only 1995 Obs. %	Total for Partic. %	1995 Obs. %
University-sponsored	44	25	30.1	21.8	26.4	21.3
Profess. Assoc. national	40	20	34.4	28.1	31.4	25.9
AAS national	30	32	38.0	43.9	32.2	40.0
AAS regional	28	18	26.9	19.7	22.3	18.1
Profess. Assoc. regional	25	13	18.6	13.8	16.8	13.2
SSRC research conference	13	2	4.2	1.4	3.2	1.0
SSRC regional seminars	10	6	5.5	4.5	4.7	3.8
Japan-specific research conf.	29	16	22.6	11.1	20.5	11.4
Conference in Japan	-	-	26.3	12.9	23.3	12.3
Sample Size	841	841	783	783	1,069	1,069

* 1984 data from 1984 Japan Foundation Report, Table 40, p. 67. Percentages for 1984 were
reported rounded to whole numbers. In both studies, each response is independent and
percentage is based on total sample.

Even when only academics are compared, attendance at all types of
professional meetings is down since 1984, with the single exception of the
annual meetings of the Association for Asian Studies. The AAS meetings are
also unusual in another respect. For every type of meeting except the national
AAS meetings, the rates for those participating in the program are higher than for
those simply observing. Some types of meetings such as SSRC-sponsored
research conferences do not encourage observers, while others such as smaller
regional meetings aim to find a participatory role for virtually everyone. An even
more important factor is that academic institutional travel support is generally
contingent upon one's active participation as a paper presenter, discussant, or
committee members, which further tilts the balance toward participation.

The fact that the AAS national meetings attract even more observers
than participants in our sample points to the central networking and
informational functions of these meetings. It is also significant that a higher

percentage of academic Japan specialists report attending the AAS national meetings than other national professional association meetings, which in most cases would be the national association of the respondent's academic discipline. While the rates for attending as a participant in AAS meetings and other national professional association meetings are relatively similar, Japan specialists are considerably more likely to attend AAS meetings even if they are not participating in the program. These figures attest to the strong pull that area studies affiliation has for Japan specialists and, conversely, hint at a degree of alienation from the disciplinary associations.

While network contacts with Japanese scholars are closely related to the ability of Japan specialists to travel to Japan, contacts with other Japan specialists are more closely associated with gatherings in the United States, such as the annual AAS meetings. As the reasons for maintaining contact with other Japan specialists make clear, such occasions provide critical opportunities to keep up with new developments in the field, both by attending formal paper presentations and through informal conversations with colleagues. For most academic Japan specialists, the national meetings of their disciplinary association simply cannot offer the same level of new information about Japan that is disseminated in the AAS meetings. At a disciplinary meeting the Japan specialist may be presenting the only paper on Japan in a comparative panel on the same subject or worse yet, stuck in a panel of "foreign papers" that have no relation to each other except that they are all about exotic subjects. With great luck, the Japan specialist might be part of a panel devoted to Japan, but if so, it is likely to be the only such panel in the entire meeting.

At the same time, younger academic Japan specialists in particular may find that participation in the AAS meetings is not given the same weight by their departments as participation in the national meetings of their own disciplinary association. They may need to write papers that will be accepted by the discipline and present them to an audience that knows nothing about Japan. Especially in the social sciences, it is not the same paper that a scholar would write for a Japan specialist audience, even if it is based on the same research. This is the kind of pressure that encourages disciplinary specialization and discourages interdisciplinary communication among Japan specialists. The loss is not simply that the research products oriented toward the discipline and presented to a disciplinary audience become less intelligible and less accessible to persons in other disciplines, but that the author loses out on all of the additional information about Japanese Studies that is shared both formally and informally at an area-centered meeting such as the AAS.

In some disciplines such as political science, a well-organized network organization composed of Japan specialists within the same discipline helps to keep scholars attached to both the disciplinary organization and the AAS. For other disciplines, such a network may not exist, or it may flourish within either the disciplinary organization or the AAS, but not both. As the number of Japan specialists within a discipline increases, it may be possible to build such an infrastructure to help scholars manage the personal and professional fragmentation that the pressures toward disciplinary specialization produce. In addition to the need for a dedicated individual who will carry the burden of organizing and maintaining such a group, the success of the efforts ultimately depends upon the strength of the friendship networks within Japanese Studies, which motivate specialists to continue to attend the AAS meetings even when the pressures of disciplinary specialization pull them the other way.

PERCEPTIONS OF JAPANESE STUDIES VIS-À-VIS DISCIPLINES

In addition to their network ties in Japanese Studies, Japan specialists also have network relations within their own disciplines. Another angle on the problem of orienting one's work to a Japanese Studies audience or to a disciplinary audience has to do with the Japan specialist's perception of the relative strength of the two fields and of the discipline's attitude toward Japanese Studies. Both the 1984 Japan Foundation survey and the 1995 survey asked respondents how they thought Japanese Studies compared to their discipline and to other area studies. The results are shown in Table 5.8.

In 1984 the majority of Japan specialists thought Japanese Studies was weaker than their discipline, with that sentiment strongest among social scientists, two-third of whom thought Japanese Studies was weaker. Only about a quarter thought the fields were about the same in strength. In 1995 the sentiment had shifted somewhat. Less than half thought Japanese Studies was weaker, but this figure was only about 40 percent in history and language and literature, and just 50 percent among social scientists. Nearly a third of respondents overall, and over 40 percent of historians, thought Japanese Studies was equally as strong as the discipline. About one in eight respondents in 1995 thought Japanese Studies was stronger than their discipline. This view was strongest among those in language and literature.

Japan specialists are somewhat more likely to regard Japanese Studies as stronger than other area studies, with a third saying Japanese Studies is stronger in both 1984 and 1995. Although there was no change in this view, there has been some positive movement at the lower end of the scale, with fewer in 1995 believing that Japanese Studies is weaker than other area studies. It is not altogether clear in this question whether strength and weakness refer to the political and economic power of the field or to its intellectual condition. In either case, views of the relative position of Japanese Studies are somewhat more favorable in 1995.

Table 5.8. Japan Specialists' Perceptions of the Strength of Japanese Studies Relative to Their Discipline and to Other Area Studies, by Disciplinary Group, 1984 and 1995*

Comparison	Stronger %	Same %	Weaker %	Not Sure %	Total N #
Discipline					
1984 Total	10	24	58	8	(784)
History	11	28	55	6	(189)
Lang. & Literature	14	24	50	12	(224)
Social Sciences	6	21	69	4	(290)
Other	10	30	43	17	(81)
1995 Total	12.8	29.4	46.9	10.8	(833)
History	9.3	41.6	42.9	6.2	(161)
Lang. & Literature	15.9	30.0	39.4	14.7	(170)
Social Sciences	11.6	32.0	50.6	5.8	(241)
Other	14.2	19.2	51.0	15.7	(261)
Other Area Studies					
1984 Total	33	29	26	11	(748)
History	40	37	19	4	(176)
Lang. & Literature	30	24	31	14	(226)
Social Sciences	32	30	26	12	(271)
Other	32	23	25	20	(75)
1995 Total	33.0	34.6	19.5	12.9	(836)
History	42.0	35.8	14.8	7.4	(162)
Lang. & Literature	30.1	30.6	23.7	15.6	(173)
Social Sciences	36.9	36.5	17.4	9.1	(241)
Other	25.8	34.6	21.5	18.1	(260)

*1984 data from 1984 Japan Foundation Report, Table 48, p. 79. 1984 percentages were reported rounded to whole numbers.

The 1995 study also asked a more direct question about the perceived attitude of other members of the respondent's discipline toward Japanese Studies. As shown in Table 5.9, a quarter of the respondents thought the discipline's attitude was very positive and another quarter thought it was indifferent. Nearly 40 percent said the discipline was mildly favorable toward Japanese Studies, and only two percent said their discipline was hostile.

Table 5.9. Perceived Attitude of Respondent's Discipline Toward Japanese Studies, by Disciplinary Group

Discipline Attitude	History %	Lang-Lit %	Soc.Science %	Other %	Total N #
Very positive	30.3	29.3	16.3	24.4	(210)
Mildly favorable	40.0	37.6	39.0	38.2	(335)
Indifferent	20.6	21.0	35.4	27.3	(234)
Hostile	1.2	1.7	3.3	2.2	(19)
Cannot judge	7.9	10.5	6.1	8.0	(69)

However, the hostile response was twice as high in the social sciences as in history or language and literature, and more than a third of social scientists said their discipline was indifferent to Japanese Studies. While social scientists said their discipline was mildly favorable to Japanese Studies in about the same proportion as other disciplinary groups, only half as many social scientists thought their discipline had a very positive attitude toward Japanese Studies. These variations in the perceived attitudes of one's disciplinary colleagues, combined with differing assessments of the strength of Japanese Studies compared to the discipline, help to explain the pressures social scientists face when they have to decide whether to orient their work to meet the expectations of Japan specialists or of their own discipline because the two do not coincide.

STRATEGY AND TOOLS FOR INDEPENDENT STUDY

This consideration of the informational aspects of personal network contacts leads us neatly into the more general issue of what kinds of materials the Japan specialist uses to maintain currency in a specialized field, and what sorts of research tools are available to make the task easier. The concern here is with maintaining a general level of expertise in the field that does not necessarily involve original research and in any event, covers a broader topical range. The 1995 survey asked several questions about how Japan specialists keep up with developments in their field, and the sorts of research tools they use in doing so, in addition to travel to Japan and the network contacts we have just discussed.

Strategies for Keeping up with New Knowledge

The 1995 survey asked Japan specialists what they need to read in order to keep up in their field. The question was not aimed at specific research projects, but rather at the general maintenance and currency of one's expertise on Japan. The question offered seven general response categories: books, journal articles, government documents, technical reports, newspapers and magazines, quantitative data, and visual materials such as picture, maps, or photographs. Each response category was further subdivided into English, translated, and Japanese materials.

Not surprisingly, over 90 percent of respondents said they had to read books in English, and almost as many (88.7 percent) said they needed to read journals in English. Although the question did not probe specifically for the content area of this reading, we can assume that it refers both to general material in one's discipline and to the English language literature on Japan. The latter has increased geometrically over the past two decades in both scale and sophistication, and has become the basic foundation for American expertise on Japan. The increase in the volume of this body of English language material on Japan also means that it is only possible to keep up with the part of it one finds most relevant or interesting; it is no longer possible to read it all. For most Japan specialists, however, keeping abreast of the English language literature on Japan through books and journal articles is just the beginning. Next in order of frequency were books in Japanese, at 62.4 percent, and English newspapers and magazines, at 62.0 percent, followed by books translated into English (58.0 percent), journals in Japanese (57.8 percent), journal articles translated into English (48.2 percent), and Japanese newspapers and magazines (43.4 percent).

A third of the respondents said they need to read quantitative data in English, while more than a quarter need to read government documents in English, translated newspapers and magazine articles, or quantitative data in Japanese. Even the least frequently selected categories of material had substantial rates of response. The high rate of response (a mean of 7.8 responses per person) plus the broad distribution of responses across all the categories, suggests that there may be some distinctly different patterns within the sample, which we must tease out by examining various subgroupings.

The patterns of response are somewhat different by employment status, as shown in Table 5.10. Since retirees have less need to keep up with the field, they are lower on all categories, with the single exception that retirees are more likely to read books in Japanese than non-faculty as a way of keeping current. In every general response category, faculty are more likely than non-faculty to read materials in Japanese, although in some categories the difference is negligible. Faculty are more likely to need to read books and journals in English to keep up with their field, while non-faculty are more likely to need to read government documents, technical reports, mass media, and quantitative data in English. There is basically no difference between the two groups in their need to read translated books and journal articles, but non-faculty are also more likely to read translated government documents, technical reports, mass media, and quantitative data.

Table 5.10. What Japan Specialists Need to Read in Order to Keep Up in their Field, by Type of Material, Language of Material, and Employment Status

Material	Faculty %	Non-faculty %	Retired %	Total %
Books				
English	94.9	87.4	78.6	91.7
Translated	59.9	56.1	49.0	58.0
Japanese	69.1	44.8	56.1	62.4
Journal Articles				
English	92.6	83.0	74.5	88.7
Translated	50.0	49.1	33.7	48.2
Japanese	64.3	43.5	44.9	57.8
Government Documents				
English	27.4	34.3	23.5	28.6
Translated	17.4	20.9	14.3	17.9
Japanese	22.5	20.0	15.3	21.2
Technical Reports				
English	21.4	27.8	17.3	22.5
Translated	10.7	17.8	8.2	12.1
Japanese	17.8	14.3	13.3	16.6
Newspapers, Magazines				
English	60.7	69.1	54.1	62.0
Translated	27.1	34.8	22.4	28.4
Japanese	44.9	43.0	33.7	43.4
Quantitative Data				
English	33.0	37.8	23.5	33.2
Translated	16.5	19.6	14.3	17.0
Japanese	27.0	23.5	23.5	25.8
Visual Materials				
English	20.7	19.1	11.2	19.4
Translated	10.3	8.3	9.2	9.7
Japanese	17.1	13.5	11.2	15.7
# Respondents	690	230	98	1,018

Table 5.11. What Japan Specialists Need to Read to Keep Up in their Fields, by Genre of Material, Language of Material, and Discipline Group (Major Groups Only)*

Materials	Humanities		Social Sciences		Professions	
	%	Rank	%	Rank	%	Rank
Books						
English	94.8	1	92.9	1	86.6	2
Translated	67.8	5	50.2	5	56.0	4
Japanese	80.3	3	54.7	4	39.6	8
Journal Articles						
English	90.9	2	90.4	2	88.1	1
Translated	55.3	6	39.2	9	50.7	6
Japanese	74.0	4	49.8	6	35.8	10
Gov't Documents						
English	13.3		39.2	9	51.5	5
Translated	7.9		24.8		31.3	12
Japanese	13.5		29.9	12	29.1	14
Technical Reports						
English	11.8		28.3	14	38.1	9
Translated	6.9		12.9		23.9	
Japanese	10.3		22.5		17.2	
Newspapers, Mags.						
English	50.6	7	69.1	3	76.9	3
Translated	24.3		28.9	13	40.3	7
Japanese	43.2	8	45.7	8	30.1	13
Quantitative Data						
English	22.1		46.0	7	35.8	10
Translated	12.3		21.9		20.1	
Japanese	19.7		35.7	11	22.4	
Visual Materials						
English	22.1		19.3		14.2	
Translated	12.0		6.8		9.0	
Japanese	18.4		14.5		10.4	
# Respondents	407		311		134	

*Remaining categories too small for separate analysis and too heterogeneous to combine. Ranks only given for categories with at least 25 percent response.

These rather modest variations suggest that the underlying difference may be the discipline rather than whether the respondent works in an academic setting. As shown in Table 5.11, there are substantial differences between humanists, social scientists, and those in professional fields, the only categories large enough for meaningful analysis. Nearly everyone reads books and journal articles in English to keep up, but beyond that the discipline groups differ considerably. Humanists need to read a much narrower range of materials than either social scientists or professionals. If we take any category with at least a 25 percent response rate as worthy of notice, humanists read in only eight categories, while professionals and social scientists read in fourteen to keep up.

Within this array, humanists read three different genres of Japanese language materials, those in professional fields four, and social scientists five. All three groups read Japanese books, journals and mass media, but social scientists and professionals also need to read government documents, and social scientists need to read Japanese quantitative data. The relative ranking of the categories also differs, as does the degree of agreement about the need for reading in a particular category (as measured simply by the percentage that cite it). We list rankings only for those with 25 percent or higher response rate.

We would expect to find differences in reading patterns depending on the Japanese language ability of the respondent, but the findings are somewhat surprising, as shown in Table 5.12. As expected, the heaviest readers of Japanese language materials are those with language skills suitable for scholarly use. The unexpected finding is the extent to which persons whose language is not yet at the level of comfortable scholarly use also feel they must read Japanese materials to keep up in their fields. Nearly a third of those with limited Japanese feel they need to read Japanese books and journal articles, a fifth have to read Japanese mass media, and more than one in seven needs to keep up with Japanese quantitative data. Persons with limited Japanese are also heavy users of translated materials, in several categories having higher rates of using translated materials than persons with no Japanese language at all. This may reflect their relatively greater commitment to the study of Japan.

Our measure of intensity of involvement in Japanese Studies, which combines language ability with time commitment, does not settle this issue, but puts it into a different light. In general, those who have high intensity of involvement with Japan are much more likely to read Japanese language materials of any type. Those with low intensity of involvement are equally likely to read translated books and journal articles as those with high intensity, but more likely to keep up by reading translated government documents, technical reports, mass media materials, and quantitative data. They are also more likely to read English government documents and technical reports, which suggests some disciplinary differences as well.

Table 5.12. What Japan Specialists Need to Read to Keep Up in their Field, by Genre of Material, Language of Material, and Respondent's Japanese Language Ability Level

Material	No Japanese %	Non-Scholarly %	Scholarly Use %	Total Sample %
Books				
English	97.3	92.5	90.2	91.5
Translated	53.3	70.7	50.8	57.6
Japanese	1.3	32.4	90.2	64.2
Journal Articles				
English	88.0	91.3	87.6	88.9
Translated	46.7	60.4	41.5	48.2
Japanese	0.0	31.8	82.7	59.4
Gov't Documents				
English	49.3	31.5	24.4	28.7
Translated	34.7	26.8	11.2	18.2
Japanese	1.3	11.5	30.7	22.1
Technical Reports				
English	30.7	22.4	21.1	22.3
Translated	17.3	17.4	8.4	12.1
Japanese	0.0	5.3	25.8	17.0
Newspapers, Mags.				
English	76.0	63.2	59.0	61.7
Translated	32.0	39.3	22.0	28.5
Japanese	0.0	21.5	63.7	44.8
Quantitative Data				
English	45.3	30.8	32.6	33.0
Translated	24.0	23.4	12.7	17.1
Japanese	5.3	16.2	34.9	26.4
Visual Material				
English	24.0	20.2	17.8	19.1
Translated	8.0	12.8	8.4	9.8
Japanese	1.3	9.0	22.0	16.1
# Respondents	75	321	573	969

Low intensity of involvement means that the person most likely spends a relatively small proportion of time on Japan, and has low or non-existent Japanese language ability. Looking again at Table 5.12 with this information in mind, we can also see that those with no Japanese ability are much more likely to be reading quantitative data in English, which means that they are likely to be specialists in fields that emphasize the interpretation of numeric data in a comparative context, such as economics and sociology. The high reliance on English government documents suggests that this category may also include specialists in policy areas in which the US government collects and disseminates data relevant to Japan. Thus as we learn more about what Japan specialists actually do, we can begin to understand how persons with quite diverse sets of qualifications—even people who might be considered not to possess some of the traditional basic qualifications—can legitimately be Japan specialists in the 1990s. We also hasten to point out that this category is quite small, and that overall the level of Japanese language ability among Japan specialists is quite high, as has already been documented in Chapter Four.

This analysis of how Japan specialists maintain their expertise has also pointed to a fairly substantial reliance on translated materials of various types. Literary translations comprise only a fraction of translated material, which includes secondary works by Japanese scholars, primary research materials of various types, and current events materials. Respondents were asked how much they use non-literary translations, and whether they trust their accuracy. About 38 percent of Japan specialists use translations occasionally, regardless of their employment status. However, 45 percent of non-faculty use translations regularly, compared to 35 percent of faculty and retirees. Slightly less than a quarter of faculty use translations in their teaching.

Table 5.13. Japan Specialists' Use of Non-Literary Translation and Beliefs About their Accuracy, by Japanese Language Ability

	No Japanese %	Not Scholarly %	Scholarly Use %	Total Sample %
Use of Translations				
Use regularly	71.6	56.8	19.0	35.7
Use occasionally	18.9	32.8	44.7	38.7
Rarely use	4.1	8.8	28.8	20.2
Use in teaching	2.7	8.4	28.8	20.0
Opinion of Translations				
Accurate and reliable	36.5	44.2	30.8	35.7
Inaccurate, unreliable	6.8	24.7	30.5	26.7
# Respondents	74	308	548	930

The use of translated materials, and attitudes about their reliability, vary sharply with the specialist's Japanese language ability, as shown in

Table 5.13, above. Only 19 percent of specialists with Japanese language skills suitable for scholarship use translations regularly, compared to 71.6 percent of specialists with no Japanese language skills at all and 56.8 percent of those with limited Japanese language skills. Those with high level Japanese language skills are more than four times as likely not to trust the accuracy and reliability of translations as those with no Japanese language ability. This finding mirrors the differences in perception of the importance of Japanese language that was chronicled in Chapter Four, and also clarifies their basis. Those without Japanese language skills rely heavily on translations and are much less likely to question their accuracy.

Those with some Japanese language also tend to use translations regularly, but are much more likely to be concerned about their accuracy. Specialists with scholarly level language ability are less likely to make regular use of translations, but they are evenly divided on whether translations are likely to be accurate. Of course, some Japan specialists in this category also produce translations themselves, so the difference of opinion about whether translations are accurate is understandable, and these specialists would no doubt prefer to reply that there are both good and bad translations available and each should be judged on its merits.

These findings about what Japan specialists do to keep up in their fields have considerable implications for American libraries, which is where American Japan specialists are most likely to turn for at least some of the materials they need. Books and journals in English are likely to be widely available, but most of the other materials are more difficult to obtain and would not be part of the general collection of libraries unless they support an acknowledged clientele of Japan specialists. Of the 1,018 persons who responded to the questions about what they must read to keep up in their field, nearly three-quarters reported a need to read some kind of Japanese language materials. The distribution within this group is enlightening, as it intensifies the patterns we have drawn out of the data up to this point.

Among those who do read Japanese materials in order to keep up with their field, books and journal articles are reported most frequently, followed by mass media, quantitative data, and government documents. Technical reports and visual materials ranked last, but were also cited by more than a fifth of those who read Japanese (Table 5.14). Even those with limited Japanese language ability report substantial need to read all of the first five types of materials. In addition, more than a quarter of those with Japanese language suitable for scholarly use also report that they need to read Japanese technical reports. The table includes six persons who reported a need to read Japanese language materials even though they report no usable Japanese language skills. While these may be data errors, it seems more likely that the respondent is reporting a need to keep up with Japanese materials that can be met with the aid of a research assistant. Certainly once suitable material has been located and marked, a person with no Japanese can read and analyze quantitative data and visual materials. If we think both of the individual specialist's need to maintain certain kinds of expertise on Japan and of the kinds of support that are necessary on a larger scale to maintain that sort of expertise in the United States, it becomes apparent that the need of persons who cannot themselves read Japanese to have access to certain kinds of Japanese language materials must be figured into the overall equation of infrastructure support for Japanese Studies in the United States.

Table 5.14. What Japanese Materials Japan Specialists Need to Read to Keep Up with their Field, by Genre of Material and Respondent's Japanese Language Ability

Material	No Japanese %	Non-scholarly %	Scholarly Use %	Total %
Books	16.7	65.4	93.2	86.4
Journal Articles	0.0	64.2	85.4	80.0
Gov't Documents	16.7	23.3	31.7	29.7
Technical Reports	0.0	10.7	26.7	22.9
Newspapers, Mags.	0.0	43.4	65.8	60.3
Quantitative Data	66.7	32.7	36.0	35.6
Visual Materials	16.7	16.2	22.7	21.7
# Respondents	6	159	555	720

In general, these findings make clear that the differentiation and specialization within Japanese Studies has broadened considerably the range of materials that Japan specialists need to read in order to maintain their expertise. We will take up this issue again, in the context of the kinds of resources Japan specialists need for research purposes, and the extent to which libraries in the United States are able to meet those needs. First, however, we will extend our inquiry from the basic ways that Japan specialists maintain their expertise to the more specialized research through which they extend and disseminate knowledge of Japan. This chapter began with the finding that teaching and research, writing, and lecturing are the most common ways that Japan specialists spend their time. Research in particular engages both academic and non-academic Japan specialists, and thus encompasses the growing differentiation and specialization of the field. In Chapter Six we will look at the research activity of Japan specialists, focusing particularly on the many kinds of research specialists do, and the different audiences to which it is now directed.

6

Research and Publications of Japan Specialists

Chapter Five concentrated on what Japan specialists do in order to acquire and maintain their expertise, but the findings about how they spend their Japan-related time also point to the ways in which Japan specialists share their expertise with others. These two processes of acquiring and communicating knowledge interact constantly. Japan specialists do research to expand and update their understanding of Japan, and then communicate that research to an audience, but the kinds of research they do and the forms in which it appears are shaped in part by perceptions of what the audience wants, needs, and expects. One classic way of communicating knowledge is through academic courses and programs of study, which we will take up in Part III of this volume. The other is through the publication of research findings and interpretations of Japan. What has changed over the past decade is the degree of interest in Japan outside of the college classroom and a readership of other Japan specialists, and thus the extent to which Japan specialists now share their expertise with much wider audiences. This chapter will examine both the audiences for knowledge and information about Japan, and the research processes through which Japan specialists create and deliver their knowledge to those audiences.

We begin by assessing changes in the audience for knowledge about Japan and the overall volume of research output produced by Japan specialists. We will then explore the different patterns of research in contemporary Japanese Studies so that the specific needs of various subcommunities can be identified, and their differing orientations and goals can be better understood. Finally, we will focus more closely on scholarly research intended for academic publication. We will consider its role in the 1990s and beyond, how it is directed to different audiences, and how accessible it is to those intended audiences.

THE EXPANDING AUDIENCE FOR KNOWLEDGE ABOUT JAPAN

The 1984 Japan Foundation survey initiated an exploration of the audiences for Japan specialists' knowledge, which we have tried to replicate and enlarge. The 1984 survey asked Japan specialists a series of questions about their perception of the degree of interest in and knowledge about Japan in several audiences. Since the 1984 survey was still primarily focused on the academic world, the audiences identified were undergraduate students, graduate students, faculty colleagues, and administrators. In the 1995 survey we have replicated these questions but added the general public as another potential audience.

Table 6.1. Japan Specialists' Perception of Changes in Interest in Japan over the Past Ten Years, by Audience, 1984 and 1995*

Year and Audience	More Interested %	About the Same %	Less Interested %	Not Sure %	Number Responding #
1984					
Undergraduates	63	22	7	8	807
Graduate Students	46	29	8	16	763
Faculty Colleagues	53	33	5	9	791
Administrators	41	33	6	19	790
1995					
Undergraduates	77.1	13.3	3.8	5.8	863
Graduate Students	62.9	22.7	2.6	11.8	849
Faculty Colleagues	57.0	32.2	3.9	6.9	849
Administrators	49.4	32.7	6.7	11.2	847
General Public	67.4	22.5	4.2	5.9	877

*1984 data from 1984 Japan Foundation Report, Table 51, p. 82. Percentages were reported rounded to whole numbers.

Table 6.1 shows the comparison for the degree of interest various audiences have in Japan. The perceived interest has increased across the board for the four academic audiences, but administrators are still perceived to be relatively less interested in Japan than the other three groups. That is, not only does the 1995 sample believe that each audience's interest in Japan has increased over the past decade, they also rate the change even more positively than respondents did a decade ago. More than half the respondents think students and faculty colleagues are more interested in Japan than they were ten years ago, and the figures for administrators lag behind very slightly. Perceptions about the increase in general public interest in Japan are even stronger, with two-thirds believing the public is more interested in Japan than it was ten years ago.

Even more important, Japan specialists believe these audiences also know more about Japan than they did ten years ago, as shown in Table 6.2. Nearly two-thirds think students, both undergraduate and graduate, know more about Japan than their counterparts did a decade ago. This is substantially higher than the roughly 40–45 percent who thought in 1984 that students knew more about Japan than they had a decade earlier in the 1970s. And in 1995, half the respondents think the general public knows more about Japan than it did a decade ago.

Table 6.2. Japan Specialists' Perception of Changes in Knowledge over the Past Ten Years, by Audience, 1984 and 1995*

Year and Audience	More Interested %	About the Same %	Less Interested %	Not Sure %	Number Responding #
1984					
Undergraduates	45	37	6	12	805
Graduate Students	42	33	5	20	761
Faculty Colleagues	44	39	4	12	788
Administrators	33	38	7	23	786
1995					
Undergraduates	63.6	22.5	5.2	8.7	866
Graduate Students	62.1	22.8	2.5	12.6	848
Faculty Colleagues	53.7	35.6	2.9	7.7	853
Administrators	37.3	41.8	8.2	12.6	849
General Public	51.5	36.1	5.8	6.6	880

*1984 data from 1984 Japan Foundation Report, Table 51, p. 82. Percentages were reported rounded to whole numbers.

While the increased interest in Japan may have been motivated by the overall internationalization and restructuring of the economic, political, and social relationships between Japan and the United States, the increase in knowledge about Japan has come about largely because of the greater availability of information about Japan in English language publications produced in the United States. Some of those publications stem directly from the research of American Japan specialists, while other publications represent a trickle down or multiplier effect, in which the English language research products of Japan specialists contribute to the background knowledge of journalists and others who write about Japan for the general public.

Already in the early 1980s Japan specialists were beginning to feel the impact of increased popular interest in Japan. In response to a question about the perceived consequences of the increased interest in Japan in the popular press and publications for specialized audiences, just under half of the respondents to the Japan Foundation survey saw an increase in students taking Japanese language, but less than a third saw an increase in students majoring in Japanese Studies or related fields. By the 1995 study, over three-fourths noted the increase in students taking Japanese language, and twice as many (62.4 percent) observed an increase in majors, as shown in Table 6.3. The 1995 respondents saw some greater administrative receptivity to more extensive Japanese Studies course offerings, but this response remained less common than their perception of increased student demand. All other perceived consequences were reported at about the same levels as in 1984. In both surveys about half the respondents noted increased demands for Japan specialists to communicate with the general public.

Table 6.3. Perceived Consequences of Increased Attention Devoted to Japan in the Popular Press and Publications for Special Audiences, 1984 and 1995*

Consequence	1984 %	1995 %
Increase in students studying Japanese language	47	78.9
Increase in students majoring in Japanese Studies	31	62.4
Increased administrative receptivity to more courses	30	42.1
Increased demands to communicate to the general public	54	52.2
Pulls specialists toward less scholarly activities	27	30.5
Increased popular demand for scholarly research findings	16	20.4
Not sure	16	11.0
Number of Respondents	799	862

*1984 data from 1984 Japan Foundation Report, Table 49, p.80.

We also replicated a question from the 1984 survey asking whether the greater emphasis on communicating to a non-academic audience had resulted in increased financial opportunities, more opportunities to present research results, or less time and energy available for scholarly work. Table 6.4 shows the comparison, with and without those who said the question did not apply to them. Including the nonresponse offers a more balanced picture of the overall impact on Japan specialists of the opportunities to communicate to the general public, while the adjusted figures provide a better view of the magnitude of the impact on those who do so.

Table 6.4. If your own activities have recently placed grater emphasis on communicating to a non-academic audience, has this resulted in:

Result	1984 Full %	1984 Adjusted %	1995 Full %	1995 Adjusted %
Increased financial opportunities	16	31.3	24.9	45.5
More opportunities to present research findings	16	31.3	19.6	35.9
Less time and energy available for scholarly work	32	62.8	32.8	60.0
Not applicable	49	--	45.3	--
Number in Sample	752	384	728	398

*1984 data from 1984 Japan Foundation Report, Table 50, p. 81. Figures recalculated after subtracting those who said the question was not applicable. Original percentages were reported rounded to whole numbers.

In both studies, nearly half the respondents said the question did not apply to them, because they were not placing greater emphasis on communicating to a non-academic audience. Among those who did reply, about 60 percent in both surveys reported that they had less time and energy available for scholarly work. About a third said they had more opportunities to present their scholarly research findings. There was about a 50 percent increase in the 1995 study in the percentage who reported increased financial opportunities as a consequence of their greater emphasis on communicating to a non-academic audience.

The findings suggest some bifurcation between those who do and do not direct their attention to general audiences. We can explore this division in more depth if we turn now to the range of publications produced by Japan specialists, after which we will explore the research processes that shape those publications for different audiences.

RESEARCH OUTPUT

Research is the broadest common denominator in the activities of Japan specialists. Although they do not necessarily spend the most time on it, both academic and non-academic Japan specialists report that they do research. Moreover, research is an important component of many of the other things Japan specialists do, such as teaching, writing and lecturing, or consulting. Not all research results in publication, but if we define the term broadly enough we can capture enough "output" to be able to assess what Japan specialists actually do when they say they are doing research. The output of course does not measure the time that went into it, nor does it capture the research that makes a general contribution to the specialist's knowledge or enhances teaching, lecturing, and consulting without leaving a tangible product behind.

The 1984 Japan Foundation survey was the first that attempted to measure publication by Japan specialists. It did not count the number of publications, but simply asked whether the respondent had published something about Japan in one of several different forms of publication. The 1995 survey asked respondents to list the number of publications of each type and format, from which we can derive both counts of the volume of publication and assessments of the proportion of Japan specialists who are engaged in publication. Only 71 percent of survey respondents answered the question by reporting their number of publications in any category. We have expressed the number reporting publications as a percentage of the total sample, even though some persons may have skipped either the question or the entire section for other reasons. The percentage reported is thus a minimal figure.

Table 6.5 shows the percentage of Japan specialists in 1984 and 1995 who reported that they have published on Japan. The first three decks of the table use the same categories for 1984 and 1995 and are thus directly comparable. However, to reflect both the differentiation of expertise within Japanese Studies and the development of new publications media, the 1995 study included several other publication forms that are presented in the lower two decks of the table. We also know that the 1995 sample contains a substantially higher proportion of non-academic Japan specialists, whose interest in research for publication may be quite different from that of academics. The table therefore shows the 1995 data separately for academic and non-academic Japan specialists. We use this variable rather than current employment because the question refers to lifetime productivity, and the academic versus non-academic variable groups emeritus faculty with current faculty.

Table 6.5. Percent of Japan Specialists Who Have Published About Japan, by Publication Type and Academic Status, with 1984 Comparison*

Publication Type	1984	Academic 1995	Non-Academic 1995	Total 1995
A. Books				
Original research	42	42.1	18.3	35.7
Volumes edited	22	22.6	12.8	20.0
General, non-scholarly	8	12.4	15.6	13.2
Other materials	8	4.1	4.5	4.2
B. Articles in Journals & Edited Volumes				
Original research	69	67.9	34.6	59.0
General, non-scholarly	7	4.3	6.9	5.0
Other materials	8	3.1	3.5	3.2
C. Articles in Other Periodicals				
Original research	32	24.5	11.8	21.1
General, non-scholarly	19	14.0	18.7	15.3
Other materials	3	0.6	1.7	0.9
D. Other Publishing Media				
Original research	--	6.9	4.5	6.3
General, non-scholarly	--	1.0	0.0	0.7
Other materials	--	1.1	2.4	1.5
Film	--	2.6	2.4	2.5
Computer software	--	1.8	2.1	1.9
E. Work for Private Clients				
Books	--	2.0	2.4	2.1
Articles	--	4.3	6.9	5.0
Total Number of Respondents	923	783	289	1,072

*1984 data from SSRC Report, Table 35, p.62.

As Deck A of the table shows, about the same proportion of academic Japan specialists in 1995 have produced either books of original research or edited volumes, while the percentages for non-academics were considerably lower. The 1995 question did not cover textbooks explicitly, and we cannot be certain how respondents treated textbooks. The percent of academics reporting the publication of general or non-scholarly books is higher in 1995 for both academics and non-academics, but the latter have the higher rate. Some textbooks may be buried in this category, but the higher rate for non-academics suggests a real increase in the publication of trade books on Japan written for non-academic and non-student audiences.

Decks B and C show a similar pattern. The percentage of academics who have published original scholarly articles is only slightly lower than the overall rate was in 1984, while the percentage of non-academics with journal articles or chapters published is about half as high. However, the percentage of non-academics who have published articles for a general audience in journals or edited volumes is about the same as the 1984 rate. Academics are twice as likely as non-academics to publish original research even in non-academic periodicals, but non-academics are more likely to produce articles for a general audience and to publish them in periodicals aimed at the general public.

Thus, while the overall percentage of specialists engaged in traditional forms of publication has dropped in virtually every category since 1984, the analysis by academic status gives a quite different picture. About the same percentage of academics are still engaged in publication of original research in the traditional venues, but non-academics are more likely to publish general material in non-scholarly outlets.

Decks D and E reveal that Japan specialists are also now publishing in new media as well as producing both article and book-scale materials for private clients. Works for private clients include legal briefs, consulting reports, stock assessments and economic forecasts, and other materials commissioned by and tailored for the needs of a specific client. While the percentage of Japan specialists producing materials either in other media or for private clients is still modest, these baseline figures from the mid-1990s will undoubtedly rise in the future.

The 1984 and 1995 comparative data show how the internal differentiation in the field can distort comparisons that do not take this change in the population into account. For 1995 we can go beyond these simple percentage figures to examine the volume of publication, but again we must distinguish between academics and non-academics to get a clear picture.

Table 6.6. Number of Publications on Japan, by Publication Type and Respondent's Academic Status

Publication Type	Academic #	Academic M	Non-Academic #	Non-Academic M	Total #	Total M
Books	1,457 (403)	3.6	367 (99)	3.7	1,824 (502)	3.6
Articles	7,565 (558)	13.6	2,163 (142)	15.2	9,728 (700)	13.9
Other Media	708 (117)	6.1	367 (35)	10.5	1,075 (152)	7.1
For Clients	369 (47)	7.9	707 (26)	27.2	1,076 (73)	14.7

As shown in Table 6.6, the respondents have produced a total of 1,824 books, 9,728 articles, 1,075 items in other media, and 1,076 items for private clients. Nearly three-quarters of the respondents in the survey sample are academics, but the distribution of those who actually publish varies by the type of publication. About 80 percent of those producing books and articles are academics, but under three-quarters of those producing other media and less than two-thirds of those producing for private clients are academics. Because of these variations it is more useful to compare the mean rate of publication among those who reported publications of specific types.

Academics and non-academics produced books at about the same average rate, 3.6 versus 3.7 per person. Non-academics produced more articles (15.2 versus 13.6 per person) and items in other media (10.5 versus 6.1 per person). The greatest difference was in production for private clients, where non-academics produced at more than three times the rate of academics (27.2 versus 7.9 per person).

Publications in Japanese

Some work by Japan specialists in the United States also finds its way into print in Japanese, when it is published primarily for an audience in Japan. The 1984 Japan Foundation survey asked whether any of the respondent's work had been translated into Japanese, or had been written originally in Japanese. The 1995 survey asked how many of the respondent's publications had been either translated into or written originally in Japanese.

Table 6.7. Percent of Japan Specialists with Publications either Translated or Originally Written in Japanese, 1984 and 1995*

Publication Type	1984 Total %	1995 Total %	Academic 1995 %	Non-Academic 1995 %
A. Japanese Translation	45	26.9	29.2	20.4
Base N of Respondents	(739)	(1,072)	(783)	(289)
Adjusted 1995 percentages	---	36.3	36.5	35.5
Adjusted 1995 Base	---	(794)	(628)	(166)
B. Written in Japanese	27	18.9	23.4	6.9
Base N of Respondents	(794)	(1,072)	(783)	(289)
Adjusted 1995 percentages	---	25.6	29.2	12.0
Adjusted 1995 Base	---	(794)	(628)	(166)

*1984 data from 1984 Japan Foundation Report, Table 37, p. 64.

This slight difference in wording makes it difficult to compare the responses, because it is not clear in the 1995 question whether persons who did not give a number of publications had no publications in Japanese or skipped the question for some other reason. It we use those who did provide the number of publications as the equivalent of a "yes" response, the problem is what base to evaluate it against. Table 6.7 gives the 1984 figures, plus several possibilities for 1995 comparison. We show the 1995 figures as a percentage of the entire survey sample of 1,072 and by academic status to more closely parallel the composition of the 1984 sample, which was almost entirely academics. Then, since the other questions in this segment of the questionnaire consistently have about 780–795 respondents, we have recalculated the percentages using the number of respondents for the next question in the survey as a base. This smaller sample also has a smaller percentage of non-academic respondents (20.9 percent as opposed to 27 percent of the full survey sample of 1,072), presumably because some of those who do not do research or do not publish skipped the whole section of the questionnaire.

These alternatives were prompted by our inability to explain the large drop in the percentage of respondents with Japanese publications between 1984 and 1995, especially given the substantial carryover between the two samples. For publications that were written in Japanese, the adjustments produce roughly comparable figures to the 1984 rate of 27 percent. For publications translated into Japanese the adjustment still produces a drop from 45 percent in 1984 to 36.3 percent in 1995, with virtually no difference between the academic and non-academic portions of the sample. We still cannot explain this finding, and are reluctant to pursue it farther. However, we can look more closely at the internal composition of the numbers reported in 1995.

As might be expected, about 95 percent of those whose writings were translated into Japanese are not native speakers. Over 40 percent of them have limited or no Japanese language ability. More surprising was the finding that less than a quarter of those whose publications were originally written in Japanese are native speakers of Japanese. About 90 percent of them report that their Japanese is suitable for scholarly use, but the remaining 10 percent who wrote in Japanese do not feel their Japanese is adequate for scholarly research. While most of these authors presumably had some assistance in polishing their work for Japanese publication, it is still rather remarkable given the earlier findings in Chapter Four that most people did not think writing in Japanese was an essential skill, and did not think they were very competent in this area.

Whether the items in question were books or articles, and translated or written originally in Japanese, more than 80 percent of these Japanese publications were produced by academics. Moreover, those who did publish for a Japanese audience tended to have done so more than once. Respondents who reported that translations of their work had been published in Japanese had published a mean of 1.9 translated books and 3.5 articles, while those who reported works written in Japanese reported a mean of 2.2 books in Japanese and 5.5 articles, as shown in Table 6.8. The overall reported volume of material published in Japanese by Japan specialists in the United States is also worthy of note, a total of 318 books and 1,815 articles.

Table 6.8. Total and Mean Number of Items Published in Japanese by Japan Specialists in the United States, by Type of Publication and Academic Status of Author

	Books		Articles	
Publication Type	*#*	*Mean #*	*#*	*Mean #*
Japanese Translation				
Academic	187	1.9	666	3.6
Non-Academic	46	1.6	126	3.0
Total	233	1.9	792	3.5
Written in Japanese				
Academic	78	2.3	877	5.3
Non-Academic	7	1.3	146	7.7
Total	85	2.2	1,023	5.5

Although it is well known that in general many more works are translated from English into Japanese than are translated from Japanese into English, the works in question here are articles or books about Japan, written largely by non-Japanese. While some of these publications may be classified as courtesy or curiosity, some part of this work also constitutes a recognition in Japan of the quality of American scholarship on Japan and of its fresh perspective. Such translations and works written in Japanese attest to the growing internationalization of American Japanese Studies, in that the audience for the research of Japan specialists from the United States is no longer limited to Americans or even the broader English-reading public.

RESEARCH PURPOSES AND AUDIENCES

Most Japan specialists in our survey report that they currently are doing research on Japan, but their goals and procedures vary considerably. If we are to begin to meet the training, library, and research support needs of this diversified community of Japan specialists, we must try to understand what sorts of research they do, for what purposes and audiences, and how they go about it. To do so we will first explore a number of different aspects of the research enterprise, looking for patterns. From these clues we will then sketch out a general picture of six different types of research that are now carried out by Japan specialists.

There is no single criterion that divides Japanese Studies into completely separate and distinct subgroups; it remains a community with a great deal of commonality and overlapping interests. However, the lines of internal variation that we have already identified also affect the research activities of Japan specialists in significant ways.

Research Purposes

Probably the most basic research distinctions arise between academics and non-academics, although even here the differences are not absolute, since many persons who are not faculty were trained as academics and do essentially the same kinds of research in other occupational positions. The distinction is sharpened if we also control for the presence of retirees. As Table 6.9 shows, faculty, non-faculty and retirees differ in the purposes for which they do research. Not surprisingly, current faculty are highly oriented to academic publishing (86.4 percent) and to teaching preparation (72.9 percent), while non-faculty are less likely to do research for these purposes. The majority of non-faculty (58 percent) report that they do research as a part of their non-academic professional work. Retirees fall between these two patterns. The high proportion of emeritus faculty is revealed by the two-thirds of retirees who still engage in research for academic publication, but retirees also report doing more research for their non-academic professional work than current faculty do.

Table 6.9. Purpose of Research, by Employment Status*

Purpose of Research	Faculty		Non-Faculty		Retired	
	#	%	#	%	#	%
Academic Publication	557	86.4	63	37.3	54	66.7
Teaching Preparation	470	72.9	35	20.7	20	24.7
Non-Academic Work	91	14.1	98	58.0	19	23.5
N of Respondents	645		169		81	

*Percentages based on respondents who report they are currently doing research. Questions are independent, so percentage totals exceed 100%.

While the differences here are unmistakable, it is also important to notice the amount of overlap. Nearly forty percent of non-faculty also do research for academic publication, and twenty percent as preparation for teaching, while fourteen percent of academics engage in research as part of their own non-academic professional work. Faculty members are somewhat more likely than non-faculty to work either with a Japanese collaborator or with other Americans in joint research projects, even though the overall percentage doing so for their current research is modest.

Several other measures help to identify those who are most centrally involved in academic research on Japan. Those who wrote dissertations wholly (88.8 percent) or partly (87.1 percent) on Japan are most likely to engage in research for academic publication, compared to those whose dissertation was on an unrelated topic (74.5 percent). However, research for teaching preparation is about the same in all three groups, as is research for one's non-academic professional work. The factor of prior dissertation research highlights an important factor in how research is carried out. Those who did not do a dissertation on Japan are about 50 percent more likely to work with a collaborator in Japan to carry out their research. About 16 percent of those whose dissertation was all or partly on Japan are working with Japanese collaborators for their current research, as compared to a quarter of those without dissertation experience that involved the study of Japan.

Table 6.10. Purpose and Type of Research, by Disciplinary Group*

Purpose of Research	Humanities	Soc. Sciences	Professions	Other
	%	%	%	%
Academic Publication	84.7	77.6	64.1	60.8
Teaching Preparation	64.9	56.0	44.7	51.2
Non-academic Work	17.7	25.4	36.9	27.2
N of Respondents	379	232	103	125
Type of Research	%	%	%	%
Basic	68.1	57.3	37.5	42.2
Applied	11.4	46.2	68.3	46.9
N of Respondents	376	225	104	128

* Percentages calculated on the basis of respondents who report that they are currently doing research. Questions are independent, so percentage totals exceed 100%.

Disciplinary differences also underlie these patterns, as shown in Table 6.10. Japan specialists in the humanities are most likely (84.7 percent) to be doing research for academic publication, with social scientists next most likely (77.6 percent) and then professionals (64.1 percent). The rates for research in preparation for teaching follow the same pattern but are less pronounced, reflecting the fact that persons in the humanities have the highest rate of employment as faculty. The proportion engaged in research for non-academic work scales in the opposite direction, highest for professionals and lowest for those in the humanities. While not quite so pronounced, the same pattern can be found by language competence and the related variable of intensity of involvement on Japan.

Research Types and Audiences

Research can also be differentiated by whether it is "basic," an endeavor of intellectual discovery, as opposed to "applied," meaning that it has some clear practical application. In American academics in general, the humanities disciplines engage primarily in basic research and scholarship, persons in the professions are most oriented to applied research, and social scientists do both types. These differences are also apparent in our sample. Japan specialists in the humanities are most likely to characterize their work as basic research, while social scientists are split, with a slight preference for basic research. Those in professional fields primarily do applied research, but more than a third report that they do basic research.

Current faculty are twice as likely to characterize their research as basic, while non-faculty are nearly twice as likely to characterize their work as applied. Likewise, those with research-level Japanese language competence are twice as likely to characterize their work as basic research.

These distinctions in the purpose and type of research were not considered in the 1970 SSRC-ACLS study, which was concerned primarily with the development of basic training resources for Japanese Studies in the United States and not with research produced by American scholars. The only question related to research asked whether Japan specialists thought the work of Japanese scholars was sufficiently known in the United States. The question hints at the fact that in the early postwar period, much research by American scholars involved the distillation and presentation for an English-language audience of work by Japanese scholars that was already published in the Japanese research literature, as well as translations into English of both fiction and non-fictional works of particular importance.

The question of research types and audiences was explored briefly in the 1984 Japan Foundation study, which reported that respondents were heavily oriented to producing basic research for the scholarly community, with a secondary interest in applied research for the scholarly community. There was less interest in either basic or applied research for government or business users.[1] We cannot compare our 1995 findings directly with the 1984 data

---

[1] See 1984 Japan Foundation Report, Table 33, p. 60.

because of differences in the way the questions were asked and a lack of information about the data reduction procedures used in 1984.

In our 1995 survey, 55.8 percent reported that they are doing basic research and 34.8 percent said they do applied research. There was only a 17 percent overlap between the two groups (representing specialists, primarily social scientists, who do both types of research). The intended audiences for those doing each type of research are shown in Table 6.11. Although there is still a strong preference for academic audiences for research, almost a third of respondents who are doing applied research aim at a business or government audience. Roughly a quarter of those doing each type of research report that it is intended for an audience of students or the general public.

Table 6.11. Research Types and Intended Audiences, 1995*

Research Type	Basic Research		Applied Research		Total	
Audience	#	%	#	%	#	%
Academic Audience	429	88.1	202	67.8	669	75.9
Business-Government	40	8.2	90	30.2	119	13.5
Students	111	22.8	78	26.2	228	25.9
Public	94	19.3	73	24.5	212	24.1
N of Respondents	487		298		881	

*Percentages based on respondents who reported that they are currently doing research. Each question is independent, so percentage totals exceed 100%. There is a 17 percent overlap between those reporting basic and applied research, but some did not respond to that set of questions.

Our findings reflect the major changes since the early 1980s in both the population of Japan specialists and the relevance of Japanese Studies to non-specialists. What has changed as a result is the availability of new non-academic audiences for different kinds of knowledge about Japan, and the increasing number of Japan specialists who provide both basic and applied research tailored to the needs of those audiences.

The question, then, is who is meeting the new demand for knowledge about Japan? In general, academic faculty remain strongly oriented to their primary audiences of scholars and students. As shown in Table 6.12, other scholars are vastly more important (85 percent) to academic faculty as an audience for research findings than students (27 percent). Faculty express minimal interest in producing research for audiences in business and government, and only a bit more interest in communicating their research to the general public. By contrast, non-faculty Japan specialists are oriented only slightly more to academic audiences (40.9 percent) than to public audiences (36 percent). In order of preference, they are next interested in business users, and then to some extent in students, and finally government. Retirees, like current faculty, are oriented to academic and student audiences. They are particularly noteworthy, however, for the interest they take in the general public as an audience for their research.

Table 6.12. Research Audiences of Japan Specialists, by Employment*

Audience	Faculty %	Non-faculty %	Retired %	Total %
Academic	85.0	40.9	75.6	75.9
Students	27.1	18.9	30.8	25.9
Business	5.8	26.8	9.0	10.0
Public	18.9	36.0	41.0	24.1
Government	4.2	9.8	7.7	5.6
N of Respondents	639	164	78	881

*Percentages based on number of respondents answering questions on research audiences. Questions are independent, so percentage totals exceed 100%.

This bifurcation of interest in academic and non-academic audiences reflects not only the isolation of the ivory tower, but also the different types of expertise that Japan specialists of various disciplines have to offer to non-academic audiences. As shown in Table 6.13, Japan specialists in the humanities are least interested in business and government audiences, which are also probably least interested in the kinds of knowledge they have to offer. Humanities specialists do have some interest in communicating their research to the general public. Although still oriented toward academic audiences, those in the professions have the greatest interest in the business audience and some interest in the general public, while social scientists are moderately drawn to public, business and, to a lesser extent, government users as research audiences. The greatest interest in both public audiences and government users comes from the catchall "other" category, which includes interdisciplinary fields such as international studies, plus the performing arts.

Social scientists appear the most scattered in their audience choices because their training and expertise equip them to direct their research either to academic or non-academic audiences. Different audiences make very different demands, however, and social scientists frequently must make training and career decisions that lead them toward one audience at the expense of others.

The extent of the non-academic audience, and the price or reward for courting it, also varies by discipline within the social sciences.

Table 6.13. Research Audiences by Discipline Groups*

Audience	Humanities %	Soc. Sciences %	Professions %	Other %
Academic	81.9	79.3	68.0	55.7
Business	3.4	12.5	30.0	9.6
Government	2.4	8.1	4.0	11.3
Students	24.7	24.7	25.0	33.0
Public	26.5	18.8	15.0	36.5
N of Respondents	381	271	100	115

*Percentages based on respondents to questions on audiences for research. Each question is independent, so percentage totals exceed 100%.

The bifurcation of academic and non-academic audiences appears logical and perhaps inevitable, but a closer look at who makes each choice reveals some troubling details when we examine the academic credentials and experience of each group. Among academics, those who wrote dissertations on topics unrelated to Japan turn out to be most interested in directing their research on Japan toward public and student audiences. This same group, we have noted earlier, has the least Japanese language competence and is most likely to conduct research with the help of Japanese collaborators.

Actually, the group with the highest interest in directing research toward the public and toward business users is the portion of the sample that is omitted from such an analysis altogether: those who do not hold a doctorate. This is a reasonable result to the extent that the non-Ph.D. category contains both specialists in professional disciplines that require a different credential than the Ph.D., and persons whose job it is to provide information about Japan to the general public or to special categories of users. However, these findings still raise some questions about who is communicating about Japan to non-scholarly audiences.

The findings on Japanese language competence and intensity of involvement with Japan reinforce these concerns, and suggest the dynamics involved. Those who have scholarly competence in Japanese are heavily oriented to academic audiences, with relatively secondary interest (around 20 percent) in students and the general public. Those who have less than scholarly competence in Japanese, or no Japanese at all, have greater interest in communicating their research on Japan to students, the general public, and to business users. Similarly, those with high intensity of involvement with Japan are most oriented to academic audiences, while those with low intensity are more interested in communicating research on Japan to student, public, and business audiences.

This division suggests that the academic Japan specialists who are the most highly trained and the most deeply immersed in the study of Japan are least willing or able to communicate to non-academic audiences, or do not have relevant kinds of knowledge for these audiences, and that others have stepped into the breach. Until very recently the study of Japan was an obscure and exotic enterprise suitable only for an elite of ivory tower academics and of little interest to anybody else. It should not be surprising that academics who were trained for this obscure and exotic activity would keep doing what they were trained to do even after Japan has lost its irrelevance within American society. The new relevance of Japan has expanded the student audience, and shifted proportionately greater attention to the disciplines that offer a foundation for the kinds of knowledge that non-academic audiences want and need. This in turn leads to the creation of new kinds of Japan specialists who are better-equipped to meet the needs of non-academic audiences. The differentiation of types of Japan specialists is part of the overall normalization of Japanese Studies in American society, in which a broader range of people in a variety of different occupations acquire and use knowledge about Japan for purposes other than academic research designed for a scholarly audience.

One side of normalization is the inclusion of people without traditional academic credentials into the category of Japan specialist. The field itself gets normalized. The other side is that traditionally trained Japan specialists are transformed from being the only specialists on something nobody cares about, to the more normal role of the academic as a certain kind of specialist who does scholarly research, teaches students, and produces publications in English that other people can use as the basis for their own broader range of pursuits. For the traditionally trained Japan specialist, normalization is a process of letting go of a tiny monopoly in favor of a modest but important role in a much larger and more complex field of action.

Differences in the Research Process

The differences in language competence and intensity of involvement with Japan that distinguish the two groups of Japan specialists suggest that they are conducting rather different kinds of research for their disparate audiences. Until quite recently, most academic Japan specialists viewed the capacity to do primary research in Japanese language sources as the sine qua non of the Japan specialist. Anyone who could not meet that standard was, by definition, not a Japan specialist. Our argument here is that there are now many different kinds of research on Japan being carried out by persons with differing expert credentials. We will explore this divide by examining the language of research materials, the types of research materials used and how they are obtained, and the relations between researchers who carry out these different types of research.

Language of Research Materials

The first issue concerns the language of research but also embodies the distinction between primary research using original sources or data, and secondary research that is based on an existing research literature of findings and interpretations already developed by others. Although as we have noted earlier, the first postwar decades of American scholarship on Japan featured a considerable amount of distillation of the secondary research literature in Japanese for the benefit of an American audience that knew virtually nothing about Japan, since the 1960s academic research on Japan has been increasingly oriented to primary research using Japanese sources.

Two-thirds of current faculty and over half of retirees report that they do primary research using Japanese language materials, as opposed to about half of non-faculty (not shown). Roughly 40 percent of both faculty and non-faculty say they do primary research on Japan using English language materials. Faculty and retirees report using Japanese and English materials for secondary research about equally, suggesting that they consult whatever is available in either language to support their work. Non-faculty, who are somewhat less likely to use Japanese materials for primary research, are far less likely to use Japanese language materials for secondary research.

Table 6.14. Language of Research Materials, by Disciplinary Group*

Research Materials	Humanities %	Soc. Sciences %	Professions %	Other %	Total %
Primary, Japanese	78.5	57.8	43.3	47.7	63.7
Primary, English	37.0	43.6	36.5	36.7	38.7
Secondary, Japanese	50.0	26.7	22.1	24.2	36.3
Secondary, English	46.3	38.7	33.7	34.4	40.8
N of Respondents	376	225	104	128	833

*Percentages based on number of respondents to questions on language of research materials. Questions are independent, so totals exceed 100%.

There are some differences by discipline. As shown in Table 6.14, over three-quarters of specialists in the humanities use Japanese materials for primary research, as do more than half of social scientists. Half of those in the humanities use Japanese sources for secondary research, compared to just over a quarter of the social scientists. Social scientists are more likely than other disciplinary groups to do primary research using English sources, but specialists in the humanities are more likely to do secondary research in English sources. Less than half of those in professional fields and other disciplines do primary research using Japanese sources, and they are also correspondingly less likely to use Japanese sources for secondary research.

Those who wrote dissertations wholly about Japan are most likely to do primary research using Japanese sources (81.6 percent), followed by those whose dissertations were partly on Japan (66.7 percent). However, about 40 percent of those whose dissertations were not related to Japan, or who do not have a doctorate, also report that they do primary research using Japanese materials. Only about a quarter of respondents in these two groups report that they do secondary and background research using Japanese materials. This suggests that they may use interviews, observational material or quantitative data for primary research, which they may collect with the help of assistants or Japanese research collaborators, but they are less likely to read Japanese scholarly materials for secondary research purposes. This would help to explain the otherwise alarming finding that 45 percent of those who do not have Japanese language skills adequate for research purposes nonetheless report that they do primary research using Japanese materials. In Chapter Five we saw that even with limited Japanese language competence these specialists do try to use Japanese materials to keep up with the field, and seem to have developed strategies that fit their disciplinary training and specific research needs.

TYPES OF RESEARCH MATERIALS

A second approach to the variations in research asks whether the research is even based on textual materials, or instead requires different types of research data that are collected or obtained in ways other than going to the library to read books. Where, then, do Japan specialists obtain the materials they need for their research? Over 80 percent rely on their own personal collection of textual materials. Just under 70 percent use their institution's collection, but nearly as many (64.7 percent) use another institution's collection. The remaining categories reflect the substantial proportion of research on Japan that does not rely on traditional library materials at all. Over 40 percent of respondents report that their research is based on data they collect themselves. Over a quarter use government materials, about one in six uses materials from private collections other than their own, and 10 percent use their collaborators' data. About 8 percent use material that is available in private or commercial databases. Academics are slightly more likely to report the use of library material from their own or an institutional collection, while non-academics are slightly more likely to report the use of non-library sources of research material.

Table 6.15. Research Sources Japan Specialists Utilize, by Discipline Group*

Resource	Human	Lang	Soc. Sci.	Arts	Interdisc.	Profess.
Personal Collection	88.6	83.3	77.9	86.2	72.7	77.4
Institution's Collection	71.4	68.8	71.5	44.8	52.3	67.9
Other Institution's Collection	78.4	54.2	52.2	48.3	54.5	60.4
Government Materials	18.4	12.5	34.7	24.1	65.9	38.7
Private Collections	17.1	16.7	13.9	34.5	25.0	16.0
Collaborators' Data	5.2	8.3	14.6	13.8	9.1	19.8
Data Respondent Collects	24.4	45.8	62.8	65.6	68.2	45.3
Private/Commerc . Databases	2.9	10.4	10.6	3.4	15.9	19.8
N of Respondents	385	48	274	29	44	106

*Questions are independent, so percentage totals exceed 100%.

These differences also reflect disciplinary variations, as shown in Table 6.15. We have presented even the categories that are too small for serious analysis to show how very different the patterns are by discipline. Specialists in the humanities, language and linguistics and the arts rely most heavily on their own collections. About 20 percent in the first three groups rely on their own institution's library collection, but humanities scholars are about 50 percent more likely to use the library collection of another institution for their research. By contrast, every disciplinary group except the humanities places substantial importance on data they collect themselves. Nearly two-thirds of social scientists and those in the arts and interdisciplinary fields collect their own data. For those in language and linguistics and the professions the figure is about 45 percent, compared to under a quarter of those in the humanities.

The pattern is similar for use of collaborators' data, only the rates are considerably lower. About one in five professionals use collaborators' data, compared to one in twenty in the humanities. About 14 percent of respondents in the social sciences and the arts report using data collected by their collaborators. One in five in the professions uses private or commercial databases for research, about double the level in language and linguistics and the social sciences, with those in interdisciplinary fields falling in between. Nearly two-thirds of those in interdisciplinary fields use government materials for their research, as do more than a third in the professions and the social sciences, about double the level in the humanities.

It is also not surprising that the research sources used vary somewhat depending upon the respondent's language ability. Persons with limited or no Japanese are nearly twice as likely to use a collaborator's data or to use private and commercial databases as are those with language skills suitable for scholarly research. And persons with even limited Japanese are more likely to collect their own data or to use material in private collections than persons with no Japanese at all. These findings are similar to those reported earlier for the materials Japan specialists must read to keep up in their field. What is most striking about this picture is how much persons with limited Japanese language are able to do. In some respects their research strategies parallel those of persons with full scholarly ability in Japanese, while in other respects they resemble the techniques used by those with no usable Japanese language skills. This middle category may include people who perceive themselves as still struggling with the language even though they do conduct research, and it may also include those who can speak but not read or, less commonly, those who can read but not speak Japanese. As suggested earlier, by working with assistants or collaborators these specialists may be able to conduct research using Japanese primary materials despite language limitations. And as we have also seen, many may rely on quantitative data, either collected from other sources or derived from their own data collection efforts, which they can analyze and interpret without having any command of Japanese.

RELATIONS BETWEEN DIFFERENT KINDS OF RESEARCHERS

A third approach is to ask how those who do meet the traditional standard of conducting research using Japanese sources relate to those who use other approaches. As noted earlier, a decade ago those who did not meet the language standard were usually defined as "non-specialists," a characterization that is appropriate when persons embark upon the study of Japan without any formal training in Japanese Studies, but does not necessarily fit after they have successfully completed and published research on Japan. At any rate, the 1984 survey included a question designed to tap Japan specialists' views about the upsurge in work on Japan by persons defined as "non-specialists." The 1984 report characterized the survey response as favorable, in that a quarter thought such work had value for both specialists and laymen, while 44 percent saw the work as having value for laymen, even if it had little value to specialists. The question was replicated in the 1995 survey, and the responses have not changed much a decade later, as shown in Table 6.16. Only a third now see such work as having value for laymen but not specialists. The shift is about equally distributed between those who think work by non-specialists does have much of value for specialists, and those who think it offers little of value for anyone. Although some write-in comments on this question expressed hostility toward work by non-specialists, many respondents expressed the more temperate view that the work in this category varies considerably, and cannot be given a single summary judgment.

Table 6.16. Attitudes Toward Non-Specialists' Work on Japan, 1984 and 1995*

Attitude	*1984 %*	*1995 %*
Contains much of value for both specialists and laymen	25	29.6
Has value for laymen but little for specialists	44	34.2
Has value for specialists, but little for laymen	1	1.8
Has little value for either specialists or laymen	16	19.9
Not sure	14	14.4
N of Respondents	817	818

*1984 data from 1984 Japan Foundation Report, Table 52, p. 83. Percentages were reported as rounded whole numbers.

If we reconfigure the responses to separate out positive and negative views of the value of non-specialists' work to specialists and laymen, respectively, a slightly different picture emerges. Respondents' evaluation of the value of non-specialists' work for laymen has become somewhat less positive, while their view of the value of such work for specialists has become less negative over the past decade.

In both the 1984 and 1995 surveys, respondents were also asked what Japan specialists should do to assist non-specialists studying and writing about Japan. These responses also have not changed much since 1984, except that Japan specialists now seem slightly more willing to provide support such as introductions and references so that non-specialists can do independent work on Japan. This also suggests that the "non-specialists" are persons who not only study and write about Japan, but do their own research.

Table 6.17. Ways of Assisting Non-Specialists Studying and Writing about Japan*

Form of Assistance	1984 %	1995 %
Serve as consultants to review their work	63	61.6
Encourage or provide language instruction	37	40.1
Provide introductions to other scholars	41	46.1
Explain existing knowledge about Japan	57	65.2
Provide references to existing research**	--	65.4
Other	4	--
Nothing	2	2.6
Not sure	6	9.6
N of respondents	815	856

*This is a multiple response variable so percentages exceed 100%. 1984 data from 1984 Japan Foundation Report, Table 53, p. 84. Percentages reported as rounded whole numbers.

**This response choice was added in 1995.

This question also provoked a rather high number of write-in responses, many of which were negative remarks. We must reiterate that this question was originally written in 1984 and directed to a sample largely composed of traditionally-trained academic Japan specialists. By the 1995 study many of the "non-specialists" who were to be assisted have met the criteria for entry in the *Directory of Japan Specialists* and consequently are part of the 1995 survey sample. We have spent much of this volume analyzing how these new specialists differ from the more traditional Japan specialists, and trying to understand their place in the Japanese Studies of the 1990s and beyond. The responses to this question suggest that while there is still some resistance, about two-thirds of Japan specialists now perceive their role as consultants and authorities who provide knowledge about Japan either directly or by referring non-specialists to the English language literature produced by trained Japan specialists.

SIX TYPES OF RESEARCH IN JAPANESE STUDIES

Having identified a number of factors that differentiate the research that Japan specialists do in terms of its purposes, audiences and procedures, we can now step back from the details of the data analysis and try to sketch out in a more general way the types of research that are being done in the 1990s by American Japan specialists, as embodied in the 1995 directory and survey data. We have identified six types, each of which can be characterized in terms of the kinds of expertise the researcher brings to the task, how the research is conducted, and the audiences to which it is directed. In addition to the quantitative analysis of the survey data presented here, we have relied on a reading of individual directory entries and our general knowledge of the field in the construction of the six types. While it is not feasible to try to classify individual Japan specialists according to these types on the basis of the survey data alone, the descriptions may help clarify what the survey findings have revealed.

Classic Japanese Studies Research

This research may be conducted on virtually any topic in Japan's past or present. It involves primary research using Japanese language materials, carried out by a formally trained Japan specialist who reads and speaks Japanese at a level adequate for research purposes. Such research is most common in the humanities and secondarily in the social sciences, but may be found in other disciplines as well. The research product normally displays a command of the English language secondary literature, and in some fields may require a command of the Japanese secondary literature as well, but it also requires original work in Japanese primary sources. Depending on the discipline and topic, these primary sources may include interviews and observational methods as well as textual materials. The research is most likely to be oriented toward a Japan specialist audience, but also may be directed toward the researcher's own discipline.

Disciplinary Expert Research

This primary research is done by an academic who is not formally trained in Japanese Studies and possesses either limited or no Japanese language skills, but is an acknowledged expert in a particular area. The disciplinary expert can carry out primary research in Japan with Japanese collaborators who collect data, or may be able to collect some types of data directly with the help of translators and assistants. Because of the transferability of the researcher's expertise in the subject matter, such research may be highly sophisticated and focused. The researcher relies on the English language secondary literature on Japan for context and cultural interpretation, and may consult directly with other American Japan specialists in addition to Japanese colleagues. Such research may be either explicitly or implicitly comparative, and is most likely to be oriented to a disciplinary audience.

International Japanese Research

This research, usually primary, concerns the relationship of Japan to some other place, context, or culture. It is done by a person who is not necessarily trained as a Japan specialist, but is trained for the study of the relevant context and culture as well as the subject matter. It usually involves the impact of Japanese phenomena in some other setting, but it might also concern a foreign element in Japan. This type of research is distinguished from the disciplinary expert type by the fact that the primary research requires a language other than Japanese, and that much of it may be done outside of Japan. Such research may rely on the English language secondary literature on Japan for cultural background, but is sometimes carried out in isolation from both the Japanese and English language secondary literature relevant to the topic. It may be basic or applied in nature, and may be directed toward either an academic (disciplinary) or a non-academic audience.

Theoretical Secondary Research

This type of research is conducted by an academic or professional expert who is not formally trained in Japanese Studies, has no usable Japanese language competence, and relies on the secondary English language literature on Japan. The research may use some available quantitative data for secondary analysis, but mostly entails a close reading of secondary and translated materials on Japan, coupled with theoretical concepts derived from the discipline. This fusion of theory with substantive information on Japan may advance new interpretations or simply reinforce prevailing views in the English language literature on Japan. Because such research relies on English language secondary materials, it tends to be oriented to disciplinary, student, and general audiences rather than Japan specialists.

Non-Academic Secondary Research

This type of secondary research is done by a non-academic who uses the English language literature on Japan as a source of basic information and standard interpretations to present to non-specialist, non-academic audiences. The researcher does not do original work on Japan, but may draw independent conclusions or interpretations from the material and incorporate them into the presentation. While not a scholar, the researcher may draw upon personal observations or informal interviewing of "natives" or "experts" to supplement the secondary sources. Such research performs an important bridging function in communicating the results of American research on Japan to non-academic and general audiences.

Proprietary and Professional Research

This highly specialized research, which may be primary or secondary, is conducted by a professional or an academic to meet the specific needs of a private client. The researcher has recognized expertise in the subject matter plus either research-level Japanese language competence or access to specialized research material of use to the client. Such research is often time-sensitive, and a premium is placed on the researcher's ability to deliver timely information that is not readily available to others. However, the primary distinguishing characteristic of this research is that it is commissioned by a client for private use, and normally does not enter the domain of public knowledge except at the client's direction.

Implications of the Six Types

The main point of this description of six types of research is to underscore the diversity and complexity of contemporary Japanese Studies research in the United States. Some of the types reflect the changed nature of Japan itself, and its new relationship to the rest of the world. The internationalized, post-industrial Japan of the 1990s raises new research questions and demands for knowledge. Moreover, those new demands pop up all over the world, and require very different kinds of disciplinary background and specialization on the part of the researcher than the traditional Japanese Studies curriculum provides. Specialists with the necessary background to answer these new questions are now an essential part of Japanese Studies in the United States.

Several of the types point directly to the normalization of Japanese Studies, in that they demonstrate the relative ease with which persons trained for other kinds of research and professional activity can now enter into Japanese Studies, develop some professional expertise, and make a contribution. At the same time, these researchers depend heavily upon the primary research in Japanese materials that is carried out by classically trained Japan specialists and published in English. Since it is the existence of that growing body of English language scholarship that makes other kinds of research as well as the training of new Japan specialists possible, the field still requires a heavy commitment to the training and support of Japan specialists with full language capability plus area and disciplinary expertise.

At the same time, disciplinary specialization and the differentiated needs of the general audience for Japanese Studies research in the United States have made it impractical, indeed impossible, for traditionally trained Japan specialists to meet all of the current needs. Informally and in response to perceived opportunities and needs, research in Japanese Studies in the United

States has been moving in several new directions at once. Over the next decade we can anticipate a clearer articulation of the special needs of each segment of this larger research community, and a new rapprochement between the various groups of specialists as they recognize and define their differences and interdependencies.

The first four of the six types of research in Japanese Studies represent different forms of academic research. Regardless of their variations in language, methods and materials, they all are largely conducted by academically trained scholars who write for academic audiences. Yet the same processes that have caused internal differentiation within Japanese Studies and greater disciplinary specialization have also created differentiated audiences for academic research on Japan, which demand more specialized research products and expect to find them in different places. We therefore return now to the issue of publication with a more specific set of questions concerning how academic research is tailored for different audiences, and how it is positioned so that they can find it.

ACADEMIC PUBLICATION IN JAPANESE STUDIES

We saw at the beginning of this chapter that the lines between scholarly and non-scholarly publication are rather ambiguous. The tabulation of publications by type and publication outlet makes it very clear that scholarly research may appear either in academic journals and edited volumes or in periodicals directed at a more general audience. Secondary research may appear in either academic or general periodicals as well. Yet even when respondents were asked specifically about where they would first try to publish their scholarly research, the responses were divided and revealed considerable underlying ambivalence. There is also some evidence that this division and ambivalence are growing.

The 1984 Japan Foundation survey asked respondents whether they would first submit an article-length manuscript reporting scholarly research findings on Japanese studies in their field to a journal devoted exclusively to Japanese Studies, an interdisciplinary journal dealing with international or comparative studies, or a journal in their own discipline. This question was replicated in the 1995 survey. Unlike many of the 1995 survey questions that encouraged respondents to "circle all that apply," this question asked for one response, only forcing a choice that many found very difficult. The results are shown in Table 6.18.

Table 6.18. Where Japan Specialists Would First Submit an Article for Publication, 1984 and 1995*

Type of Journal	1984 %	1995 %
Exclusively on Japanese Studies	30	16.4
Interdisciplinary, International or Comparative	27	16.4
Disciplinary Journal	43	33.7
Not sure, depends on content	7	33.5
N of Respondents	(809)	(781)

*1984 data from 1984 Japan Foundation Report, Table 39, p. 66.

In the 1984 survey, respondents were most likely to send an article first to a disciplinary journal (43 percent), but a journal exclusively on Japanese Studies was not too far behind at 30 percent, and an international or comparative journal was selected by more than a quarter of the respondents as well. There was little ambivalence about these choices, with only 7 percent not sure where they would first send an article. By 1995 the selection of all three journal categories had dropped, and the number unable to choose had skyrocketed. Of the 781 Japan specialists who responded to this question in 1995, a third selected a journal in their own discipline, and another third were evenly divided between a journal devoted exclusively to Japanese Studies and an interdisciplinary journal dealing with international or comparative studies. A third of the respondents said they were not sure, since it would depend upon the content. The question also generated an unusually high number of write-in responses, most of which simply added one of the responses they did not select the first time.

Non-academics were somewhat less likely to select an area-focused journal, and more likely to express ambivalence about where to send their work, although some wrote in the response that they would not send it to any kind of academic journal. There were also strong disciplinary differences, with those in the humanities relatively more likely to choose a Japanese Studies journal (28.6 percent) than social scientists (5.3 percent) or professionals (3.6 percent). Conversely, those in the professions (56.6 percent) and social sciences (43.6 percent) were far more likely to send an article to a disciplinary journal than were persons in the humanities (21.5 percent). Similar differences between the humanities and social sciences were also reported in 1984, although the disciplinary groupings were not quite the same.

The extent of competence in Japanese language also had a strong effect on the choice of a publication outlet, in part because it is an indicator of how connected a specialist is to the interdisciplinary Japanese Studies community as an intellectual and social network. As shown in Table 6.19, those with scholarly level Japanese language competence were only slightly more likely to send an article to a disciplinary journal (29.6 percent) than to a Japanese Studies journal (23 percent), but a third were uncertain where they would send their work. Persons with limited Japanese were also likely to be uncertain about where to send their work, but more than a third would choose a disciplinary journal, while the second choice was an interdisciplinary journal publishing international or comparative research. The small group of respondents with no Japanese language who answered this question was much less likely to be ambivalent about where they wanted to publish. Half of them would choose a disciplinary journal and a third an interdisciplinary international or comparative journal.

Table 6.19. Where Japan Specialists Would Send an Article Reporting Their Scholarly Research, by Japanese Language Competence of the Author

Language Level and Publication Type	No Japanese %	Not Scholarly %	Scholarly Use %	Total Sample %
Japanese Studies Journal	2.0	8.6	23.0	16.9
Interdisc. International Journal	33.3	19.2	12.5	16.1
Disciplinary Journal	49.0	37.1	29.6	33.4
Not Sure, Depends on Content	15.7	35.1	34.9	33.6
N of Respondents	51	245	456	752

Both the 1984 and 1995 surveys also asked respondents to whom they would turn to critique a manuscript they had written about their research findings on Japanese Studies in their field. The choices covered persons in and outside the respondent's discipline, and in and outside of Japanese Studies. In the 1995 survey this question permitted up to three responses, but the average was just under two per respondent. The published 1984 responses to the same question total just slightly over 100 percent, so apparently multiple responses were acceptable, but infrequently given. The 1995 question also included additional response choices to cover Japanese colleagues in and outside the respondent's discipline.

As shown in Table 6.20, all responses were up considerably in 1995, but the general pattern remained the same. The most common response, selected by 70 percent of respondents in 1995, was a Japan specialist in the respondent's own discipline. The second most common response (42.6 percent) was a person in the same discipline who was not a Japan specialist, while the third-ranked response (31.5 percent) was a Japanese colleague in the same discipline. One in five respondents in 1995 said they would seek a critique from a Japan specialist in a different discipline.

Table 6.20. Persons to Whom Respondents Turn for Critique of a Manuscript They Had Written, 1984 and 1995

Critique Requested From:	1984 %	1995 %
Japan specialist in respondent's discipline	57	70.0
Non-Japan specialist in respondent's discipline	21	42.6
Japanese colleague in respondent's discipline	--	31.5
Japan specialist in some other discipline	10	21.9
Non-Japan specialist in some other discipline	2	12.3
Japanese colleague in some other discipline	--	6.8
Not sure	13	10.1
N of Respondents	(808)	(794)

*1984 data from 1984 Japan Foundation Report, Table 38, p. 78. Percentages reported as rounded whole numbers.

The general rank order of responses holds for both academics and non-academics, and also across all three employment statuses. Academics, and especially current faculty, have higher rates of response in all of these categories. Most notably, one in four would seek a critique from a Japan specialist in another discipline, as opposed to less than one in six among those who are not academics, or are not currently employed as faculty (including retirees). These differences most likely reflect the relatively greater access that academics, particularly current faculty, have to colleagues either in the same discipline or in Japanese Studies in general.

There are some differences by discipline. More than three-quarters of those in the humanities would seek a critique from a Japan specialist in the same discipline, as opposed to just under two-thirds of those in the social sciences or the professions. This may partly reflect variations in the sheer availability of Japan specialist colleagues within the same discipline. However, over half of the social scientists (54.5 percent) would turn to a disciplinary colleague who is not a Japan specialist, as opposed to just under 40 percent of humanists and less than 30 percent of professionals. Social scientists were also more likely to turn to a Japanese colleague in the same discipline, reflecting the greater degree of international collaborative research on Japan that is conducted by social scientists. Both of these differentials point to the strong orientation of social scientists to their own discipline. Still, both social scientists (25.6 percent) and humanists (23.6 percent) were considerably more likely than those in professional fields (16.1 percent) to seek a critique from a Japan specialist in another discipline.

As shown in Table 6.21, the findings by Japanese language competence contained one surprise: the greater the Japanese language competence, the more likely respondents were to seek a manuscript critique from any of these sources! This finding suggests the greater network connections within Japanese Studies, which operate both within and across disciplinary lines. Of those with scholarly level competence in Japanese, three-quarters would seek a critique from another Japan specialist in the same discipline (as opposed to two-thirds of those with limited Japanese), and nearly a quarter would seek a critique from a Japan specialist in another discipline (as opposed to about a fifth of those with limited Japanese). Yet those highly competent in Japanese are also slightly more likely to seek a critique from someone in their discipline who is not a Japan specialist.

Table 6.21. To Whom do Japan Specialist Turn to Critique Their Manuscripts, by Language Competence of the Manuscript's Author

Language Competence Critique Requested From:	No Japanese %	Not Scholarly %	Scholarly Use %	Total Sample %
Japan specialist in own discipline	56.6	65.6	74.3	70.3
Non-Japan specialist in discipline	32.1	41.4	45.4	43.2
Japanese colleague in discipline	22.6	31.6	32.6	31.6
Japan specialist, other discipline	22.6	19.3	23.5	22.1
Non-Japan specialist, other disc.	7.5	11.9	13.0	12.2
Japanese colleague, other disc.	7.5	10.7	5.2	7.1
N of Respondents	53	244	463	760

In general, these findings indicate some division between those who orient their research toward other Japan specialists and those who orient their work toward their own discipline. In some fields the two are more or less "nested," and as the number of Japan specialists grows, it is possible to orient one's work toward a recognizable subset of specialists on Japan within the discipline and not experience any conflict between area specialization and disciplinary obligations. In other cases the discipline does not acknowledge "Japan" as a subfield of disciplinary specialization, so the specialist must choose to orient research toward one audience or the other, or try to straddle the two. Since the two audiences may make rather different demands on the Japan specialist scholar, the choices not only affect the kind of research that is produced, but may have material consequences for the academic careers of younger scholars. We have touched on this topic in Chapter Five, in the context of Japan specialists' orientation to area or disciplinary meetings and the different networks associated with them. The same hard choices follow the social scientist in particular all the way from the framing of a research topic and the search for funding to the final form and venue of publication.[2]

The conflict is revealed in these data in several ways. First, social scientists are more likely to be oriented to their own discipline to the extent of seeking critiques from disciplinary specialists who are not Japan specialists, or from Japanese colleagues in the same discipline. Second, they are more likely to orient their publications to disciplinary journals or comparative journals. And third, the high rates of uncertainty about where to send a manuscript suggest that many respondents are trying to straddle intellectual networks that make conflicting demands. Those with greater Japanese language competence and more ties to the Japanese Studies community are most likely to try to meet both sets of demands by seeking multiple critiques of their work, and directing their research findings to separate specialized audiences through different publication outlets. The competition within their own disciplines comes increasingly from scholars with limited or no Japanese language competence, who are fully oriented to their discipline and publish work that is more likely to be based on quantitative data, in either disciplinary or international and comparative journals.

These findings about the varied publication outlets for research in Japanese Studies and the conflicting demands placed on researchers suggest that there may be difficulties in connecting academic research publications on Japanese Studies to their intended audiences. If the researchers themselves are ambivalent about where to publish their findings, we should not be surprised to learn that the intended audiences have a hard time finding them. Japan specialists with active research networks usually find out about new research through informal channels, but the external audience for academic research in Japanese Studies published in English must rely on the standard information location methods of the American library system. Academic materials in Japanese Studies are unusually difficult to locate for two reasons.

First, some of the work that is most highly regarded among specialists appears in edited volumes, which constitute a particularly important form of publication in Japanese Studies. Twenty-two percent of academic Japan specialists have edited a volume of essays, a number that has remained stable

---

[2] See Patricia G. Steinhoff, "Who Knows? Who Wants to Know? Doing Japanese Studies in the 1990s: Colleagues and Collaboration" Kyoto Conference on Japanese Studies 1994, (International Research Center for Japanese Studies and The Japan Foundation, 1994), pp. 353-363 for a fuller discussion of these dilemmas.

since the 1984 Japan Foundation study. The Japan specialists in our survey sample report that they have produced 532 edited volumes and have published over 2,000 chapters or essays in edited volumes. The edited volume, or conference volume, became an important vehicle for collaborative research in Japanese Studies because it provided a vehicle for coordinating work on related topics by Japan specialists based in different institutions located throughout the United States.

Whereas academics doing research on more standard topics frequently can form a critical mass of scholars at one academic institution or research institute to work on a topic of common interest, Japan specialists were too few and too scattered, and their research too esoteric, to support such a critical mass working on one topic at a single institution. Instead, from the 1960s through the early 1990s, there has been some funding available, primarily from the Social Science Research Council, the Japan-U.S. Friendship Commission, and The Japan Foundation, to bring groups of Japan specialists together to plan a coordinated research effort, meet for a few days in a conference to present their individual papers and critique them, and then to have the papers edited into a volume for publication. As funding for conferences and their associated published volumes has become scarce in the past few years, some scholars have produced edited volumes of essays without a conference, often presenting some of the papers as panels at national meetings. Other groups have held formal conferences, but opted to publish groups of their papers in special editions of journals rather than through a formal conference volume in book format. Though the days of the classic conference volume may be waning, it is nonetheless the case that much of the premier scholarship on Japan in English is found in such edited volumes.

The difficulty these volumes pose for the research audience is that books are indexed by book title and editor, but not by chapter author and chapter title. Thus unless one knows that a particular author wrote an essay on a particular subject in a specific edited volume, there is no ready way to find it. Neither the cataloguing systems for books nor the current online and CD-ROM indexing systems for periodical articles index the individual essays in edited volumes by their author, title, and subject. Hence a student who specializes in Japanese Studies will learn the authors in certain fields and become familiar with their research through course readings, but the student or scholar who wants to find material on a particular topic in Japanese Studies may only come upon seminal material by chance, or by reading the footnotes in other publications.

The second reason Japanese Studies materials are hard to find is that the work that appears in periodicals is widely scattered across a range of publication outlets associated with many different disciplines and topics. While there are a few journals specifically devoted to Japanese Studies, the findings about where Japan specialists try to publish their work makes clear that very little of the total volume of research in Japanese Studies appears in periodicals that are in any way marked as being about Japan. Most of the articles about Japan turn up unexpectedly in journals that reach either a disciplinary audience or a more generic international and comparative studies audience. And since both the authors and the journals are selectively emphasizing certain qualities that will enhance the "fit" between journal and manuscript, the regular reader of a disciplinary or comparative journal is likely to find there only those materials about Japan that least disturb underlying assumptions or undermine prevailing theoretical approaches.

Given the vast number of specialized academic publications in the United States and the relative scarcity of academic publications about Japan, it is also unlikely that the regular reader of any particular disciplinary or interdisciplinary international and comparative journal will find a great deal of material about Japan. Hence anyone who wants to find out about a particular topic in Japanese Studies will have to launch a broader search through an unknown range of periodicals. The problem is not that such a search produces nothing. On the contrary, the standard American library search technique using online or CD-ROM bibliographic databases turns up a peculiar assortment of material in rather overwhelming quantities, especially in the social sciences.

Using "Japan" or "Japanese" as the basic search criteria and publication dates of 1988-1992, we searched the standard CD-ROM bibliographic databases available in academic libraries in the United States. For the social sciences, the Social Sciences Index had about 850 entries per year; PAIS (Public Affairs Information Service) an average of about 475; Sociofile an average of 200 pieces per year; ERIC, the education database had about 230 entries per year; and ABI INFORM, a full-text database covering business and management journals, a whopping 1,300 or more entries per year.[3] Both PAIS and ABI INFORM heavily index the popular press, so most of what turns up in these searches is not academic research at all, and was written by journalists rather than Japan specialists of any sort. By contrast, the more academic Humanities Index averaged a little over 100 items per year, and the MLA International Bibliography, covering literature and language materials, carried about 275 items each year on Japan.

Our five-year search of standard bibliographic databases produced over 13,700 items which, even after removing foreign items and duplicates, totals well over 10,000 entries. By contrast, the lifetime total of both academic and non-academic articles produced by our sample of Japan specialists was less than 10,000 articles. Work by Japan specialists did turn up in these database searches, but it was buried in an avalanche of other material of widely varying quality. The fact that so much material is readily available on Japan certainly

---

[3] PsycLit, the psychology database, also contained over 800 entries per year, but most of them were totally irrelevant since the search picked up any psychology paper with an author living in Japan. These are not included in the totals.

attests to the normalization of the field and its general accessibility in contemporary American society. Information about Japan is now part of the general information glut that puts knowledge about everything at one's fingertips, but provides few clues for deciding what is accurate, useful, or insightful. The burden is clearly on the reader, or searcher, to dig through it all and find something relevant. But determining what is worthwhile requires an educated reader with some standards and criteria against which to evaluate the materials.

Fortunately, the same processes of normalization that have generated the great demand for material about Japan, and have brought new and different kinds of specialists into Japanese Studies, have also expanded the availability of academic study of Japan. In Chapter Two we traced that process through the extension of Japan specialists to a wider range of academic institutions throughout the United States. In the next three chapters we will look more closely at how the study of Japan has become normalized within American academic institutions through the proliferation of courses, the expansion of formal academic programs, and the increase in Japan specialist staff that makes these offerings possible.

PART III:

ACADEMIC PROGRAMS IN JAPANESE STUDIES

7

Academic Courses on Japan

Up to this point we have concentrated largely on professional specialists on Japan, but now we shift to the main institution through which their expertise is transmitted to others, American colleges and universities. In Chapter Three we looked at the presence of a Japan specialist at an academic institution as a very rough measure of the availability of expertise on Japan. We now inquire more specifically about the actual transmission of basic knowledge about Japan through academic instruction. Some American colleges and universities began offering a few courses on Japan in the early part of the twentieth century, but as with Japan specialists, the real growth in instruction on Japan is a postwar phenomenon. In this chapter we will trace that postwar growth, beginning with the mid-1970s but focusing particularly on changes since 1984 and the current situation.

For this analysis we are restricted to the academic institutions that provided data for entries in the *Directory of Japanese Studies Institutions in the United States and Canada*. Our unit of analysis will be the semester (or sometimes quarter) course, a metric that is fairly standard across college campuses despite wide variation in course content. Since the American college curriculum generally allows students to choose a certain number of elective courses outside the major as well as offering some course flexibility within majors and graduate degree programs, single courses on Japan constitute the minimal amount of instruction available to the widest range of students. An institution can also offer isolated courses even if there is no formal program of study on Japan and no degree offered in Japanese Studies.

Unlike the situation in Japan, where permission of the national Ministry of Education is required to add a single course, American colleges can add and subtract courses from the curriculum quite easily as a local initiative in response to faculty and student interest. Consequently, the number of courses offered at any one time provides a reasonably good measure both of the availability of faculty to teach courses on Japan and of the student demand for such instruction. We will look first at regular disciplinary or area courses on Japan, and then at Japanese language courses. We will then return to our survey of Japan specialists to see how they view their current teaching conditions.

167

COURSES AND INSTITUTIONS

The 244 academic institutions that participated in the 1995 directory study reported a total of 4,506 courses related to Japan. The number of courses offered at a single institution ranged from one (seven cases) to over a hundred (two cases). The course lists were edited for comparability to produce a separate entry for each semester or quarter. Responding institutions were asked to code the courses as lower division, upper division, or graduate level. When the institution did not do so, we were able to make the assignment based on available information.[1] About a third of the courses were offered at the lower division level and half at the upper division level, with the remainder at the graduate level, as shown in Table 7.1. Eighty percent of the courses reported to the study (including language courses) were exclusively about Japan. The remainder covered a wider area of Asia, encompassed a more general international theme with substantial Japan content, or were systematically comparative.

Table 7.1. Courses Related to Japan, by Course Level and Extent of Content on Japan, 1995

Level	Lower Division		Upper Division		Graduate		Total	
Content	#	%	#	%	#	%	#	%
Exclusively on Japan	1,260	35.2	1,695	47.3	629	17.6	3,584	79.5
Multinational with Japan	285	30.9	474	51.4	163	17.7	922	20.5
Total on Japan	1,545	34.3	2,169	48.1	792	17.6	4,506	20.5

Using the course numbering system, department, and course title, the courses were coded according to the same disciplinary categories used by Japan specialists participating in the study to identify their own disciplines. The courses were distributed among 42 disciplines, except for 128 (2.8 percent) coded as "other." By far the largest category was Japanese language, which accounted for 1,580 or a third (35.1 percent) of all the courses. Over half of these (57.4 percent) were lower division first- and second-year language courses. A third (35.3 percent) of the language courses were classified as upper division, with 7.3

[1] In general, first- and second-year Japanese language courses were coded as lower division and third- and fourth-year Japanese language courses as upper division, except when special introductory language courses were explicitly designated as being for graduate students.

percent at the graduate level. However, this classification does not include graduate-level courses and seminars reading Japanese literature in the original language, which were coded as literature courses. Language courses also accounted for nearly 60 percent of all lower division courses; hence non-language classes are even more heavily skewed toward the upper division and graduate level.

Table 7.2. Japanese Area Courses in Disciplines with 25 or More Courses, by Course Level, 1995*

Course Level Discipline	Lower Division #	%	Upper Division #	%	Graduate #	%	Total #	%
History	166	28.1	333	56.3	92	15.6	591	20.2
Literature	76	17.7	241	56.0	113	26.3	430	14.7
Art History	67	30.5	104	47.3	49	22.3	220	7.5
Political Science	25	12.8	132	67.7	38	19.5	195	6.7
Japanese Studies	51	33.6	78	51.3	23	15.1	152	5.2
Religion	53	37.6	68	48.2	20	14.2	141	4.8
Buddhist Studies	22	15.9	77	55.8	39	28.3	138	4.7
Anthropology	24	23.5	59	57.8	19	18.6	102	3.5
Linguistics	7	7.0	46	46.0	47	47.0	100	3.4
Sociology	22	28.9	36	47.4	18	23.7	76	2.6
Business Managemt.	2	2.9	20	29.4	46	67.6	68	2.3
Economics	6	8.8	42	61.8	20	29.4	68	2.3
Women's Studies	11	18.6	41	69.5	7	11.9	59	2.0
Film Studies	9	16.1	39	69.6	8	14.3	56	1.9
Philosophy	12	30.8	23	59.0	4	10.3	39	1.3
Asian-Amer. Studies	10	25.6	23	59.0	6	15.4	39	1.3
Asian Studies	11	34.4	16	50.0	5	15.6	32	1.1
International Studies	5	15.6	15	46.9	12	37.5	32	1.1
Law	1	3.3	4	13.3	25	83.3	30	1.0
Performing Arts	3	10.0	20	66.7	7	23.3	30	1.0
Music	8	29.6	15	55.6	4	14.8	27	0.9
All Other	44	14.9	178	60.1	74	25.0	296	10.4
Total	635	21.8	1,610	55.1	676	23.1	2,926	99.9

*This table excludes Japanese language courses, but includes all area courses either on Japan exclusively or including coverage of Japan in a multinational course. Disciplines are ordered by number of courses reported.

When Japanese language classes are removed, over half the remaining courses (55.1 percent) are offered at the upper division level, and nearly a quarter (23.1 percent) at the graduate level, with just over a fifth (21.8 percent) at the lower division level. The largest category of area courses was history, with 591 courses, followed by literature with 430. As shown in Table 7.2, above, in both cases slightly over half of the area courses were offered at the upper division level, but the next largest category for history was lower division courses, often on generic East Asian history, while for Japanese literature the second largest category was graduate courses, primarily advanced seminars reading Japanese literature in the original.

Next in scale were art history with 220 courses, nearly a quarter at the graduate level and nearly half upper division, and political science at 195, two-thirds at the upper division level and a fifth at the graduate level, followed by general or interdisciplinary Japanese Studies courses (152), which were even more heavily undergraduate. Religion and Buddhist studies were next at 141 and 138 courses, respectively, but if combined they would easily outpace the art history and political science offerings. There was some natural division of labor, however, in that religion courses were more skewed toward general lower division courses, while Buddhist studies accounted for twice as many graduate courses as did religion. Anthropology (102) and linguistics (100) courses were similar in number, but about half of the linguistics courses were at the graduate level. Almost a quarter of the 76 sociology courses and nearly a third of the 68 economics courses were offered at the graduate level, compared to over two-thirds of the 68 business management courses. These disciplines were followed in order by women's studies, film studies, philosophy, Asian-American studies, Asian studies, international studies, law, performing arts, and music, but the numbers become too small for reliable comparison of course-level distributions.

Three points about this overall ranking and distribution are worth noting. First, there is a relationship between the availability of disciplinary specialists and courses offered in that field, but it is not as close as one might expect. Beyond the top disciplines of Japanese language, history and literature, the number of courses being offered in a particular discipline does not seem to be closely correlated with the number of Japan specialists in that discipline or even at the institution.[2] There seem to be two reasons for this: disciplinary differences in how finely subject matter is divided; and what else Japan specialists may be required to teach. In the social sciences, for example, it is unusual for more than one or two upper division courses on Japan to be offered in one discipline, while in the humanities the courses are more likely to be divided up by time period or genre, resulting in more courses, perhaps offered less frequently.

The lower half of the ranking includes several interdisciplinary fields plus a number of specialized areas in the arts, and in this respect the distribution of

---

[2] The same observation was also made in the 1977 CULCON Report, p. 24.

area courses currently offered reflects the increase in Japan specialists who identify themselves as specialists in these disciplines. Moreover, all of the disciplines ranked in Table 7.2 together account for 90 percent of the courses offered, but only half of the disciplines in which courses were reported. In other words, there are a small number of courses being offered in a very wide range of other disciplines. That long tail includes traditional Japanese Studies disciplines such as geography, plus fields such as East Asian Studies, art, architecture, journalism, and communications.

Second, the disciplines vary considerably in their relative distribution of lower division, upper division, and graduate courses. Not surprisingly, law and business management courses are offered predominantly at the graduate level. The high proportion of graduate courses in linguistics seems to be due to their close association with graduate programs in Japanese language and literature. The ranking of disciplines would be rather different if one were looking at the fields where students are most likely to gain their first exposure to Japan. Religion, Asian studies, and Japanese studies would move up in the rankings, followed by the traditional social science disciplines of sociology and anthropology. Literature and political science would drop in rank.

Third, these course counts and the disciplinary rankings based on them include both courses exclusively on Japan and multinational courses with some coverage of Japan. To get a clearer picture of how Japanese Studies is developing, we need to distinguish these two types of courses more carefully. This in turn requires combining disciplinary categories into larger clusters so there are sufficient cases to analyze.

Courses Exclusively on Japan

To gain some sense of how course offerings have expanded over time, we have recoded the courses according to a disciplinary scheme utilized in the 1977 CULCON Report, and modified slightly for the survey of Japanese Studies in the United States commissioned by The Japan Foundation through the SSRC-ACLS Joint Committee on Japanese Studies, which was published in 1984. This permits us to compare courses across three decades. We have not included the 1989 directory survey in this comparative series for two reasons. First, because the current study was designed and managed as an update to the 1989 edition of the directory, some data such as course listings for 1989 are difficult to reconstruct from our computer records. Second, the 1984 survey of Japanese Studies institutions had a higher participation rate than the 1989 directory survey of institutions, and in fact matches fairly closely the combined list of 1995 entries that had either a primary or secondary listing in the 1989 directory. Thus the 1984 survey seems to be a more appropriate base for comparison of course data.

Tables 7.3 and 7.4 show the classification by disciplinary group of area courses exclusively on Japan and the number of institutions reporting them, for 1977, 1984, and 1995. The first general point to be made is that following a relatively flat period from 1977 to 1984, the number of area courses exclusively on Japan has more than doubled since 1984, while the number of institutions reporting the courses has increased by less than 20 percent. Courses have tripled in sociology, anthropology, and culture and civilization, as shown in Table 7.3. They have doubled in religion and philosophy, literature, performing arts and economics, and nearly doubled in art and art history. The only disciplines showing more modest rates of growth are history at 54 percent and political science at 27 percent. In absolute numbers, however, the largest increases were in literature (224 courses) and history (153 courses). There is a drop in the overall number of courses reported from 1977 to 1984, and we do not know whether this was a real decrease in the number of courses or was due to underreporting in the 1984 study. Even if the change from 1984 to 1995 is slightly overstated because of underreporting in 1984, this still represents a dramatic increase in the depth and breadth of Japanese Studies programs in a little over a decade.

Table 7.3. Area Courses Focusing Exclusively on Japan in 1977, 1984, and 1995, by Discipline

Year	1977		1984		1995		1984–95 Change	
Discipline	#	%	#	%	#	%	#	%
Art, Art History	81	8.2	97	10.8	179	8.9	+82	+85
Literature	168	16.8	167	18.6	391	19.5	+224	+134
Performing Arts	39	3.9	44	4.9	90	4.5	+46	+105
Relig-Philosophy	61	6.1	55	6.1	131	6.5	+76	+138
Anthropology	23	2.3	24	2.7	72	3.6	+48	+200
Economics	33	3.3	20	2.2	40	2.0	+20	+100
History	292	29.3	282	31.3	435	21.7	+153	+54
Political Science	87	8.7	71	7.9	90	4.5	+19	+27
Sociology	24	2.4	14	1.6	53	2.6	+39	+279
Business	6	0.6	--	--	37	1.8	(+31)	(+517)
Culture, Civiliz.	--	--	46	5.1	153	7.6	+107	+233
Other	184	18.4	80	8.9	333	16.6	+253	+316
Total	998	100.0	900	100.1	2,004	99.8	+1,104	+123

*1977 figures from 1977 CULCON Report, Table 5, p. 23; 1984 figures from 1984 Japan Foundation Report, Table 15, p. 35. Percentages for 1984 were recalculated and rounded to the first decimal place. Data for 1977 include only institutions for which enrollments were reported, so this may slightly undercount courses.

One dimension of program expansion is the depth of offerings within a discipline, which can be measured as the average or mean number of courses per institution.[3] In 1984 the highest average was 3.0 courses in literature, followed by 2.2 in history and performing arts. By 1995, this average has increased to 4.2 in literature, 2.9 in history, 2.5 in art and art history, and 2.2 in culture and civilization. Performing arts and religion both averaged 2.1 courses per institution.

A second dimension of expansion is breadth: more institutions are now offering courses in disciplines that were not included in their programs a decade ago. As shown in Table 7.4, the increase in the number of institutions offering courses is most dramatic for literature (37) and culture and civilization (33), followed by religion and philosophy (26), anthropology (25), history (24), sociology (23) and performing arts (22). The percentage increase is greatest for sociology, simply because it was by far the smallest discipline a decade ago. While the addition of literature or culture and civilization courses are likely to be associated with the core development of new programs, the additions in religion and philosophy, anthropology, and sociology are more likely to reflect the expansion of existing programs into a wider range of disciplines.

Table 7.4. Number of Institutions Offering Area Courses Focusing Exclusively on Japan in 1977, 1984, and 1995*

	1977*		1984	1995	Increase, 1984–95	
Discipline	*#UG*	*#Grad*	*#*	*#*	*#*	*%*
Art, Art History	36	10	52	71	+19	+37
Literature	36	13	56	93	+37	+66
Performing Arts	12	6	20	42	+22	+110
Religion, Philosophy	29	6	35	61	+26	+74
Anthropology	12	6	19	44	+25	+132
Economics	11	11	15	28	+13	+87
History	101	41	127	151	+24	+19
Political Science	37	20	39	53	+14	+36
Sociology	12	9	9	32	+23	+256
Culture, Civilization	--	--	35	68	+33	+94
Other**	32	20	28	93	+65	+232

*1977 data recalculated from 1977 CULCON Report, Table 5, p. 23; 1984 data from 1984 Japan Foundation Report, Table 15, p. 35. 1977 data were presented separately for undergraduate and graduate courses so the total number of institutions for each discipline could not be determined. In most cases the larger number is probably the total. 1977 data only for institutions that reported enrollment figures, so this may undercount slightly.

**Business included in "Other" for 1984 and 1995; 1 undergraduate and 3 graduate institutions reported for 1977 omitted because it could not be determined whether those institutions were already counted in "Other."

[3] These figures are not shown in the table, but were calculated from the raw numbers therein.

A further indicator of the growing breadth of Japanese Studies programs is their expansion into new disciplines that were not identified separately in 1977 and 1984. In the 1977 report the "other" category accounted for 19.0 percent of courses. By 1984 this had dropped to 8.9 percent, and there was a decrease in the actual number of such courses, which may be largely due to the use of the new category of culture and civilization courses in 1984. By 1995 the proportion of "other" courses was back up to 18.5 percent, and the actual number of "other" courses was nearly double that reported in 1977. As the variable rates of growth by discipline suggest, most of this growth in the "other" category between 1984 and 1995 has come at the expense of history, which dropped from 31.3 percent of area courses exclusively on Japan in 1984 to 21.7 percent in 1995, and political science, which decreased from 7.9 percent to 4.5 percent of the total. The distribution showed only minor shifts for the remaining disciplines, except that the sharp increase in literature courses together with the much slower growth in history has put literature almost at parity with history.

In the original coding of 1995 courses by discipline, only 5.2 percent of the area courses exclusively on Japan were classified as "other" because they could not be placed in a discipline code. The increase to 18.5 percent "other" in this table arose because nearly 14 percent of the 1995 courses did not fit into the ten discipline groups identified in the 1984 survey. These unclassifiable courses were primarily located in two fields: linguistics (90 courses) and women's studies (42). While there were undoubtedly some courses in these fields that were also classified as "other" in 1984, we have no way of comparing the numbers directly. Women's studies is unquestionably an area that has come to occupy a much larger place in Japanese Studies during the past decade. It should also be noted that our coding represents the discipline or subject matter of the course, regardless of the department through which it is offered. It is therefore possible that some courses previously identified as history or political science were reclassified as women's studies in 1995.

The large number of linguistics courses can be understood, along with much of the increase in literature courses, as an indirect effect of the increased demand for Japanese language instruction, and the overall upgrading of language programs during the past decade. To the extent that academic institutions have met the increased demand for Japanese language instruction by hiring PhDs, they have necessarily ended up primarily with specialists in Japanese literature or linguistics, who want to offer courses in their own academic specialty as well as language skill courses. In fact, as noted earlier, a good part of the phenomenal increase in literature courses is attributable to advanced courses in which Japanese literary works are read and discussed in Japanese by students whose language skills are very advanced. The increase in such courses is also testimony to the increasing depth and quality of Japanese language programs in the United States.

Multinational Courses

Tables 7.5 and 7.6 offer further insight into the pattern of expansion of area courses. From 1984 to 1995 the number of reported multinational courses with coverage of Japan has increased only 8 percent, from 862 to 922. However, this masks a 15 percent drop in the number of institutions offering multinational courses with coverage of Japan, from 174 to 148. The pattern by discipline is mixed.

Table 7.5. Multinational Courses with Coverage of Japan in 1984 and 1995, by Discipline*

	1984		1995		Increase	
Discipline	#	%	#	%	#	%
Art, Art History	66	7.7	80	8.7	+14	+21
Literature	49	5.7	39	4.2	-10	-20
Performing Arts	25	2.9	28	3.0	+3	+12
Religion-Philosophy	172	20.0	187	20.3	+15	+9
Anthropology	29	3.4	31	3.4	+2	+7
Economics	28	3.2	28	3.0	0	0
History	169	19.6	156	16.9	-13	-8
Political Science	114	13.2	105	11.4	-9	-8
Sociology	11	1.3	23	2.5	+12	+109
Culture & Civilization	59	6.8	86	9.3	+27	+46
Other	140	16.2	159	17.2	+19	+14
Total	862	100.0	922	99.9	+60	+7

*1984 figures from 1984 Japan Foundation Report, Table 16, p. 36. Percentages were recalculated and rounded to the first decimal place.

The number of multinational courses with coverage of Japan dropped in history, political science, and literature, but grew in several other disciplines. The number of institutions dropped precipitously in several disciplines, as shown in Table 7.6. What seems to have happened is that some institutions that previously offered only partial coverage of Japan have developed new area courses wholly on Japan in the central disciplines, and either have discontinued multinational courses or no longer report them. This is offset to some degree by new institutions initiating some basic coverage of Japan through multinational courses, and by programs expanding into new disciplines by offering multinational courses with some Japanese content.

Table 7.6. Number of Institutions Offering Multinational Courses with Coverage of Japan in 1984 and 1995, by Discipline*

Discipline	1984	1995	Increase #	Increase %
Art, Art History	50	49	-1	-2
Literature	29	26	-3	-10
Performing Arts	17	22	+5	+29
Religion-Philosophy	110	81	-29	-26
Anthropology	18	22	+4	+22
Economics	23	18	-5	-22
History	109	82	-27	-25
Political Science	81	62	-19	-23
Sociology	7	16	+9	+12
Culture & Civilization	41	44	+3	+7
Other	66	69	+3	+5

*1984 figures from 1984 Japan Foundation Report, Table 16, p. 36.

This trend of shifting from multinational courses to courses exclusively on Japan constitutes a significant strengthening of Japanese Studies programs, since the overall course time devoted to Japan is greatly increased, with corresponding opportunity for greater depth of coverage. A student who takes four courses exclusively on Japan has presumably spent at least twice as much time studying Japan as would have been the case if the same student had taken four multinational courses that included coverage of Japan. The tradeoff, of course, is less contextualizing of Japan, either within East Asia or through some other systematic comparison.

The overall trend can be seen more clearly in Table 7.7, which shows the distribution of number of disciplines in which institutions offered courses about Japan in 1984 and 1995. The number of schools reporting courses exclusively on Japan increased only slightly from 1984 to 1995, but the distribution changed dramatically. In 1984, nearly 40 percent of schools offered courses exclusively on Japan in only one discipline. The number of schools offering courses dropped sharply at each level after that, and only 5 percent of schools offered courses exclusively on Japan in eight or more disciplines. By 1995 only a quarter of all schools offered courses exclusively on Japan in only one discipline, while a fifth of them offered courses in eight or more disciplines. Thus most schools added not only courses but additional disciplines to their Japanese Studies programs, and the number of full-scale programs with Japan-specific courses in eight or more disciplines more than quadrupled in just over a decade.

Table 7.7. Distribution of Number of Disciplines in which Institutions Offered Courses About Japan, 1984 and 1995*

Type	Courses Exclusively on Japan				Multinational Courses			
Year	1984		1995		1984		1995	
	#	%	#	%	#	%	#	%
One	63	38.7	48	24.6	36	21.2	32	21.6
Two	34	20.9	31	15.9	40	23.5	32	21.6
Three	24	14.7	28	14.4	37	21.9	22	14.9
Four	13	8.0	14	7.2	22	12.9	9	6.1
Five	12	7.4	16	8.2	14	8.2	17	11.5
Six	6	3.7	11	5.6	10	5.9	7	4.7
Seven	2	1.2	7	3.6	6	3.5	8	5.4
Eight or more	9	5.5	40	20.5	5	2.9	21	14.2
Total	163	100.1	195	100.0	170	100.0	148	100.0

*1984 figures from 1984 Japan Foundation Report, Table 17, p. 38, percentages recalculated and rounded to one decimal place.

The number of institutions reporting multinational courses dropped from 170 to 148 during the same time period, but the percentage reporting courses in one or two disciplines remained about the same. The changes were mixed for programs offering multinational courses in three to seven disciplines, but there was a substantial increase in programs offering multinational courses in eight or more disciplines. In 1984 there were only a few more institutions reporting multinational courses on Japan than there were institutions reporting courses exclusively on Japan. By 1995 the number of institutions reporting courses exclusively on Japan was nearly a third larger than the number of institutions reporting multinational courses. Since there is considerable overlap between institutions reporting the two categories of courses, the implication is that many institutions with substantial offerings exclusively on Japan either no longer offer multinational courses or no longer report them as part of their Japan program. Closer inspection of the pattern of reporting by institutions reporting either multinational or Japan-specific courses in eight or more disciplines confirms that many large Japanese Studies programs no longer are reporting many multinational courses, as shown in Table 7.8.

Table 7.8. Reporting of Japan-specific and Multinational Courses by Institutions with Large Japanese Studies Programs, 1995

Type	Description of Category	#
I.	Reported 8 or more disciplines with multinational courses, less than eight with Japan-specific courses (two reported only one discipline with Japan-specific courses)	5
II.	Reported 8 or more disciplines with multinational courses AND 8 or more disciplines with Japan-specific courses	16
III.	Reported 8 or more disciplines with Japan-specific courses, less than 8 with multinational courses (three reported no multinational courses at all, and 2 reported only one discipline with multinational courses)	24

Both Japan-specific and multinational courses are often reported in the same discipline, suggesting that even as larger programs focus more attention exclusively on Japan, there are still opportunities for students to place Japan into a larger context. However, the three categories of programs in Table 7.8 reflect different program emphases. Category I programs may offer a broad exposure to Asia or East Asia, but have less developed resources on Japan. Category II programs have strong resources on Japan but also maintain a broad multinational focus. Category III programs appear to be stronger on the Japan-specific side. What cannot be determined is whether institutions in the third category no longer offer multinational courses in certain disciplines, or simply no longer regard such courses as part of their Japanese Studies program, perhaps because such courses are not staffed by Japan specialists. Conversely, large programs in Categories I and II that continue to report multinational courses may have a programmatic emphasis on Asia or East Asia rather than Japan, and thus an intellectual preference for multinational offerings.

Although courses on Japan are certainly not yet available at all or even most American colleges, the dramatic increases in the number of courses, the greater range of disciplines in which courses are offered, and the greater mean number of courses per institution all attest to the trend toward normalization of the study of Japan. At least at these institutions, the general student who is not intending to become a Japan specialist is increasingly likely to come across a course on Japan either within the major field or as an available elective. In this sense, the study of Japan becomes a part of the normal curriculum of the college student. At the same time, the shift toward more courses exclusively on Japan and fewer multinational courses considered as part of the curriculum on

Japan, plus the greater number of courses on Japan offered within a single discipline, point to a greater tendency for specialization on Japan, and more opportunity for students to concentrate on Japan within a discipline. The greater breadth and depth of courses makes possible a more intense and comprehensive study of Japan, and has brought that potential to students at a greater number of institutions.

As we saw in Chapter Two, these opportunities tend to be available at larger academic institutions offering both undergraduate and graduate degrees, that are at least moderately selective in their admissions. This strategic location of Japanese Studies courses maximizes their impact, for two reasons. First, because such courses are offered at larger institutions, they are available to a relatively large pool of students, making them more cost-effective to the institution (and therefore also increasing their stability in the curriculum). Second, because of the more selective nature of these institutions, the students most likely to take courses on Japan will comprise the most highly educated segment of the labor force, where knowledge of Japan will have a potentially greater impact on decision-making in both the public and private sectors.

COURSE ENROLLMENTS

The massive increase in the breadth and depth of Japanese Studies programs that is revealed in the course data could only have been fueled by substantial student demand. Course enrollment figures provide a more direct measure of that demand. Institutions were asked to provide enrollment data for the 1992–93 academic year, but data were only reported for 40.3 percent (1,817) of the 4,506 courses reported. Some schools did not report any enrollment figures, but a more common pattern was for enrollment to be reported for some but not all courses, presumably because many courses are not offered every year. Excluding language courses, a total enrollment of 17,301 was reported for 667 area courses exclusively on Japan (33.3 percent reporting), and enrollment of 13,742 was reported for 327 multinational courses that included coverage of Japan (35.5 percent reporting).

Table 7.9 shows comparative enrollment data from courses exclusively on Japan from the 1977, 1984, and 1995 studies. In each case, the base for enrollment percentages is the number of courses for which the enrollment data were provided, which is smaller than the total number of courses. For 1977, course data were only reported for courses that also reported enrollment figures, so Tables 7.3 and 7.9 refer to the same base, but we do not know how many additional courses were omitted from the data used for both tables. It is not clear what proportion of the courses reported enrollments for 1984, but since the total enrollment numbers are only slightly smaller than the underreported 1995 totals, they probably represent a considerably higher proportion of all courses than the 1995 data.

Table 7.9. Enrollment Distribution (%) for Courses Exclusively on Japan in 1977, 1984, and 1995, by Discipline and Student Level*

Discipline	1977	1984	1995
A. Undergraduate			
Art, Art History	16.0	13	8.4
Literature	8.7	10	17.5
Performing Arts	1.7	3	4.4
Religion-Philosophy	5.4	5	4.2
Anthropology	3.5	2	9.9
Economics	1.8	1	2.4
History	40.7	40	27.6
Political Science	6.6	9	4.8
Sociology	1.5	1	2.7
Business	0.3	--	1.0
Culture-Civilization	--	9	7.6
Other	14.1	6	9.5
Total	100.3	99	100.0
	(13,021)	(11,873)	(14,838)
B. Graduate			
Art, Art History	3.8	9	10.5
Literature	11.3	13	18.1
Performing Arts	1.8	2	0.7
Religion-Philosophy	4.3	4	1.1
Anthropology	0.87	2	2.4
Economics	4.0	5	8.4
History	30.0	14	17.1
Political Science	19.6	17	6.0
Sociology	2.5	2	2.2
Culture-Civilization	--	2	2.9
Business	7.3	--	10.4
Other	14.9	31	20.1
Total	99.9	101	99.9
	(2,079)	(1,999)	(2,463)

*1977 data recalculated from 1977 CULCON Report, Table 5, p. 23, as enrollment in courses designated as primarily undergraduate or primarily graduate courses; 1984 data from 1984 Japan Foundation Study, Table 15, p. 35, based on undergraduate or graduate students enrolled in courses, but course levels are not distinguished; 1995 data based on undergraduate or graduate course level (same as 1977).

Thus, while the comparative totals in the table might suggest that the doubling of courses on Japan in the past decade has been accompanied by only a small increase in enrollment, a more likely explanation is that the rate of reporting enrollments has decreased. We know that the 1977 CULCON survey was particularly zealous in seeking course information from institutions, while the 1984 Japan Foundation study was unable to do such extensive follow-up. In our own two directory studies we have found it increasingly difficult to obtain detailed information from institutions, particularly those with large Japanese programs that now are spread across many disciplines.

Caution is also advised because the undergraduate-graduate distinction in the 1984 study was based on the enrollment status of the student rather than the level of the course. We have recalculated the 1977 data to match the same course-level distinction used in 1995, but did not have sufficient information to do this for 1984. Although this undoubtedly shifts some enrollment in 1984 from the undergraduate to the graduate column, it would only have an effect on the shape of the distribution if the crossover enrollment differed systematically between disciplines. For 1977, where we could recalculate the data both ways, the difference between using undergraduate students and undergraduate courses was negligible. However, using graduate students rather than graduate courses inflated the percentage of enrollment in art history, performing arts, anthropology and "other," but decreased it in religion and political science. We therefore draw our graduate-level comparisons largely from 1977 to 1995, looking only for some consistency in 1984.

The change in the enrollment distribution at the undergraduate level is quite clear and systematic. Enrollment in art and art history courses has dropped to half the 1977 proportion of the distribution, while literature course enrollment has doubled. The proportion of enrollment attributable to history courses has dropped by a third, with the difference spread among several small fields: performing arts, religion, anthropology, economics, and sociology. The "other" field has grown since 1984, but the 1977 "other" category appears large because it includes culture and civilization courses that were recorded separately in 1984 and 1995.

The picture is quite different for graduate-level courses. At the graduate level, enrollments in both art history and literature courses have come to occupy a substantially larger share of the total. History and political science, which had the two largest segments of enrollment in 1977, have both shrunk dramatically. Among the smaller fields, economics has doubled its share, while performing arts, religion, and anthropology have decreased. The "other" category now holds the largest share of graduate enrollments. However, the dominance of the "other" category in 1984 is cut considerably by the separation of business in 1995, where it accounts for about a ten percent share of graduate enrollments.

It must be remembered that we are comparing shares of a pie that has grown larger, although for reasons discussed above the actual enrollment data we have to work with have not increased that much from 1977. If we allow for the greater amount of underreporting of enrollment data in 1995, it seems likely that rather than an absolute reduction in enrollment in some fields, there is simply proportionally greater growth in others.

Although we have not presented the absolute enrollment numbers in the comparative analysis, we can use those numbers for 1995, despite the overall undercount, for a more detailed internal comparison and examination of mean enrollment levels. Table 7.10 shows 1995 enrollment figures by discipline for area courses exclusively on Japan. Data are provided separately for undergraduate and graduate courses, and mean enrollments are also given. History and literature draw the largest undergraduate enrollments, paralleling their top showing in number of courses offered. Anthropology had the third largest undergraduate enrollment of any specific discipline group, followed by art and art history, and culture and civilization courses, but the latter two were outranked slightly by the "other " category.

Table 7.10. Enrollments in Courses Exclusively on Japan in 1995, by Discipline and Course Level*

Year	1995 Undergraduate Courses				1995 Graduate Courses			
Discipline	Courses	Enroll.	Mean	%	Courses	Enroll	Mean	%
Art, Art History	37	1,240	33.5	8.4	16	259	16.2	10.5
Literature	85	2,602	30.6	17.5	45	447	9.9	18.1
Performing Arts	24	652	27.2	4.4	3	17	5.7	0.7
Relig-Philosophy	23	625	27.2	4.2	4	28	7.0	1.1
Anthropology	24	1,476	61.5	9.9	5	58	11.6	2.4
Economics	8	353	44.1	2.4	8	207	25.9	8.4
History	113	4,096	36.2	27.6	25	422	16.9	17.1
Political Science	23	718	31.2	4.8	11	148	13.5	6.0
Sociology	15	403	26.9	2.7	5	53	10.6	2.2
Business	6	147	24.5	1.0	9	257	28.6	10.4
Culture-Civiliz.	43	1,122	26.1	7.6	7	71	10.1	2.9
Other	79	1,404	17.8	9.5	49	496	10.1	20.1
Total	480	14,838	30.9	100	187	2,463	13.2	99.9

*1995 data based only on undergraduate and graduate level courses for which enrollment data were provided.

The high enrollments for anthropology courses are particularly surprising because the overall number of anthropology courses was much lower than the number of art and art history or culture and civilization courses, a differential that holds even for the smaller number of courses for which enrollments were reported. The mean enrollment in undergraduate-level anthropology courses exclusively on Japan was 61.5, substantially higher than the mean enrollment for comparable courses in other disciplines. The closest second was economics, with a mean of 44.1. At the graduate level the "other" category accounted for 20.1 percent of enrollments with 496, and literature (447 or 18.1 percent) slightly outpaced history (422 or 17.1 percent) for second place. Art and art history were next with 259, followed by economics at 207 and political science with 148, accounting for 10.5 percent, 8.4 percent and 6.0 percent of graduate enrollments, respectively. Graduate-level economics classes were the largest, with a mean enrollment of 25.9, followed by history at 16.9 students and art and art history at 16.2 students.

Even though the enrollment figures undoubtedly undercount the actual numbers, the data can still be interpreted as a reflection of the general enrollment pattern because much of the missing data seems to be from courses that are not offered every year. Only one discipline, economics, has less than ten undergraduate courses for which enrollment data are available. Since the student demand as measured by mean enrollment is quite high, this may well be due to the scarcity of Japan specialist economists available to teach such courses at the undergraduate level. At the graduate level, the majority of the disciplines have less than ten courses with enrollment figures reported. This suggests that while there is considerable undergraduate demand for instruction about Japan in most disciplines and faculty are available to teach the courses, graduate training in some disciplines is limited to a very small number of institutions.

Table 7.11 presents similar information for multinational courses with coverage of Japan. The major findings in the table are, not surprisingly, the heavy weight of undergraduate enrollments in religion and history survey courses. Multinational courses are also more prevalent at the undergraduate level in art history, political science, and general culture and civilization courses. By contrast, while religion-philosophy and culture and civilization courses are also quite common at the graduate level, 20 percent of graduate enrollments fall into the "other" category, while a third of the multinational courses at the graduate level are in business. Many of these are general courses in international business subjects, in which the extent of Japan content is not known. Mean enrollments are substantial in all of the multinational undergraduate disciplines, and most of the graduate fields as well.

Table 7.11. Enrollment Distribution (%) for Multinational Courses with Japan Coverage in 1995, by Discipline and Course Level*

Discipline	Undergraduate Courses				Graduate Courses			
	Course #	Enroll #	Mean Enroll.	% Dist.	Course #	Enroll #	Mean Enroll.	% Dist.
Art History	22	1,020	42.8	8.2	2	7	3.5	0.5
Literature	8	162	20.3	1.3	1	9	9.0	0.7
Performing Arts	9	253	28.1	2.0	4	89	22.3	6.7
Relig.-Philos.	60	3,111	51.9	25.1	15	163	10.9	12.2
Anthropology	9	246	27.3	2.0	2	59	29.5	4.4
Economics	4	291	72.8	2.3	2	24	12.0	1.8
History	50	2,213	44.3	17.8	2	24	12.0	1.8
Polit. Science	32	1,279	40.0	10.3	5	41	8.2	3.1
Sociology	9	586	65.1	4.7	3	40	13.3	3.0
Business	7	1,010	144.3	8.1	15	460	30.7	34.4
Culture-Civ.	14	1,135	81.1	9.1	7	144	20.6	10.8
Other	33	1,101	33.4	8.9	12	275	22.9	20.7
Total	257	12,407	48.3	99.8	70	1,335	19.1	100.1

*Based on all courses for which enrollment data were provided.

Overall, the mean enrollments for courses exclusively about Japan are quite high at the undergraduate level and respectable at the graduate level. In many fields, the mean enrollments for Japan-specific courses are higher than for multinational courses. Such strong student demand ensures that the courses will continue to be offered, and strengthens the case for maintaining Japan specialist faculty and expanding courses on Japan. It attests to the new relevance of Japan for American students, and provides further evidence of the growing normalization of the study of Japan. At the same time, the overall increase in graduate course enrollments and the high mean enrollments in graduate courses exclusively on Japan in most disciplines point to the expectation of students that knowledge about Japan will be a marketable skill. For many students, area knowledge goes hand in hand with Japanese language skill, to which we now turn.

JAPANESE LANGUAGE COURSES

Both the number of institutions offering Japanese language and the depth of the language offerings have increased dramatically in recent years. As shown in Table 7.12, the number of institutions reporting that they offer courses in Japanese language has increased more than a third over the past decade. The number of institutions offering only one year of introductory Japanese has remained fairly constant since 1977, with a steady increase in institutions offering two years of Japanese and an apparent doubling of the number of institutions offering four or more years of Japanese language instruction just since 1984. The size of the increase at the top level may be deceptive, however. The 1984 study reported that the top level of language instruction could not be established clearly for 23 schools, or 15 percent of the total, presumably because of ambiguities and inconsistencies in the naming and numbering of advanced courses. If these institutions are added to the number offering three or four years of Japanese in 1984, there has not been too much change in the overall picture.

By contrast, the apparent stability at the lower end masks a certain amount of succession and replacement, as institutions that formerly offered only a year of Japanese have expanded their offerings, and new institutions have begun teaching first-year Japanese.

Table 7.12. Highest Level of Japanese Language Courses Available at Schools Offering On-Campus, In-Classroom Language Instruction, 1977, 1984, and 1995*

Highest Level of Japanese	1977 #	1977 %	1984 #	1984 %	1995 #	1995 %	1984–95 Increase #	1984–95 Increase %
First Year	30	27.8	29	19.0	31	14.8	+2	+6.9
Second Year	22	20.4	34	22.2	59	28.2	+25	+73.5
Third Year	23	21.3	34	22.2	46	22.0	+12	+39.4
Fourth Year or higher	33	30.6	33	21.6	73	34.9	+40	+121.2
Not Clear	--	--	23	15.0	--	--		
Total	108	100.1	153	100.0	209	99.9	+56	+35.5

*1977 data from 1977 CULCON Report, Table 4, p. 17; 1984 data from 1984 Japan Foundation Report, Table 18, p. 38.

In the 1995 study a total of 1,580 Japanese language courses were reported by 243 institutions. Courses were coded by language level and specialized type, based on the course title and number. Normally every semester or quarter was entered as a separate course, although a few institutions listed full-year courses. The latter are roughly offset by the extra listings for institutions on the quarter system, so the numbers approximate the total number of semesters of Japanese language instruction available.

As shown in Table 7.13, only half (53.4 percent) of the courses were staple first- and second-year Japanese language courses. A quarter (26.3 percent) were regular third- and fourth-year Japanese courses. Another 3.7 percent were accelerated courses, generally at the introductory and intermediate levels. The remainder were specialized advanced courses and courses tailored to the needs of particular audiences. Forty-six courses in classical Japanese and kanbun were reported, in addition to 90 courses in business or technical Japanese. The range and depth of offerings, particularly at large graduate training institutions, underscore the variety of demands placed on Japanese language programs in the 1990s.

Table 7.13. Japanese Language Courses and Course Enrollments, by Level and Type*

Level	Courses #	Courses %	# Courses	Enrollments Total	Enrollments Mean Enroll.	Enrollments %
First Year	459	29.1	268	17,748	66.2	55.0
Second Year	385	24.4	205	7,740	37.8	23.9
Third Year	270	17.1	129	3,830	29.7	11.9
Fourth Year	146	9.2	80	1,290	16.2	4.0
Advanced, Special	79	5.0	28	392	14.0	1.2
Classical	46	2.9	20	257	12.9	0.8
Accelerated	58	3.7	33	356	10.8	1.1
Business, Technical	90	5.7	37	588	15.9	1.8
Directed Reading	47	3.0	16	146	9.1	0.5
Total	1,580	100.1	816	32,347	39.6	100.2

*Enrollments based on number of courses for which institutions reported enrollment figures for 1992–93 academic year.

Enrollments for the 1992–93 academic year were reported for 55.1 percent of the Japanese language courses. This was a somewhat higher rate of reporting of enrollments than was found for Japanese area courses, presumably because more of the language courses are offered every year. Enrollments were slightly more likely to be reported for introductory and accelerated introductory courses, as opposed to advanced specialized courses, but the differences were slight. We are reluctant to try to adjust the enrollment figures to account for the unreported courses, and have simply reported them with their own base number (# of courses) for comparison with the overall course numbers.

Enrollments in first-year Japanese courses account for 55 percent of all language enrollments, with second-year Japanese accounting for another 23.9 percent. In general, each successive year of Japanese reduces the enrollment level by half. This pattern has been reported previously for the drop from first- to second-year Japanese, but it also holds for third- and fourth-year Japanese, as well as for the move from fourth-year to more advanced specialized and classical Japanese courses.

When these figures are expressed as the average enrollment per course, however, it is apparent that even very advanced and specialized Japanese language courses are holding their own. The average number of students per course drops from 66.2 to 29.7 over the first three years of Japanese language courses, but holds steady in the 12-16 student range for all types of advanced and specialized courses. Enrollments in accelerated courses are slightly lower, at 10.8 students per course, but still quite solid. These figures represent total enrollment for each course, regardless of the number of sections; hence actual class size may be much smaller, particularly in lower-level courses.

Perhaps the clearest indicator of the instructional burden now placed on Japanese language teachers is the astonishing mean enrollment of 9.1 students for advanced directed reading courses. Although students doing advanced independent work with various instructors may be subsumed under one course number, there is clearly a strong demand for such individualized instruction, despite the vast array of advanced courses available at many institutions.

Although the enrollment figures reflect a very high demand for first-year Japanese, a small but growing number of students now enter college Japanese language courses with prior exposure to Japanese. More important is the fact that most of those with prior exposure obtained it through their own activities, rather than through family circumstances. As shown in Table 7.14, an average of less than five percent of entering Japanese language students grew up in Japan and learned Japanese as children, or use Japanese at home with a native-speaking parent. Somewhat larger percentages of students have previously studied Japanese at another college or university, or have lived in Japan for a year or more. Over nine percent on average have studied Japanese in high school. While previous study at another college and previous residence in Japan may be more closely associated with older transfer and graduate students who enter the largest Japanese programs, the phenomenon of entering students who have studied Japanese in high school affects all undergraduate institutions offering Japanese language. This is certainly one of the factors encouraging institutions to initiate and expand Japanese language instruction. Unfortunately, no comparable data on these measures are available for earlier periods, so we cannot see precisely how these aspects of Japanese language study have changed over time.

Table 7.14. Estimated Percentage of Students Entering Japanese Language Programs Who Have Prior Japanese Language Exposure*

Type of Prior Exposure to Japanese	# of Institutions	% of Students
Grew up in Japan, learned as a child	100	3.37
Use at home with native-speaking parent	114	4.78
Studied at another college or university	110	6.44
Lived in Japan one year or more	123	7.39
Studied Japanese in high school	118	9.21

*Percentage given is the average of percentages reported by all institutions (# of Institutions) responding to the question. This was a multiple response question, so neither numbers nor percentages can be added.

Overall, the sharp increase in the number of institutions offering Japanese language, coupled with the increased depth of these language programs, constitutes a major strengthening of Japanese Studies in the United States over the past two decades and particularly since the mid-1980s. The overall enrollment figures, and the mean enrollments per course, once again reflect very strong student demand, to which institutions have responded by initiating Japanese language instruction, adding sections to meet demand, and adding language levels as students advance. The fact that nearly ten percent of students enter college having studied Japanese in high school is in itself strong evidence of the normalization of the study of Japanese language and of Japan itself in American education.

What seems most significant about the sharp drop in language enrollments after the first year of Japanese is not that so many students find it too hard and quit, but rather that so many are willing to study it in the first place. The growth of Japanese language courses at community colleges and the general scale of undergraduate Japanese language enrollments attest to the transformation of Japanese from its former image as a language so difficult and exotic that only graduate students and gifted linguists should tackle it, into a language still difficult to master, but accessible enough for undergraduates to use to fulfill their language requirement. This normalization of Japanese language study is due in no small measure to the internationalization of Japan and of Japanese Studies, our shorthand term for all the changes in Japan's relationship to the United States, and the greater sense of accessibility and physical proximity between the two countries. Undergraduates in American colleges today study Japanese because they think it will be economically and socially advantageous to do so: they expect to visit Japan, and to have occasion to interact with Japanese people. Yet to the extent that students choose Japanese over French or German to meet their language requirement, they may have fairly low expectations about both the level of proficiency they will achieve and the effort they are willing to make to reach those goals. That, too, is an inevitable concomitant of normalization.

What relationships can we see between the increases in Japanese language courses and disciplinary courses exclusively about Japan? If we assume that language students normally take two semester courses per year, and divide the number of language course enrollments by two, we can estimate that about 16,000 students are taking Japanese language in an academic year. The number is surprisingly close to the total annual enrollment in area courses exclusively on Japan. There is undoubtedly a substantial degree of overlap between the two enrollment categories. If the overlap were total, each Japanese language student would also be taking one area course per year. While we are unable to test this at the individual level, we do have some evidence from institutions.

There is the relationship one would expect to find between the depth of the language program and the availability of area courses on Japan at an institution. In general, institutions offering area courses exclusively on Japan in four or more disciplines offered at least two years of Japanese language. Without exception, those offering area courses exclusively on Japan in six to eight disciplines offered at least three years of Japanese language. Institutions offering area courses exclusively on Japan in more than eight disciplines invariably offered four or more years of Japanese language instruction. Conversely, only a handful of schools reported offering three or four years of Japanese language instruction but no area courses exclusively on Japan. The correlation was not quite as close for multinational courses. These relationships will be explored in more detail in Chapter Eight, where they will serve as criteria for the classification of Japanese programs at the undergraduate level. Now we turn instead to the question of how faculty are coping with the greater student demand for instruction on Japan, and the conditions under which they teach.

TEACHING CONDITIONS

Satisfaction with Teaching

The 1995 survey replicated several questions about teaching that were first asked in the 1984 Japan Foundation study. Respondents in 1995 were generally satisfied with the number of courses they are teaching about Japan. Despite the great increase in courses and enrollments, the distribution of responses has changed only slightly from the 1984 survey. The change is in the expected direction: a reduction in those teaching fewer courses than they would like, and slight increases in the other two categories.

This overall stability masks a sharp difference between respondents who are currently teaching courses on Japan and those who are not. Two-thirds of those not currently teaching courses on Japan would like to be teaching them more, while two-thirds of those who are teaching courses on Japan are satisfied with their current level and only 6.3 percent would like to teach less, as shown in Table 7.15.

Table 7.15. Survey Respondents' Satisfaction with Teaching About Japan, 1984 and 1995, by Current Teaching Status for 1995*

		1995 Teaching on Japan		
Teaching Satisfaction	*1984 %*	*Teaching*	*Not Teaching*	*Total*
Teaching more courses than would like	3	6.3 (40)	0.6 (1)	5.0
About as many courses as would like	56	66.5 (423)	32.1 (51)	59.7
Fewer courses than would like	41	27.2 (173)	66.7 (106)	35.1
N of Respondents	676	636	158	794

*1984 data from 1984 Japan Foundation Report, Table 10, p. 31.

There is a striking change since 1984 in the reasons respondents report for teaching fewer courses on Japan than they would like, as shown in Table 7.16. While the most commonly reported reason in both surveys, "other demands on the respondent's time," is remarkably stable at about 59 percent, there has been a sharp change in all response categories that reflect general interest in and support for courses on Japan. "Insufficient student interest," which was the second most common response in 1984 at 45 percent, has dropped to 15 percent in 1995, next to last place on the list. "Insufficient administration interest" has dropped from more than a third to less than a quarter, and "insufficient interest among colleagues" has dropped from 24 percent to 14.2 percent to land in last place.

Table 7.16. Reasons for Teaching Fewer Courses About Japan Than Respondent Would Like, 1984 and 1995*

Reason Given	1984 %	1995 %
Other demands on time	59	58.8
Insufficient student interest	45	15.0
Insufficient administration interest	36	23.7
Lack of resources	25	29.9
Insufficient interest among colleagues	24	14.2
Other	8	23.7
N of Respondents	284	274

*1984 data from 1984 Japan Foundation Report, Table 10, p. 31. Data for both years limited to those who reported teaching fewer courses on Japan than they would like.

These changes attest to the remarkable shift in the general academic climate regarding the study of Japan that has occurred during the past decade. Two response categories have increased. Lack of resources rose slightly from 25 to 29.9 percent, while the "other" category has tripled, from 8 to 23.7 percent. In the 1984 survey the "other" category was apparently a collection of several different responses, but in 1995 this category is solely attributable to one response: the respondent does not hold an academic appointment and therefore cannot teach courses on Japan.

There was little difference between those currently teaching and those not currently teaching courses on Japan in their perception of student, collegial, and administration interest in such courses. Those currently teaching were twice as likely to point to lack of resources and 50 percent more likely to cite other time demands as reasons for not teaching more courses on Japan. Those not currently teaching were five times as likely to attribute the problem to their lack of an academic appointment.

All of these data are from respondents who say they are currently teaching fewer courses on Japan than they would like. However, 51 persons who said they are currently teaching about as much as they would like on Japan also replied to the question, and over three-quarters of them pointed to other demands on their time. At the risk of reading too much into this response configuration, it suggests that the respondents acknowledge that other commitments reduce their ability to teach courses on Japan, but they are relatively satisfied with the resulting balance. These are the same respondents who in the previous table were not teaching courses currently, but reported that this was about as much as they would like to be teaching.

Taken together, all of these survey responses suggest that Japan specialists generally remain committed to teaching courses on Japan, and during the past decade students, academic colleagues, and even academic administrators have come to recognize the value of such courses.

Satisfaction with Teaching Materials

There has been little change in survey respondents' evaluation of the adequacy of available teaching materials for Japanese Studies since 1984, but considerable improvement since 1970, when the 1970 SSRC-ACLS study reported that there was not a 50 percent satisfaction rate for any type of teaching material. The 1995 evaluations of the adequacy of Japanese language teaching materials are virtually identical to the 1984 distribution, with materials generally rated good (35–36 percent) or fair 20 or 19.8 percent). About a quarter of the respondents declined to rate Japanese language teaching materials in both surveys (see Table 7.17).

Table 7.17. Adequacy of Teaching Materials for Japanese Studies, by Subject, 1984 and 1995*

| | 1984 % | | 1995 % | | |
Evaluation	Language	General	Language	Own Disc.	General
Excellent	14	10	13.6	21.5	7.8
Good	35	45	36.0	45.8	54.3
Fair	20	32	19.8	32.5	27.2
Poor	8	9	7.5	9.1	5.1
Not sure	23	5	23.0	1.1	5.6
Base N	569	673	469	661	591

*1984 data from 1984 Japan Foundation Report, Table 19, p. 39. Percentages were reported as rounded whole number.

In the 1995 survey, respondents were asked about teaching materials in their own discipline as well as in the field in general. Response patterns were similar, but as might be expected, respondents seemed to make sharper distinctions in their own discipline. The 1984 survey asked only about the field in general, but curiously, the response pattern for that question in 1984 was almost identical to the 1995 response pattern for teaching materials in the respondent's own discipline.

In both surveys, about one-third of the respondents reported that readings in Japanese are required in at least one of their courses, as shown in Table. 7.18. The percentage of respondents reporting that they required Japanese language materials has increased for Japanese language and literature specialists (from 76 percent to 81.5 percent), and for the social sciences (from 9 percent to 12.8 percent), but has remained about the same for history and the arts. Two new disciplinary categories were added for 1995. It is not clear how these fields might have been categorized in 1984, if they were included at all. In the new category of philosophy and religion, 28.8 percent reported using Japanese materials, as did 17.0 percent of those in the professions (law, business, and education).

Table 7.18. Use of Japanese Language Materials Required in Courses, by Disciplinary Group, 1984 and 1995*

Discipline	1984			1995		
	Yes %	No %	Total N	Yes %	No %	Total N
History	20	80	173	19.0	81.0	142
Lang. & Lit.	76	24	200	81.5	18.5	162
Arts	20	80	65	21.3	78.7	61
Social Science	9	91	235	12.8	87.2	172
Phil. & Relig.	--	--	--	28.8	71.2	59
Professions	--	--	--	17.0	83.0	47
Total Sample	33	67	659	34.2	65.8	652

*1984 data from 1984 Japan Foundation Report, Table 20, p. 39. Percentages were reported as rounded whole numbers. 1995 Disciplinary distinctions based on primary discipline of respondent.

Overall, these findings reflect the expansion of higher level language and literature courses and the general increase in students in other disciplines who are able to read Japanese language materials. At the same time, the increase in area courses directed at the general student population necessarily limits the opportunity to teach courses in which enrollment is restricted to students with advanced Japanese language ability. Hence the normalization of Japanese Studies in the curriculum militates against the use of required Japanese language readings, even as the number of students who could actually read them increases. Current innovations in teaching language across the curriculum may help to resolve this dilemma in the future. It may also be appropriate for surveys to begin asking more carefully about optional Japanese reading assignments and informal encouragement for the use of Japanese language materials in courses that do not require them.

The question of using Japanese language materials in disciplinary courses touches on the larger issue of how language skills and knowledge about Japan become integrated as students become more specialized and expert in their study of Japan. We have reached the limit of what can be learned from the examination of single courses on Japan. The next logical step is to look at how academic institutions offer organized programs of study that lead to some kind of certification of expertise about Japan.

8

Academic Programs in Japanese Studies

Statistics on individual courses give some sense of the volume of instruction available on Japan and student demand for it. The accumulation and integration of knowledge about Japan, however, depends upon the availability of structured programs of study. In the American academic environment of the 1990s, such programs of study are offered through a variety of institutional arrangements, culminating in several different forms of academic certification at three degree levels. We will explore each of these elements separately, and then combine them in an overall assessment of program strength at the undergraduate and graduate levels, comparing the current situation with data from previous studies using the same criteria. After looking more closely at the range of graduate-level program options available, we will examine the actual distribution of doctorates awarded by institutions. We will extend this analysis to the institutions that are currently training the samples of doctoral candidates from 1989 and 1995 that we first introduced in Chapter Two.

INSTITUTIONAL ARRANGEMENTS

The survey of institutions asked how instruction about Japan was organized at each institution.[1]

The question and response choices followed the format used in the 1984 study to facilitate comparison, but some new response categories were added to reflect the development of Japan-related instruction in professional degree programs such as business and law, and of cooperative programs involving multiple institutions. Survey responses to this question were obtained from 197 of the 249 institutions included in the 1995 directory. The missing cases included 21 institutions that did not submit a new questionnaire to update their 1989 directory information and consequently did not respond to this question. Most of the remaining nonrespondents offered only a few courses and did not have

---

[1] At large programs these data were collected from each unit involved in Japanese Studies that submitted a separate questionnaire, but they have been combined in the present analysis.

formal academic programs in Japanese Studies. This was a multiple response variable, since many institutions offer multiple program options in Japanese Studies and thus have multiple forms of administration. The mean number of responses was 1.64 per institution.

As shown in Table 8.1, the most common form of instructional organization is an interdisciplinary degree, which was reported by a third of the institutions. This was followed by a department of Japanese or East Asian Languages or East Asian Studies, reported by 28.4 percent of institutions, and a list of courses without further linkage, which was reported by 22.3 percent. Nearly a fifth reported that they offer instruction on Japan in only one department.

Table 8.1. Organization of Instruction about Japan at Academic Institutions, 1984 and 1995*

Year	1984		1995		Change	
Organization	#	%	#	%	#	%
Japanese, E.Asia Lang/Area Dept.	36	16	56	28.4	+20	+55.6
Interdisc. Degree Program	46	21	66	33.5	+20	+43.4
Non-degree with minor offered	9	4	29	14.7	+20	+222.2
Coordinating Committee	22	10	21	10.7	-1	-4.5
Course List but no formal links	51	23	44	22.3	-7	-13.7
No Coordination between depts.	33	15	20	10.2	-13	-39.4
Courses only in one department	30	14	38	19.3	+8	+26.7
Professional Program	-	-	11	5.6	-	-
Professional Degree	-	-	8	4.1	-	-
Other Organiz.	24	11	7	3.6	-17	-29.2
[Other Organiz. including Profs.]	[24]	[11]	[26]	[13.3]	[+2]	[+8.3]
Not applicable	4	-	7	-	-	-
Total N	220		197			

*1984 data from 1984 Japan Foundation Report, Table 8, p. 28.

This constitutes considerable change and upgrading of programs since 1984, despite the fact that a smaller number of institutions responded to the question in the current survey. In 1984 the most common form of organization was a simple list of courses, followed by an interdisciplinary program without a department. A full department was third, followed closely by no coordination at all, and courses in only one department. In 1995, interdisciplinary degree programs were most common and their absolute number had increased by over 40 percent. Departmental degrees had risen from third place to second, with an increase of 55.6 percent. The simple list had dropped to third place, and the actual number of institutions reporting this very basic form of organization decreased by 13.7 percent, while the number of institutions reporting no coordination of instruction on Japan dropped by nearly 40 percent.

Because of the very general nature of the question, these figures are useful only for evaluating the overall pattern of organization of instruction about Japan and do not tell us much about the types, content, and quality of instructional programs. More complete data on these matters in available from the program data and narrative program descriptions provided by institutions for their directory entries, to which we now turn. We will first try to evaluate the general strength and quality of instructional programs. The measures we use were developed to assess undergraduate and graduate programs in Japanese Studies, but in fact they measure the instructional resources available at the institution in quite general terms.

UNDERGRADUATE PROGRAMS

The 1970 SSRC-ACLS Report listed 61 American institutions with "undergraduate area programs" in Japanese Studies, but did not report criteria for inclusion or make any further distinction among programs.[2] Subsequently Elizabeth Massey and Joseph A. Massey, authors of the 1977 *CULCON Report on Japanese Studies at Colleges and Universities in the United States in the Mid-1970s*[3] developed a categorization scheme for undergraduate programs concerned with Japan that was based on four factors: the availability of Japanese language instruction, the number of disciplines in which courses wholly about Japan are offered, the size of the faculty specializing in Japan, and whether an undergraduate major offering study of Japan is available. Utilizing various combinations of these criteria, they established four program levels: minimal undergraduate program, limited undergraduate program, undergraduate area program, and full undergraduate program. This scheme was applied with minor improvements in the 1984 Japan Foundation study.

By the CULCON criteria of 1977 as modified in 1984, a **minimal undergraduate program** offers either disciplinary courses or language courses, or one year of language and only one disciplinary course. A **limited undergraduate program** offers either courses exclusively on Japan in several disciplines but only one year of language, or several years of language but only

[2] 1970 SSRC-ACLS Report, Appendix 21, p. 107.
[3] CULCON Report, pp. 29-31.

one disciplinary course, or two years of language and several disciplinary courses, but fewer than two faculty specialists on Japan. The difference between the first two categories is that a minimal program generally offers either language or area courses, but not both. A limited program offers both, but only one in depth. An **undergraduate area program** offers courses exclusively on Japan in two disciplines and two years of Japanese language, and has a minimum of two faculty Japan specialists. A **full undergraduate program** offers courses exclusively on Japan in three or more disciplines and at least three years of Japanese language instruction, and regularly offers a BA for work on Japan, through an undergraduate major in Japanese or East Asian Studies, or by offering a major on Japan as part of an interdisciplinary program (such as international studies). Institutions qualifying for this category also have more than two faculty Japan specialists.

Table 8.2. Classification of Undergraduate Programs in Japanese Studies, 1977, 1984, and 1995*

Year	1977		1984		1995	
Program	#	%	#	%	#	%
Minimal	64	41.0	91	46.2	98	40.7
Limited	37	23.7	46	23.4	25	10.4
Area	24	15.4	22	11.2	37	15.4
Full	31	19.9	38	19.3	81	33.6
Total	156	100.0	197	100.1	241	100.1

*Sources: 1977 figures taken from 1977 CULCON report p. 30 and reprinted in 1984 Japan Foundation Report, Table 13, p. 33 based on data for 1974–75 academic year. The latter is also the source for the 1984 data, which is based on the 1981–82 academic year. Percentages recalculated for 1977 and 1984 data. 1995 data from the present study are based on reports for the 1992–93 academic year.

The 1984 Japan Foundation Report found little change from the 1977 CULCON Report findings, except for a small increase in the number of institutions with full undergraduate programs. We have applied this same classification scheme to the 248 institutions for which the current study provided directory data. Seven institutions did not report program data that would meet the minimum undergraduate program level.[4] Data for the 241

[4] Six of these institutions had no undergraduate program. One did not report course and staff data but may have a program. It is not clear whether institutions that fell below the minimum criteria were excluded in the two previous studies or were included in the lowest category even if they did not meet its threshold. Given the higher standards of current programs it seems most appropriate to exclude them from the classification, but this would skew the comparison, so we have included them in the minimal category.

programs that met the classification criteria are shown in Table 8.2, above, with the 1977 and 1984 data for comparison.

While the number of institutions offering undergraduate programs in Japanese Studies has grown only modestly since the early 1980s, the strength of the programs has increased markedly. In both the 1970s and 1980s the distribution of programs across the four categories was quite similar: just under one-fifth were classified as full undergraduate programs, less than 15 percent met the standard for undergraduate area programs, and just under a quarter were classified as limited undergraduate programs. The bottom category of programs with very minimal offerings accounted for over 40 percent of all programs in both of the earlier studies. The higher figure of 46.2 percent for minimal programs in 1984 presumably reflected new growth: institutions where Japanese Studies programs were just beginning to develop.

By 1995, the proportion of minimal programs remained about the same (40.7 percent), but the rest of the distribution had changed substantially as programs became stronger. A third of all programs now qualify for the top classification of full undergraduate program, which represents a doubling of the number of institutions at that level in just a decade. There was also growth in the number of institutions in the second highest category of undergraduate area programs, but their proportional share remains at 15.4 percent of institutions offering undergraduate Japanese Studies programs. Limited programs shrank from almost a quarter of all programs to a mere ten percent, and the actual number of programs classified at this level dropped substantially.

Appendix B lists the institutions with undergraduate programs in each of the four classifications. Because the classification of programs is based on information submitted by the institutions for their program listings in the institutional directory, our list is inevitably incomplete. The list of "Other Academic Institutions with Japan Specialist Staff," which was created from the directory entries of Japan specialists whose institutions did not submit program listings for the institutional directory, suggests that there may be a fair number of additional instructional programs in the United States. We are confident that virtually all of the full undergraduate programs are included in our study, and nearly all of the undergraduate area programs, but we have probably missed a substantial number of limited or minimal programs. In a subsequent chapter on staffing of academic programs we develop a strategy for estimating this undercount, but in the absence of program data we cannot do much more than that.

Comparison of the current classifications with the categories assigned in the 1984 study provides a measure of the stability or fluidity of undergraduate instructional programs over time. The 1984 Japan Foundation study found that just under half of the 116 schools that submitted data in both the 1977 and 1984 studies remained in the same category. There was substantial upward movement from the three categories that could move upward, and substantial downward movement only in the limited undergraduate program category. However, their turnover analysis omitted both institutions new to the 1984 survey and those that participated in the 1977 and not the 1984 survey, so the overall patterns of movement could not be determined.

Table 8.3. Turnover Table for Undergraduate Programs as Classified in 1984 and 1995*

1995 Program Status	Not Included in 1984	Minimal Program in 1984	Limited Program in 1984	Under-grad Area Prog. in 1984	Full Under-grad in 1984	Total for 1984
Not Included	[2,793]	67 (78.6%)	18 (40.0%)	4 (19.0%)	4 (10.8%)	93 (27.2%)
No Program	6 (4.1%)	--	--	1 (4.8%)	1 (2.7%)	8 (2.3%)
Minimal Program	90 (60.8%)	7 (7.7%)	1 (2.2%)	--	--	98 (28.7%)
Limited Program	19 (12.8%)	3 (3.3%)	2 (4.4%)	1 (4.8%)	--	25 (7.3%)
Undergrad Area Prog.	15 (10.1%)	5 (5.5%)	11 (24.4%)	4 (19.0%)	2 (5.4%)	37 (10.8%)
Full Undergrad	18 (12.2%)	9 (9.9%)	13 (28.9%)	11 (52.4%)	30 (81.1%)	81 (23.7%)
Total	148 (100%)	91 (100%)	45 (99.9%)	21 (100%)	37 (100%)	342 (100%)

*1984 program classifications taken from 1984 Japan Foundation Report. Appendix 5, pp. 125-129. 1995 classifications from the present study. Both sets of classifications were added to date on 3,135 academic institutions in the United States, from which the table was generated.

For the present study, we have included all programs that appeared in either the 1984 or 1995 survey, so that all movement can be evaluated. Table 8.3, above, shows the turnover in undergraduate Japanese Studies programs between 1984 and 1995. In order to include programs that appeared in one study but not the other, the table was generated using the master list of 3,135 academic institutions in the United States. There were 2,793 institutions that did not participate in either study, most of which do not have a Japanese Studies program. To avoid swamping the percentages for the 342 institutions that did have classified programs in one or both studies we have removed this cell from the calculations. The percentages shown are based on 1984 program status.[5] Just over one quarter (27.2 percent) of the programs classified in 1984 did not participate in the 1995 study. However, 148 (43.2 percent) of the institutions that did participate in the 1995 study had not been included in the 1984 study.

The table reveals two very significant processes. First, there is great instability in the participation of institutions with minimal offerings in Japanese Studies in studies such as this, which does not necessarily mean there is corresponding instability in the programs themselves. Nearly three-quarters (67) of the institutions that were classified in 1984 but did not participate in the 1995 study had minimal programs in 1984, while over 90 percent of the programs classified as minimal in 1995 (90 programs) did not participate in the study or had no program in 1984.

This discovery casts new light on the earlier finding that about 40 to 45 percent of the undergraduate programs have been classified as minimal in each of the three major studies of the state of Japanese Studies that have been carried out since the 1970s. The percentage may be quite stable, but the actual programs being counted are different in each study! For example, only seven programs, or 7.7 percent of the minimal programs in 1984, retained that same status in the 1995 study. Conversely, those same seven programs constituted only 7.1 percent of the programs classified as minimal in 1995. We do not know how much of this apparent instability is due to actual fluctuation in the existence of programs, and how much is attributable to instability in the reporting of minimal Japanese Studies programs by institutions, even though the programs survive. The list of "Other Institutions with Japan Specialist Staff" in the institutional directory suggests that variation in reporting may be a major factor. On the other hand, the attrition rate for programs that participated in the 1984 study is highly correlated with the scale of the program, ranging from 78.6 percent loss for minimal programs to 40.0 percent for limited programs, and 19.0 percent for undergraduate area programs, and down to 10.8 percent for full undergraduate programs. This suggests that the smaller programs may be more vulnerable to faculty movement and other economic pressures, and may indeed disappear at a higher rate.

The second major finding in the table is that despite the instability at the minimal program level, most programs that did participate in both studies had upgraded to a higher classification by 1995. Even with some attrition in the 1995 study, over half of all those institutions that had limited or undergraduate area programs in 1984 had a higher program classification in 1995. In the top classification of full undergraduate program it was not possible to move upward, but over 80 percent retained their classification in 1995. Most of the

---

[5] The two programs that appear as outliers with no 1995 program in the upper right corner of the table are Michigan State University and the University of Virginia, both of which still do have Japanese Studies programs in 1995, but did not provide course lists to the study and therefore could not be classified properly.

remainder either did not participate in the study or did not provide enough data to be classified in 1995, rather than suffering an actual decline in program status.

This extensive upgrading reflects the huge increase in Japanese language courses and area courses wholly on Japan that was documented in Chapter Seven. Table 8.3 reveals that this upgrading has taken place across the board, and has been so extensive that institutions have not simply moved into the adjacent program category. In fact, only a little more than a third of all the institutions classified in 1995 as having a full undergraduate program had held that status in 1984, and only 13.6 percent had been classified in the adjacent category of undergraduate area program. The other half of the 1995 full undergraduate programs had been classified as minimal or limited programs, or had not been included at all, in the 1984 study.

Most institutions that have a full undergraduate program in Japanese Studies in 1995 exceed the criteria for that classification by a considerable margin. Unquestionably, American institutions have succeeded in creating undergraduate programs in Japanese Studies that exceed the wildest dreams of the field in the 1970s, as measured by both number of programs and program scale. That in turn raises the issue of whether we have outgrown the criteria of the 1970s, and ought to increase the standards for undergraduate programs in Japanese Studies as we approach the 21st century. In the conditions of the 1970s, a relatively high proportion of institutions with undergraduate programs in Japanese Studies also offered graduate degrees, so in some sense the criteria that were developed to assess graduate programs provide such a set of higher standards. We will therefore return to this question after we have investigated the current situation of graduate programs in Japanese Studies at American academic institutions.

GRADUATE PROGRAMS

The 1977 CULCON study also developed a classification system for graduate programs in Japanese Studies, using a multi-factor approach similar to the undergraduate classification system to evaluate the instructional resources available for graduate training at an institution. They distinguished three categories of graduate program: MA program, limited Ph.D. program, and complete graduate program. These are best understood in descending order. An institution with a **complete graduate program** has Japanese language library holdings of 25,000 volumes of more; offers courses exclusively on Japan in four or more disciplines; has a minimum of eight faculty specialists on Japan; offers Japanese language instruction at all levels; and demonstrates a commitment to Japanese Studies from at least four disciplines in addition to those offering courses exclusively on Japan. The last criterion presumably means four departments in addition to the requisite minimum of four, and would therefore not apply to institutions that already offer courses exclusively on Japan in eight or more disciplines. Such a program regularly offers both MA and Ph.D. degrees in which there is concentration on Japan.

An institution with a **limited Ph.D. program** offers the Ph.D. regularly in several disciplines, or else offers an interdisciplinary Ph.D. with concentration on Japan. It is distinguished from a complete graduate program by its relative weakness in one or more of the following areas: less than 25,000 volumes in Japanese in its library collection; Japanese language offered only through the second or third year; courses exclusively on Japan in three or fewer departments; or less than eight Japan specialists on its faculty. An institution is classified as having an **MA program** if it regularly offers an MA degree for work on Japan; has faculty Japan specialists in at least four disciplines; offers courses exclusively on Japan in at least two disciplines; and offers at least two years of Japanese language.

In the mid-1990s, 51 academic institutions in the United States have graduate programs in Japanese Studies that meet these standards. We have classified 17 institutions at the MA program level, 15 as having limited Ph.D. programs, and 19 as having complete graduate programs. Appendix C lists all of these institutions by category. Comparison with earlier time periods is a bit difficult because the 1984 Japan Foundation study did not use this classification system, but simply noted changes since 1977 in the specific institutions that reported graduate programs. We therefore have to go back nearly two decades to make a systematic comparison, but the results are illuminating.

As shown in Table 8.4, the number and distribution of institutions with graduate programs in Japanese Studies has changed only slightly between 1977 and 1995. The small number of additional institutions has been distributed across all three program categories, but with a slight tendency toward expansion of the top category of complete graduate programs. That trend is consistent with the general tendency we have noted for existing Japanese Studies programs to deepen and expand over the past decade. The 1984 study reported a larger number of institutions with graduate programs, but since no criteria were applied, we suspect that they may have included some programs that did not meet the minimal standards set in 1977.[6]

---

[6] The criteria are sometimes difficult to apply, and since the 1984 study was contracted out to a commercial survey research firm rather than being done by Japan specialists, they may have simply abandoned the attempt to classify programs.

Table 8.4. Classification of Institutions with Graduate Programs in 1977, 1984, and
1995 Studies*

Year	1977		1984		1995	
Program	#	%	#	%	#	%
MA Program	16	35.6	-	-	17	33.3
Limited Ph.D.	14	31.3	-	-	15	29.4
Complete Program	15	33.3	-	-	19	37.3
Total	45	100.2	57	100.0	51	100.0
Change from 1977	-	-	+12	+26.7	+6	+13.3

*Sources: 1977 data summarized from 1977 CULCON Report, Appendix K, pp. 112-114;
1984 data from 1984 Japan Foundation Report, Appendix 6, p. 130.

Analysis of program turnover since 1977 clarifies this. The fifteen complete graduate programs of 1977 have remained absolutely stable, with no institutions moving out of the top category. Of the four new institutions that have joined them, two have moved up from MA programs in 1977 and one from a limited Ph.D. program, while one was new to the (unranked) list in 1984. All of these programs exceed the faculty and course requirements for a complete graduate program by a wide margin. The fifteen older programs have not rested on their laurels, and most have grown steadily over the past decade despite the loss of a large cohort of senior Japan specialist faculty to retirement. These fifteen programs still dominate graduate education in Japanese Studies.

There is substantially more fluidity in the middle category. Just over half of those classified as having a limited Ph.D. program in 1977 remain in that position in 1995. Two did not submit program entries for 1995, but at least one would probably have remained at the same level if it had done so.[7] Three programs moved down to the MA program classification, but two from the MA level have moved into the middle category, along with two more institutions that first appeared on the list in 1984. One program has moved up from the limited to the complete graduate program category, while three new programs have entered the listing at the limited doctoral program level. From this middle position programs move easily in either direction as they fall above or below the rather narrow bounds of the criteria.

[7] The 1977 study listed the Claremont colleges collectively as having a limited doctoral program. The 1995 directory received an entry from one of the colleges (Pitzer) and listed faculty from two others (Pomona and Scripps) in the list of "Other Academic Institutions with Japan Specialist Staff." The combined staff total is sufficient for the limited doctoral program level, but unfortunately we do not have enough other information to make a judgment.

As with undergraduate programs, the entry-level category shows the greatest instability. Of the 16 institutions classified as having MA programs in Japanese Studies in 1977, half had dropped off the list completely by 1995, and only a quarter remained in the same position they had held two decades earlier. Two institutions moved up to the limited doctoral program category, and two had expanded into complete graduate programs by 1995. There were 13 new programs at the MA level by 1995, two having moved down from the limited doctoral program category and four having first appeared on the unranked 1984 list of graduate programs on Japan. With fewer faculty resources to begin with, these programs can be destabilized completely by the departure of one or two faculty members, but they can also be energized by a strategic or serendipitous new hire. Relatively little institutional commitment is required to bring a program up to this level, but considerably more is needed to sustain or go beyond it.

That is why the same fifteen institutions that produced most of the new doctorates in Japanese Studies two decades ago still play the same role today. They have been joined by four additional institutions whose programs have grown considerably, but it seems unlikely that the list will expand much in the next decade. Developing a complete graduate program in Japanese Studies is an enormous financial commitment for an institution. The cost in faculty resources is far outweighed by the prohibitive costs of library development, since one assistant professor's salary for a year would only cover the cost of purchasing and cataloguing about 500 Japanese books. By the standards of 1995, the entry-level criterion of 25,000 volumes of Japanese language materials is low compared to the size of the collections built over several decades by the fifteen major institutions, but it is enormously expensive to accomplish today. Two of the new institutions with complete graduate programs have only recently cleared the library hurdle of 25,000 Japanese language volumes, while the other two are substantially beyond it with collections around the 50,000 volume mark. The next program in line is still about 20 percent short of the goal.

But library resources are not the only obstacle to developing a complete graduate program in Japanese Studies. Ten of the institutions in the limited doctoral program category already have Japanese library collections of more than 25,000 volumes. Most of the institutions that have remained in this middle category for the past two decades already had substantial second-tier Japanese library collections in the 1970s. Their problem has been developing and sustaining the faculty and graduate student resources for a complete graduate program, which is largely a matter of institutional commitment to build a strong program in this area as opposed to another. It is not surprising that the majority of the new programs in the limited doctoral program category, the ones that have grown rapidly in the past decade, are located in California, where such an institutional commitment is easier to justify economically, socially, and politically.

The relatively slow growth in the number of institutions with graduate programs in Japanese Studies contrasts sharply with the picture we have been drawing of rapid expansion in undergraduate programs. Comparison of the undergraduate and graduate program classifications for 1995 clarifies the current pattern, as shown in Table 8.5. Less than a quarter of the institutions with any level of undergraduate program in 1995 also have a graduate program, and just over 40 percent of the 117 institutions with undergraduate area or full undergraduate programs also have a graduate program. This is a profound change from the situation two decades ago, when 55 institutions had full undergraduate or undergraduate area programs, and 45 institutions had some kind of graduate program, with over 75 percent nesting of graduate and undergraduate programs at the same institutions. The current pattern of narrowly concentrated graduate programs and steady proliferation of undergraduate programs is likely to continue, since most of the expansion of Japanese Studies now takes place at four-year colleges without the infrastructure for graduate programs.

Table 8.5. Graduate Program Status by Undergraduate Program Classification, 1995

Graduate Program	None	Undergrad Minimal	Program Limited	Area	Full	Total
None	[2,894]	97 (99.0%)	25 (100.0%)	33 (91.7%)	35 (43.2%)	190 (78.8%)
MA level*	1	1 (1.0%)	-	3 (8.3%)	12 (14.8%)	17 (7.1%)
Limited Doctoral	-	-	-	-	15 (18.5%)	15 (6.2%)
Complete Graduate	-	-	-	-	19 (23.5%)	19 (7.9%)
Total	1	98	25	36	81	241 (100.0%)

*The two outliers are institutions that did not provide sufficient course data for proper classification of their undergraduate programs, but appeared to meet the criteria for MA-level graduate programs.

Table 8.5 shows the expected relationship between graduate and undergraduate programs. All of the institutions classified as having limited doctoral or complete graduate programs also have full undergraduate programs. The picture is slightly more varied for institutions at the MA level of graduate program classification. The undergraduate programs of two institutions at this level were underclassified because their directory entries did not contain sufficient course list information to assess the undergraduate program. One did not submit a course list, while the other listed only the graduate courses offered within a highly specialized graduate program, so the undergraduate offerings available at the institution could not be assessed fully. Three other MA-level institutions were classified as having undergraduate area programs rather than full undergraduate programs, either because the institution offered only three years of Japanese language training, or because the program did not encompass a large enough number of disciplines and faculty, factors which would not preclude offering an MA degree through one discipline.

The pattern shown in Table 8.5 suggests that at present, the graduate program categories offer a natural progression of criteria for programs that have developed well beyond the threshold of the full undergraduate program, with a certain amount of overlap in criteria at the MA level. There does not seem to be any particular reason to raise the criteria for a full undergraduate program at institutions that have no intention of expanding into graduate education. For those that do, the graduate program criteria remain generally appropriate. However, one might well question whether in the future at least the Japanese language criterion for MA-level programs ought to be raised to reflect current expectations of language proficiency.

While the application of the existing institutional criteria for Japanese Studies programs at the undergraduate and graduate levels has been a useful device for assessing the stability and growth of the field, there is a fundamental limitation to this analysis in the 1990s. Even though the number of institutions with graduate programs has not increased much at all in the past two decades, the internal differentiation of the larger Japanese Studies institutions can no longer be captured effectively by these global, institutional criteria. "Program" today means not just the sum of the resources for Japanese Studies at one institution, but may also be used to designate a variety of different undergraduate and graduate degrees and academic program options within one institution. We must therefore now use a different strategy to examine the scope and variety of such options.

TYPES AND LEVELS OF ACADEMIC PROGRAMS AVAILABLE

The directory entries for academic institutions provide narrative descriptions of undergraduate and graduate degree programs and certificate programs, based on information provided by the institution. In earlier studies this information could be summarized at the institutional level in terms of the span of the program (Asia, East Asia, or Japan), the level of degree offered, and whether the degree was offered through a department or an interdisciplinary arrangement. By the 1990s, the range and complexity of academic programs in Japanese Studies had outgrown this categorization at the institutional level, because larger institutions now offer many degree options in Japanese Studies, with different combinations of these dimensions.

For this analysis we have therefore coded each degree or certificate program along several dimensions, based on the information from the narrative description in the directory.[8] If an institution reports, for example, that MA degrees with concentration in Japan are offered in history, art history, religion and political science, each of these is treated as a separate degree option. If undergraduate degrees are offered in Japanese language and literature by a language department and in Japanese Studies through an interdisciplinary program, these are also treated as separate degree options.

This coding produced a total of 590 program options, divided almost equally between undergraduate and graduate levels. They include 170 undergraduate majors, 88 undergraduate minors, and 28 undergraduate certificates. At the graduate level, there are 164 MA degree programs, 130 doctoral degree program options, 9 graduate-level certificate programs, and one professional degree listed in the directory.[9] These options are offered by the same 241 programs whose classifications we have just considered. Since the undergraduate majors are offered essentially by institutions with undergraduate programs at the undergraduate area or full undergraduate level, this is a ratio of 2.5 undergraduate major options per institution. Assuming that all institutions with graduate programs offer an MA, this would be a ratio of 3.2 MA options per institution. At the doctoral level, degrees are awarded by a more limited number of institutions at a ratio of 3.8 per institution. Of course the degree program options are not even distributed across all institutions, but these ratios illustrate why a global description of "programs" offered by an institution is no longer adequate. Instead, we must now consider the level (BA, MA, or Ph.D.), the span (Japan, East Asia, or Asia) and the venue (language department, interdisciplinary program, or disciplinary department) of each degree option.

At the undergraduate level, nearly half of the majors and minors are offered through interdisciplinary area studies programs, with a small fraction offered through other interdisciplinary programs that have some area component as a secondary feature, such as international affairs or international studies programs. The remainder are offered either by a separate department of Japanese or East Asian languages and literature (often with a

---

[8] Unfortunately, this was done after publication of the directory, so the more detailed information was not used to index the programs in the directory.

[9] This total undercounts program options to some extent, since a number of institutions reported degree options available in "several departments" but did not specify them, and thus such programs were counted only once. Assuming that "several" means a number between two and five, the undercount would be from 60 to 120 additional degree options, again about evenly divided between undergraduate and graduate levels.

culture or civilization component as well), or by regular disciplinary departments. The pattern is reversed for undergraduate certificates, a less common alternative that is similar to a minor, but may have more prescribed requirements. The undergraduate certificates are offered most frequently by disciplinary or language departments, and less frequently as interdisciplinary programs.

The situation is strikingly different at the graduate level, where most program options involving the study of Japan are offered through disciplinary departments. At the MA level, over half (56.7 percent) of the degrees are offered by disciplinary departments, and another 21 percent by Japanese or East Asian language or language and culture departments. Twelve percent of the MA degree options are interdisciplinary area programs with the remainder either interdisciplinary non-area studies programs or programs offered by professional schools. The small number of graduate certificate programs is distributed across all the options, so they will henceforth be considered along with MA programs.

At the doctoral level the trend toward disciplinary degrees is even more pronounced. Eighty percent of doctoral degrees concerning Japan are offered through disciplinary departments, with most of the remainder offered through Japanese or East Asian language or language and culture departments.

We should not overestimate the significance of the large number of departmental or disciplinary degree options. At the MA level, a relatively small number of interdisciplinary programs at key institutions probably produces as many degree students as the much larger number of disciplinary program offerings. What is significant is the fact that it is now possible to concentrate on Japan within a wide range of disciplinary degree programs. It means, in effect, that there are Japan specialists and Japan-related courses available in these departments and, equally important, that the department will recognize such a specialization as a legitimate field of concentration within the discipline.

In earlier studies, tabulations of degree programs encompassed both concentration on Japan and a broader concentration on East Asia, since the program designations differ by institution. Degree programs change more slowly than individual courses, and the institutional rubric for the degree does not necessarily reveal the degree of specialization that actually occurs within it. For this analysis we have included programs designated as Asian, East Asian, or Japanese Studies, so long as they appeared to include coursework wholly on Japan. As we have seen, over the past decade there has been a marked increased in courses wholly on Japan. We can distinguish whether degree programs are labeled Asia, East Asia or Japan, but since the distinction was not clear in the statistical tables of the earlier studies, we cannot evaluate whether degree programs in 1995 are more likely to focus on Japan alone than in previous decades. What is clear in 1995 is that the higher the level of the degree, the more likely that the concentration will be solely on Japan, rather than on East Asia or Asia.

At the undergraduate level, just over a quarter of the degree programs concentrate solely on Japan, and a quarter on East Asia. Another quarter provide for a concentration on Japan within a broader Asia or East Asia program. Hence just over half of the undergraduate programs now encourage or permit a student to concentrate specifically on Japan. The degree programs with Japan concentration are almost equally divided between interdisciplinary area programs (39.3 percent) and Japanese or East Asian language or language and culture departments, with another 20 percent offered through disciplinary departments. Programs in which the narrowest official focus is East Asia are more likely to be offered through interdisciplinary area programs (45.6 percent) than language and culture departments (26.3 percent) or disciplinary departments (21.0 percent).

At the MA level, about 60 percent of all programs facilitate concentration solely on Japan, while a quarter focus more broadly on East Asia. In either concentration, more than half of the degree options are offered through disciplinary departments, and a quarter or less through language or language and culture departments. At the undergraduate and MA levels, about 14 percent of programs officially offer concentration only on Asia in general. This number drops to 10 percent at the doctoral level. We have left these programs in the overall tabulations because they offer some coursework wholly on Japan, even if the degree requires a broader focus.

If they are removed, the remaining 140 MA programs offer concentration on Japan or East Asia in a wide range of fields, but with few programs in any specific discipline. At the MA level, the most common are East Asian Studies (20), Asian Studies (9), or Japanese Studies (7) programs, generally offered either by language and culture departments or as interdisciplinary programs. Next most prominent are 13 programs in business or international management and six in law. While these options might be considered terminal degrees, most of the remaining disciplinary degree options at the MA level are primarily intermediate options for students en route to a doctorate.

At the doctoral level, 70 percent of programs offer concentration specifically on Japan, while less than 20 percent have an East Asia focus. However, over 80 percent of these degrees are offered through disciplinary departments, so they are essentially disciplinary doctoral programs within which one may focus on Japan. These are legitimately counted as "Japanese Studies" degree programs, since they are the programs producing Ph.D.-level Japan specialists. The nature of the area specialization differs considerably depending upon the discipline involved. In some disciplines that are internally organized along geographic or cultural lines, concentration on Japan or East Asia may constitute nearly the entire doctoral program. In other disciplines, particularly in many social sciences, the core of the program is devoted to general issues of theory, methods and substantive specializations, and area concentration on Japan or East Asia must be achieved in addition to major program requirements.

If we eliminate the 14 doctoral programs offering concentration on Asia in general, the remaining 116 degree programs offered by 34 institutions comprise the options currently available for producing new Ph.D. Japan specialists in the United States. All but two degree options are located within departments, rather than being interdisciplinary programs that cross departmental lines. Nineteen options are offered by language and literature or language and culture departments, with the remainder at regular disciplinary departments. Because there is considerable overlap between the two types in terms of disciplinary specialization, we will dispense with the distinction and simply consider all of them as disciplinary degrees offered by departments.

Given the degree of concentration of doctoral training in Japanese Studies by institution, it should not be surprising that few options are available for any specific disciplinary degree. The most widely available degree is in history, with doctoral-level concentration on Japan or East Asia available at 14 institutions. Literature is available in eight programs, with Japanese language and literature designated at another four. Nine doctoral programs in linguistics offer concentration on Japanese, four other programs offer Japanese language, and two offer a doctorate in Japanese language teaching. Opportunities are more restricted in other arts and humanities disciplines, with four programs offering Japanese or East Asian concentration at the doctoral level in art history, three in philosophy, two each in performing arts, art and music, two in Buddhist Studies, and one in religion. However, these arts and humanities options are supplemented by eight doctoral-level programs titled East Asian Studies and another three in Japanese Studies, the majority offered through language and culture departments, within which students generally pursue topics in the arts and humanities, including history.

The most widely available social science doctorate with concentration on Japan is political science, which is offered at eight different programs. The directory lists seven doctoral programs in anthropology, six in economics, and four in sociology. One program each is available in industrial relations, archaeology, and urban studies with concentration on Japan or East Asia. Doctoral-level degrees in professional fields with Japanese concentration are also quite restricted. There are four doctoral-level programs in business management or international management, two each in education and law, and one each in agriculture, journalism, and architecture.

ESTIMATING STUDENT NUMBERS

These figures count the number of degree programs in existence, not the number of students they enroll or graduates they produce. Many of these programs exist only as theoretical possibilities that accommodate an occasional student, while others attract a steady stream of matriculating students. The growth in formal program opportunities suggests that the number of students trained through Japanese Studies programs has likewise increased. Unfortunately, as Japanese Studies program offerings expand it becomes more difficult to obtain reliable enrollment and graduation figures for them. Large institutions do not know how many students are pursuing an undergraduate major or minor related to Japan until the credits are calculated for graduation. Even then, it may not be possible to retrieve the information for students in interdisciplinary programs or disciplinary departments other than language and literature, because no one keeps such a count specifically for Japanese or East Asian Studies. The situation is similar at the graduate level, where it is very difficult to track and count students who specialize in Japanese Studies but obtain a degree through a disciplinary department.

More than half of the schools that responded to our survey did not even try to answer the questions regarding program enrollments and degrees awarded. The distribution of institutions that reported data did not offer a solid basis for estimation of overall numbers. About the only thing we can say from these partial data is that compared with the total number of program enrollments and degrees awarded that were reported in 1984, data from less than half as many institutions in 1995 produced roughly similar totals. There is no question that the overall numbers are higher than they were a decade ago, but we cannot get much closer than that for undergraduates, master's degree candidates, and certificate recipients.

A clear illustration of the difficulties institutions have in counting the number of students involved in Japanese Studies programs is the fact that the survey respondents reported a total of 304 doctoral candidates and 53 doctoral degree recipients specializing in Japan, while the directory project was simultaneously compiling a list of names, departments, and dissertation topics of doctoral students at these same institutions that totaled 784 current doctoral candidates and 57 new PhDs.[10] The directory's list of doctoral candidates is

---

[10] The latter is not intended as a complete count of recent PhDs. Rather, it is an acknowledgment of degree completion for those who finished too recently to have a complete entry in the Japan specialist directory. If their names were removed from the list of doctoral candidates upon graduation, the directory would have no record of them as Japan specialists, so they are retained in a separate section of the doctoral candidates list. The discrepancy in counts of new PhDs is due to degrees awarded after the questionnaire was turned in and reported in subsequent follow-ups by the study staff just prior to publication of the directory. However, the close match between the two counts of new PhDs indicates that this is the one remaining point at which institution staff can refer to readily available institutional records (graduation lists) from which it is possible to identify and count doctoral degree recipients who have written a dissertation concerning Japan.

compiled by asking both the institutional survey respondents and individual Japan specialists to report doctoral candidates. There is of course a high degree of overlap between the two lists, but they are far from identical, and faculty provide many names that the institutions do not list. If the institutional representatives and faculty can no longer keep track of their doctoral candidates, it is a sure bet that neither of them can keep track of undergraduates anymore.

The only reliable numbers that might be used to estimate the number of students in Japanese Studies programs are the course enrollment figures that were analyzed in Chapter Seven. Assuming that most undergraduate institutions do not demand more than two years of foreign language for their general education requirements, enrollments in third-year Japanese (3,830) might serve as a rough approximation of the number of students who are pursuing a major or minor involving Japanese Studies. Even if we regard these as semester enrollments and divide them by two, that still suggests that close to 2,000 students each year may be concentrating on Japanese Studies at the undergraduate level. This is enormously higher than the 123 undergraduate degrees in Japanese language and 213 undergraduate degrees in East Asian Studies (a number that includes students concentrating on Chinese) reported in the 1984 study. An estimate based on third year language enrollments may be on the high side, but it must be recalled that the total enrollment in Japanese language courses reported to the present study from 55 percent of the listed language courses was 32,349, virtually triple the total reported in the 1984 study from the best available source.[11] In addition, the number of institutions offering undergraduate degree programs in Japanese Studies has doubled since the early 1980s while course offerings solely on Japan have more than doubled, as reported earlier. If twice as many institutions are now offering Japanese Studies majors, and each is now enrolling twice as many majors as a decade ago, the number of undergraduate majors could easily have quadrupled.

If we assume that most of the 784 students on the current doctoral candidates list have completed most of their coursework and are working on their dissertations, then the enrollments in graduate-level courses exclusively on Japan would represent students either at the master's level or at an earlier stage in their doctoral programs. The total enrollment for graduate-level area courses wholly on Japan was 2,463, to which should be added fourth-year, advanced special, and classical Japanese language course enrollments of 1,939, even though some fraction of that enrollment can be attributed to undergraduate majors. If we subtract about 400 from the combined total to allow for undergraduate enrollments, that leaves a total graduate course enrollment of approximately 4,000 per year. In a few fields graduate students

[11] The 1984 Japan Foundation Report presented language data from the 1977 and 1980 Modern Language Association surveys, reportedly the most comprehensive available on language course enrollments. See 1984 Japan Foundation Report, Table 23 and table notes, pp. 43-44.

might enroll in six courses per year solely on Japan, while in some disciplinary programs students would be able to take only one or two because of their other program requirements. In addition, some graduate area courses may enroll students in disciplinary graduate programs who are not specializing on Japan at all. If we assume an average of four course enrollments wholly on Japan per year would encompass these various factors, that would translate into an enrollment of 1,000 graduate students in addition to the 784 advanced doctoral candidates previously mentioned. This is about a one-third increase over the total number of graduate students enrolled in Japanese Studies programs as reported in the 1984 study. Since the total number of institutions engaged in graduate education related to Japan has remained relatively constant over the past decade, we would expect a more modest rate of enrollment growth at the graduate level than at the undergraduate level. The two sets of estimates based on course enrollments are therefore relatively consistent with the pattern of program expansion traced above. Nonetheless, they remain very crude and unverifiable estimates. Unfortunately, they are as close as we can get at present to estimating the current number of students below the doctoral level.

PRODUCTION OF DOCTORATES IN JAPANESE STUDIES

As we cautioned earlier in this chapter, the fact that an institution reports the availability of a particular graduate program option in Japanese Studies does not give us any information about how many students actually utilize that option. Our efforts to get counts of students enrolled in particular programs are frustrated by the complexity and scale of activity at the institutions where most of the students are concentrated. We can use a different strategy to get at changes over time in the involvement of institutions in the production of new doctorates in Japanese Studies. As reported in Chapter Two, we have data on current doctoral candidates for 1989 and 1995. We also have data from the previous studies on the institutions from which Japan specialists obtained their doctorates, and similar data is also available for the 1995 directory sample. By putting these figures together as a series, we can see how the institutional configuration of doctoral-level training has changed over time, and how the increase in the production of Ph.D. Japan specialists has been absorbed differentially by various types of institutions.

First, however, we need to take note of variations in data collection procedures that affect the comparability of the numbers in the series. The 1970 SSRC-ACLS study began with a count of the doctoral institutions of their survey respondents, but supplemented this with data from the 1969 edition of Shulman's *Doctoral Dissertations on Asia*, to produce a fairly complete list of 348 US doctorates from 43 institutions. The 1977 CULCON report did not survey individuals at all, but instead did a thorough count of two successive editions of *Doctoral Dissertations on Asia* to produce a virtually complete count of 825 US doctorates related to Japan from 1945 to 1975. This count is therefore higher than any numbers based on survey respondents, but provides a useful alternative measure. The 1984 Japan Foundation study reported only the doctoral institutions of its own survey respondents, generating a count of 655 US doctorates for which the institution could be determined. The difference between the 1977 count and the figures reported just a few years before and after can be attributed to a combination of survey non-response and the loss from the largely academic survey pool of people who did not take academic positions in Japanese Studies after completing their doctorates.

The 1995 directory survey also collected data on the doctoral degree year and institution of its respondents, and thus is comparable to the 1984 data. However, as we have documented in previous chapters, since the 1980s a growing number of people have become identified as professional Japan specialists after the completion of a doctorate that was not related to Japan. While a count of doctoral dissertations related to Japan will include many people who do not turn up in a survey of Japan specialists, the survey strategy will now catch a number of people who did not train in Japanese Studies at the doctoral level, hence it is not necessarily a measure of the production of doctorates in Japanese Studies. Either measure contains some slippage. Acknowledging the difference between the first two counts and the latter two, it is still instructive to compare them. If we extend the comparison to the doctoral candidate samples for 1989 and 1995, the additional data becomes more like the first two sets of data from the 1970s, in that it is a count of those who are actually writing a dissertation on Japan. Since they are not yet finished, however, we do not yet know what the ultimate attrition rate will be, and how many of those who do finish their dissertations will stay in the United States and work as Japan specialists, let alone how many will respond to the next survey of Japan specialists.

What makes a comparison of these rather mismatched sets of data worth doing, and the results so compelling, is the remarkable degree of institutional consistency they reveal. Table 8.6 presents a number of simple statistical calculations based on the institutional distribution of doctorates either on Japan or earned by Japan specialists (depending on the data set).

By 1970, eight institutions had each awarded ten or more doctorates to Japan specialists, and another four institutions had awarded between five and seven doctorates related to Japan. The institutions that had awarded ten or more degrees accounted for 70 percent of all Japan specialists in the United States. Adding the slightly smaller programs that had awarded 5-9 degrees brought the total up to 79.3 percent. We already know that Japanese Studies was a small, highly concentrated and quite elite field in the early postwar period, so this finding in itself is old news. The number of Japan specialists with doctorates tripled over the next 25 years, so we would not necessarily expect this early pattern to persist, even though there is some cumulative effect because we count the same Japan specialists in each successive study.

Table 8.6. Institutional Concentrations of Doctorates and Doctoral Candidates in Japanese Studies, 1970–1995*

Measure**	1970	1977	1984	1995	1989 DC**	1995 DC**
Institutions with 10 or more doctorates	8	19	15	22	14	18
Institutions with 5–9 doctorates	4	14	12	11	5	6
Institutions with 1–4 doctorates	31	58	8	50	32	36
Total # Institutions awarding doctorates	43	91	35	94	51	60
Number of US PhDs in Sample	348	825	655	1,072	445	803
# from institutions with 10 or more doctorates	246	638	493	887	361	701
% from institutions with 10 or more doctorates	70.7%	77.3%	75.3%	82.7%	81.1%	87.3%
# from institutions with 5–9 doctorates	30	NA	78	71	33	45
% from institutions with 5–9 doctorates	8.6%	NA	11.9%	6.6%	7.4%	5.6%
% from institutions with 5 or more doctorates	79.3%	NA	87.2%	89.3%	88.4%	92.9%
% from original 8 institutions with 10 doctorates in 1970	70.7%	56.7%	55.9%	53.5%	54.2%	44.7%
% from original 12 institutions with 5 doctorates in 1970	79.3%	65.7%	68.1%	66.4%	60.7%	52.2%
% with 10 or more doctorates that are public institutions	41.7%	50.0%	44.4%	51.5%	57.9%	62.5%
% of PhDs from public institutions with 10 or more doctorates	43.5%	NA	40.1%	37.6%	50.9%	53.5%

*1970 data recalculated from 1970 SSRC-ACLS Report, Appendix 2j, Table 1, p. 102; 1977 data recalculated from 1977 CULCON report, Appendix N, Table 23, pp. 118–119; 1984 data recalculated from 1984 Japan Foundation Study, Table 4, pp. 16–17. 1977 data did not provide number of doctorates at institutions with less than 10 degrees awarded.

**For 1989 and 1995 Doctoral Candidates (last two columns on right) the calculations are based on counts of current doctoral candidates, not degrees awarded.

Just a few years later, the 1977 CULCON report found that the field was opening up in terms of the number of institutions awarding degrees, but students remained highly concentrated at a small number of institutions. Although the 1977 study counted more than twice as many degrees as its predecessor, almost two-thirds of them came from the same 12 institutions. The number of institutions that had awarded ten or more degrees related to Japan increased to 19 in the 1977 study, and those 19 institutions accounted for over three-quarters of the degrees awarded.

The 1984 survey reported a smaller number of doctorates (655) and of institutions that had awarded ten or more degrees (15) in its sample of academic Japan specialist survey respondents, but it found a 77.3 percent concentration of doctorates from those 15 institutions. Moreover, two-thirds of the respondents' doctorates still came from the original 12 institutions that had awarded five or more degrees related to Japan prior to 1970.

By 1995 the number of institutions that had awarded 10 or more doctorates to the current survey's respondents had grown a bit more, to 22, but so had the concentration: over eighty percent of the respondents had obtained their doctorates from those 22 institutions, and the original 12 doctoral institutions still accounted for about two-thirds of all the doctoral degrees awarded to the respondents.

By this time, however, the two figures can be interpreted as measuring rather different phenomena. The persistence of two-thirds of the respondents with doctorates from the original 12 institutions tells us that those institutions have remained major producers of Japan specialists, and therefore that a very high proportion of currently active Japan specialists have had essentially similar graduate training at the same institutions and with the same faculty. The expansion of the number of institutions that have awarded ten or more doctoral degrees to Japan specialists shows that the range of available options for doctoral training is gradually widening, but the fact that over 80 percent of the degrees came from that small pool of institutions also tells us that most doctorates are still coming from institutions that do have specialized resources and a track record in Japanese Studies. Both the training received and the networks created during graduate school still have a high degree of commonality despite the gradual increase from 12 to 22 institutions.

Adding the two sets of data on doctoral candidates to the series shows these trends even more clearly. While the proportion of students doing doctorates at the original 12 Japanese Studies institutions had dropped slightly to 60 percent, over 80 percent of the 1989 doctoral candidates were studying at 14 institutions that each had ten or more current doctoral candidates. The latter is a different measure than the previous calculation based on how many doctorates the institution had ever granted, but it taps the same institutions. In the 1995 doctoral candidates sample, with a pool twice as large as in 1989, just over half the students were at the original 12 institutions but 87 percent were studying at 18 institutions that currently have ten or more doctoral candidates in Japanese Studies.

The concentration at a small number of specialized institutions remains exceedingly high, but the share of the original 12 institutions is decreasing. This part of the pattern becomes apparent if we trace the fate of the smaller set of eight institutions that had produced 10 or more doctorates in Japanese Studies by 1970. That set of institutions—Harvard, University of Michigan, Columbia, University of California at Berkeley, Stanford, University of Washington, Yale, and University of Wisconsin—accounted for 70 percent of the doctorates in 1970, but dropped almost immediately to about 56 percent in the 1977 and 1984 studies, to less than 55 percent in the 1995 survey of specialists and the 1989 doctoral candidates group, and finally to just under 45 percent in the 1995 group of doctoral candidates. The remaining four original institutions, those having awarded 5-9 doctorates in Japanese Studies by 1970, absorbed the difference to keep the total at about two-thirds of all doctorates awarded prior to 1995. But in the two groups of current doctoral candidates the share of both the core eight institutions and the larger group of 12 institutions from 1970 is shrinking. In other words, while the original institutions still dominate the totals of doctorates awarded because of their cumulative impact, their share in the current production of doctorates in Japanese Studies is lower, and still dropping. The expanding demand for doctoral-level training on Japan is now being met by a relatively small number of other institutions that have begun training PhDs in the field since the mid-1970s. Because such a high proportion of all Japan specialists trained in the United States are still alive today, the cumulative total representing past doctorates awarded, while useful for understanding certain characteristics of contemporary Japanese Studies, provides a rather distorted picture of current doctoral training.

We can see this more clearly if we now put names to the institutions and specific numbers to their counts of doctorates and doctoral candidates. Table 8.7 shows the top 33 institutions producing doctorates in Japanese Studies as of 1995, ranked in order of the number of specialists in the 1995 directory who had obtained their doctorates from those institutions, which represents the latest cumulative total.[12] The table includes all of the institutions ranked as having full graduate programs in 1995 except the University of Kansas and University of Pittsburgh, which have produced a smaller number of doctorates to date. As we pointed out earlier in discussing the movement of institutions between graduate program categories over the series of studies, there is strong overall consistency at the top of the rankings, but many institutions have shifted position in the rankings slightly over time.

---

[12] The 1977 data only provided specific numbers for institutions with 10 or more doctorates and a list of institutions that had awarded 1-9 degrees, plus a summary count of institutions that had awarded 5 or more degrees. All of the institutions without a number for 1977 had awarded between one and nine doctorates related to Japan prior to 1970 except SUNY-Buffalo.

Table 8.7. Top 33 Institutions Awarding PhDs in Japanese Studies and Cumulative Number of Doctorates Awarded up to 1970, 1977, 1984, and 1995, by 1995 Rank Order*

Institution	Ph.D. 1970	Ph.D. 1977	Ph.D. 1984	Ph.D. 1995	Grad. Prog.
Harvard University	54	102	89	129	Full
Columbia University	46	101	63	102	Full
University of Michigan	47	90	60	82	Full
University of Chicago	8	31	48	78	Full
Stanford University	19	38	33	73	Full
Univ. of California, Berkeley	37	53	44	64	Full
Yale University	15	30	32	58	Full
University of Washington	17	34	22	33	Full
University of Wisconsin	11	20	23	32	Full
University of Pennsylvania	8	15	10	29	Limited
Univ. of California, L. A.	4	14	15	27	Full
Princeton University	4	13	13	27	Full
Cornell University	3	*	8	23	Full
University of Illinois	4	16	15	21	Full
Univ. of Hawaii at Manoa	0	*	12	20	Full
New York University	6	12	8	16	*
Indiana University	8	17	14	15	Full
University of S. California	4	13	6	13	Limited
University of Minnesota	3	10	7	13	Full
Johns Hopkins University	4	*	6	12	Full
Claremont Colleges (combined)	4	13	7	10	*
Ohio State University	0	*	3	10	Full
University of Texas at Austin	2	*	5	9	Limited
Massachusetts Inst. of Tech.	4	*	7	8	*
University of Arizona	0	*	7	8	Limited
The American University	3	*	7	8	None
Northwestern University	3	*	2	7	None
Michigan State University	2	16	4	6	*
Univ. of North Carolina	0	*	0	5	None
Duke University	2	*	5	5	Full
State Univ. of NY, Buffalo	0	0	0	5	Limited
Univ. of CA, Santa Barbara	0	*	1	5	Limited
University of Oregon	2	*	4	5	Limited

*1970 data from 1970 SSRC-ACLS Report, Appendix 2j, Table 1, p. 102; 1977 data from 1977 CULCON Report, Appendix N, Table 23, pp. 118–119; 1984 data from 1984 Japan Foundation Report, Table 4, pp. 16–17. 1977 data did not provide number of doctorates at institutions with less than 10 degrees awarded, so those institutions listed as having awarded 1-9 doctorates are marked with an asterisk. Institutions whose graduate programs could not be evaluated due to missing data are also marked with an asterisk.

These shifts can be tentatively projected into the future if we compare the ranking in Table 8.7 with the rank ordering of institutions by their current number of doctoral candidates in 1989 and 1995. The overall shift in ranking of institutions by number of completed doctorates will of course be much more gradual because of the cumulative effect of degrees previously awarded. We will first compare the rank order of institutions training current doctoral candidates in 1989 and 1995, and then consider the relationship between these rankings and the ranking of institutions by completed doctorates shown in Table 8.7.

The concentration of students at a relatively small number of doctoral training institutions has stayed at virtually the same level despite the substantial growth in the number of doctoral candidates over the past decade. In both 1989 and 1995 the top six institutions accounted for half of the current doctoral candidates, the top thirteen accounted for over three fourths, and the top eighteen accounted for 87.3 percent of the students. The full rankings are shown in Table 8.8 for 1989 and 8.9 for 1995.

Table 8.8. 1989 Rank Order of Institutions by Number of Doctoral Students in Japanese Studies, with Percent and Cumulative Percent

Rank	Institution	#	%	Cum. %
1.	University of Hawaii	51	11.4	11.4
2.	University of Michigan	45	10.1	21.5
3.	Columbia University	44	9.9	31.4
4.	Stanford University	36	8.1	39.5
5.	Yale University	35	7.8	47.3
6.	University of California at Berkeley	29	6.5	53.8
7.*	Harvard University	26	5.8	59.6
7.*	Cornell University	19	4.3	63.9
9.	Princeton University	17	3.8	67.7
10.	University of Washington	15	3.4	71.1
11.	University of Chicago	12	2.7	73.8
12.	University of California at Los Angeles	11	2.5	76.3
12.	University of Wisconsin	11	2.5	78.8
14.	Indiana University	10	2.2	81.0
15.	University of Kansas	8	1.8	82.8
16.	University of Pennsylvania	7	1.6	86.0
16.	Ohio State University	7	1.6	84.4
18.	Johns Hopkins University	6	1.3	87.3
19.	University of Illinois	5	1.1	88.4
Plus	32 schools with less than 5 students		11.6	100.0

* These institutions were tied for seventh place.

Table 8.9. 1995 Rank Order of Institutions by Number of Doctoral Students in Japanese Studies, with Percentage of Students and Cumulative Percent

Rank	Institutions	#	%	Cum. %
1.	University of Hawaii	106	13.2	13.2
2.	Columbia University	74	9.2	22.4
3.	Cornell University	61	7.6	30.0
4.	Univ. of California at Berkeley	60	7.6	30.0
5.	Stanford University	55	6.9	44.4
6.	Yale University	49	6.1	50.5
7.	University of Michigan	41	5.1	55.6
7.	Harvard University	41	5.1	60.7
9.	University of California, Los Angeles	37	4.6	65.3
10.	University of Chicago	28	3.5	68.8
11.	University of Washington	27	3.4	72.2
12.*	Ohio State University	21	2.6	74.2
12.*	Indiana University	21	2.6	77.4
14.	University of Pittsburgh	20	2.5	79.9
15.	University of Illinois	19	2.4	82.3
16.	Princeton University	17	2.1	84.4
17.	University of Wisconsin	12	1.5	85.9
18.	University of Pennsylvania	11	1.4	87.3
19.	Duke University	9	1.1	88.4
19.	University of California at San Diego	9	1.1	89.5
21.	State University of New York-Buffalo	8	1.0	90.5
22.	Johns Hopkins University	7	0.9	91.4
23.	University of Minnesota	6	0.7	92.1
23.	University of Kansas	6	0.7	92.8
Plus	36 institutions with less than 5 students		7.2	100.0

* These institutions were tied for twelfth place.

The same institutions hold the top eight positions in 1995, but their rank order in terms of number of doctoral candidates has changed. All but one has more students in 1995, but the extent of the increase varies considerably. The University of Hawaii, which holds the top position in both surveys, has more than doubled its doctoral candidates, from 51 in 1989 to 106 in 1995. The University of Michigan, which was ranked second with 45 students in 1989, has dropped to a tie for seventh place with Harvard University, both of which now report 41 doctoral candidates. Columbia was just behind Michigan in 1989, but has subtantially increased its student numbers since then to hold the number two position. The largest increase in rank was registered by Cornell University, which tripled its doctoral students and moved from eighth place to third.

In the second tier of ten institutions ranked from ninth to eighteenth place in 1989, there have been even greater changes. Two institutions that did not increase their 1989 student numbers appreciably (the University of Kansas and Johns Hopkins University) have dropped to 22nd and 23rd place, to be replaced by the University of Pittsburgh and the University of Illinois, whose doctoral programs have grown substantially in recent years.

There has been some expansion of the number of institutions that are marginally involved in doctoral training in Japanese Studies. The total number of institutions with doctoral candidates in Japanese Studies has grown from 51 to 60, and even institutions with fewer students have shared proportionally in the increased student load. In 1989, the eighteenth-ranked institution had six doctoral candidates in Japanese Studies, and an additional 33 institutions reported five or fewer students, including 18 schools with only one doctoral candidate working on Japan. In 1995, the two institutions that tied for twenty-third place in the rankings each reported six doctoral candidates in Japanese Studies, and an additional 36 institutions reported having less than five students working on Japan, including 23 with only one doctoral student.

Not surprisingly, the institutions at the top of the rankings in terms of number of students correspond closely to those coded earlier in this chapter as having complete graduate programs. The top nineteen rank positions correspond to the nineteen institutions with complete graduate programs in 1995, except for the University of Kansas, which has dropped in the ranking since 1989, and the University of Pennsylvania, which was ranked sixteenth in 1989 and eighteenth in 1995. It is classified as having a limited doctoral program because it has fewer than eight faculty Japan specialists. Both of these institutions, like most others between ranks 18 and 23, have excellent resources for doctoral programs in specific disciplinary areas, and attract students in those areas of strength. Each of these programs is a valuable contributor to the still-limited national resource for doctoral training in Japanese Studies, and the size ranking should not be confused with quality.

The comparison of specific institutions by size of doctoral program is significant because it brings to light what may be a critical element of the changing distribution of doctoral degrees: a gradual but unmistakable shift from private to public institutions. Among those institutions that awarded five or more doctorates to Japan specialists, the proportion that are public institutions has grown steadily from 41.7 percent in 1970 to 51.5 percent in 1995 (shown at bottom of Table 8.6). During that time the share of specialists who had obtained their doctorates at those public institutions decreased from 43.5 percent to 37.6 percent, largely because of the cumulative effect of older specialists who were educated at private institutions.

When the number of doctoral candidates was smaller and support for doctoral training in Japanese Studies was more readily available from both private and federal sources, it did not matter so much where a student went, because the training was largely supported by fellowships that covered tuition and partial living expenses. However, the rising demand for doctoral training in Japanese Studies over the past decade has also coincided with a decrease in the available fellowship support. Private institutions that are committed to the full support of their doctoral students have therefore either held steady or very slowly increased the number of doctoral students in Japanese Studies to match available levels of financial support. On the other hand, public institutions admit more students who do not have full funding or expect it, feel more of an obligation to expand student numbers in response to an increase in qualified applicants, and also have somewhat lower tuition rates and more provisions for waiving tuition for qualified students. The combination of their greater attractiveness to students because of lower costs and their willingness to admit qualified students even if they cannot guarantee financial support means that public institutions have been absorbing a larger share of the increase in student demand for doctoral training in Japanese Studies.

Public institutions comprised 57.9 percent of the institutions with five or more doctoral students in 1989, which grew to 62.5 percent by 1995. At the same time, the proportion of all students who were studying at public institutions increased from 50.9 percent to 53.5 percent. This gradual shift also reflects on a small scale the normalization of Japanese Studies, in that doctoral training in Japanese Studies now has become more accessible through these public institutions to students who cannot afford to attend private institutions. In an earlier time these students would have received financial support at either public or private institutions, because there was much more funding available relative to the demand. In fact, the federal funding through the National Defense Education Act, which supported most Japan specialists of the post-GI Bill generation who were trained in the 1960s and early 1970s, was originally intended to entice students into a field for which there was no demand at all. Now that there is some perceived economic value to doctoral-level training in Japanese Studies, potential students are more likely to seek the training even at considerable personal sacrifice. But this too has its costs in delayed degree completion and divided attention, as students work full-time while going to school or writing their dissertations.

Particularly at large state institutions and in fields other than history and Japanese literature, the way that doctoral candidates enter programs also reveals the subtle effect of normalization of Japanese Studies. Such students often simply apply for entrance and are accepted into a regular departmental doctoral program without any prior contact with the institution's formal Japanese Studies program or personnel. Department personnel committees also may regard the study of Japan as less exotic than they did formerly, and may admit a good student with a background or interest in Japan without treating it as a special case that ought to go through the Japanese Studies program. The students may not identify themselves to the Japanese Studies program until much later in their graduate career, and may not even be aware of funding that is specifically designated for the study of Japan. Under these circumstances, it is no wonder that the Japanese Studies program staff has trouble keeping a good count of students who have already been admitted, and has no control over the numbers who enter. And since the job market for trained Japan specialists is no longer limited to and defined by the academic market (another aspect of normalization), there is less reason to limit enrollment in Japanese Studies except when it exceeds the limits of available resources.

The shift toward public institutions for doctoral training has significant implications for the funding of Japanese Studies that already affect not only doctoral students directly, but the overall structure of the field, as part of the general issue of coping with the growth and normalization of Japanese Studies. The growth in the number of courses offered that was documented in Chapter Seven and the concomitant growth in programs and doctoral students that we have traced in this chapter all have a heavy impact on faculty time and workload, as well as on the infrastructure and institutional resources available for Japanese Studies. At the same time, the need to staff Japanese Studies programs to meet strong student demand creates academic positions for new Ph.D. Japan specialists, and the demand for other services and support activities in Japanese Studies creates additional positions for those with Japanese Studies training. We will take up these issues in the next two chapters; Staffing in Chapter Nine, and Infrastructure and Resources in Chapter Ten.

9

Staffing of Japanese Studies Programs

The major annual expense for any academic Japanese Studies program in the United States is the cost of faculty and staff salaries. The nature of those positions and their stability within the academic institution in large measure determine the strength and stability of the Japanese Studies program. This chapter will examine what kinds of staff are associated with various types and levels of Japanese Studies programs, and the extent to which formal Japanese Studies programs acknowledge the Japan specialists affiliated with their institution. Since academic institutions remain the major employer of Japan specialists in the United States, we also need to consider the present and future staffing of academic Japanese Studies programs as an indicator of the job market for new PhDs trained in Japanese Studies.

STAFFING

American academic institutions with Japanese Studies programs that were listed in the directory reported a total of 1,452 affiliated faculty and staff members. Two-thirds are listed as faculty members at the regular academic ranks of assistant, associate or full professor, and another 16.7 percent are instructors or lecturers. The remainder are administrators, librarians, emeritus or visiting faculty, and research or staff associates of specific programs.

As shown in Table 9.1, over two-thirds of all listed staff members are affiliated with institutions that have full undergraduate Japanese Studies programs. At these institutions, over two-thirds hold regular faculty academic rank. Another 13.4 percent are lecturers or instructors, and the remainder hold a wide variety of administrative and staff positions. The proportion of faculty in regular academic ranks is about the same for institutions with limited undergraduate programs, undergraduate area programs, and full undergraduate programs. However, institutions with minimal undergraduate programs have a lower proportion of staff in regular faculty ranks, and both minimal and limited undergraduate programs have a higher proportion of staff at the lecturer or instructor level. At institutions with limited Japanese Studies programs, the ratio is 63 percent regular faculty rank to 25 percent instructors and lecturers. At institutions with minimal Japanese programs the balance is 43 percent in regular academic ranks to 34 percent instructors and lecturers.[1]

Table 9.1. Distribution of Staff Positions at Institutions with Instructional Positions in Japanese Studies and Staff Ratios, by Undergraduate Program Classification*

Program	Instructor, Lecturer %	Professor Ranks %	Other Staff %	Total Staff %	Number of Programs (& % Dist.)	Faculty-Program Ratio
Minimal	34.2 (67)	42.9 (84)	23.0 (45)	100.0 (196)	42.0 (101)	0.83
Limited	25.0 (19)	63.2 (48)	11.8 (9)	100.0 (76)	10.0 (24)	2.0
Undergrad Area	11.8 (23)	69.7 (136)	18.5 (36)	100.0 (195)	15.8 (38)	3.6
Full Undergrad	13.4 (129)	67.7 (651)	18.9 (182)	100.0 (962)	32.1 (77)	8.5
All Programs	16.7 (238)	64.3 (919)	19.0 (272)	100.0 (1,429)	100.0 (240)	3.8

*Staff (n=23) at institutions listed in the directory without instructional programs have been excluded from the table.

Although the number of Japan specialist faculty only enters into the criteria for classification of undergraduate programs at the level of the undergraduate area program, it is apparent that many Japanese Studies programs are "minimal" or "limited" because they lack academic faculty to teach the necessary courses. The 101 minimal undergraduate programs have a total of only 84 staff of academic faculty rank among them, or 0.83 per institution, while the 24 limited undergraduate programs have only 48, or 2 per school. At the 38 institutions with undergraduate area programs, by contrast, the total number of faculty holding academic rank is 136, or 3.6 per school, while the 77 institutions with full undergraduate programs have a total of 651 faculty holding academic ranks, or 8.5 per school. In the latter

---

[1] These figures may underestimate the number of lecturers and instructors associated with Japanese Studies programs in the two highest classifications (full undergraduate and undergraduate area program) since institutions with large numbers of regular faculty may not list all of the instructors and lecturers who hold non-permanent positions, particularly in language instruction. However, the difference between those with minimal and limited programs would not be affected by this omission.

category the number is actually even higher, because of the additional presence of academic administrators, researchers, and other staff at the largest research institutions who also hold academic rank but were classified here by their position to distinguish them from teaching faculty.

This pattern of staff distribution has two strong implications. First, many "minimal" Japanese Studies programs appear to have been prompted by student demand for Japanese language instruction, which can be provided through instructors, lecturers, or even teaching assistants, but these programs will not be able to develop further without the addition of Japan specialist faculty holding academic rank. We will return to this issue after taking a broader look at faculty resources for Japanese Studies instructional programs.

A second implication of this skewed staffing pattern is that because of the heavy concentration of faculty in institutions with full undergraduate programs, the overwhelming majority of academic faculty who are teaching in Japanese Studies programs (84 percent) have Japanese Studies colleagues available at the same institution. This calculation, however, does not take into consideration those Japan specialists who are isolated at institutions with no Japanese Studies program and no Japan specialist colleagues. They cannot be incorporated into the current assessment based on staff lists provided by institutions with Japanese Studies programs.

The undergraduate program classifications were necessarily based on course lists, staffing, and other program data provided by institutions in their directory entries. It is important to remember that these staffing data, while the best available by far, are not complete. Comparing the information provided by Japan specialists for their individual directory entries with the staffing data provided by institutions offers a strategy for estimating the overall faculty resources in Japanese Studies programs more precisely. For the specialist data, the sample for this analysis includes anyone residing in the United States who listed any level of postsecondary faculty status as their primary occupation, a total of 964 persons out of the total US directory sample of 1,554. For the institutional dataset, the sample includes anyone reported as a staff member at a listed institution whose position was identified as instructional (including instructor, lecturer or equivalent, and the three traditional academic ranks), a total of 1,157 out of 1,452 staff listed by institutions.

Table 9.2 shows the faculty and staff data from the two sources, by undergraduate program classification. The data form overlapping sets, with about 30 percent of the names appearing on both lists, 41 percent only on the staff lists, and 29.1 percent only on the specialist list. We do not know what proportion of the persons reported only on the staff lists would meet the criteria for inclusion in the Japan Specialists directory, since some appear to be specialists in other areas who also teach courses either wholly or partly on

Japan. In the overlapping category there is further ambiguity, because during the directory editing process if there was any question about whether the specialist directory entry submitted offered sufficient evidence that an individual met the criteria for inclusion in the specialist directory, the presence of the person's name on an institutional staff list, as a form of local peer review, was deemed sufficient evidence for inclusion. By contrast, those persons who submitted individual directory entry forms as Japan specialists but did not appear on an institution's staff list were evaluated on the basis of the achievements they reported in their directory entry forms. These criteria were not necessarily rigorous, but they could easily encompass persons who do research on Japan but do not teach Japan-related courses.

Table 9.2. Japan Specialists with Faculty Occupations and Program Staff Lists as Alternative Measure of the Teaching Staff of Academic Japanese Studies Programs, by Undergraduate Program Classification, 1995

Source	Specialist Only		Both Sources		Staff List Only		Program Totals		Grand Total
Program	#	%	#	%	#	%	#	%	%
Full	163	17.3	365	38.7	415	44.0	943	68.4	57.7
Area	24	13.1	72	39.3	87	47.5	183	13.3	11.2
Limited	6	8.2	16	21.9	51	69.9	73	5.3	4.5
Minimal	29	16.1	35	19.4	116	64.4	180	13.1	11.0
Total in Prog.	222	16.1	488	35.4	669	48.5	1,379	100.1	
No Prog. Reported	254		-		-		254		15.6
Grand Total	476	29.1	488	29.9	669	41.0	1,633		100.0

Despite these caveats, the combined dataset totaling 1,663 faculty clearly offers a better sense of the overall size of the faculty engaged in Japanese Studies than does either source by itself. The staff lists offer nearly a 70 percent improvement over the specialist directory alone, while the specialist directory entries offer a 41 percent improvement over the staff lists alone, and includes faculty affiliated with institutions that did not submit a program entry for the directory.

Addition of the undergraduate program classification further clarifies the situation, but also raises new questions. Three points require additional explication. First, as shown in Table 9.2, the pattern of reporting of faculty was very similar for full undergraduate programs and undergraduate area programs, while a different pattern held for limited and minimal undergraduate programs. The proportion of faculty listed only in the specialist directory but not on institutional staff lists is relatively similar across all four categories, except for the limited undergraduate program category, in which the overall numbers are quite small and thus the percentages may be unreliable. The difference therefore centers on what proportion of the total appears on both lists, which is in some sense a measure of whether the staff list submitted by the institution is actually composed of Japan specialists. Appearing on the staff list only may also be a measure of faculty forgetfulness or anti-questionnaire sentiment, but there is no particular reason to expect that this would vary by program classification. For full and area programs, the area of overlap is about 40 percent of the total, while at limited and minimal programs it is only about half that. We have already observed that at these smaller programs a higher percentage of the staff are instructors and lecturers. It seems probable that a greater proportion of the program staff from these institutions did not submit specialist questionnaires to the directory either because they did not think they met the directory criterion of holding the highest degree in the field, or because they did not consider themselves to be specialists on Japan. This hypothesis needs to be explored further.

Second, while there is not much difference by program classification in the percentage of faculty whose names did not appear on the staff lists of their institutions, one group does stand out because of its sheer size. Due to the heavy concentration of Japan specialists at institutions with full undergraduate programs, this category contains a sizable number of individuals (163) who were not reported by their institutions as program staff. At large institutions with many Japan specialists, there may be many faculty members who do research on Japan but do not teach Japan courses regularly. This might explain the absence of some faculty from program staff listings. We noted earlier that many large institutions with extensive course offerings exclusively on Japan no longer list multinational courses that include Japan. The faculty who teach such courses might also fall outside the purview of the Japanese Studies program and thus not be listed as program staff. Or, alternatively, the omissions might simply reflect the lack of centralized organization of Japanese Studies at large institutions, the inability of Japanese Studies staff to keep track of everyone, and variations in the degree to which busy faculty in far-flung departments seek out ties to the Japanese Studies program. These possibilities also require further exploration.

The third important category illuminated by this analysis is the group of 254 Japan specialists in the specialist directory who report their occupation as faculty but whose institutions did not submit a program entry for the directory. Since these institutions clearly do have Japan specialists on their faculty, the question is whether they offer any courses related to Japan and if so, whether there is any appreciable difference between these institutions and those with program listings in the directory.

The survey portion of the specialist questionnaire permits us to investigate further the ambiguous findings of our comparison of staff lists and specialist listings, albeit with a more limited sample. Within the survey sample, we can determine whether Japan specialist faculty are currently teaching courses about Japan. Unfortunately the question in the survey does not permit us to distinguish whether the courses are wholly or only partly on Japan. We can, however, look at the level of instruction and the disciplines in which the courses on Japan are offered.

Table 9.3. Courses on Japan Reported by Specialist Survey Respondents Currently Teaching about Japan, by Program Classification and Staff List Status*

Program Staff Listing	No Program	Minimal	Limited	Area	Full	Total
Instructor-Lecturer	4	3	-	4	53	64
# specialists	(1)	(1)		(1)	(9)	(12)
mean	4.0	3.0	-	4.0	5.9	
Academic Faculty	27	119	43	163	906	1,258
# specialists	(5)	(27)	(12)	(41)	(201)	(286)
mean	5.4	4.4	3.6	4.0	4.5	
Non-faculty	-	2	1	21	81	105
# specialists		(1)	(1)	(5)	(22)	(29)
mean		2.0	1.0	4.2	3.7	
Not Listed	5	69	15	25	249	363
# specialists	(1)	(21)	(2)	(11)	(77)	(112)
mean	5.0	3.3	7.5	2.3	3.2	
Total	36	193	59	213	1,289	1,790
# specialists	(7)	(50)	(15)	(58)	(309)	(439)
mean	5.1	3.9	3.9	3.7	4.2	4.1
Persons at unlisted inst.	-	-	-	-	-	540
# specialists						(205)
mean						2.6
Grand Total	-	-	-	-	-	2,330
# specialists						(644)
mean						3.6

* The question asked how many *different* courses on Japan were offered in the 1991–92 and 1992–93 academic years. A separate question tabulating the number of repeat offerings of these courses is not included here. The two-year span was used to reflect the normal range of courses a faculty member might offer, comparable to an institutional course list in which some courses are not offered every year. The figure in parentheses is the number of faculty members reporting courses in the category. The mean is the average number of different courses on Japan taught by faculty members in the category. It is not a measure of faculty course load.

Of the 1,072 specialists who responded to the survey, 644 reported that they are currently teaching courses on Japan.[2] About one in eight of those currently teaching do not list their primary occupation as faculty at an academic institution. In most cases these are either emeritus faculty who still offer courses, or persons holding administrative or staff positions at an academic institution. Table 9.3 shows the number of courses these survey respondents reported, by program classification and the respondent's academic position as reported on the program's staff list.

Table 9.3 provides some support for the speculation advanced earlier, that staff at institutions with minimal or limited Japanese Studies programs are less likely to meet the directory's listing criteria. We noted earlier that such programs rely more heavily on instructors and lecturers who may not hold the highest degree in their field. In this table, only a tiny fraction of the specialists reporting that they teach courses on Japan are instructors or lecturers—2.7 percent of this sample of specialists who are currently teaching at listed institutions, or 3.7 percent of just those who appeared on staff lists. This is much lower than the proportion of instructors and lecturers reported on institutional staff lists (Table 9.1).

Also, the survey data demonstrate that many of the Japan specialist faculty at institutions with academic programs listed in the directory who are not reported on the institutional staff lists are indeed teaching courses on Japan. However, these unlisted specialists are somewhat less likely to teach Japan courses at all, and those who do teach offer somewhat fewer different courses on Japan than those who appear on institutional staff lists. The unlisted specialists have a teaching rate of 80 percent compared to 90 percent for specialist faculty who are on the staff lists. The 112 specialists who were not listed by their institutions but say that they are currently teaching courses on Japan report a total of 363 courses, or an average of 3.2 courses each. This is somewhat lower than the overall average of 4.4 different courses reported by specialists who are included on their program's staff list.

As indicated earlier, this category is dominated by faculty at institutions with full undergraduate programs. Respondents affiliated with institutions that have full undergraduate programs comprise two-thirds (68.8 percent) of the teaching specialists not listed by their institutions, and offer 68.5 percent of the courses reported by nonlisted specialists. Within the category of specialists affiliated with full undergraduate programs, however, they account for one-quarter of the sample but just under 20 percent of the courses, suggesting that they may be less centrally involved in teaching courses about Japan in the Japanese Studies program than their colleagues.

---

[2] Depending on whether you include or exclude those who did not respond to the question, this comprises either 60.1 percent or 71.7 percent of the total.

The survey questions on teaching are not as precise as the course lists provided by institutions, but the number of courses was reported by course level. The 77 survey respondents at institutions with full undergraduate programs who were not listed as staff by their institutions reported that they teach 92 different lower division undergraduate courses, 106 upper division undergraduate courses, and 51 graduate courses on Japan, as shown in Table 9.4. This is about 20 percent of all the undergraduate courses specialist respondents reported teaching at institutions with full undergraduate programs, and 17 percent of all the graduate courses. The results skew the actual distribution of courses taught at these institutions because so few courses taught by instructors and lecturers, such as basic language courses, are included. However, this omission should not seriously affect the comparisons among the other three categories.

In this survey sample, faculty of academic rank who were reported on the staffs at institutions with full undergraduate programs taught a progressively greater proportion of courses offered at higher levels (from 65.9 percent for lower division courses to 75.3 percent for graduate and professional school courses). The corresponding decrease of higher-level courses among the nonlisted faculty was not nearly as sharp as that found among the smaller categories of instructors or non-faculty personnel. This suggests that the nonlisted faculty were not institutionally marginal by virtue of their academic positions, but rather may be regarded as less central to the Japanese Studies program, perhaps because they teach courses that are not wholly about Japan, teach outside the traditional Japanese Studies disciplines, or are not considered as full specialists in Japanese Studies by the program personnel because they specialize more heavily in some other area.

Table 9.4. Distribution of Courses Reported by Specialist Survey Respondents at Institutions with Full Undergraduate Programs, by Course Level and Staff List Position of Respondent

Level	Lower Div.		Upper Div.		Graduate-Prof.		Total	
Staff List	#	%	#	%	#	%	#	%
Instructor-lecturer	29	6.4	17	3.2	7	2.3	53	4.1
Academic faculty	300	65.9	380	71.2	226	75.3	906	70.3
Non-faculty	34	7.5	31	5.8	16	5.3	81	6.3
Not listed	92	20.2	106	19.9	51	17.0	249	19.3
Total	455	100.0	534	100.1	300	99.9	1,289	100.0

Unfortunately, the survey question does not permit a precise analysis of the nature of each course reported through which these alternatives could be investigated. Respondents were asked one general question about the disciplines or fields in which the reported courses were taught. About a quarter of the fields reported were in the social sciences and another 12 percent in the professions, for a combined total of over one-third in these fields. However, we have no way of weighting this distribution by the number of courses, so it remains impressionistic.

The one firm measure available is the discipline of the respondent. While at institutions with less developed Japanese Studies programs the fields in which survey respondents reported teaching courses did not necessarily correspond to the respondent's discipline, the correspondence was quite high at institutions with full undergraduate programs, where the level of faculty specialization is much greater. Compared to academic faculty at institutions with full undergraduate programs who were listed on the program's staff list, unlisted faculty are less likely to be teaching in Japanese language and literature, or in the arts and humanities. As shown in Table 9.5, they are 40 percent more likely to be in the social sciences, 47 percent more likely to be in linguistics, and more than six times (638.5 percent!) as likely to be in a professional field such as law or business. The percentage of historians was about the same in both faculty categories.

Table 9.5. Courses Offered by Listed and Unlisted Academic Faculty at Institutions with Full Undergraduate Programs by Discipline of Specialist Respondent

List Status	Academic Faculty		Unlisted Faculty		% Change
Discipline	#	%	#	%	
Social Sciences	144	15.9	56	22.5	+41.5
History	201	22.2	58	23.3	+4.9
Arts & Humanities	126	13.9	10	4.0	-71.2
Linguistics	94	10.4	38	15.3	+47.1
Lang. & Literature	329	36.3	59	23.7	-34.7
Professions	12	1.3	24	9.6	+638.5
Other	-		4	1.6	
Total	906		249		

The differences between the two distributions offer some evidence for all three of the factors that we have suggested might distance unlisted faculty from the Japanese Studies program. The unlisted faculty are more likely to be offering courses in disciplines outside the traditional arts and humanities core, and they are more likely to be in disciplines that encourage cross-national comparison rather than concentration on a single language and culture. In history, where their proportional strength is the same, the unlisted faculty are much less likely to be teaching graduate courses than their listed counterparts, suggesting that they may be less specialized in Japanese history.

What then of the third issue of concern, persons who are listed in the specialist directory as faculty members at institutions that did not submit a program entry for the institutional directory? The critical question is whether these specialists at unlisted institutions are in fact teaching courses on Japan. We saw in Table 9.3 that 205 of them are indeed teaching, which at 58.5 percent of those who completed the survey is considerably lower than the 71.6 percent at listed institutions who currently teach courses about Japan, but still a substantial representation. The 205 respondents who are currently teaching reported a total of 540 different courses on Japan, an average of 2.6 per person, which again is considerably lower than the average of 4.1 courses reported by all specialists affiliated with institutions whose programs are listed in the directory, but still substantial.

The distribution of these courses by discipline of instructor, as shown in Table 9.6, closely resembles the distribution of courses reported by specialists at institutions with minimal, limited, or no program (combined). Both differ from the disciplinary distribution of listed faculty at institutions with full undergraduate programs shown above in Table 9.5 in the greater weight given to arts and humanities courses, and the smaller proportion devoted to linguistics, language and literature, or other subjects.

Table 9.6. Distribution of Courses Offered, as Reported by Survey Respondents from Unlisted Institutions and Listed Institutions with Minimal, Limited, or No Programs, by Disciplinary Group

Affiliation	*Unlisted Institution*		*Minimal, Limited, No Prog.*	
Discipline	#	%	#	%
Social Sciences	87	16.3	23	8.2
History	132	24.7	82	29.2
Arts & Humanities	106	19.8	64	22.8
Linguistics	12	2.2	15	5.3
Lang. & Literature	119	22.2	72	25.6
Professional	40	7.5	10	3.6
Other	39	7.3	15	5.3
Total Courses	535	100.0	281	100.0

Japan specialists who are affiliated with academic institutions that do not have a regular program listing are listed in the institutional directory's secondary list of "Other Institutions with Japan Specialist Staff," so they have been included in the broadest measure of presence of Japanese Studies in Chapter Three. Comparison of these "other institutions" with those listed in the directory as having limited or minimal programs suggests strongly that the difference between the two groups is more a matter of institutional questionnaire submission than of actual program resources.

The number of Japan specialist faculty at "other institutions" ranges from one to six, with most having only one current faculty member listed in the directory. This suggests that a very few of these institutions might have an undergraduate area program or even a full undergraduate program in place, but the vast majority would fall into the limited or minimal undergraduate program classifications if the data were available to make the assignment. Even though a smaller proportion of the specialists at unlisted institutions are currently teaching courses on Japan, it appears that most of the institutions have at least one person teaching. While we cannot extrapolate any further from the available data, the findings suggest that our initial measure using the simple presence of a Japan specialist listed in the specialist directory as a basic measure of the extension of Japanese Studies to academic institutions in the United States is not far off the mark. While it may slightly overestimate the number of institutions at which courses on Japan are offered, this gap may be smaller than the degree of underestimation that results from using only program data submitted by institutions.

The slippage in the number of programs reported results from our inability to get a 100 percent response to the survey of institutions. The directory project expended considerable effort to get the response to its final level through targeted follow-up to all institutions from which specialist entries had been received, including sending institutional questionnaires directly to many of the specialists. The most intensive follow-up was directed toward institutions with five or more Japan specialists in the directory. One measure of our success is the fact that only five US institutions on the "other institutions" list have more than four specialists listed in the directory. In addition to the difficulties busy individual faculty members may have had in either getting an institutional response or gathering the necessary information themselves, there is the problem of the specialist's own subjective definition of what constitutes a Japanese Studies program. Faculty members who received their own training at institutions with well-developed Japanese Studies resources may well believe that their current institution has "no program" when the courses they teach would have warranted a program listing in the institutional directory.

As we have observed earlier, the expansion of Japanese Studies during the past decade has resulted both from the extension of some Japanese Studies presence to new, usually smaller, institutions, and from the intensification of

Japanese Studies, as measured in courses, staffing, and program options, at institutions where there was already some program in place a decade earlier. Roughly 15–17 percent of the growth of each type seems to be institutionally invisible, either because the institution does not report all of its faculty who are engaged in Japanese Studies, or because the institution does not report that it has any Japan specialist faculty or courses at all. Both of these forms of institutional invisibility are likely to persist at least at the current level. What we do not know is whether our current estimate of a 15–17 percent invisibility factor is likely to remain stable or to increase over time.

To the extent that Japanese Studies becomes normalized in American academics as a subject that is neither exotic nor restricted to a dedicated intellectual elite, the invisibility factor is likely to increase over time. How many American academic institutions could readily report, for example, how much of a German Studies program they have, using the same criteria of language and area courses, degree programs, and program staff that we have used for Japanese Studies?

PROSPECTS FOR FUTURE GROWTH IN INSTITUTIONAL PROGRAMS

We noted earlier in the analysis of Japanese Studies programs classified as minimal or limited, that many of these programs offer Japanese language and little else. The existence of such programs appears to be driven by student demand for Japanese language instruction, often delivered by instructors and lecturers. By definition, these programs cannot develop much further without the addition of area faculty. Since the undergraduate program criteria are based on a language and area model, both elements are required by definition for a program to advance beyond the limited undergraduate level.

It would be theoretically possible for a program at the minimal level not to offer any Japanese language instruction and for one at the limited level to offer only one year of language. However, the programs we have classified at this level are far more likely to have begun with language. It is possible that some of the institutionally invisible programs we have just examined, that have one or two Japan specialists but no institutional directory listing, tilt in the other direction and have area courses but do not offer Japanese language. Indeed, both faculty and institution might have concluded that in the absence of Japanese language instruction they do not yet have a Japanese Studies program.

The strong program priority placed on language instruction becomes even clearer when the distribution of courses on Japan in the institutional course lists is examined by program level.[3] In minimal undergraduate programs 62.1 percent of all courses exclusively on Japan are Japanese language courses. This rises to 68.2 percent for limited undergraduate programs, but drops to 52.9 percent for undergraduate area programs and to 37.5 percent for full undergraduate programs. Even though programs in the latter two classifications offer more levels of language instruction and a wider array of specialized language courses, these increases are outweighed by increased breadth in area course offerings.

A similar calculation reinforces this finding and clarifies its mechanism, by relating the percentage of Japanese language courses to the number of disciplines in which area courses exclusively on Japan are offered. When area courses on Japan are offered in only one discipline, nearly three-fourths of all courses are Japanese language courses. When area courses are offered in two or three disciplines the proportion of language courses drops to just over half of all courses. When area courses are offered in four to six disciplines, language courses account for about 45 percent of the total, and when seven or more disciplines offer area courses, the proportion of language classes decreases to about 35 percent. Finally, in the largest programs, where more than fifteen disciplines are represented, language courses decrease to just over a quarter of the total, completely reversing the pattern of the smallest programs.

While the initial priority of Japanese language courses in the establishment of Japanese Studies programs is clear, it is difficult to discern a consistent pattern to the sequence in which other disciplines are added. History is definitely the most common discipline in Japanese Studies after language, accounting for between 10 and 20 percent of all courses regardless of the number of disciplines in which area courses on Japan are available. Within this range the percentage of history courses fluctuates erratically, with only slight evidence of a drop as the number of disciplines increases. Literature is the next most frequent discipline, but it shows an upward trend from under 10 percent of courses when less than six disciplines are represented in the program, to 10-20 percent thereafter. The increase in the percentage of literature courses as programs expand is due to the fact that advanced Japanese courses in which literature is read in the original are counted as literature, rather than language courses.

No other single discipline comes close to the proportions of courses offered in language, history, and literature. In fact, the four main social science disciplines of anthropology, economics, political science, and sociology

---

[3] The data for this calculation include courses exclusively on Japan at all levels of the curriculum, crosstabulated by undergraduate program classification. Because much of the curriculum expansion at larger institutions involves upper division area courses and advanced language courses open to both graduate and undergraduate students, this approach seems more meaningful than restricting the sample to undergraduate courses.

combined generally account for only 5 to 10 percent of all courses on Japan,[4] and show no clear pattern as the number of disciplines in the program increases. The formula therefore seems to be that language and history are basic, some representation of social sciences and other humanities disciplines helps to expand the program, and literature courses proliferate as the language program adds advanced courses.

The relatively random order in which Japanese Studies programs expand into new disciplines seems to be a product of three main factors. First, beyond the disciplines of history and language and literature, there has always been a relatively small supply of Japan specialists in any given discipline. If every program tried to expand in a particular disciplinary order, there simply would not be enough specialists available to meet the demand, even if it were spread out across a number of years. Consequently, even programs with a dozen or more Japan specialists do not have the same disciplinary array, and smaller programs exhibit even greater variety in their configurations.

Second, there are both disciplinary and local departmental variations in receptivity to the very notion of hiring a "Japan specialist." The conceptual maps of some disciplines are naturally configured in terms of geographic, political, linguistic, or cultural areas that facilitate the notion of "Japan specialist," while the conceptual maps of other disciplines are less receptive, or even hostile, to such a notion because they seek faculty specialization according to entirely different dimensions. To this general variation among disciplines must be added the particular needs and priorities of the local department that would accommodate a Japan specialist in that discipline. Even a department in a discipline that is organized by cultural area may feel that it needs a Russian specialist more than a Japan specialist, while a department whose discipline is not organized geographically may not understand why anyone would want a "Japan specialist," when what they need is someone who does network analysis.

Third, and partly as a consequence of the first two factors, a fair amount of the program expansion in Japanese Studies is due to serendipitous hiring. Conversely, program losses due to resignation or retirement may not be replaced with an equivalent Japan specialist. The survey data permit us to explore all three of these factors and their interrelations.

The institutional survey provides additional insight into the problems of staffing Japanese Studies programs. During the past five years, institutions responding to the survey reported losing through separation or retirement a total of 216 faculty positions at 82 institutions, a mean of 2.63 per institution. A total of 145 of these positions at 65 institutions had been filled with another Japan specialist, presumably in the same field. In addition, about a third of

[4] The few instances in which the figure appears to exceed 10 percent are statistical anomalies due to the small number of institutions represented.

those responding to the survey reported that their institution had added new faculty positions in Japanese Studies during the same time period. The 70 newly created positions in Japanese Studies were overwhelmingly in language and literature or language and civilization, with a small scattering in history, social sciences, or Japanese Studies with discipline not further specified. Nearly 50 institutions reported that they are currently trying to fill one or more Japan specialist positions. Half of these were in language, with the remainder in social sciences (10), humanities (8), history (6), and literature (3).

Independent of these deliberate staffing changes in Japanese Studies, 41 institutions (21.6 percent of those responding to the question) reported that they had filled 48 positions with Japan specialists who had not been recruited specifically for their expertise on Japan. About 40 percent of these serendipitous hires were in the social sciences. They included six political scientists and seven sociologists, fields where there is some resistance to the concept of hiring an area specialist. Nearly the same percentage were specialists in the humanities, especially in religion (7) and history (4). The disciplinary pattern of these serendipitous hires stands in sharp contrast to the fields in which deliberate program expansion has proceeded.

In terms of disciplines, then, the overall picture is of new Japanese Studies positions being created and filled largely in language, with a much smaller number going to disciplinary specialists in social sciences and humanities. Serendipitous hiring of Japan specialists, by contrast, produced a substantial number of new positions in the social sciences and humanities. This pattern reflects both the huge demand for Japanese language instruction during the early 1990s, and the nature of the disciplines involved in accidentally hiring a Japan specialist. It would be rather unlikely for an institution to acquire a Japanese language teacher serendipitously, but much more likely that a social science or humanities department seeking either a generalist or a person with a particular specialization within the discipline might find someone whose research centered on Japan. If the department could accommodate it, such an individual might be willing, even eager, to develop and offer courses on Japan.

The extent to which non-language positions in Japanese Studies are filled by serendipity has important implications both for program development and for the strategies of Japan specialists entering the job market. It helps to explain why programs show no clear sequence of development by discipline, other than the fact that they generally begin with language and then add history. It also suggests that some Japanese Studies programs develop without clear institutional commitment, or expand unintentionally in particular directions. Moreover, the instability of minimal undergraduate programs in Japanese Studies, which are predominately programs offering only language instruction, may be partly due to the fact that some institutions by sheer chance either already have or subsequently acquire a faculty Japan specialist in a field other than language, while other programs that depend solely on language instructors can neither sustain their activity nor develop further without an accidental hire.

From the perspective of the job-seeking Japan specialist, this recruitment situation suggests strongly that candidates need to search beyond the small pool of positions marked specifically for Japan specialists, and to present themselves in terms of their disciplinary expertise rather than or along with their area expertise on Japan.

Institutional survey respondents also reported a variety of other recruiting complexities, most of which militated against the successful hiring of a Japan specialist. The 95 institutions responding to the multiple response question about recruiting problems offered a total of 221 responses, or an average of 2.3 responses per institution. Forty-one percent reported that they had hired a Japan specialist away from another institution, which means that one hire caused a vacancy elsewhere that might or might not be replaced by another Japan specialist. Only seven percent reported that they had failed in an attempt to hire a Japan specialist away from another institution. This discrepancy may reflect a reluctance to advertise failures rather than the probability that such attempts usually succeed. When the question was asked in the opposite direction, over a third of the respondents reported that another institution had hired a Japan specialist away from their institution, while nearly 20 percent reported a failed attempt to do so.

A third of the responding institutions reported difficulty in getting a Japan specialist in a particular discipline because the department did not want to hire a Japan specialist, but very few got into a situation where the department did not like a particular candidate for a Japan position. Much more common was the situation where there were no suitable candidates available. More than a fifth of the institutions reported filling a Japan position with a visitor because they could not find someone suitable for a permanent appointment.

About 18 percent reported having lost a Japan specialist who failed to obtain tenure, but only one percent of institutions reported gaining a Japan specialist who had failed to obtain tenure elsewhere. And finally, 11.6 percent reported that an effort to hire a Japan specialist had been complicated by the need to hire the candidate's spouse, while a slightly smaller number (8.4 percent) reported that they had obtained a Japan specialist through a spousal hire.

Since these reports refer more to the institution's deliberate attempts to hire or replace a Japan specialist, they suggest that even when there is an institutional commitment to a particular Japanese Studies position, there may be additional internal or external barriers to filling the position successfully. In some cases it may be easier and more effective to expand the Japanese Studies program through serendipitous hiring than to overcome all the barriers to a successful search for a Japan specialist.

In another sense, the serendipitous hiring of Japan specialists also points to the normalization of the study of Japan within the American academic world. The fact that a prospective candidate for a disciplinary position happens to do research on Japan may be regarded as interesting, but much less important than the length of the candidate's publication record and how the candidate's particular subspecialty fits into the department's needs. The recruiting department might not even realize that the candidate would like to offer a course specifically on Japan, but would expect that the research on Japan would be incorporated as examples into whatever disciplinary courses the candidate taught. Disciplinary colleagues would regard the candidate's knowledge of Japan as an intriguing case against which to compare their own theoretical ideas or research experiences, without according expertise on Japan any status as an organizing principle either within or outside the discipline.

While accidental or serendipitous hiring of Japan specialists can stabilize small Japanese Studies programs and ensure academic employment for more young Japan specialists, it does leave programs with some long-term uncertainty, because the institution has not necessarily made a commitment to the development of Japanese Studies in those disciplines. We can examine this question further by considering what will happen to such a position when the Japan specialist leaves. The 1984 Japan Foundation study, which was directed to academic Japan specialists, asked respondents whether they planned to stay in the academic world until retirement or would leave before retirement. Eighty percent planned to stay until retirement, 4 percent expected to leave sooner, and 16 percent were not sure.[5] For the broader sample of the 1995 study the question was adapted to cover those working in business and government as well as academics. Twenty percent of the respondents still could not fit themselves into these categories, either because they were too young to know (12.2 percent), already retired (7.5 percent), or are not employed in one of these three sectors.

Still, two-thirds of the sample said they would remain in academics until retirement, and only 3.4 percent said they would leave academics before retirement. Much smaller percentages reported that they would stay in business (3.8 percent) or government (1.5 percent) until retirement. Just under one percent each reported that they would leave business or government before reaching retirement. A small fraction reported plans for a combination of academic and business activity post-retirement, or said they were continuing in academics even after retirement. It is apparent from this distribution that most of those responding to the question were academics.

Academic respondents were also asked in both surveys what would happen to their position after they retired. In 1984, 59 percent reported that their position would be filled, 13 percent said it would be dropped, and 29

[5] 1984 Japan Foundation Report, Table 55, p. 86.

percent were not sure what would happen to the position. In 1995 we offered a slightly more complex set of responses in order to clarify whether the position would be filled with another Japan specialist. Only 41.5 percent of the respondents were confident that their position would be filled by another Japan specialist when they retired, while a quarter said the position would be filled but the replacement probably would not be a Japan specialist. Another 7.8 percent said the position probably would not be filled at all, and slightly more than a quarter were not sure. Because of the ambiguity of the 1984 question we cannot evaluate the results comparatively, but it is clear that considerably less than half of the 1995 respondents expect that their positions will be filled by Japan specialists after they leave.

Some part of this expectation is based on the fact that the institution hired a Japan specialist not as the result of a purposeful search for one, but as an accidental result of a search for a specialist on something else. The differences by discipline clarify this, as shown in Table 9.7. Nearly three-quarters of the language and literature specialists and over half of the historians expect that their vacated positions will be filled by Japan specialists, compared to just over a quarter of the social scientists. Language and literature specialists express the least uncertainty, since their positions are generally located in language-based programs with high student demand for Japanese. In very few cases did respondents think the position would not be filled at all. Hence the critical difference is in whether the position will be filled by someone who is not a Japan specialist. While a very small proportion of the historians and language and literature specialists thought their positions would be filled by someone who is not a Japan specialist, more than a third of the social scientists expected that would happen.

Table 9.7. What Will Happen to Academic Position After Respondent Retires, by Disciplinary Group

	History %	*Lang. & Lit.* %	*Social Sci.* %	*Other* %	*Total* %
Replace with Japan specialist	53.2	73.0	28.2	26.1	41.5
Will not fill with Japan specialist	15.4	5.2	36.6	31.8	24.5
Position will not be filled at all	6.4	3.4	9.3	10.0	7.8
Not sure what will happen to position	25.0	18.4	26.0	32.1	26.3
Total	100.0	100.0	100.0	100.0	100.0
# Respondents	156	174	227	280	837

This difference points to two characteristics of the social scientists in the sample. First, many of those who were trained as Japan specialists obtained their academic positions because of their general social science credentials and not through a purposeful search for a Japan specialist; hence the position is not defined institutionally as a Japan position. Second, the social science group also includes many social science generalists who have always done comparative work, or who began studying Japan after completing a dissertation on another topic. They, too, were hired because of their credentials as social scientists and not because they specialized on Japan. Both of these types of social scientists will likely be replaced by someone who has a similar subspecialty in the discipline, with little consideration given to the candidate's geographic area of research and expertise. The pattern in the catchall "other" category looks very similar to that in the social sciences, but with a higher level of uncertainty.

The picture looks somewhat brighter when we look at what institutions plan to do over the next five years to phase out or expand their Japanese Studies offerings.[6] They reported plans to phase out only 23 Japan-related positions: ten in social sciences, five each in Japanese language and in humanities disciplines, two in Japanese linguistics, and one in business. By contrast, more than four times as many potential new positions (96) were reported, although we cannot distinguish a genuine institutional commitment from the hopes and desires of the Japanese Studies program.

About a third of the potential expansion positions are in Japanese language, and some of them may be filled with part-time instructors rather than full-time academic faculty. The institutions reported that they hoped to add eight positions in Japanese history and six in Japanese literature. The most commonly reported expansion plans were in other humanities or in social sciences, both of which had 22 potential new positions identified. The social science positions were most commonly specified as anthropology or sociology, while the humanities positions were most often designated as art history or religion. Six expansion positions in the professions were also identified, four in business and two in law.

Taken together, all of these bits and pieces suggest that Japanese Studies programs will continue both to extend to new institutions and to expand at institutions where they already exist. Some of this growth will be deliberate and some will come about through routine hiring that accidentally produces a position filled by a Japan specialist. While some positions currently filled by Japan specialists may be phased out and others may not go to another Japan specialist when the current incumbent leaves, the overall trend is toward more academic positions. Furthermore, the current hiring and

---

[6] We received some responses to the institutional survey from institutions that do not at present have a Japanese Studies program that could be included in the directory, but hope to add one in the future and may have had some level of program in the past. Their responses are included in this tally.

future expansion plans of institutions suggest that once the basic demand for Japanese language is filled, institutions seek specialists in a broad array of disciplines. It is neither feasible nor necessary to try to direct future cohorts of doctoral candidates into one discipline rather than another, so long as there are no artificial barriers that keep students from training or finding employment in the discipline of their choice.

The reports from institutions also suggest strongly that there is not a serious problem in finding academic employment for new PhDs in Japanese Studies in the mid-1990s. The 1984 survey was conducted at a time when the employment pattern for Japan specialists was changing, but the implications of the changes were not yet clear and there was considerable concern that new PhDs would not be able to find suitable academic employment. That survey provided some fragmentary information on where recent graduates had found employment. As noted earlier, in 1995 we were fortunate just to be able to identify Ph.D. candidates and track whether they had completed their degrees between 1989 and 1995. Our data on what positions graduates have taken, based largely on reports by their faculty advisors, are too fragmentary for any quantitative analysis beyond that presented in Chapter Two.

We were able to replicate an impressionistic question from the 1984 survey that asked Japan specialists why they thought recent PhDs were accepting non-academic positions. The comparison is shown in Table 9.8. Whereas in 1984 respondents felt that new PhDs were taking non-academic positions because there were no tenure-track positions available, or no academic positions at all, neither of these reasons was accorded nearly as much weight in 1995, although the lack of tenure-track positions remained the most important reason offered. The 1995 respondents cited more often the low salaries of academic compared to non-academic positions, and gave some weight to the lack of security in academics and the lack of positions in certain geographic areas. The person's own preference for non-academic work was given almost no weight in 1984, but received more attention in 1995, particularly from those who are not academics themselves (not shown). Overall, fewer respondents answered this question in 1995, and far fewer thought any of the reasons offered was a major factor. Family considerations gained in importance as a secondary consideration, but were rarely seen as a major factor. Many wrote in comments indicating that all of their graduate students had found academic positions, and more than one referred to students taking academic positions in Japan. The responses indicate that in the mid-1990s, respondents see no crisis in employment for new PhDs, and perceive non-academic employment as a choice made largely as a matter of economic advantage or personal preference.

At this very general level, it appears that market forces and the personal inclinations of graduate students will produce a reasonable match between supply and demand in the academic marketplace. That certainly does not guarantee every new PhD the desired academic position at the opportune time. The pools for both positions and candidates are very small, so there will most likely be mismatches of supply and demand for particular disciplines every year, even though the overall picture seen from a greater distance looks relatively well coordinated.

Table 9.8. Percent Distribution of Perceived Reasons New PhDs Accept Non-Academic Employment, 1984 and 1995

Reason	Major Reason	Some Importance	Little Importance	Not Sure	# Responding
1984 Survey*					
No tenure track positions available	65	24	4	7	725
No positions available in geographic area	23	42	25	11	676
No academic positions of any sort available	58	23	9	10	712
Low salary compared to non-academic posts	22	43	26	9	692
Lack of security and future in academics	31	44	15	10	696
Family considerations (spouse's employment)	5	37	32	26	638
Prefer non-academic work	6	29	41	25	635
1995 Survey					
No tenure track positions available	39.5	28.5	8.5	23.6	636
No positions available in geographic area	19.8	37.0	13.5	29.8	587
No academic positions of any sort available	20.8	24.8	23.3	31.1	557
Low salary compared to non-academic posts	35.6	30.2	11.0	23.2	626
Lack of security and future in academics	21.8	31.2	20.6	26.4	587
Family considerations (spouse's employment)	9.6	42.2	13.4	34.7	573
Prefer non-academic work	16.0	29.2	18.5	36.3	531

*1984 data from 1984 SSRC Report, Table 58, p. 88. Percentages were reported rounded to whole numbers.

One structural problem clearly looms on the horizon. As we have noted, doctoral-level training in Japanese Studies remains highly concentrated at a relatively small number of institutions, even as undergraduate-level Japanese Studies is extending steadily into smaller schools and schools with less restrictive entrance requirements throughout the United States. Although we see some signs of normalization of graduate education in the shift toward more doctoral training in Japanese Studies at public institutions, there is still a growing disjuncture between the academic environment of graduate training and the qualifications of these highly trained new PhDs on the one hand, and the academic settings of the available positions, on the other. There may well be years when the top graduates from elite institutions in particular fields will judge that there are no jobs in Japanese Studies, because the available positions are beyond the range they are willing to consider. Given the international academic job market for American-trained Japan specialists plus non-academic job possibilities now open to Japan specialists both in the United States and internationally, some highly qualified new PhDs will most certainly choose not to take employment in American academic institutions, at least initially.

As a result, the available positions in US academic institutions that represent the extension of Japanese Studies into the normal, non-elite mainstream of higher education are more likely to be filled by the "normalizing" segment of doctoral candidates at large public institutions, or by graduate students from other countries who have trained in Japanese Studies at US institutions and are happy to find any opportunity to remain in the United States. Thus normalization and internationalization are intertwined, both in graduate training and in the future staffing of Japanese Studies programs in the United States.

10

Libraries, Other Activities, and Funding of Japanese Studies Programs

This chapter will assess the infrastructure for the study of Japan in the United States. We will concentrate primarily on academic institutions of higher education, since they comprise the central institutions that support both academic training and research in Japanese Studies, and are therefore the primary suppliers of both human capital and new knowledge to meet the nation's need for information and expertise on Japan. We will first examine library resources as the most critical element of the infrastructure of Japanese Studies. We will look briefly at other aspects of Japanese Studies programs, such as opportunities for study abroad, the domestic and international cooperative relations between programs that permit them to stretch limited resources, and the services that larger Japanese Studies programs offer to primary and secondary schools, business, the mass media, nonprofit organizations, and the general public. Finally, we will consider some aspects of the available funding for Japanese Studies under the conditions of growth and development that we have been documenting throughout this study.

LIBRARY RESOURCES

After Japanese Studies staff, the most important element of the infrastructure for the study of Japan in the United States is the category of library and information resources. The core resource is without question the collections of Japanese language library materials that are maintained by the Library of Congress, academic institutions, and a few other institutions. However, as the body of English language materials on Japan has grown, as the number and types of users of information about Japan have expanded, and as information technology has developed, new kinds of resources have become essential to the infrastructure for Japanese Studies.

Earlier chapters have identified a number of different purposes for which library and information resources about Japan located in the United States are essential, and it would be useful to list them again here. First, Japan specialists need to keep their knowledge current, and to do so they must read a wide variety of materials in both English and Japanese. Second, Japan specialists conduct research for academic and non-academic publication, for their teaching, and to meet the needs of clients and special audiences. To carry out these professional activities they not only need to collect materials themselves in Japan, but also must have access to library and information resources in both English and Japanese for primary and secondary research in the United States. Third, the growing number of students in Japanese Studies courses and programs of study depend upon library and information resources in the United States to meet course requirements and to develop their own expertise on Japan. Advanced Japanese language students and graduate students in particular depend upon the Japanese collections in the United States to develop their Japanese reading and research skills, and to conduct their own research using Japanese language materials. These same students also depend heavily on American library collections for access to the English language literature on Japan. Fourth, as the study of Japan becomes normalized in American society, a wider range of non-specialists need access to the English language materials on Japan, and effective ways to search for them using the ordinary resources of American libraries. Fifth, both specialists and non-specialists need access to information resources such as statistical data that can be used with minimal Japanese language skills, but can only be obtained through Japanese language library and information channels. Sixth, as Japanese Studies has differentiated into new fields and research in all aspects of Japanese Studies has become more specialized and sophisticated, Japan specialists and specialists-in-training require access to very different kinds of highly specialized materials depending upon their academic discipline or professional field.

As this enumeration makes clear, the problem is not simply one of maintaining high quality collections of standard Japanese library materials at a small number of well-staffed institutions, but of providing effective search tools and access mechanisms for both Japanese and English language materials, so that users throughout the United States can identify the items they need and obtain them for their own use, with reasonable speed and at reasonable cost. Developments in Japanese Studies over the past decade have broadened the range of both Japanese and English language library and information resources that American Japan specialists need, placing new burdens on libraries to collect unfamiliar types of materials and to make them available to new classes of users.

In addition to the general advances in library and information technology in the United States that have brought nationally accessible online catalogs and bibliographic databases, and the interlibrary loan system that links libraries throughout the country to provide local access to materials in distant collections, the Japanese libraries in the United States and their dedicated staffs have been working together for several years to coordinate collection development and find innovative solutions to mounting access problems for the very specialized materials in their collections.

Growth in the Number and Size of Collections

Previous surveys of Japanese Studies in the United States have routinely documented the size and location of the major Japanese language library collections. Two different size criteria have been used to rank these collections. The first, established by the 1977 CULCON study as part of its categorization of graduate programs, set 25,000 volumes in Japanese as the minimum library size for a full graduate program. By 1995, 28 libraries met that standard, but a few of them fell slightly short of other criteria in our assessment of graduate programs in Chapter Eight. The 1984 Japan Foundation Report noted that the Joint Committee on Japanese Studies regarded 40,000 volumes in Japanese as a necessary minimum for comprehensive research purposes.

Table 10.1. Japanese Language Collection in the United States, by Number of Volumes in Japanese, 1977, 1984, and 1995*

Volumes in Japanese	1977	1984	1995 Academic	1995 Other
1,000 to 19,999	31	33	31	5
20,000 to 39,999	8	9	9	
40,000 and over	12	16	21	2
Total	51	58	61	7

*Figures for 1977 and 1984 taken from 1984 Japan Foundation Report, Table 26, p. 49, which calculated the 1977 figures from numbers provided in the 1977 CULCON Report, Appendix V, Table 33, p. 137. The 1977 figures were originally from collection surveys by Japanese librarians. The 1984 figures were from that study's questionnaire, supplemented by 1975 data for institutions that did not return the questionnaire. For 1995, small collections reported size figures on the questionnaire, but figures for the larger staffed collections were taken from the 1984 Annual Report of the Committee on East Asian Libraries to ensure comparability. We have adapted the practice of the 1984 Japan Foundation Report and included in our count the earlier library data for any institution with a primary or secondary listing in the 1995 directory, but we have omitted two institutions with small Japanese collections reported earlier, for which we have no evidence of current Japanese Studies activity.

Table 10.1 shows the number of schools with Japanese collections of various sizes in each of the three studies. The 1995 study also included collections at non-academic institutions, which are reported separately for purposes of comparability with the earlier figures. The five new academic collections above the 40,000 volume mark in 1995 are at the University of Oregon, University of Texas at Austin, Indiana University, University of Kansas, and the Ohio State University. The two non-academic libraries in that size classification are the Library of Congress and the New York Public Library. In the 20,000 to 39,999 volume category all of the collections are over 25,000 volumes except the University of California, San Diego. That institution and the University of California at Santa Barbara are completely new to the listings in 1995, while Georgetown, Duke, The University of Iowa, and the University of Pittsburgh have moved up from the under 20,000 volumes category. Just as we have found for small academic programs, the library collection reports for small Japanese collections fluctuate from study to study.

Seven of the small academic collections in the 1995 study were not reported in the earlier studies, while two of those reported earlier had neither a regular nor a secondary listing in the 1995 directory. Most of the institutions with small collections reported in earlier studies did not submit library data for the 1995 study, but we have included them in the list on the basis of their earlier reports. If we add back all the academic collections ever reported as having over 1,000 volumes, there are a grand total of 75 Japanese collections at American colleges and universities with 1,000 or more volumes, plus another 4 with more than 500 volumes. That means that less than one in three academic institutions in the United States that currently offers some kind of a Japanese Studies program has any Japanese library collection at all, and less than one in ten has a comprehensive research collection.

While the overall picture looks rather bleak, there is some room for optimism in the growth of the larger collections. In particular, some of the collections that have moved into the comprehensive research category have demonstrated vigorous collection development over the past decade. These are institutions that have made a strong commitment to the development of Japanese Studies through increased staffing, courses, and graduate programs. Some of the institutions in the second tier have embarked upon a similar effort to expand their Japanese Studies programs, and the results should be apparent by the end of this decade.

The Needs and Frustrations of Library Users

The 1995 study tried to go beyond simple collection numbers in order to investigate the problems of the library and information infrastructure in more detail, through survey questions directed at both Japan specialists and the librarians who staff Japanese collections. Some of the questions directed to specialists have already been utilized to identify the wider range of users of library and information resources on Japan, and to clarify their special needs. Here we will explore in more detail how specialists meet their resource needs, how they use information technology, and the fit between user strategies and the practices and priorities of Japanese library collections in the United States.

First we need to put into perspective the role of library materials in the research activities of American Japan specialists. As reported in Chapter Six, just under 70 percent use their institution's libraries and collections, but nearly as many (64.7 percent) use libraries and collections at other institutions. About 70 percent of specialists in the humanities, language and linguistics, social sciences, and the professions rely on their own institution's library collections. Humanists are more likely (78.4 percent) to use the library collections of other institutions for their research than specialists in other fields, but even in other fields about half of the respondents report using materials in other library collections. Thus even though specialists in all fields except the humanities rely heavily on their own collection of data and other non-library materials, they also make heavy use of library collections in their work.

Respondents to the specialist questionnaire were asked whether there is a library collection of research materials on Japan either at the respondent's own institution or readily accessible. Eighty percent of respondents had ready access to a collection of research materials on Japan. Those with access to a collection were then asked about how well this collection meets their research needs for English and Japanese language materials. The results are shown in Table 10.2.

Table 10.2. Satisfaction with Materials on Japan in Library Collection At Own Institution or That Is Readily Accessible to Respondent, by Language of Materials*

Degree of Satisfaction	English Materials		Japanese Materials	
	#	%	#	%
Meets all needs	116	17.2	50	8.8
Meets secondary research needs	128	19.0	79	13.9
Meets most needs	307	45.5	156	27.4
Meets half of needs	100	14.8	96	16.8
Sometimes useful	99	14.7	172	30.2
Completely inadequate	16	2.4	63	11.1
# of Respondents	675		570	

*Respondents were permitted to select up to two responses from a list including reasons they did not use the collection at all, so the number of responses slightly exceeds the number of respondents. Percentages based on number of respondents.

Survey respondents were not particularly satisfied with the library resources available to them in either English or Japanese, but the English collections were relatively more satisfactory. About 45 percent of respondents said the library they use meets most of their needs for English language materials, and another 17 percent said it meets all of their needs. One in five said the English collection meets their needs for secondary materials. The remainder were less satisfied, finding that the library meets half or less of their needs, but very few (2.4 percent) judged it to be completely inadequate.

Respondents were less satisfied with the Japanese materials in the collection they use. Since 11 percent of respondents said they did not use Japanese materials, 1.8 percent said they did not need library materials for their research, and 3 percent said there were no Japanese materials in the library at all, we have calculated satisfaction with the Japanese collection only on the basis of the 570 respondents who do use such materials. Only 8.8 percent of these respondents reported that the Japanese collection they use meets all their needs. About 14 percent felt the collection meets their needs for secondary materials. More than a quarter reported that the Japanese collection they use meets most of their needs, and another 30 percent offered the lukewarm response that the Japanese collection is "sometimes useful." Eleven percent have found the collection to be completely inadequate.

If one in five specialists has no ready access to a library collection with materials on Japan and few of those that do have such access are completely satisfied with what is available, where do Japan specialists obtain the research materials they need? The 1995 survey asked specialists how they obtain the research materials they need if there is no library accessible or the library does not meet their needs completely. This was a multiple response question to which 696 respondents gave an average of 2.6 responses. Over half the respondents said they obtain materials at their own library through interlibrary loan. One in five said they borrow the materials from colleagues at another institution, while one in ten borrow materials from a colleague at their own institution.

A substantial proportion go to other institutions to get the materials they need. While a quarter of the respondents reported that they travel to the nearest collection, smaller percentages travel to the institution where they obtained their doctorate or to a particular institution that has the specialized materials they require. Nearly half the respondents report that they obtain materials directly from Japan, either by traveling to Japan (46.1 percent) or by asking a colleague in Japan to send them (45.0 percent), or by getting a photocopy from the National Diet Library (9.3 percent). The fact that nearly half of the respondents obtain materials by asking a colleague in Japan to send them sheds new light on the importance of maintaining personal network ties with Japanese colleagues, while the extent of borrowing among colleagues in the United States points to the network relations among American Japan specialists.

Despite all these strategies, nearly a quarter of the respondents said they buy all their own materials and do not depend on library collections. A small number of respondents said they do not need to use library materials for their research, or that they cannot do research because they are unable to obtain the materials they need.

Although over half the respondents use interlibrary loan, the level of use to obtain Japanese language materials is not high. Just under half say they do so less than five times a year, and only 4.4 percent use it more than 25 times a year. About sixty percent say their institution pays all interlibrary loan charges, while a third say they have to pay the entire expense with their own funds. Very small numbers either share the costs or get a grant to cover them. Nearly 85 percent use interlibrary loan to obtain books in Japanese. About 40 percent use it to obtain photocopies of recent articles, while just under 20 percent obtained bound volumes of serials, or photocopies of non-circulating materials. Roughly ten percent obtained government publications or photocopies of sections of books.

Those who did not use interlibrary loan to obtain Japanese materials cited a variety of problems. More than a quarter said they needed to browse the collection to find out what they wanted, while another quarter said the materials they needed were not available through interlibrary loan. About twenty percent each said they needed to see the table of contents to determine if there was anything relevant in a publication, that the materials they needed did not circulate and they could not specify the pages without seeing the volume, or that interlibrary loan takes too long. Five percent said they needed small portions of materials from a series of volumes, and the holding library could not provide this level of research service for them. Small percentages of respondents also reported very fundamental barriers to access, such as the high cost of interlibrary loan services, having no access to an institution through which to request interlibrary loan, the local library's inability to handle their requests for Japanese materials, having no access to online catalogs in order to specify the materials they wanted, or not being able to find out where the materials might be available because they did not have access to a reference librarian who could search for Japanese materials.

Respondents were asked to list all the libraries or research collections in the United States or Canada, other than their own institution, that they have visited in the past five years for research purposes, and then to rank the three they have used the most. They produced a combined total of 1,415 reports of libraries that have been visited in the past five years, an overall average of two per respondent. Of these, 683 were ranked 1, 2, or 3 to designate the first, second, or third most-used collection. Although there was some clustering of responses on the major Japanese collections, it was not as concentrated as might have been expected. In fact, 83 different libraries were ranked number one, as the library respondents have used the most. Since some respondents listed a specific library and others listed only the name of the institution, we have combined the reports for all libraries at one institution. We report only those that were ranked 1-3, with no weight given to the ranking.

Harvard University was ranked by the largest number of respondents, 78. Many of these specifically designated the Harvard-Yenching Library, but several other Harvard libraries were also listed. University of California at Berkeley was chosen second most often, with 49 ranked selections. The Library of Congress was third with 45, and Columbia University was fourth with 37 selections,. Several other universities with major Japanese collections (Stanford University, University of California at Los Angeles, University of Michigan, University of Chicago, and Princeton University) each received between 21 and 25 reports as one of the three libraries the respondent had used the most. University of Washington, Yale University, New York Public Library and the University of Hawaii were named between 14 and 16 times. The National Archives, University of Illinois, Indiana University, Duke University, Cornell University and the University of Oregon all received between 7 and 11 rank designations. These are generally the largest Japanese collections in the United States, and nearly all of them have 50,000 or more volumes in Japanese. Duke University's collection is half that size, but it is the largest collection, indeed the only large collection, in the south. The National Archives is not normally listed among Japanese collections, but as the repository for US government documents and diplomatic papers concerning relations with Japan, it is the most important collection for certain fields. This measure does not tell us how frequently the respondent visited the named collection, but it does suggest that the largest collections do indeed serve a broad constituency beyond their own institutions.

Finally, respondents were asked for a global assessment of their satisfaction with the quantity and quality of materials on Japan that they obtain from various sources, using 5 as the highest rating and 1 as the lowest. The mean rating for English materials obtained at the respondent's own institution was 3.5, and for English materials obtained through interlibrary loan was 3.9. Japanese materials obtained from the respondent's own institution were rated 2.6, those obtained through interlibrary loan a 3.3, and Japanese materials found by the respondent at other US collections a 3.7. Japanese materials found at collections in Japan were rated 4.2, the same as Japanese materials the respondent buys in Japan.

These finding highlight the stubborn realities of doing research on Japan in the United States. First, most researchers cannot get all the materials they need at their own institution. While many researchers are able to obtain material through interlibrary loan, others find this an unsatisfactory solution because of the nature of their needs or other barriers to access. Consequently, researchers must rely on their colleagues or travel to other collections to get the material they need.

Second, both the high use of interlibrary loan and the high percentage of researchers who travel to other collections underscore the importance of treating the Japanese library collections in the United States overall as a national resource serving researchers regardless of their location or institutional affiliation. At a certain point, however, this concept runs up against the reality that, except for the Library of Congress, the Japanese collections are staffed and funded largely out of the budgets of individual institutions. The findings reinforce the importance of current cooperative activities through which Japanese librarians are coordinating their activities and stretching scarce resources for collection development, but they also point to the inherent limitations of trying to meet the expanding library needs of the entire United States with woefully inadequate resources.

Third, Japan specialists in the United States remain highly dependent on travel to Japan and direct requests to Japanese colleagues to meet their research resource needs. The great increase in access to Japan over the past decade makes these direct means of obtaining materials much more feasible than they were in the past, not only because researchers can get to Japan to obtain materials themselves, but also because they are better able to maintain the personal contacts with colleagues in Japan that allow them to ask for occasional favors.

The significance of the need to obtain material directly from Japan is underscored by the fourth finding, that a quarter of the respondents rely entirely on their personal collections rather than on library resources. While this may reflect personal preferences and the highly specialized nature of the materials they need, this response undoubtedly also reflects a frustration with the limited availability of library materials.

The Potential for Technological Solutions

Twenty-five years ago, the research tools of a Japan specialist were quite simple. One needed to know how to use a Japanese dictionary in order to read things in Japanese. The entire body of English language works on Japan was modest enough that after a heavy immersion in graduate school, one could keep up with a reasonable amount of effort and a library card. Knowing how to use an English typewriter was useful but not essential, and not even Japanese scholars knew how to use a Japanese typewriter. Today, the tremendous proliferation of information about Japan available in English and Japanese, and the advent of the computer age, have changed all of that. The problem of the information glut is how to find selectively what one needs, but the computer makes many more research tools readily available to help in the search.

We asked our survey respondents about various ways they might use a computer in their work on Japan. Over eighty percent use a computer for English word-processing, and only ten percent said they do not use a computer at all. Ten percent now use a dedicated Japanese word-processor, but 27.9 percent do Japanese word-processing on a general purpose personal computer. The survey was completed just before the advent of the World Wide Web and the explosion of popular interest in the internet, but even at that point, nearly 40 percent of Japan specialists used the computer for e-mail. The same proportion reported using computers to access online library catalogs, through which access is available not only to one's home institution catalog but to a number of major U.S. collections of Japanese materials as well as the national Diet Library collection in Japan.

Over half of our respondents use a computer to store their own research notes and data in English, and about 16 percent use it to store research data in Japanese. Twenty-eight percent use a computer to obtain English online data from American sources, but only one-fourth as many obtain English language data from Japanese sources. The percentage accessing Japanese data by computer is even lower: five percent obtain Japanese data by computer from a U.S. source, and even fewer (3.4 percent) obtain online Japanese data from Japanese sources. About ten percent of the respondents use the computer for quantitative data analysis. Although there is no data from earlier studies to compare with these figures, they constitute a baseline that will undoubtedly rise in the future.

As might be expected, computer usage rates are lowest among retirees, nearly a third of whom do not use a computer at all. Usage rates are generally higher for faculty than for non-faculty, with 85 percent doing English word processing, nearly half using e-mail, and almost a third able to do Japanese word processing on a personal computer. About one in five faculty Japan specialists stores research data on a computer in Japanese. While the high use of e-mail and online library catalogs by faculty reflects the amenities available at American colleges and universities, the fact that faculty are no more likely than non-faculty to use online databases in either Japanese or English, from either US or Japanese sources, points to the relative inaccessibility of these resources. The data resources certainly exist, but Japan specialists either do not know about them, cannot get access to them, or find the costs prohibitive. We will explore these possibilities in more detail below.

Some of these computer tools are obviously only relevant for those with the language skills to use them, as shown in Table 10.3. Of those Japan specialists with Japanese language ability suitable for scholarly use, 41.1 percent do Japanese word-processing on a personal computer and nearly a quarter store Japanese research data on computer, but still only 3.9 percent obtain Japanese online data from Japanese sources, and 5.9 percent obtain Japanese data from U.S. sources.

This question also offers another clue to the divergent research methods of Japan specialists with varying degrees of language skill. While about ten percent of Japan specialists with limited or full Japanese language capabilities use the computer for quantitative data analysis, the percentage is double that among Japan specialists who do not know Japanese. Surprisingly, some computer uses that do not require Japanese language skills also vary with the user's degree of language competence. Those with no Japanese language skills are less likely to use a computer for English word-processing, e-mail, access to online library catalogs, or to store English research data, and more likely not to use a computer at all.

Table 10.3. Japan Specialists' Use of Computers, by Japanese Language Ability

Computer Use	No Japanese	Not Scholarly	Scholarly Use	Total
Do not use computer	22.2	10.8	6.2	9.0
English word-processing	70.8	83.2	82.6	81.9
Japanese on dedicated word processor	0.0	3.8	15.3	10.3
Japanese word-processing	0.0	12.4	41.1	28.5
E-mail communication	26.4	36.8	42.5	39.4
English data, US source	34.7	28.6	28.3	28.9
English data, Japanese source	5.6	11.1	6.6	8.0
Japanese data, US source	0.0	5.4	5.9	5.3
Japanese data, Japanese source	1.4	3.2	3.9	3.5
Online library catalogs	26.4	37.5	41.3	38.9
Quantitative data analysis	20.8	10.2	9.6	10.6
Research data, English	43.1	57.5	59.3	57.4
Research data, Japanese	1.4	7.3	23.0	16.1
N of Respondents	72	315	562	949

In a separate question, respondents were asked more specifically about their use of computerized research aids for their research on Japan. This question has a somewhat lower response rate of 616, but seems to have had responses from those most likely to use new technology. Two-thirds said they use the online catalog of their own library, and more than a quarter use the online catalogs of other libraries. Only 7 percent said online catalogs were available but they did not use them, nearly 10 percent said they did not know how to use online library catalogs, and 5 percent said such resources were not accessible to them through their institution. About one in eight respondents had used the RLIN catalog and one in seven had used the OCLC catalog, both of which are national union cataloguing systems that provide listings of Japanese materials with full Japanese characters. These systems are somewhat more difficult to use, which suggests that the respondents had both Japanese language skills and some training in the use of these systems. However, the number is far too large for them all to be librarians. Nearly one in eight respondents had used citation indexes. Very small numbers reported the use of specific online or CD-ROM bibliographic databases and dictionaries, full text databases, or document delivery services. Almost 20 percent of the respondents said they did not know how to use online databases.

In another question, respondents were asked if they had ever used Japanese databases for their research on Japan. Ten percent had used Japanese databases in Japan, and almost 10 percent had used them in the United States. Half said they had not done so, but were interested. Almost a quarter said they had not, and were not interested in doing so. Fifteen percent said no, because they had no access, while 5 percent said they were deterred by the cost.

A follow-up question asked for the names of specific Japanese databases that respondents had either used in the past or wanted to use. By far the most frequently cited were the Nikkei economics and current events databases. The NACSIS bibliographic databases were also mentioned by about a dozen respondents. Several people also reported having used the Diet Library serials database, and smaller numbers mentioned either other library databases in Japan or general databases available to online service subscribers in the United States. In general, the listings reflected about an even split between databases that contain economic and current events information of relevance to social scientists and those in the professions, and bibliographic databases that facilitate the identification and location of library materials in special collections.

Although the number of Japan specialists who currently use or are eager to use such tools is small, both of these aspects of information technology are certain to become more important to researchers in Japanese Studies in the second half of the 1990s. Providing inexpensive, ready access to such standard Japanese information resources as the Nikkei and NACSIS databases and the Diet Library databases through normal online channels in the United States would vastly improve the research tools available to Japan specialists and their students, and is the sort of technological solution that could be centrally implemented by a funder for general national use. It is particularly attractive because it circumvents some of the problems of local institutional support and puts the information resources directly in the hands of the individual specialist no matter where he or she is located.

The Librarian's Perspective

The 1995 survey included a separate module sent directly to librarians that asked about the nature of their Japanese collection, its accessibility to outside users, their collection priorities, and the kinds of support they offer users. Much of the basic information concerning collection size, special strengths of collections, and accessibility is reported individually in the library entries in the Volume II of the *Directory of Japan Specialists and Japanese Studies Institutions in the United States and Canada*. We concentrate here on survey questions that are particularly relevant to the issues raised by Japan specialists' needs for library and information resources.

Sixty-two librarians responded to at least some parts of the survey, but not all of them are Japanese Studies librarians who staff a Japanese collection. Some are general librarians whose collections include a relatively small amount of Japanese material, and they rely on students and faculty with Japanese language skills to identify, order, and catalog them. Their responses are important for helping us understand the situation of Japan specialists whose institutions do not have a staffed Japanese collection.

In general, librarians thought that acquisitions, staffing, and infrastructure support had remained about the same over the past five years, as shown in Table 10.4. Less than a third reported increases in acquisitions and infrastructure support, and only 16 percent had seen an increase in staffing. More than one in five reported a decrease in acquisitions and staff budgets, but very few reported decreases in infrastructure support.

Table 10.4. Librarians' Perception of Changes in Library Support in Past Five Years

Type of Support	Decreased %	About Same %	Increased %	Total N #
Acquisitions support	21.1	47.4	31.6	57
Staffing support	23.6	60.0	16.4	55
Infrastructure support	3.6	66.1	30.4	56

These figures are remarkable in light of the increases in virtually every aspect of Japanese Studies that we have documented in previous chapters. Library support clearly has not kept pace with the growth in students, faculty, programs, and publications. Moreover, during this same period the cost of obtaining Japanese language library materials from Japan has nearly tripled due to the sharp de facto devaluation of the US dollar plus some modest inflation in the actual yen price of the materials. Thus libraries are able to buy much less with the same dollars, even as they face rising demand from faculty and students. The frustrations of library patrons are well-grounded in fact.

How do librarians set priorities for these very limited funds? Respondents were asked what they do when a user wants material the library does not have, the counterpart of our earlier question asking researchers what they did when the library did not have what they needed. This is a multiple response question with an average of 4.3 responses to the seven alternatives offered. The vast majority of the librarians (87.3 percent) said they would encourage the patron to use interlibrary loan to get the material, and nearly as many (85.5 percent) said they would check the RLIN or OCLC online catalogs (the two major national union cataloguing systems for Japanese language materials that give listings with Japanese characters) to see what library has the material. Two-thirds reported that they would check other university online catalogs to see who might have the material, since several of the large Japanese collections now have their catalogs online and accessible through the internet.

Three-quarters said they would arrange to purchase the material. About half said they would contact other librarians to try to get the item, and nearly half would encourage the patron to contact another Japanese librarian directly. Less than one in five said they would contact colleagues in Japan to obtain the materials, an option often chosen by Japan specialists themselves.

The responses varied with the size of the Japanese collection. The 28 respondents from collections with 25,000 or more Japanese books, the entry level for a full graduate program, were nearly universal in turning to RLIN or OCLC to check what institutions have materials, and they were also likely to contact other librarians in pursuit of material. Librarians at collections with less than 10,000 Japanese books were far less likely to check either the two national Japanese catalogs or the online catalogs of major universities. While they would not normally have access to the two Japanese cataloguing systems, which are fairly expensive and specialized services, they would have free access to university online catalogs. All except the librarians with less than a thousand items in Japanese, however, encourage interlibrary loan requests and try to arrange for the purchase of the materials.

Thus the effects of not being at an institution with a large Japanese collection cumulate, making it more and more difficult to obtain Japanese language materials. The small collection is not staffed by a Japan specialist librarian with both personal network ties and access to Japanese language online resources through dedicated terminals. These non-specialist librarians are also less likely to check online catalogs of other institutions, or to arrange to buy the material. They even are less willing to courage the patron to use interlibrary loan, perhaps, as some specialist respondents complained, because they are unable to find out where the materials are located. These findings add weight to the responses of discouraged library patrons who said they could not get material because they did not have access to a reference librarian who could help them search for materials.

Librarians also were asked to rank ten possible collection development priorities on a scale of 1 (high) to 5 (low). The mean ranks by collection size are shown in Table 10.5. Meeting faculty requests was the highest general priority, followed closely by purchasing basic reference materials for general use. Meeting graduate student needs and maintaining serials and standing orders were tied, followed by meeting undergraduate needs and maintaining special strengths of the collections. Building new special strengths was tied with fulfilling a cooperative collection plan. At the bottom of the list were meeting community needs for Japanese reading materials and acquiring rare materials, both luxuries these collections cannot afford.

The responses varied with collection size. The research level collections placed much higher priority on meeting faculty research needs, acquiring basic reference materials for general use, meeting graduate student needs, and maintaining serials and standing orders. Those with smaller Japanese collections placed relatively higher priority on meeting the needs of undergraduates, and some wrote in comments indicating that there were no graduate students using their collections. The smaller collections rated fulfilling cooperative collection plans at the bottom of the list, because they do not participate in these activities, which have been devised to stretch the acquisitions budgets of the large Japanese collections that collectively must meet the national need for Japanese language resources.

While there are no major surprises here, it is clear that the librarians who manage Japanese collections are hard-pressed to meet the wide range of conflicting collection development demands with their overstretched budgets. Although they say that their highest priority is meeting faculty research needs, they also must purchase general reference materials and maintain serials and standing orders, which may also be defined as serving both faculty and graduate students' research needs at the most fundamental level.

The responses to the multiple response question about what they do when their library does not have something a patron needs tell a slightly different story. Japanese collections cannot simply buy whatever faculty members need; they have to encourage their patrons to make the best use of shared, scarce resources, primarily through the use of interlibrary loan, but also through direct requests to other librarians for photocopies of materials. In this context, the Japanese librarian's function as a reference librarian who has the tools, expertise, and personal networks to locate the needed material becomes critical. It is this personalized service to which Japan specialists at smaller institutions lack direct access.

Table 10.5. Mean Acquisition Priorities of Librarians Purchasing Japanese Library
        Materials in Rank Order, by Size of Collection

Acquisition Priority	Smaller Collections	Larger Collections	All Collections	Total N
Meet faculty research needs	1.8	1.1	1.5	51
Basic references for gen'l use	1.9	1.4	1.6	52
Meet graduate student needs	2.8	1.9	2.2	43
Maintain serials, stand. orders	2.8	1.8	2.2	42
Meet undergraduate needs	2.1	2.7	2.4	49
Maintain special strengths	3.3	2.0	2.5	44
Build new special strengths	4.1	3.4	3.7	40
Fulfill cooperative plan	4.8	3.0	3.7	36
Meet community needs	3.9	4.5	4.2	47
Acquire rare materials	4.5	4.4	4.4	42

The earlier findings concerning the extent to which Japan specialists return to the collection of their doctoral institution, or travel to other collections, take on additional significance in this light. Those libraries not only have more books; they also have reference librarians to help Japan specialists find what they need, and developing and maintaining a personal relationship with a knowledgeable reference librarian may be as important as simply browsing the stacks. This, too, suggests that sending the researcher to the books may often have a larger payoff than sending the books to the user. In reality, researchers use a combination of the two strategies, since one brief trip to a major library to search and browse can become the foundation for a long series of interlibrary loan requests and for personal queries about problems in the future.

In this sense Japanese librarians, in addition to having their own professional networks and cooperative relationships, are also part of the personal networks of the Japan specialists who use their services. The high institutional concentration of graduate training in Japanese Studies is unquestionably a function of the limited number of research-level Japanese library collections in the United States, but that same concentration creates large personal networks between the librarians who staff the collections and whole generations of Japan specialists who have trained at these institutions.

Because of disciplinary variations in the nature of specialists' dependence on library materials, these networks tend to be strongest among those in the humanities. The latent problem here is that librarians who see less of social scientists may generalize from the specialized needs of scholars in the humanities, and misconstrue the research needs of social scientists and those in the professions. These latter researchers may visit the Japanese collections less, but they are equally dependent upon them for certain basic resource needs. Because of the quite different nature of their research and the way they use research materials, it is much harder for social scientists to specify exactly what books they need, since they are not looking for particular classic titles, the works of particular authors, or scholarly commentary on particular subjects.

Social scientists are much more likely to be looking either for material that is presented as collected data and research results, or for material that can be used or treated as primary data for the researcher's own analysis. Outside of certain standard kinds of government reports and statistical compilations, such material does not come packaged in titles that the researcher knows in advance, or even by specific topics or subjects that can be clearly defined. Hence the communication between social scientists and Japanese librarians is likely to be frustrating for both parties unless the librarian also has social science training and understands what kinds of material the researcher needs and how he or she might use them.

This discussion may help to clarify the earlier findings that social scientists use the library less, by suggesting that they are less likely to find what they want there, and thus more likely to conclude that they have to go to Japan and get it themselves, either by collecting their own data directly, or by finding the kinds of material they need at libraries and bookstores in Japan. It may well be that it is far more efficient and natural for most social scientists to collect their own research materials and not expect to find them in Japanese collections in the United States. Yet Japan specialists and graduate students in the social sciences and the professions do not have greater independent resources for collecting data and buying books in Japan. They should be able to depend upon the library collections in the United States for some basic part of their research needs, even if they still need to collect data in Japan. Meeting the needs of social scientists will require greater communications efforts on both sides, at a time when there are more and more competing demands on scarce library dollars as well as on the librarian's time.

Some of the new solutions to these chronic problems will come from greater use of new information technologies. At the time of our survey, access to Japan-related databases was quite scarce. The vast majority of Japan specialists reported that they use computers, but most did so for word-processing and data storage, although over half were on e-mail and used online library catalogs. Many specialists reported an interest in exploring Japanese databases, but little opportunity to learn how or gain access. Much of that has changed in the past two years, even though there are still some barriers to access to Japanese language databases.

Since librarians are now on the forefront of much information technology, the distance barriers for Japan specialists at small institutions may be bridged by a combination of online catalog access, e-mail communication with reference librarians at major Japanese collections, and access to downloadable full-text databases to supplement the use of photocopies and faxes. Even with the free internet access that most academics enjoy, there are still a variety of costs at the provider's end, ranging from the reference librarian's time to the cost of faxes and photocopies, let alone the expense of setting up and maintaining table of contents or full-text database services for Japanese language materials. And in a world where information about Japan has economic value, tension will inevitably arise over whether to provide these services free or at cost in the academic model, or to undertake them as profit-making enterprises that will serve corporate needs but may be priced beyond the reach of academic institutions, students, and faculty.

It is already the case that a great deal of proprietary, time-sensitive material about Japan is readily available to anyone who can pay for the services. The Nikkei databases fall into this category. Part of the normalization of Japanese Studies involves just this sort of trade-off, in which Japanese information services are in sufficient demand to attract investors and clients, and to provide good jobs for trained Japan specialists. Some of that information is tailored to the needs of very specific clients, who pay specifically to obtain time-sensitive material that is not readily available to others. Academics cannot produce information at that speed, and may have trouble with the very idea of proprietary information, but they often can make use of it for research purposes even after it has lost its economic and political value.

Technology will not solve all the problems of access to research materials in Japan and the United States, but it can change the cost and time factors in ways that permit creative new approaches to old problems. The strategies Japan specialists currently use to solve their research problems suggest that it may be more efficient and even cost effective to bring the person to the materials rather than try to deliver the materials to the person. Yet what is efficient and cost effective for the individual may not be as effective in the long-run for the maintenance and development of a critical national resource that has to meet the needs of larger and larger number of users.

Librarians as a Resource

The survey results have revealed the central role of Japan specialist librarians in the infrastructure of Japanese Studies in the United States. In recent years a number of advertised positions for Japan specialist librarians at academic institutions have remained unfilled, prompting considerable concern about the future of staffing for Japanese library collections. Our survey sample included 55 Japan specialist librarians, three-quarters of whom are employed at academic institutions. The sample consists of persons who are already working as Japan specialist librarians, most of whom are probably not in the job market. Analysis of the characteristics of this small sample offers some clues to the nature of the current and future staffing problem, and what can be done about it.

Among the 51 librarians for whom age was reported or could be estimated, the age distribution was about the same as that of the entire US sample, with 43.2 percent aged 55 or older and 25.5 percent under 45. A few have already retired. Two-thirds of the sample of Japan specialist librarians were born outside the United States. Over half were born in Japan, with smaller numbers from China (4), Taiwan (2), Korean (1) and the Netherlands(1).

While the age distribution does not suggest a complete absence of younger persons going into the field, part of the concern is that library positions in the United States are unlikely to attract native speakers and readers of Japanese as they did in earlier decades. On the other hand, the pool of American Japan specialists with strong Japanese language skills is now large enough to meet US needs, if training and professional opportunities can be made sufficiently attractive to recruit them into the field. Our findings suggest that there may be two pools of potential Japan specialist librarians: those currently in doctoral programs or holding a doctorate in a Japan-related field who want an alternative to employment as academic faculty; and students with BA and MA-level training in Japanese Studies who are looking for career opportunities related to Japan.

The question, then, is what professional credentials potential Japan specialist librarians will need, and how difficult it will be to obtain them. Just half of the librarians in our sample hold a degree in library science, but 18 percent have earned a doctorate. Most of those with doctorates do not have a library science degree, suggesting that for some positions it may serve as an alternative professional credential. However, the absence of either a PhD or a library science degree would preclude professional level employment in most academic libraries. The proportion of librarians now working outside of academia, about the same as that for Japan specialists as a whole, suggests that there is also likely to be growing private sector demand for persons trained in library and information science who have expertise in working with Japanese materials.

At least three or four of the academic institutions with full graduate programs in Japanese Studies and research-level Japanese library collections also offer degrees in library science, and thus have the capacity to offer the necessary academic and practical training for this profession. The missing element seems to be sufficient information and incentives to attract potential candidates into this field of Japanese Studies. One possible model would be the special fellowship programs of the 1980s that successfully recruited and trained Japan specialists for professional careers in law, business, and economics.

ANCILLARY PROGRAMS AND SERVICES

Japanese Studies programs do more than offer courses and facilitate the research of individuals. They organize and run ancillary programs of various types for their own students and faculty as well as for external constituencies, and maintain relationships with other institutions. They also engage in fundraising and grant-seeking to support all of these activities. In this section we report briefly on some of these ancillary programs and services. It should also be noted that these activities are one reason for the presence of additional non-teaching staff positions, particularly at institutions with large Japanese Studies programs.

Study Abroad Programs

No matter how well-developed and sophisticated Japanese language programs in the United States become, they cannot duplicate the impact of full immersion in the language and culture of Japan that extended study and residence in Japan provides. Although there are still many barriers to study abroad in Japan, some of which are currently being addressed in other studies and initiatives and are beyond the scope of this report, we can present some indication of the current scope of study abroad opportunities from our institutional survey.

In general, study abroad programs appear to be widely available and well utilized. Three-quarters of institutions responding to the survey question reported that they offer their own study abroad program or participate in a consortium that does so. The 105 institutions reported a total of 169 study abroad programs to which they send students, but some institutions listed several programs, and many programs were listed by more than one institution. Kansai Gaidai was named by twelve institutions, and various programs at Waseda University were named by seven institutions. The Inter-University Center for Japanese Language Studies in Yokohama and the Kyoto Center for Japanese Studies, both administered through Stanford University, and Nanzan University were each named by six institutions. The Associated Kyoto Program and Sophia University were each named by four institutions, while Keio

University and International Christian University were named by three. For several of these named programs, such as the Inter-University Center, the survey tally is considerably lower than the number of institutions that actually have consortial relationships with the program, suggesting that these figures seriously undercount the real extent of current participation in study abroad programs in Japan.

The overwhelming majority of study abroad programs are offered for academic credit. Half were academic-year programs and a quarter were one-semester programs. The remainder were offered either for an academic quarter (10 percent) or for less than twelve weeks (14 percent). Survey respondents reported sending a total of 753 students from their own institutions to study abroad programs during the 1992–93 academic year. They also reported the participation of 555 students from other institutions in programs they administer, but this number contains an unknown amount of overlap with the first figure and thus cannot be evaluated.

The opportunities for study abroad in Japan fall into several categories: "bubble" programs in Japan administered by American academic programs with their own staff and curriculum; exchange relationships through which students from an American university and a Japanese university pay tuition at their home institution but attend the other institution on a reciprocal basis; Japanese institutions with special programs for foreign students to which American students apply directly; and Japanese branch campuses of American institutions. All four types of study abroad programs were reported, but their relative representation cannot be estimated from these data.

What is perhaps most impressive about the current array of study abroad options is the fact that they are by no means limited to institutions that have strong on-campus Japanese Studies programs or to students with career goals that involve the study of Japan. In fact, many institutions with virtually no Japanese Studies program available on campus reported arrangements through which their students can study in Japan. Many of these are reciprocal exchange relationships with particular institutions, while others involve participation in consortial arrangements. The proliferation of such arrangements, and their availability at a wide range of academic institutions even without on-campus Japanese Studies programs, certainly attests to the normalization of the study of Japan as an educational experience that is not necessarily connected to formal specialization in Japanese Studies.

At the same time, the separation of many of these study abroad programs from on-campus Japanese Studies programs also attests to their limited academic goals in terms of developing Japanese language skills and expertise on Japan. They are largely intended as a general cultural exposure for students without prior international experience, and not as an integral part of building higher levels of proficiency in Japanese language or of preparing future Japan specialists. However, they also serve as a recruiting field for students who decide as a result of their experience in Japan to study the language more seriously and perhaps to incorporate further study of Japan into their career plans. A much smaller number of programs, especially the ones specifically identified above, have been developed with more rigorous language training and pre-professional goals in mind. Although those programs collectively can accommodate a relatively small number of students each year, they have had a major impact on the upgrading of students' Japanese language skills, and on the professional development of Japan specialists in the United States.

The institutions participating in the survey also reported a broad array of relationships that they maintain with other institutions. Forty-one said they participate in consortia for activities in the United States, and 50 for activities in Japan. An additional 118 institutions reported formal ties with an institution (sometimes several) in Japan. Many of these exchange relationships in Japan have been aggressively initiated by the Japanese partner during the past decade as part of the Japanese government's policy of internationalization, and the Japanese academic institution's perception of the benefits to its own students of having such an association. In general the survey reports suggest that the American institutions also see some benefit, and that some of the relationships are quite active and reciprocal.

Outreach Services

In addition to any special programs they may provide for the benefit of their own students and alumni, institutions with well-developed Japanese Studies programs also provide a variety of outreach services to external constituencies in their own communities and occasionally on a wider scale. Institutions were asked about the services they provide to primary and secondary schools, business, the media, and nonprofit groups and the public, replicating a question asked in 1984 with the addition of one new type of service, translation and interpretation. The results are difficult to interpret and especially to compare, because respondents report every type of service separately for every type of user. Hence any summary to some extent inflates the responses of any service provided to more than one category of user, even though some categories apply to specific categories of users and others do not.

Following the practice of the 1984 survey, we have presented the absolute number of institutions reporting each type of service for each type of user, rather than the percentage distribution. The comparative results are shown in Table 10.6. A total of 94 academic and two non-academic institutions reported an average of 7.25 types of service in the 1995 survey. Some institutions reported services provided by several different units associated with Japanese Studies, but here we have combined them in the institutional count. The most common form of service provided to primary and secondary schools is training teachers to teach about Japan, which was reported by 40 percent of the institutions. A quarter of them provide language instruction to primary and secondary institutions, and produce educational materials on Japan, or maintain audio-visual resource centers.

Table 10.6. Number of Institutions Providing Various Types of Services Concerning Japan, by Type of User, 1984 and 1995*

Service	Schools	Business	Media	Public
1984 Survey				
Teacher training	37	7	5	10
Educational materials	26	15	7	12
Classes for better students	11	4	3	5
Consulting	23	43	27	36
Language instruction	31	35	16	55
Training, orientation courses	26	37	18	32
Public affairs programs	12	23	18	47
Press releases	5	8	14	11
TV productions	4	9	8	26
Film series	9	9	8	26
Commissioned research	4	11	2	10
Other	3	2	0	4
1995 Survey				
Teacher training	37	5	2	9
Educational materials	24	12	8	12
Classes for better students	10	5	3	5
Consulting	23	38	19	29
Language instruction	24	27	6	16
Training, orientation courses	17	29	4	18
Public affairs programs	19	21	16	28
Press releases	6	7	17	9
TV productions	5	10	9	9
Film series	7	2	2	6
Commissioned research	3	10	3	8
Translation, interpretation	9	18	9	15
Audio-visual resource center	25	11	5	17
Other	2	4	1	1

*1984 figures from 1984 Japan Foundation Report, Table 25, p. 48.

The most common service for business users is consulting, reported by 40 percent of institutions. Thirty percent of the institutions provide training or orientation courses for business, and a slightly smaller percentage offer language instruction for business. About 16–20 percent of institutions offer public affairs programs, or translation and interpretation services to business. The media are less frequently the clients for services, but about 20 percent of institutions provide consulting for mass media, and a slightly smaller percentage of institutions provide press releases or offer public affairs programs for students.

The most common service provided to nonprofit organizations or the general public are consulting and public affairs programs, each offered at about 30 percent of institutions. About 15–18 percent of institutions offer training or orientation courses, language instruction, audio-visual resources or translation and interpretation services to the general public.

There was a decrease from 1984 in the absolute number of institutions reporting that they do consulting, or offer language instruction, training and orientation courses, and public affairs programs. Most other categories remained at about the same level as in 1984. However, we cannot evaluate the percentage decrease because we do not know the number of institutions that reported service data in 1984. From comparison with the data reported in institutional directory entries and enumerated below, it is also apparent that this listing from survey responses seriously undercounts the number of institutions offering some types of services and programs. Although we cannot be very confident of these numbers, the relative decrease in the number of academic institutions that report the provision of certain kinds of services may be due to the increased commercial availability of these same services, as indicated by the non-academic employment of many Japan specialists in precisely these areas.

Providing certain kinds of outreach services, especially to primary and secondary schools, has long been a requirement for institutions that receive federal funding from the US Department of Education as designated National Resource Centers for East Asia. The number of such centers has ranged from roughly 12 to 15 since the early 1980s, but the pool of institutions competing for the National Resource Center grants for East Asia has grown during the same period from about 16 to 25, more or less paralleling the growth in the number of institutions that have full graduate programs in Japanese Studies, since the same grants also offer fellowship support for graduate students. For most categories the number of institutions reporting that they provide the kinds of outreach services recognized in the National Resource Center grant competition falls within this range. The only exception is the category of teacher-training, which may also be reported by undergraduate institutions with large degree programs in education.

In addition to these services, 35 institutions (20 percent of those responding) reported that they had organized a local or regional special seminar on Japan in the previous year, and 54 (31.4 percent) reported organizing and hosting a one-time event related to Japan.

The national infrastructure for Japanese Studies also includes a number of museums, freestanding libraries, research institutes, and nonprofit organizations with special resources and professional Japan specialist staff. Many academic institutions maintain museum collections or research institutes with similar focus on Japan, so the line between academic and non-academic institutions blurs at this point. Collectively, these institutions offer an impressive range of special programs and services, which are indexed by institution in Volume III of the *Directory of Japan Specialists and Japanese Studies Institutions*. To enumerate briefly some of those not covered already in this discussion of special services, 31 institutions offer Japanese performing arts programs, 38 provide a faculty research seminar, 71 run a film series, 66 offer a lecture series, 25 present a summer institute for teachers, 31 a summer language institute, and 8 produce films on Japan. Their publications programs are also extensive. Forty-six publish a newsletter, 16 publish a journal, 29 an occasional paper series, 22 publish research reports, 15 a monograph series, and 31 do some other form of publication. Given this impressive array of special activities and services, it is no wonder that Japan specialists complain about a lack of time for their own research.

FUNDRAISING, FELLOWSHIPS, AND FUNDING PRIORITIES

Many of the special activities that Japanese Studies institutions provide require special funding beyond the normal institutional budget, which means that Japanese Studies program and library staff must often engage in fundraising and grantsmanship either to support their own projects or as part of their institutional responsibilities. During the past decade there was also a great surge of interest in seeking institutional donations from Japanese sources, an activity that now appears to have run its course.

Survey respondents were asked whether they had been expected to participate in such fundraising activities from various sources, other than for their own research needs. Sixty percent said they had not been expected to do fundraising at all. More than a quarter were expected to seek funding from US agencies and foundations that support research and training, and about the same percentage were expected to seek funding from similar agencies and foundations in Japan. About twenty percent were expected to fundraise from Japanese corporations in the United States, or from Japanese corporate sources in Japan. Nine percent had been expected to seek funding from Japanese sources, but not for Japanese Studies purposes.

The institutional survey attempted to obtain more specific information about major gifts and grants that had been obtained in recent years from these various sources. Over a hundred institutions reported the receipt of a major gift or grant to support Japanese Studies since 1980. Twenty-six institutions also reported major gifts from Japanese sources that were not intended for support of Japanese Studies. Many of these gifts were from Japanese corporate sources, rather than from agencies and foundations that routinely support research and training.

Table 10.7. Japan Specialists' Perceptions of Funding Levels in Japanese Studies, 1984 and 1995*

Funding Level	*1984 %*	*1995 %*
Less plentiful	44	26.0
No change	16	14.6
More plentiful	17	34.9
Not sure	24	24.5
Total	100	100.0
# of Respondents	831	840

*1984 data from 1984 Japan Foundation Report, Table 27, p. 52.

Appreciation for this flow of support is clearly reflected in Japan specialists' perception of the funding situation. About a third of Japan specialists thought funding for Japanese Studies had become more plentiful in recent years, a quarter thought it had become less plentiful, a quarter were not sure, and the rest thought there had been no change. That in itself was a major change from perceptions in 1984, when, as shown in Table 10.7, respondents were much more pessimistic about funding for Japanese Studies.

Grants and Fellowships

These measures were intended to assess institutional funding for Japanese Studies. We also have a rather rough measure for evaluating how successful Japan specialists have been in obtaining fellowship and grant support for their own research. Both the finding that high proportions of researchers collect their own data in Japan and the finding that half of the researchers obtain library materials or buy text materials in Japan underscore the importance to Japan specialists of being able to go to Japan for research purposes. In Chapter Five we observed that Japan has become substantially more accessible in the past decade, and that specialists now go to Japan rather frequently. We also discovered that half the researchers had used their own funds for their last trip to Japan.

The need to travel to Japan for research purposes, plus the need for researchers to travel within the United States to obtain research materials from other library collections both point to the need for research support. While the survey did not ask about fellowships, for their directory entries Japan specialists were asked to report their fellowships and grants and the source of the funds. The 1,552 Japan specialists in the 1995 directory sample reported a total of 2,969 fellowships, grants, and awards, or an average of 1.9 per person. Since most of these are academic research grants and fellowships, the rate is much higher among academics (2,553 or 2.3 per person) than non-academics (416 or 1.1 per person).

Table 10.8. Major Sources of Fellowships, Grants, and Awards Reported by Japan Specialists

Source	Number	Percent
Fulbright	391	13.2
Japan Foundation	371	12.5
Social Science Research Council	274	9.2
National Endowment for the Humanities	259	8.7
Ford Foundation	125	4.2
USDOE & DOE Fulbright	106	3.6
National Science Foundation	106	3.6
American Council of Learned Societies	105	3.5
Japan-US Friendship Commission	72	2.4
Japan Society for the Promotion of Science	48	1.6
Northeast Asia Council, Association for Asian Studies	47	1.6
Guggenheim Foundation	46	1.5
Rockefeller Foundation	43	1.4
Japanese Ministry of Education (Monbusho)	34	1.1
Subtotal	2,027	(63.3)
Other	942	31.7
Total	2,969	100.0

Table 10.8 shows the fourteen granting agencies that were each responsible for one percent or more of the awards. Collectively these fourteen grantors accounted for two-thirds of the total reported. Since the data were collected for directory entries and respondents were asked to list all fellowships, grants, and awards they had received, not all of those listed were necessarily for work related to Japan, let alone for work conducted in Japan. It is therefore not possible to compare this listing directly with the findings reported in Chapter Five about the shift in sources of funding for travel to Japan. Most of the listed funding agencies, however, do fund research in and on Japan, or have in the past.

Just over a third of the awards were made by US government agencies, and 27.7 percent by private US foundations. Japanese government agencies provided the funding for 14.1 percent of the awards, and private Japanese foundations were the source for 3.8 percent. The remainder were provided by local institutional sources and other funders that could not be further identified. Some of those awards also may be traceable to US or Japanese government or private sources, but we did not have sufficient information for a reliable determination.

These figures and percentages refer only to the number of awards reported. We have no information on their monetary value. We also could not produce a reliable assessment of how the number of awards has changed over time. The 1989 directory questionnaire asked for the same information on grants and fellowships, but did not ask for the year of the award. We included the year in the 1995 questionnaire, and thus we can track awards by year from about 1988 with some certainty. Since not everyone chose to update the directory information they had provided earlier, however, we are missing the year for a substantial proportion of the reported awards. Although the award data for which the year is available appears to increase over time, as one would expect from the growing number of Japan specialists, given the shortcomings of the data we are reluctant to offer it as a reliable measure.

Funding Priorities

In both the 1984 and 1995 surveys, Japan specialists were asked to rank priorities of a number of different purposes to which funding in Japanese Studies could be directed, but the method of ranking and the list of purposes differed somewhat. The 1984 survey asked respondents to assign first, second, or third priority to a list of seven items. The 1995 study offered these seven items plus three more, and asked respondents to rank them from one (highest) to ten (lowest). Despite a number of write-in complaints about having to make such hard choices, they did so. Table 10.9 presents the 1995 results with rank order for academics, non-academics, and the total sample. To make the 1984 data comparable we have presented just the rank order based on the weighted sum of priorities assigned. The list is presented in the order of the 1995 priorities.

Table 10.9. Japan Specialists' Funding Priorities, 1984 and 1995, in 1995 Rank Order*

Purpose	1984	1995 Academics	1995 Non-Academics	1995 Total Sample
Language Study in Japan, Study Abroad	--	1	1	1
Graduate Student Support for Dissertation Research	2	2	3	2
Support for Additional Faculty Positions	1	3	3	3
Graduate training, prior to dissertation	--	4	2	4
Library and museum acquisitions	5	5	5	5
Expanding Japanese Studies to small colleges	--	7	6	6
Research grants for established scholars	3	6	10	7
Postdoctoral fellowships for younger scholars without jobs	4	8	9	8
Support for conferences and seminars	6	9	7	9
Outreach and Public Affairs programs	7	10	8	10

*1984 ranks based on 1984 Japan Foundation Report, Table 29, p. 54.

Funding priorities have changed rather dramatically since 1984. The top priority in 1995, for both academics and non-academics, is support of language study in Japan and study abroad opportunities, a choice not offered in 1984. This priority can be read both as general support for more study abroad opportunities that offer solid language training in Japan, and as a strong vote for continued support of the Inter-University Center for Japanese Language Studies in Yokohama, the premier but very expensive institution providing professional-level language training in Japan for American Japan specialists.

The second priority overall is support for dissertation research, although non-academics ranked it slightly lower. Faculty positions in Japanese Studies ranked third, a drop from first priority in 1984. Fourth was graduate training at the pre-dissertation level, which was ranked even higher by non-academics. Library and museum acquisitions ranked fifth, and expansion of Japanese Studies to small colleges sixth. Research grants to established scholars, postdoctoral fellowships for younger scholars without permanent positions, support for conferences and seminars, and outreach and public affairs programs rounded out the bottom of the priority list.

It is important to remember that this is an overall priority ranking based on a forced choice, and it does not necessarily mean that Japan specialists would begrudge any specific program that funds one of the lower ranked items. The significance of the ranking lies in the priorities at the top of the list, particularly the overall priority given to student support, which garnered three of the top four priority positions. This set of priorities suggests that Japan specialists feel relatively secure about their own economic position and professional opportunities, and are looking forward to the future of the field in the 21st century. The top priorities also reflect a recognition of the many years of rigorous training now demanded of Japan specialists, and the need for strategic forms of support at different stages of the student's development: strong language training in Japan, support for the early part of graduate training to ensure that the commitment to language and area studies remains firm in the face of disciplinary pressures, and finally dissertation support for original research in Japan.

Table 10.10. Preference for Funding Allocation Between Larger and Smaller Institutions, 1984 and 1995*

Allocation of Funds	1984 %	1995 Smaller %	1995 Larger %	1995 Total %
Greater proportion to larger institutions than at present	20	7.3	25.3	19.4
Same proportion to larger and smaller institutions as at present	22	26.0	41.5	34.8
Greater proportion to smaller institutions than at present	38	66.7	33.2	45.8
Not sure	20	--	--	--
Total	100	100.0	100.0	100.0
# of Respondents	811	192	431	623

*1984 data from 1984 Japan Foundation Report, Table 28, p. 52.

There were some variations in the ranks selected by academics and non-academics. Non-academics gave somewhat higher priority than academics did to support for pre-dissertation graduate training, outreach and public affairs programs, and to conferences and seminars. On the other hand, non-academics ranked research grants to established scholars last, while academics placed it sixth.

In a separate question, Japan specialists were asked their preferences regarding the overall allocation of funding between larger and smaller institutions. The comparison with 1984 is shown in Table 10.10. Respondents in 1995 were not offered a change to express uncertainty, which seems to account for most of the percentage change in the distribution. In both surveys the same proportion, about 20 percent, thought more funding ought to be allocated to larger institutions. Nearly half the respondents (45.8 percent) in 1995 thought a larger share of funding ought to go to smaller institutions.

However, as shown in Table 10.10, a little more than a third thought the proportional allocation should remain about the same. Both of these represent an increase from the 1984 distribution, but the preference runs consistently toward smaller institutions. However, closer inspection of these responses reveals that it is largely respondents from smaller institutions (less than 10,000 total student enrollment) who wanted more resources to go to smaller institutions. Two-thirds of them selected this response, as opposed to one-third of respondents at institutions with 10,000 or more students. Neither group favored more of the resources going to the larger institutions, but a strong plurality of those at larger institutions preferred that the allocations remain about the same. As the number of respondents at smaller institutions grows, we can expect the desire for a reallocation of resources to increase. This is an area of potential conflict within the Japanese Studies community. Although the Japan specialists themselves do not really control the allocation of resources that flow to academic institutions from outside sources, they do sit in elective and appointive positions that conduct the peer review for some types of grants. The balance of representation from large and small institutions is therefore likely to become a more sensitive issue in the future.

Despite the influence of respondents from smaller institutions in the question regarding the overall allocation of resources, "expansion of Japanese Studies to smaller institutions" ranked only in sixth place in the specific priorities ordered by essentially the same respondents. However, the number-one priority given to language study in Japan and study abroad opportunities would also benefit smaller undergraduate institutions. An alternate reading of the two sets of responses is that the preference is for providing more support to existing programs at smaller institutions, as opposed to using funding to expand Japanese Studies into smaller institutions that have not yet initiated Japanese Studies on their own.

The growing demand for a shift toward funding smaller institutions clearly reflects the pattern of growth we examined in Chapter Three, which has put a proportionately larger number of Japan specialists in smaller institutions. We noted in that analysis that Japanese Studies programs at smaller institutions will have different needs than the strong programs at large institutions now have. These sentiments indicate that the special needs of smaller institutions are not yet being met, and some reallocation of resources will be needed. Since there are not sufficient resources for Japanese Studies in the United States to provide the same level of support to the growing number of programs at smaller institutions that a much smaller number of more concentrated programs at large institutions has enjoyed in the past, the great difficulty will be how to address these new problems creatively, to achieve maximum impact for the limited resources that are available.

There are some long-standing models of success in introducing Japanese Studies into the curriculum of smaller colleges, and of consortia and cooperative arrangements that supplement classroom study with many different kinds of cultural exposure. Some of these cooperative and reciprocal arrangements may even work better at small institutions than large ones, because they can be carefully nurtured with personal contact. During the next decade we will need not only to continue to support those successful initiatives, but to expand upon, learn from, and replicate them.

Overall, our assessment of the infrastructure for Japanese Studies in the United States suggests that the scale and scope of institutional activity and support for Japanese Studies has grown significantly since the previous study in the early 1980s. More institutions support Japanese Studies programs, and most programs are significantly larger and stronger than they were a decade ago. The range of ancillary activities that Japanese Studies institutions maintain has expanded, in part due to an infusion of new financial support from Japanese sources.

Yet the increased scale of activity has also been very much a response to strong external demand for more knowledge about Japan by students, special constituencies, and the general public. While the core resources of trained Japan specialists and library resources have certainly grown, it is not at all clear that they have grown fast enough to meet the increased demand, or that they can continue to do so in the future. Library and information resources have certainly not been able to keep up, and there are some indications that Japanese Studies staff are also overburdened by the demands of more courses, more students, more services, and more external requests.

The era of sudden financial windfalls for Japanese Studies appears to be over for now, but fortunately many of the gifts from Japanese sources were in the form of permanent endowments that will continue to support Japanese Studies in the future and if invested carefully, will grow steadily. Part of the strain in the 1990s arises out of the difficult transition from exotic, obscure Japanese Studies to normal, relevant Japanese Studies. As the study of Japan becomes normalized in American society, more of its costs will be absorbed by the regular budgets of institutions without the necessity for special pleading.

As this discussion of funding reveals, the current problems of Japanese Studies are interrelated products of a decade of very impressive growth. The downside of that growth is that the problems involve hard trade-offs in the face of limited resources. In the concluding chapter we will try to draw together the threads of this many-faceted examination of Japanese Studies in the United States in the mid-1990s for a final overview of the problems and prospects of the coming decade.

11

Japanese Studies in the 1990s and Beyond

Throughout this volume we have pursued five themes of change in Japanese Studies in the United States. In this final assessment we summarize the evidence that we have found for each process of change, and what it portends. We conclude by identifying five challenges for the 1990s that arise out of the confluence of these changes.

THEMES OF CHANGE REVISITED

Growth

Japanese Studies has grown tremendously in the United States during the past decade. There are more Japan specialists, more doctoral students, more institutions with a resident Japan specialist. The number of publications on Japan has also increased. There are many more courses exclusively on Japan offered at American colleges and universities, as well as many more Japanese language courses. Enrollments are much higher in all of these courses, including even advanced Japanese language courses. Academic institutions offer more programs of study on Japan, at both the undergraduate and graduate levels, and more institutions are actively engaged in doctoral-level training in Japanese Studies.

The expansion of the past decade reflects Japan's "loss of irrelevance" for the United States, and the corresponding increase in the demand for the knowledge Japan specialists have to offer, whether it is transmitted through academic courses, publications, the services provided by academic institutions, or the Japan-related services that clients can now purchase from individuals and companies. While the rate of growth may be leveling off, we see no indication that the demand for knowledge and information about Japan will decline. There is now a continuing market demand for expertise on Japan that provides employment opportunities for persons with training in Japanese Studies, and thereby offers incentives for students to study Japanese language and take courses about Japan. Substantial gifts from Japanese sources have supported some of the institutional growth of the past decade, primarily at large institutions with well-developed Japanese Studies programs. While this largesse is unlikely to continue for the remainder of the 1990s, the income from wisely invested endowments will continue to support Japanese Studies at these institutions well into the 21st century.

However, the growth of the past decade has brought Japanese Studies to many new academic institutions with much more modest resources and a more limited commitment to the development of Japanese Studies. Whether Japanese Studies can be sustained at these institutions will depend upon their ability to attract and retain Japan specialist staff, and on the capacity of the national infrastructure of Japanese Studies in the United States to extend external support to their faculty and students. Our analysis revealed considerable turnover among institutions with fledgling Japanese Studies programs. It seems likely that many of the institutions identified as having a minimal or limited Japanese Studies program in the 1995 study will disappear from the lists over the next decade, but they will probably be replaced by an equivalent number of other institutions initiating minimal Japanese Studies programs.

We also found that while there is considerable enthusiasm on the part of institutions for initiating one or two years of Japanese language, the hiring of Japan specialists in other disciplines at these institutions is often serendipitous. Thus the growth in institutions with a resident Japan specialist does not equate to growth in institutions with a firm commitment to the development of Japanese Studies programs. Yet whether the institution has made a deliberate commitment or not, there are Japan specialist faculty at these institutions teaching students and doing their own research. They need external support all the more if the institution is not able to make available the opportunities that reinforce learning for students and the resources that enable Japan specialists to maintain and expand their expertise.

The one area where growth does not seem to have kept pace is in library resources, the most essential and expensive part of the Japanese Studies infrastructure. Libraries have suffered more than any other segment of Japanese Studies in the United States from the massive drop in the purchasing power of the dollar over the past decade, which also coincided with a sharp decrease in the availability of yen grants from the main provider of external support for Japanese language libraries in the United States, the Japan-US Friendship Commission. The Japan Foundation has increased its support, and at the urging of these two major funders the professionally staffed Japanese libraries have developed cooperative collection development and access arrangements to stretch and share their resources more effectively. Still, the fact remains that there are only a small number of large Japanese collections at major centers, while Japan specialists and Japanese Studies programs are now dispersed much more widely throughout the United States.

It is not just the book budgets of the Japanese collections that have failed to keep pace; library staff has also remained fairly level. This is not simply a function of limited institutional budgets; there is a national shortage of trained Japanese librarians who can fill the shoes of the generation of librarians who are now beginning to retire. There are MA and doctoral-level Japan specialists with the language skills and understanding of the field to fill some of these positions, but they must also acquire professional library degrees to do. Special incentive programs could help to fill this need, as they have for other professional fields such as law and business that emerged as Japanese Studies specializations in the 1980s.

The library crisis affects growth at both ends of the Japanese Studies institutional continuum: the extension of Japanese Studies into smaller institutions with a limited commitment or ability to support Japanese Studies even with minimal library development; and the development of graduate programs at larger institutions with strong Japanese programs. Each of these issues needs to be explored in a bit more detail.

Library Access for Smaller Institutions: The problem of making basic library resources for Japanese Studies accessible to the growing population of Japan specialists and students outside of the major centers remains intractable. As Japanese Studies expands to more and more institutions, the demand will increase steadily for basic library resources for the study of Japan, including both English language materials to support undergraduate instruction and basic reference materials in Japanese to support advanced language study and faculty research. While some of the costs will be absorbed by the institutions, the entry-level cost to support new Japanese Studies programs is simply beyond the level that most small institutions can devote to a single area. It is also in some sense an invisible cost that the institution may not anticipate when it decides to offer first-year Japanese language or to hire a Japanese historian. Only after the program begins to develop does this basic weakness become apparent. The Japan Foundation currently has several programs designed to address the library needs of small institutions in particular, but the demand continues to outstrip available resources.

Developments in information technology seem to offer the only hope for ameliorating the current disjuncture between the growth of Japanese Studies programs at many more institutions and the inability of library resources to keep pace. These technological strategies also carry high price tags, especially if they must be developed independently in the United States rather than through the extension of access to information systems already available to users in Japan. In addition, they will require some level of user support from Japanese reference librarians or information specialists who can help isolated users learn to utilize these systems independently.

   Libraries and Doctoral Training: Although the number of institutions training doctoral students in Japanese Studies has increased slightly, there are only a very small number of other institutions with Japanese language library collections at or near the level necessary for a full graduate program. Hence the expansion of graduate programs to additional institutions will soon be limited by library resources. Over the past decade a few institutions have made major commitments to the development of full undergraduate and graduate programs in Japanese Studies. They have increased faculty, doubled the size of their Japanese collections, and built strong new programs. While it remains possible that more institutions will take a similar initiative, the costs are higher now and the arguments for doing so may not seem as compelling if there is less chance of attracting massive outside support from Japanese donors. Future development of new graduate programs in Japanese Studies is likely to be more selectively focused on a cluster of related disciplines rather than following the traditional language and area studies model. This in turn may require a reevaluation of the criteria for evaluating graduate programs, since the number of faculty, the number of disciplines, and the size and nature of the library collection would be different under such circumstances. In fact, there may already be institutions following such a strategy that have been classified as limited graduate programs in this study.

   Since the growth in Japanese Studies is now driven by external demand (rather than by national policy operating in the absence of any external demand as was the case earlier), growth in programs and library resources are likely to remain out of synchronization into the next century. Even as there will be more demand to shift resources to support the library needs of smaller institutions directly, the burden on the larger collections will increase because they are the primary resource to which specialists all over the country can turn for essential materials that cannot possibly be made available at every institution.

Differentiation

   Along with sheer growth in scale, Japanese Studies in the United States has become considerably more internally diverse over the past decade. There are now more women with doctorates in Japanese Studies fields, which has been one of the forces expanding specialization on Japan into new academic disciplines, interdisciplinary fields, and professional fields. The range of courses reflects this new diversity, as does the range of programs in which specialization on Japan is offered. We see it also in the range of specific subject matter areas in which Japan specialists claim expertise, and in the extent to which styles of research and other aspects of the practice of Japanese Studies differ systematically by discipline group.

Running through this general proliferation of new areas in which Japan has become a subject of special interest is a more general fault line differentiating academic from non-academic Japanese Studies. What was once a tiny minority of Japan specialists working outside of academia has now become a substantial, vibrant segment of the field, with its own needs, interests, and clientele. The division is far from absolute. Some Japan specialists move back and forth between the two worlds, while many more who were trained in academic Japanese Studies now work in government, the private sector, or for non profit organizations. However, some non-academic Japan specialists have acquired their expertise on Japan on the job, after training in a discipline or professional field that was unrelated to Japanese Studies. They are likely to have the fewest formal ties to academic Japanese Studies, but are not necessarily the least sympathetic.

The differentiation between academic and non-academic Japanese Studies appears in many areas: in the different subject matter specializations on which Japan specialists have expertise; in the different kinds of publications in which material about Japan now appears; in the different specialized audiences to which Japan specialists communicate; in the demands for knowledge about Japan from non-academic audiences; in the kinds of research that academic and non-academic Japan specialists do; and even inside the academy, in the different kinds of training demanded by students who intend to work as Japan specialists outside of academia in the future.

In the latter half of the 1980s when special programs and fellowship incentives were developed to produce Japan specialists in law, business management, and economics, there was some resentment from academic Japan specialists who felt that scarce resources in Japanese Studies were being expended on students who were not willing to devote sufficient attention to Japanese language and area studies, and would probably not use their Japanese training once they had finished professional degree programs at Japanese Studies expense. It is now clear that those concerns were largely misplaced. Japan specialists in these professional fields now meet a growing demand for specialized knowledge about Japan combined with professional skills, a demand that traditional academic Japan specialists cannot possibly meet. The new Japan specialists know different things, and they address them to different audiences. A person who spends every day analyzing companies in the Japanese stock market to advise investors, or helping American companies negotiate trade deals in Japan, is no less a Japan specialist than someone who teaches Japanese poetry to college students, but the two are not interchangeable.

At the most basic level, the issue is simply one of mutual respect for these differences within Japanese Studies. At another level, colleges and universities in the United States will continue to play a central role in preparing students for Japan-related occupations. When virtually the only occupation for Japan specialists was college teaching, academic Japan specialists understood the goal and how to get there. As the potential careers for Japan specialists diversify, academic Japan specialists must discover anew what their students need to learn and how best to prepare them for non-academic careers related to Japan. The larger Japanese Studies programs have been experimenting and adjusting to this new situation over the past decade, but it may soon be time to evaluate the outcomes and take stock of what has been learned about integrating expertise on Japan with professional training. Part of this stock-taking necessarily involves educating both students and faculty to the wide range of career options now available to those with expertise on Japan, if they combine their Japanese Studies expertise with appropriate professional certification.

A second fault line is beginning to develop within academic Japanese Studies, as the study of Japan extends to smaller institutions that are isolated from major centers with diverse staff and strong libraries. We have already raised one aspect of this issue as a problem of uneven growth of faculty and courses as opposed to the basic infrastructure of library and information resources. The concept of differentiation highlights another aspect, the differing needs and interests of Japan specialists at large and small academic institutions as they compete for scarce external resources. These differences are real and structural, hence they are potential sources of conflict and division if they are not addressed.

Some of these needs at small institutions have already been recognized, and a number of existing programs, such as regional Japan seminars and the AAS Northeast Asia Council's small grants, are intended to assist Japan specialists at smaller institutions. The Japan Foundation also has several grant programs that provide institutional support to smaller institutions through library grants and salary support for new language and area faculty positions. All of these programs were initiated in an era when the proportion of Japanese Studies programs and specialists at small institutions was considerably less than it is now. Our survey results show that specialists at small institutions no longer think the current balance of resource allocations is adequate. They want a larger share of the overall pie, but specialists at large institutions think the current balance is fine. In the survey sample that answered this question, two-thirds were from large institutions. Although their majority is steadily shifting, specialists from large institutions still dominate the positions from which the allocation of resources is decided through grant allocations.

Because of the high concentration of graduate training in Japanese Studies, most of the Japan specialists who now teach at smaller institutions were formerly students at large institutions. They share a common background and participate in common networks with their former teachers and classmates, and with other specialists in the field who do research on similar topics. The issue, then, is not a fundamental division between groups of people with no connection and no sense of common identity, but rather the fact that their current institutional environments create different interests. In short, it is largely a matter of representation of those interests in the arenas of collective decision-making within the field. Some of this representation comes about naturally, either because the committees involved are elective and thus reflect the demographics of the field, such as NEAC, or because of the stature and recognition of individuals. To the extent that participation in such collective bodies is appointive and invitational, however, it will be the responsibility of the appointing agencies to take this factor into consideration. The fact that women have been smoothly integrated into all of these decision-making bodies over the past 20 years suggests that the representation of the interests of Japan specialists at smaller institutions can be managed just as effectively.

Specialization

We have also found considerable evidence of increasing specialization within Japanese Studies. There is more specialization on Japan alone, as opposed to Asia or East Asia, as indicated by more academic courses offered solely on Japan, and more academic programs, particularly at the graduate level, that encourage or permit concentration solely on Japan. The drop in reporting of multinational courses that include Japan is a further indicator of this tendency; the courses have not necessarily disappeared from the curriculum, but they are less likely to be reported as part of the Japanese Studies program. We also found that the majority of Japan specialists do not report expertise on Japan in relation to any other countries or geographic regions. The increases in higher-level Japanese language courses and in literature courses reading Japanese texts point to greater expectations of Japanese language competence, which further reinforces specialization on Japan alone.

There are also signs of increased disciplinary specialization within Japanese Studies, which goes hand in hand with disciplinary and professional differentiation. Instead of, or in addition to, the broad general exposure to Japan offered by a language and area studies approach, the trend since the 1970s has been to encourage the study of Japan plus strong disciplinary training. There are now more opportunities to do specialized graduate work on Japan within particular academic disciplines, and fewer graduate degree options in Japanese language and culture or language and civilization programs that blur disciplinary boundaries. The number of courses offered on Japan within individual disciplines has increased, suggesting that a higher degree of specialization is encouraged. As the number of Japan specialists within a discipline increases, the opportunity arises to combine a more intensive focus on Japan alone with greater disciplinary specialization, creating a nested specialization with its own reference group within the discipline. Where such a critical mass does not exist, specialization on Japan and disciplinary specialization tend to operate somewhat at cross-purposes.

A more general indicator of both specialization on Japan and specialization within Japanese Studies is the fact that new Japan specialists now take longer to complete their doctorates and enter the field at a later age, presumably because of higher training requirements and performance expectations. A further indicator is the proliferation of new subject matter specializations reported by Japan specialists, particularly in areas where previously there were few specialists or recognized specializations.

In one sense, these indications of increased specialization are measures of the growing sophistication, professionalization, and depth of Japanese Studies. To the extent that specialization on Japan and disciplinary specialization are nested, they may encourage narrowness, but do not pose conflicts of priority for Japan specialists. However, when the demands of specialization on Japan and specialization within a discipline diverge, as is frequently the case in the social sciences, they give rise to a cluster of problems for Japanese Studies. This is the major fault line of specialization that we have identified throughout this study.

Some part of the problem is the misapplication of humanities standards for Japan specialists to social scientists, which has to be addressed within the Japanese Studies community. The greater part of the problem is more intractable; it is a structural misfit between the disciplinary organization and expectations of the social sciences and the holistic demands and expectation of specialization in Japanese Studies. These fundamental differences in perspective make some social science disciplines less receptive to the training needs of doctoral candidates who want to specialize on Japan, and less interested in hiring faculty who specialize on Japan. At a more proximate level, they place conflicting demands on those who want to combine the study of Japan with disciplinary specialization in terms of how research topics are framed and pursued, how research results are presented, where they are published, and how they are evaluated within the discipline. Since individual careers are dependent upon the successful negotiation of these hurdles over a period of many years, these constitute significant barriers to the development of a stronger Japanese Studies presence in certain disciplines.

In effect, conflicting demands of specialization show up in Japanese Studies as the relative absence of Japan specialists in certain disciplines. In many cases promising young specialists reduce their commitment to Japan in order to meet the demands of the discipline because employment opportunities flow largely through disciplinary channels. Because of resistance by the discipline to hiring Japan specialists, they are more likely to have been hired without reference to their specialization on Japan, for a position not identified as a Japanese Studies position. Ironically, a certain prominence as Japan specialists may also draw individuals away from their discipline. In sociology, for example, a number of prominent Japan specialists have moved out of sociology departments to take attractive positions in business schools, where their credentials as Japan specialist sociologists are more highly valued than they are within the discipline. Much the same has happened in economics, where the higher market value of specialization on Japan has created a much more favorable environment for Japan specialist economists in the private sector than in the largely indifferent academic departments. For Japanese Studies, then, the problem is how to train and keep specialists in these social science disciplines in the face of divergent demands for specialization by the discipline.

Normalization

The evidence for the normalization of Japanese Studies in the United States is also compelling. We see it in the employment of Japan specialists in non-academic positions in the mainstream of society, not because they could not find work as Japan specialists, but precisely because the mainstream economy needs their expertise on Japan. A related factor is the extent to which academic Japanese programs provide services to business, mass media, and the general public. The great surge of public interest in Japan, and the perceived growth of general knowledge of Japan among various audiences over the past decade, also attest to the normalization of knowledge of Japan as part of common or accessible knowledge rather than esoteric, elite knowledge. This general demand for knowledge about Japan can be measured in the volume of non-academic publications about Japan, and in the demands for Japan specialists to communicate with the general public, as well as in the perceptions of specialists.

We see the same kind of normalization in the increased desire to study Japanese language, the larger number of students who have studied Japanese in high school, and the introduction of Japanese language courses at a broad range of academic institutions with no prior interest in or commitment to the development of Japanese Studies programs. Further indicators are the number of small institutions that have exchange agreements or provide opportunities for study abroad in Japan as general cultural exposure, even though they do not have extensive on-campus Japanese Studies programs. More generally, the high enrollments in both Japanese language courses and subject matter courses exclusively on Japan suggest that students who do not plan to become professional Japan specialists are taking courses on Japan for general knowledge. Even the fact that Japanese Studies programs at large institutions can no longer keep track of their students indicates that the study of Japan has become a part of the normal curriculum, and that such students are no longer marked as a special group.

Among Japan specialists as well there are indicators of normalization in the increased number of academics entering Japanese Studies in mid-career because of an interest in comparative research or to pursue a particular topic. The large body of research on Japan now available in English makes it possible for such people to work on Japan as a normal extension of their other academic interests. This is related also to the finding that many specialists are able to do research and professional work on Japan without high-level language skills, either because the nature of their work does not require extensive use of Japanese language materials, or because they have support systems or other strategies for overcoming language deficiencies. All of this evidence points to the growing accessibility of Japan as a normal subject of study in the United States, for both specialists and non-specialists.

Normalization at academic institutions is more advanced in certain parts of the country, and at certain kinds of institutions. We can see traces of institutional normalization in the high rate of penetration of Japanese Studies at more elite academic institutions, and in its spread into more mainstream institutions accessible to the average college student. Conversely, normalization as a phenomenon helps to institutionalize Japanese Studies as a part of the regular curriculum, and to spread its costs into the regular institutional budget lines that pay for faculty and courses, books for the library, and graduate fellowships and teaching assistantships. At some institutions these processes are already well advanced, while at others Japanese Studies may still be compartmentalized, dependent on special funding, and vulnerable to budget cuts as a luxury item. These are topics we have not been able to explore directly in this study, but they are consequences of the process of normalization, which we have documented.

While normalization is a positive process for the future of Japanese Studies in the United States, it requires some adjustments on the part of Japan specialists. The first adjustment is in addressing the subject matter of Japanese Studies to a broader range of students who may have less preparation and more diverse expectations because they do not intend to specialize on Japan. Courses on Japan have always attracted some students with only nominal interest in the subject, but as the subject becomes normalized, the proportion of such students increases. At the same time, normalization also means that more students think they need to know something about Japan, but there may be much more variation in what they want to know and why they want to know it.

A second adjustment concerns the relations between those who were trained in Japanese Studies as graduate students and those who enter the field in mid-career and are treated initially as "non-specialists." The normalization of Japanese Studies implies that professional specialization on Japan becomes more accessible to the latter group, and that they do have something to contribute to the field of Japanese Studies, or can use material on Japan to make a contribution to some other field.

Both of these adjustments have to do with the role of the traditionally trained academic Japan specialist as the steward of knowledge about Japan, or the source of an exotic and exclusive expertise. With the general normalization of knowledge about Japan, that role changes to a more modest position. Along with academic specialists in other "normal" fields, the academic Japan specialist becomes simply one of many purveyors of widely available knowledge; a person who has a certain kind of expertise about a subject that many people might want to learn about for a variety of purposes. This does not necessarily change what academic Japan specialists do, but it may alter the context in which they do it and thus its purpose and meaning in relation to other kinds of knowledge and other knowers.

Internationalization

The evidence of internationalization of Japanese Studies in the United States is all around us, even if there are fewer indicators of it in our survey data. That evidence ranges from increased study abroad and exchange relationships linking a wide range of American academic institutions and their students to institutions and individuals in Japan, increased frequency of travel to Japan by Japan specialists, and strong bonds of friendship between American Japan specialists and Japanese scholars. We see it in foreign graduate students from Europe, Asia, and every other part of the world who come to the United States to enroll in Japanese Studies programs, and in American Japan specialists who take regular jobs in other countries after completing their degrees in the United States. Further traces of internationalization can be found in subject matter specializations that address Japanese phenomena outside of Japan, or non-Japanese phenomena inside Japan, and geographic specializations that compare Japan with countries other than China and the United States. These traces of internationalization point to the changed position of Japan in the world, and also to the changing position of Japanese Studies in the United States.

These indications of internationalization have two implications for the future of Japanese Studies in the United States. The first reinforces the findings on normalization, by emphasizing that the study of Japan no longer takes place only in and about Japan proper, and no longer only involves those traditionally trained as Japan specialists. As Japan has moved out into the world, so has the study of Japan become relevant and accessible in many other places. The definitions and boundaries of what constitutes the study of Japan have to adjust accordingly.

The second implication is that the United States is now training Japan specialists for a much more internationalized world, in which national boundaries, national identities, and national entitlements are increasingly irrelevant to the real business of gaining and sharing knowledge about Japan. Yet those boundaries, identities, and entitlements affect who can teach, who can study, who can be supported, and who pays for that support. At the level of graduate education, the internationalization in Japanese Studies is part of a much larger phenomenon in American education that particularly concerns public institutions and public sources of funding. Despite these more general connections, there is a need to look carefully at the relationship between available sources of funding for Japanese Studies in the United States and the growing internationalization of Japanese Studies.

CHALLENGES FOR THE 1990S

After a decade of remarkable growth, in the mid-1990s Japanese Studies in the United States is in relatively good condition. Yet this is certainly not a time to rest complacently. Throughout this study we have pointed to various potholes, bumpy spots, and unmarked curves in the road. In this chapter we have used a summary assessment of five themes of change as a further device for locating the major trouble spots that lie ahead. Our final task is to refocus these bits of trouble into a clear set of challenges.

The challenges of the 1990s arise partly from recent internal developments within Japanese Studies, and partly from the changing national and global environment. Some are old problems with new twists, while others have only recently emerged. Although each can be characterized as a distinct challenge, like everything else in our complex contemporary world they are all to some degree interdependent. All five challenges need to be addressed now, so that Japanese Studies will be well-positioned to meet the new challenges of the 21st century.

I. The Challenge of Providing Japanese Library and Information Resources for Japan Studies in the United States

The problem of providing Japanese library and information resources for use in the United States is perhaps the biggest challenge facing Japanese Studies in the 1990s, and it has received special attention in this survey. Despite the greater ease and frequency of travel to Japan by American Japan specialists which the study has documented, and the extent to which researchers collect their own data or obtain their own research materials in Japan, a wide range of Japanese language materials still must be available in the United States to support Japanese Studies. There are three inter-related aspects to this daunting problem.

(1) Making available for use in the United States an ever-widening range of Japanese language library and information resources to meet the research and training needs of an expanding and diversifying Japanese Studies clientele, even as the cost of the materials escalates.

(2) Providing rapid, efficient, and economical nationwide access to Japanese language library and information resources from a relatively small number of large library collections and resource sites, because it is no longer possible to meet the needs of Japan specialists and students throughout the United States through their local library collections.

(3) Training a new generation of Japanese language library and information specialists to staff the large Japanese language library collections in the United States, and to maintain and support Japanese language information resources for use in the United States.

There are no easy solutions to the serious problems of library resources and access that the Japanese library community and the major funders of Japanese Studies in the United States have been working on for several years and that this study has now documented in greater detail. However, we can build on the high level of computer literacy and the widespread use of personal computers among American Japan specialists, to find innovative technological solutions that will centralize and rationalize resource investments while decentralizing and democratizing access.

II. The Challenge of Supporting Japanese Studies and Japan Specialists at Smaller Academic Institutions

As this survey has documented, Japanese Studies is currently expanding into smaller undergraduate colleges, sometimes through a combination of local demand for Japanese language instruction and serendipitous hiring of Japanese area specialists in disciplinary departments. This expansion is shifting more Japan specialists to academic institutions without major Japanese Studies programs and Japanese Studies library collections, and creating student constituencies without access to basic infrastructure for Japanese Studies. The challenge here is three-fold:

(1) to help build coherent and effective Japanese Studies programs when the institutions are committed to doing so;

(2) to support the research and teaching of individual Japan specialist faculty at smaller institutions, regardless of whether the institution plans to develop a formal program in Japanese Studies;

(3) to reduce disparities of opportunity between large and small institutions and potential conflicts of interest between Japan specialists affiliated with large and small Japanese Studies programs.

III. The Challenge of Integrating Japanese Studies in the Social Sciences

The increasing differentiation and specialization of Japanese Studies in the 1990s have added new pressures to the chronic problem of integrating Japanese Studies into the social sciences, as the research methods and materials of the social sciences become more distinctively different from those of the humanities. On the one hand, it is becoming more difficult for aspiring Japan specialists in the social sciences to achieve research-level Japanese language skills and conduct substantive research using Japanese sources, while simultaneously meeting high professional demands of their disciplines that often lead them in different directions. These conditions vary within the social sciences, and may extend to a reluctance to hire "Japan specialists" for academic positions in some disciplines and departments. On the other hand, many social scientists without training in Japanese Studies have become interested in the study of Japan, which they pursue through English language resources and cooperative arrangements with others.

The survey has also found that those who do not achieve research-level Japanese language competence during graduate school are likely to have greater difficulty maintaining their language skills later, while those who come to the study of Japan in mid-career are unlikely ever to achieve high levels of language competence. These language barriers, which differentially affect social scientists, in turn limit the scope and depth of specialists' research and teaching on Japan, and serve as disincentives for continued involvement in Japanese Studies. Initiatives from Japanese Studies cannot readily change the internal structure and worldview of social science disciplines, but they can provides incentives and support that may enhance the role of Japanese Studies and strengthen the training of Japan specialists within the social sciences. The key aspects of the challenge are thus:

(1) to support the Japanese Studies and particularly Japanese language training of social science students to ensure that they have research-level language competence and a broad understanding of Japan before undertaking dissertation research;

(2) to ensure the employability of social scientists who are trained as Japan specialists, by making certain they meet the high professional standards of their discipline as well as of Japanese Studies and by encouraging the development of targeted academic positions for Japan specialist social scientists.

(3) to support the research needs of social scientists for different types of Japanese language materials than those customarily used in the humanities, in particular for quantitative and statistical materials, and for primary materials that can be used for original social science analysis of contemporary Japan. In addition, to make English language research on Japan more visible and accessible to American social scientists.

IV. The Challenge of Supporting Larger Numbers of Students to Reach Higher Standards of Achievement in Japanese Studies

This survey has documented the increased student interest in Japanese Studies courses, the great increases in enrollment in Japanese language courses even at advanced levels, and the increased opportunities for study abroad. While these increases represent successes in their own right, they have created an increasing need for student support in a period when financial resources for Japanese Studies in the United States are likely to remain relatively flat. Survey respondents expressed this dilemma by ranking various forms of student support as three of their top four funding priorities. The three forms of student support specifically identified were:

(1) support for language training in Japan and study abroad, which encompasses undergraduate study abroad programs and also includes strong support for the Inter-University Center for Japanese Language Studies in Yokohama;

(2) dissertation support for doctoral candidates, which refers mainly to support for dissertation research in Japan, but also encompasses support for the completion of dissertations and other programs that bring doctoral students together for workshops and conferences that enhance their professional qualifications;

(3) pre-dissertation student support, which can also be understood to include support for students who seek professional degrees other than the doctorate and special programs to encourage students to undertake additional training in areas of particular need.

V. The Challenge of Adjusting to the Normalization and Internationalization of Japanese Studies in the United States

The survey has pointed to numerous indicators of the normalization and internationalization of Japanese Studies in the United States, as new phenomena of the 1990s that stretch the traditional boundaries of Japanese Studies. These changes require some rethinking and institutional readjustment of academic Japanese Studies, as well as new relationships and support systems that extend beyond academia and even across international borders.

(1) Japanese Studies programs and professional schools need to work together, with advice from Japan specialists employed outside of academics, to prepare students better for non-academic employment related to Japan. The problem extends from the simple question of how to inform undergraduates of the opportunities for work related to Japan and the background and credentials they will need in order to pursue them, to the more complex question of how to provide training in Japanese Studies that is relevant and appropriate for students in professional programs, without making it so narrow and superficial that it fails to provide an adequate foundation for their future development.

(2) Better systems are needed to help the growing range of people seeking knowledge and information about Japan find and gain access to the solid English-language literature on Japan that is being produced by American Japan specialists. The survey has identified a large audience of non-specialists plus an intermediate level of professionals who need good access to this literature, but has also pointed to serious problems in current methods of searching for it.

(3) American academic institutions face new problems in supporting the advanced training of aspiring Japan specialists from other countries, who fall between the cracks of arrangements designed for a two-way flow between Japan and the United States. Students from Europe and Asia whose first or second language is English often choose to receive at least part of their training in Japanese Studies at American institutions. At present Japanese Studies programs at American institutions of higher education are open to students from any country who meet the entrance criteria, but available fellowship support for Japanese Studies at the graduate level is frequently restricted by citizenship or residency requirements, and general fellowship support for foreign students does not favor subjects such as Japanese Studies. Neither Japan nor the United States should bear full responsibility for supporting such students, but their combined leadership is needed to resolve a problem that will only grow larger over time.

These, then, are the challenges of the 1990s for Japanese Studies in the United States. They will not all be resolved before the end of the decade, but we can and must begin to address them all, in order to be prepared for the new challenges that the 21st century will bring.

Appendix A

Methodology

As noted in the introduction, this study combined the data collection for the 1995 update of the *Directory of Japan Specialists and Japanese Studies Institutions in the United States and Canada* with the collection of additional survey data that did not appear in the directory entries. The study is based on three separate questionnaires sent to Japan specialists, Japanese Studies institutions, and librarians of Japanese collections, respectively. Information on doctoral candidates was collected through the first two instruments, with some follow-up directly to the candidates to determine whether they had completed their degrees. Methodological information will be presented separately for each of these four categories, with the greatest amount of detail reserved for the two major surveys directed at Japan specialists and Japanese Studies institutions.

JAPAN SPECIALISTS

In the textbook version of the survey research process the researcher creates an abstract definition of the category to be studied, identifies a specific pool of subjects that closely approximates the definition, and samples systematically within it. Our research strategy was different for two reasons. First, because we were simultaneously producing a directory and conducting a survey of the people in that directory, we were aiming for a census of all Japan specialists rather than a systematic sample within that pool. Second, because there is no identifiable comprehensive list of Japan specialists other than the directory itself, our task was to find and define the current pool as we surveyed it. Our strategy was therefore to cast a wide net with an overly inclusive mailing list of possible Japan specialists, and then to rely on a combination of self-selection (by the persons who received the questionnaire and decided themselves whether to respond to it) and committee selection (to set the final limits among those who did respond to the questionnaire) to establish the parameters of the category "Japan Specialists in the United States in the 1990s."

297

Mailing List

Developing the mailing list was an iterative process of adding and subtracting possible names on the basis of new information. The starting point for the specialist questionnaire was the mailing list that had been created for the original directory in the late 1980s. That list was based on all known potential sources of directory entrants, and thus it included a great many people with only marginal connections to Japanese Studies, who would not consider themselves to be Japan specialists. The old list of about 4,000 names was cross-checked against the current Association for Asian Studies membership mailing list for changes of name, changes of address, and deaths. Any new AAS members who had indicated primary specialization in Northeast Asia (the AAS category that encompasses Japan) were added to the list, but persons on the old list with only a secondary interest in Northeast Asia were dropped. Updated mailing lists were also solicited from various regional and disciplinary organizations in Japanese Studies, and from disciplinary organizations with membership records that might identify persons who specialized in Japan.

The primary source of new Japan specialists was the list of doctoral candidates in the previous directory. Information on doctoral candidates had been reported by both specialists and academic programs for the 1989 directory. In their update questionnaires, specialists and institutions that had reported doctoral candidates in 1989 were asked for follow-up information on those individuals. Persons who had completed their degrees were added to the specialists mailing list as their current whereabouts became known. Many were already on the AAS membership list.

New Japan specialists were also discovered through the faculty and staff lists reported by institutions as they submitted their entries to the directory. The packet sent to institutions included additional copies of the specialist questionnaire and a list of persons whom our computer had identified as Japan specialists affiliated with the institution. The staff person responsible for the directory entry was asked to update the list, and also to distribute questionnaires to any appropriate individuals who were not on our list. Hence some people were added to the "mailing list" when they sent in a completed questionnaire.

Although we were cognizant of the increasing range of professionals who have developed expertise on Japan over the past decade, we did not have very effective means of reaching them beyond our academic-centered channels and networks. These channels do reach beyond the traditional academic boundaries of Japanese Studies, however, as evidenced by the substantial number of non-academic specialists in the 1989 directory and the even larger number in the current study. What we lacked were the powerful cross-checking techniques we were able to apply to locate academic Japan specialists. It is for this reason that we presume our list is less complete for non-academic Japan specialists. If they did not appear on one of our initial mailing lists, we had no indirect ways of finding them.

We tried to put out the welcome mat for those non-academic Japan specialists who did receive a questionnaire, specifically inviting them to complete and return it if they fit the definition of "Japan specialists of professional status (generally individuals who hold the highest academic degree or major professional degree in their field, and who work or carry out research on Japan)". Our invitation added, "The study of Japan has been changing rapidly, and there are now many professionals who meet these criteria, but do not consider themselves to be 'Japan specialists' in the traditional sense. We invite such professionals also to complete both the directory and survey portions of the questionnaire. Only through the broad inclusion of all persons engaged professionally in the study of Japan can we properly assess the current state of the field and plan for its future needs. In addition to your own entry, we invite you to submit the names and addresses of any Japan specialists we may have missed."

Through these various approaches we generated a final mailing list of 4,442 persons in the United States who might possibly be Japan specialists eligible for inclusion in the directory, although we were quite certain that the actual but unknown number of Japanese specialists in the United States was probably less than half that figure.

Questionnaire

The questionnaire was designed in two parts, reflecting the study's dual purposes of updating the directory and surveying the field. The first half of the questionnaire was designated as the directory entry form and contained basic biographical information covering the individual's training, areas of specialization, professional experience, and personal accomplishments related to Japanese Studies. The second half, identified clearly as a survey whose contents would not appear in the directory or be associated with the individual respondent, contained more detailed questions about the individual's life and work as a Japan specialist, plus a number of questions asking for the respondent's opinion or judgment about various conditions in the field. The content of the directory entry form portion remained virtually the same as for the 1989 directory. The main changes were the addition of space for entering fax numbers and e-mail addresses, and the pre-coding of additional fellowships and subject matter specializations based on the 1989 directory responses. We also added space for reporting the year in which a fellowship was held.

The survey portion replicated most questions in the 1984 Japan Foundation survey. The exceptions were instances in which essentially the same information was already covered in the directory entry section of the questionnaire. In several cases we reproduced the fixed responses used in the 1984 questionnaire, but added new choices to reflect the broader options available in the 1990s and the wider range of Japan specialists we expected the survey would reach. In a few cases we changed the question format in order to obtain more complete and flexible data, such as by asking for the number of publications of a particular type rather than simply asking whether the respondent had published anything of that type. New questions were added to assess the various ways that Japan specialists utilize the time they devote to Japan, the specific Japanese language skills they need for their work, and the professional relations they maintain. Because library and information resources in the United States have become a major concern in Japanese Studies, the study added a number of questions that were designed to explore more thoroughly how Japan specialists do research, what kinds of resources their work requires, and how they obtain them. We worked closely with Japanese librarians to develop appropriate and accurate questions concerning the use of library and information resources. New questions were also written to cover skills and experiences that were likely to have been added to the Japan specialist's repertoire since the previous survey, such as personal computer use and fundraising from corporate sources.

Data Collection and Processing

All specialists who had entries in the 1989 directory received an "update" version of the directory entry form that was produced by computer and contained the information they had submitted previously, with space for making changes. An attachment contained the list of subject matter specializations plus the survey questions. All others on the mailing list received regular questionnaires containing both the directory entry and survey questions. Two follow-up mailings were sent out. Specialists were also linked to the identification code of the institutions with which they were affiliated, to facilitate cross-checking and additional institutional analysis.

After the data had been entered in the computer database, cleaned and proofread, and the Japanese romanization standardized, preliminary galley proofs of the directory entries were sent to all the entrants for correction, at which time many respondents made additional changes to the directory information, including some who had not previously responded to the 1995 questionnaire administration. During these various checks we also discovered that some people had sent in multiple questionnaires, while a number of others had filled out update questionnaires originally sent to someone else, creating data problems that took considerable time to untangle.

Since the collection, inputting of data, and correction process took far longer than we had anticipated, we also spent a great deal of time tracking Japan specialists as they moved from one institution and address to another, and trying to keep the data current. This exercise exemplifies the Heisenberg principle that it is possible either to fix the location of atoms or to trace their movement, but it is not possible to do both simultaneously. The tracking was undertaken to ensure that the directory information was current at the time of publication, but would not have been necessary for the survey alone. In fact many of the problems we worked so hard to correct probably occur in any survey, but without the sort of triangulation and individualized tracking we were able to do, they simply remain in the database as unknown errors.

Sample Definition, Sample Size, and Data Presentation

The sample for this survey analysis is defined as all persons in the 1995 directory sample with an address in the United States. We therefore need to review the procedures that were used in the compilation of the directory to include or exclude individual entries. There are two distinct aspects of this selection. The first concerns whether to include entries from individuals who responded to the questionnaire but might not meet the criteria established for inclusion in the directory. The second concerns individuals who were included in the 1989 directory, but did not respond to the 1995 questionnaire administration.

As a final step in the compilation of the 1995 directory, all entries were reviewed to determine whether they met the criteria for inclusion. Questionable entries were flagged at several points as the data were being entered and corrected, and all entries were also reviewed by the editors. A committee of Japan specialists from several institutions then carefully examined all questionable entries. For this process we were sometimes able to use additional information from the survey to help establish the individual's degree of professional involvement in Japanese Studies. Although this was necessarily a matter of judgment, the committee looked for Japanese language facility where it would be relevant to professional performance, field experience in Japan, amount of professional time devoted to Japan, and publication or other professional experience related to Japan as evidence of professional expertise sufficient for inclusion of an entry in the directory. Persons who were judged to be primarily specialists on China, Korea or South Asia were generally not included, unless their area of specialization dealt significantly with Japan. However, anyone whose entry was included in the 1989 directory (which employed a similar review process) was automatically accorded that status in the current edition. In addition, anyone who appeared on the faculty and staff list submitted by an institution and who also submitted a directory entry was included.

The entries of persons who submitted regular entries to the directory but were identified as doctoral candidates in Japan-related programs also received special scrutiny. If they were already working in some capacity as professional Japan specialists, independent of their status as doctoral candidates, their entries were included in the directory. Those who were judged to be primarily doctoral candidates received additional follow-up faxes and telephone calls to determine if they had received their degrees, or would do so before the directory was published. Whenever possible, we have included their full entries. If they did not meet the criteria for directory entry at press time, they were not included in the regular entries, but were retained on the doctoral candidates list.

The Japan specialists listed in the directory are in most instances currently resident in either the United States or Canada. Those resident in Canada were automatically excluded from the survey analysis. In some cases, Americans who are currently working in Japan were included in the directory because they remain actively a part of the intellectual community of Japan specialists in North America, but they also have been excluded from the survey analysis. We have, however, reported the size of this growing expatriate group and discussed its implications briefly in Chapter Two. Conversely, foreign nationals who work more or less permanently in the United States are included, but short-term visitors have been excluded.

An additional problem was whether to include the old data from the 1989 directory in cases where we had been unsuccessful in obtaining updated information. For specialists, we were able to use several techniques to make the final determination. Persons who had reported that they were no longer active in the field, or whose death or incapacitating illness had been reported by others, were of course removed as soon as their status was known. Persons whose mailings had been returned from the post office as undeliverable, and for whom no forwarding address could be found, were reluctantly recoded as lost when we had exhausted all methods of locating them. These entries were not reprinted.

However, there were about three hundred persons whose mail was not returned, but who did not respond to any of our mail inquiries. Our initial mailings had implied that the entry would be reprinted without change if we did not receive an update, but we were reluctant to reprint an entry that might no longer be appropriate, so these cases were all traced individually until a determination could be made about whether to include the old data. If the specialist remained on the updated faculty and staff list of the same institution, and the information in the specialist entry appeared to be still applicable, we reprinted the data. If the specialist was located on the staff list of another institution and we were able to verify that information, we updated the affiliation and reprinted the entry. The remaining individuals fell outside the purview of our limited list of institutions with updated staff information. We then conducted an intensive telephone follow-up to determine whether the person was still at the same location and there was some indication of continuing activity in Japanese Studies. If the telephone number listed in the 1989 directory did not lead us to the person, we used a national telephone listing on CD-ROM to find a more current telephone number. Through this intensive telephone tracking we were able to make direct or indirect contact with virtually all of the persons on the list, and to make a final determination of whether to reprint the entry.

Through these complex procedures we produced a final sample of 1,552 Japan specialists resident in the United States, for whom we have at least the basic biographical data of the directory entry portion of the questionnaire. For most of the sample this information is either new in 1995 or was updated by the respondent in 1995 from the 1989 entry, but for about 15 percent of the sample the information was collected in 1989. For purposes of this survey analysis the basic biographical information remains valid, and we have been able to confirm or update addresses, affiliations, and retirements.

From this sample of 1,552 specialists we have usable survey data from the survey section of the 1995 questionnaire for 1,072 persons. About half of the missing cases are persons who completed or updated the directory entry form but declined to fill out the survey section of the questionnaire. The remainder are persons who did not respond to the 1995 questionnaire administration at all, and for whom we have used the 1989 directory data after confirming that the individual was still an active Japan specialist. There do not seem to be any major differences in the overall composition of the survey sample as compared to the larger directory sample. It is as least as representative, and probably considerably larger, than the sample we would have obtained if the two parts of the study had been conducted independently and we had simply sent a separate survey mailing to everyone in the directory.

However, respondents answered the survey questions rather selectively, particularly when the questions appeared to deal with aspects of Japanese Studies that were not relevant to their personal situation. In particular, non-academic Japan specialists did not answer some questions that seemed most applicable to academics, and those without usable Japanese language skills tended not to answer questions about the use of Japanese language materials. The whole instrument was also very long, and some people did not make it all the way to the end. Consequently, the sample size varies for each part of the analysis. We have reported the relevant number of respondents in each table, and have discussed in the text any instances where it seemed that response bias might have affected the results. In most cases the data are presented as a comparison of different categories of respondents, so the percentage comparisons should remain valid even if the number of respondents from a particular category is lower than their overall representation in the directory sample. Where comparisons have been made with data from earlier studies, we have frequently presented the data for the 1995 study separately for academics and non-academics to improve the comparability.

We have not applied any sampling statistics to the data tables because despite the documented gaps between the size of the mailing list and the sample, and between the directory and survey sample sizes, these data still represent something much closer to a census than a random sample. The basic data in the directory portion of the data probably represent somewhere between three-fifths and three-fourths of all the Japan specialists who are really "out there," and the questionnaire sample is two-thirds of that. Significance tests that are designed to test whether the results obtained from a tiny systematic sample of a huge immeasurable population were likely to be badly distorted by chance are simply not appropriate in this situation. Opinion surveys representing the entire population of the United States, for example, are frequently carried out using samples smaller than the 1,072 Japan specialists from whom we have survey data. We therefore present the survey results with considerable confidence that they reflect the general parameters of the field at the time the data were collected, taking into the consideration the limitations we report both here and in the discussion of each analysis.

JAPANESE STUDIES INSTITUTIONS

As with Japan specialists, our goal was to conduct a census rather than a sample survey of Japanese Studies institutions, but this posed a new set of "universe" problems for academic and non-academic institutions, which we have addressed with several different strategies.

Mailing Lists

Academic Institutions. For its institutional mailing list, the 1989 directory had followed the practice of previous surveys of Japanese Studies in the United States and Canada and had presumed that there was a relatively small, known universe of Japanese Studies programs. However, in compiling the 1989 directory we had been surprised at the number of Japan specialists who were teaching at academic institutions that fell outside of our roster of known programs, and had added a supplemental list of "academic institutions with Japan specialist staff" to the institutions volume of the directory, based on the institutional affiliations of specialists. We were also aware that by the early 1990s many smaller academic institutions were seeking staff so they could offer at least elementary Japanese language courses, and possibly other Japanese Studies courses, to meet student demand.

Since we could no longer rely on personal knowledge as the basis for identifying institutions with Japanese Studies programs, we needed a different strategy to capture the explosion of institutional interest in Japanese Studies. Starting from the other end of the problem, we utilized a purchased mailing list of 3,139 institutions of higher education in the United States as the core academic mailing list. While this strategy produced a high rate of non-response to our questionnaires, it also has made it possible to include in the survey many Japanese Studies programs that might otherwise have escaped our notice, as well as to locate the programs we have identified within a fairly clear universe.

Non-academic Institutions. In 1989 we had supplemented the AAS list of Asia-related academic programs through a library search for museums, libraries, research institutes and other associations likely to have programs or resources related to Japan. This list became the base for the non-academic institutional mailing list, supplemented by the business addresses of specialists who were employed at similar non-academic institutions. The latter list did not include law firms or corporations, unless they appeared to have an explicit program related to Japan. Most governmental agencies and departments were also excluded on the assumption that they would not submit an institutional entry to a directory of the type we were producing.

Questionnaire

Both academic and non-academic institutions received the same questionnaire. Like the specialist questionnaire, the first half of the instrument comprised the directory entry form and the second half the survey questions. The directory portion contained basic contact information for the program, plus some pre-coded categories and space for narrative descriptions of various kinds of academic programs, facilities, and other activities that might be maintained or conducted by a Japanese Studies program. The instrument also asked for complete lists of the staff, courses, and doctoral candidates associated with the program. The directory portion of the instrument paralleled the 1989 directory entry form closely, except that detailed questions about library holdings were moved to a separate instrument which was sent directly to librarians. Space was added for fax numbers and e-mail addresses, and enrollment figures and a course level code were added to the information requested about all courses relating to Japan. In addition, two questions that were actually part of the survey and not to be published in the directory were inserted in the directory portion of the questionnaire. These questions asked how instructional and non-instructional activities were organized at the institution, and their placement was intended to assist in the management of directory data for large institutions with complex Japanese Studies programs that might be submitting multiple institutional questionnaires for different units. Since much of the information requested was likely to be available in institutional publications or lists,

306 *Appendix A*

programs were encouraged to submit available materials rather than recopying the information into the questionnaire.

The survey section of the questionnaire asked about the number of students in the program, and included more specific questions about various kinds of academic and non-academic programs. There were a number of questions concerning relations with other institutions, institutional support, faculty recruitment, hiring, and loss over the past several years and future plans for expansion or contraction of the program. Some questions were replicated from the 1984 Japan Foundation survey, but many were either new or were asked in a somewhat different way in order to obtain more complete data.

Data Collection and Data Processing

All academic and non-academic institutions on the mailing list were sent a packet of materials including the institutional questionnaire, a list of any Japan specialists that our computer had linked to the institution, and several copies of the specialist questionnaire to distribute to any other Japan specialists at the institution. The institutional respondent was asked to update the list of specialists and provide information on the current location of persons who were no longer with the institution. As with the specialist questionnaire, institutions that had submitted an entry for the 1989 directory received an "update" version of the directory entry form produced by the computer and containing the information they had previously submitted, with space for changes, plus the new survey section of the questionnaire. The "update" version also asked specifically for further information on all doctoral candidates reported to the 1989 directory project.

Institutions with large Japanese Studies programs were contacted in advance so the study could identify the appropriate staff person to whom the materials should be sent. Their packets included several copies of the institutional questionnaire, with instructions that different units such as a language department and a center should submit separate questionnaires for their own programs, but one institutional entry should contain general information for the institution as a whole.

A second mailing was sent to all institutions that did not respond to the first questionnaire, but subsequent follow-ups were more focused, since we expected that most institutions receiving the mailing would not have any Japanese Studies program. A computer program was developed to link the number of specialists associated with a particular institution who had returned questionnaires, the number of institutional questionnaires that had been returned, the number of Japan specialists reported on the institution's staff list, and whether a library questionnaire had been returned. The program then categorized these combinations so that more intense follow-up could be concentrated on institutions with some documented Japanese Studies activity, and missing materials for each institution could be readily identified. Follow-up was most intense for programs that had submitted an entry for the 1989 directory, and for institutions from which several Japan specialists had submitted questionnaires, but the institution had not responded. Through this focused follow-up system we were able to obtain an institutional questionnaire from virtually all institutions with five or more resident Japan specialists.

Data entry for the institutional entries was time-consuming because in many instances the narrative for the directory entry portion was extracted from institutional materials and edited by the project staff to fit the directory entry requirements. We also edited course lists to eliminate irrelevant courses and standardize the reporting format. Some institutional staff lists were edited to remove persons who were quite clearly not Japan specialists and who had not submitted directory entries. These were most often either specialists in other parts of Asia or persons associated with professional school programs who were teaching general courses that were not specifically related to Japan. After the data were entered, cleaned, and proofread, galley proofs of the directory entry were sent to each institution for a final check. Some staff changes and completion of doctorates were reported at this point, leading to another round of changes in the institutional, specialist, and doctoral candidates data.

Sample Definition, Sample Size, and Data Presentation

The institutional sample is defined as all institutions in the United States that were included in the 1995 directory. As with the specialist data, we must therefore review how the final selections for the directory were made. The institutional data also posed problems of sample definition. Two of these problems, how to define the limits for marginal cases and whether to reprint old data for non-responding institutions, paralleled the basic sample definition problems of the specialist data. The use of a national mailing list of academic institutions raised problems of inclusion when institutions submitted entries that included some useful survey data, but did not yet constitute a program in Japanese Studies. Mindful that many of our large Japanese Studies programs began with one or two courses just a decade or two ago, we have included entries that reported at least one academic course in either Japanese language or Japanese Studies, but have excluded those that offer only more general Asian Studies courses with some Japanese content. In some instances we received an entry from a library but not from the parent institution. In most cases the library did not actually have a Japanese collection, but in one or two cases we judged that the library was sufficiently important to warrant an institutional entry, so we constructed one by using as much general information about the institution's Japanese Studies program as we could find. These were cases where there were clearly Japan specialist faculty and a program at the institution, but we had not been able to get an entry from the institution despite repeated requests.

Similar measures were used with the handful of institutions that did not update their entries despite repeated requests. When we could verify that the same faculty and staff members remained at the institution and there was reason to believe that the program continued to exist, we reprinted the entry after removing from the staff list any persons who were known to have left that institution. The institutional data were therefore as current, accurate, and complete as we could make them, but some information was inevitably out of date the day after the directory was published.

The 1995 directory sample includes data from 333 institutional units at 247 academic and 28 non-academic institutions in the United States. These figures do not include libraries, which are tabulated separately below. In the 1995 directory the data from different institutional units, including libraries, were assembled in a fixed sequence and printed separately under the main institutional entry. For the survey analysis we have retained all the data from separate units, but have edited out any duplications in reporting, such as two units reporting the addition of the same faculty position. Some parts of the data, such as course and staff lists, were already constituted as data from a single institutional entity. In some other cases, such as academic program descriptions, we have combined the information from different units in order to produce a single institutional unit for analysis. Since much of the analysis centers on programs at academic institutions, and even some of these either do not have or did not report certain kinds of data, we report the relevant sample size for each segment of the analysis and for every table. For some parts of the institutional analysis we use the combined total of all items reported by all institutions, and these numbers are also reported as they occur in the text and tables.

Most of the survey analysis is restricted to those institutions whose entries appeared in the directory, but there are three notable exceptions. First, we retained for the survey analysis 99 questionnaires submitted by institutions that do not currently have a Japanese Studies program that would meet the minimum criteria for entry in the directory. Data reported by these institutions were incorporated into the analyses of institutional relations and of staff losses, gains, and future plans in order to produce a more complete picture of current and future Japanese Studies activity.

Second, despite our greater effort to solicit entries from academic institutions, there were still several hundred scholars in the specialist directory who were affiliated with academic institutions that did not submit a regular institutional entries. We have therefore once again compiled a separate listing of "other academic institutions with Japan specialist staff" from the institutional affiliations reported by specialists By adding to our database some systematic information on nearly all of the institutions on our national mailing list of academic institutions, we have also been able to use the minimal data we have on Japanese Studies at these 193 institutions (i.e., the bare fact that there is a resident Japan specialist at the institution) for a more comprehensive analysis of the spread of Japanese Studies. These additional data, taken from Peterson's Guides to Two-Year and Four-Year Colleges in the United States, enable us to make systematic comparisons of the rate of Japanese Studies presence at institutions with different characteristics, such as difficulty of entrance, size of the student body or faculty, and the availability of graduate degrees.

Third, we also compiled for the 1995 directory a supplemental list of "other non-academic institutions with Japan specialist staff" based on non-academic institutional affiliations reported by Japan specialists. This list of 149 institutions was particularly interesting because the affiliations listed range so far beyond the limits we had previously used to define "non-academic Japanese Studies institutions" for the questionnaire mailing list. We have been able to utilize this additional data in the survey analysis by coding the type of institution, although in this case we could not project the data against a national base as we could for the academic institutions.

JAPANESE STUDIES LIBRARIES

We greatly expanded our coverage of the library resources for Japanese Studies in the United States, both by asking a broader range of questions about access to library and information resources, and by posing those questions directly to the librarians with a separate questionnaire and mailing.

Mailing List

The same commercial mailing list of academic institutions in the United States, augmented by the list of non-academic institutions described above, was used for a separate mailing to the librarians at those institutions. For institutions known to have a staffed Japanese collection, the name and address of the appropriate staff person as reported in the directory published by the Committee on East Asian Libraries was substituted for the generic institutional library addressee.

Questionnaire

The library questionnaire was developed in close cooperation with the National Coordinating Committee for Japanese Libraries. Like the other instruments, the library questionnaire contained both directory information and survey questions. The directory entry data included the questions on the size of the collection in both Japanese and western languages, and the descriptions of special collection strengths that were part of the regular institutional directory questionnaire for the 1989 directory, plus additional questions on online catalogs and the accessibility of the collection to outside users, and on how the Japanese collection is staffed and shelved. The survey section contained questions about collection use, acquisition priorities, institutional support for the library, faculty input into acquisitions decisions, and how librarians assist users who need materials that are not in the collection.

Data Collection, Data Processing, and Sample Definition

Library questionnaires were sent directly to librarians at the institutions on the national mailing list. Each mailing also included copies of the Japan specialist questionnaire so that qualified library staff would be included in the Japan specialist directory and survey. A copy of the library questionnaire was also included in the institutional mailing. At the suggestion of Japanese librarians we also eliminated some duplicate work for them and standardized our reporting of collection size by utilizing the data they already report annually to the Committee on East Asian Libraries. This covered only the reporting of Japanese language materials held in all of the staffed Japanese collections. The reporting of western language materials on Japan, and of Japanese and western language materials at smaller collections that do not have a specialized Japanese librarian, was handled directly through the questionnaire administration. This produced some obvious anomalies that made us reluctant to use the data on western language materials, which some librarians seemed to be reporting for the entire library and not for materials specifically about Japan.

Except for a small number of free-standing libraries and libraries attached to non-academic institutions, the library information was considered to be a segment of the institutional entry, so the follow-up was conducted primarily through the coordinated follow-up procedure described above for institutions. In addition, we had a good list of the staffed Japanese collections in the United States, so there was much less chance of discovering a large unknown Japanese library collection through the general survey than of discovering an unknown Japanese Studies program. Rather, the purpose of the broad mailing was to clarify just how limited the library resources for the study of Japan are, and to find out what support librarians provide when the needed library materials are not available locally. The librarians at staffed Japanese collections provided excellent cooperation with the study, and little follow-up was needed. For institutions with small Japanese Studies programs and no Japanese librarian, we used the library questionnaire if we received one, but did not engage in intensive follow-up to obtain one. Library follow-up was thus focused on the few staffed Japanese collections that required a reminder, and institutions with mid-sized Japanese Studies programs but without a Japanese librarian, where the availability of library materials and support could be the most problematic aspect of the program. A few institutions with substantial Japanese Studies programs also reported library data independently for two separately-administered library collections or divisions. Thus the library sample contains 72 library units at 58 academic and 10 non-academic institutions. However, some of these units have very small, specialized collections.

We also received 82 library questionnaires from institutions with no Japanese Studies program and virtually no materials on Japan in any language. These questionnaires were not included in the directory because they were not connected to an institutional entry and did not contain sufficient independent information to warrant inclusion. We retained their data for the survey analysis, but were unable to make much use of it except to make the important negative point that these institutions have no library resources on Japan.

Doctoral Candidates

The study did not attempt to collect data directly from doctoral candidates. Instead, following the strategy used in the 1989 directory, both Japan specialists and Japanese Studies institutions were asked to report basic information about doctoral candidates in Japan-related fields. The requested information included the name of the candidate, departmental affiliation, and the topic or title of the dissertation. As noted above, both individual Japan specialists and Japanese Studies institutions that had entries in the 1989 directory received an update version of the 1995 questionnaire produced by the computer, which contained the information they had submitted in 1989 on doctoral candidates and asked for follow-up information. They were also asked to report both current doctoral candidates and any candidates not previously reported who had completed their dissertations in the interval between the two directories and might have slipped through the cracks in both surveys.

Data from the institutional and specialist sources was combined and cleaned of duplicates to produce a single list of 803 current doctoral candidates for the 1995 directory. The follow-up data on candidates previously reported in the 1989 study, along with additional information from external sources, was used to trace completion and drop-out rates for the 1989 cohort of doctoral candidates and to identify the amount of overlap between the 1989 and 1995 doctoral candidate lists. The data are somewhat ambiguous because institutions and even departments at the same institution vary considerably in the point at which they identify graduate students as doctoral candidates. Given the indirect nature of the data collection procedure we did not attempt to eliminate candidates from the list, so long as they had been identified by either the institution or a faculty Japan specialist as working in Japanese Studies.

The more difficult problem was deciding when they no longer belonged on the list. As noted earlier, many doctoral candidates also submitted questionnaires for the Japan specialist directory. Following the practice of the 1989 directory study, we excluded from the Japan specialist directory entries from persons who were primarily graduate students, but we accepted entries from persons who were working in a professional capacity as Japan specialists before completing their degree, and of course from those who had completed their doctorate. These determinations wee made after the data had been entered and cleaned. Before the publication of the directory we conducted a final round of follow-up queries with institutions and the candidates themselves, to determine which doctoral candidates had completed their degrees. If the degree was completed and the individual had already submitted an entry for the Japan specialist directory, we simply recoded the entry as accepted and included it in the directory. However, if the candidate had completed the degree but had not submitted a directory entry, we did not want to eliminate that person from both listings and thereby lose track of a legitimate Japan specialist. We therefore retained such new doctorates in the doctoral candidates list, marking their names with an asterisk in the published list to indicate completion.

Because of these data collection and data management procedures the doctoral candidates list is also a significant source of data for the survey analysis. We have not used it for a separate chapter on doctoral candidates, but instead have used relevant parts of the data on doctoral candidates to extend the overall analysis at several points.

Appendix B

UNDERGRADUATE PROGRAMS IN JAPANESE STUDIES

Minimal Undergraduate Program

Adams State College
Antioch College
Arkansas State University
Bakersfield College
Bentley College
Bradley University
Bridgewater State College
Brookdale Community College
Bucks County Community College
California State University at
   Bakersfield
California State University at
   Northridge
California State University at
   San Bernardino
Centenary College
Central Missouri State University
Central Washington University
Cleveland State University
College of Wooster
Columbia College
County College of Morris
Dakota Wesleyan University
Danville Community College
Don Bosco Technological
   Institute
Drake University
Elizabethtown College
Eureka College
Francis Marion College
Fresno Pacific College
Illinois Central College
Illinois Wesleyan University
International Training College
Johns Hopkins University
Juniata College
Kansas City Art Institute
Kapiolani Community College
Kent State University

La Grange College
La Verne University
Lewis-Clark State College
Lincoln University
Lindenwood College
Loyola University
Loyola University of Chicago
Marylhurst College
Maryville College
Metropolitan State University
Miami-Dade College New World
   Center
Mills College
Mission College
Missouri Southern College
Moberly Junior College
Montgomery Jr. College
Morgan State College
Mt. Hood Community College
Muhlenberg College
Naval Postgraduate School
Nazareth College
North Carolina Agricultural and
   Technical University
Northampton County Area College
Northeastern Junior College
Northwood College Institute
Oakland Community College at
   Auburn Hills
Otterbein College
Pennsylvania State University,
   State College Campus
Pasadena City College
Pepperdine University at Malibu
Pitzer College
Polk Community College
Purdue University, Calumet Campus
Saddleback Community College
St. Bonaventure University

Santa Barbara City College
Scottsdale Community College
Seattle Central Community College
Shippensburg State University
Siena Heights College
Sinclair Community College
Snow College
South Dakota School of Mines
and Technology
Southeastern Massachusetts
University
Southeastern State University
Southern California Institute of
Architecture
Southwestern University
State University of New York
College at Oneonta
Stephens College

The American University
Tidewater Community College
Union College
Union University
University of Alaska at Juneau
University of Arkansas
University of Pittsburgh at
Johnstown
University of Tennessee at
Chattanooga
University of Tennessee at Martin
University of Tulsa
University of Wisconsin at
Whitewater
Virginia Polytechnic State
University
West Georgia College
Wheeling College

Limited Undergraduate Program

Augustana College
Baylor University
Bowdoin College
Brandeis University
Clark University
Colby College
College of St. Benedict
De Paul University
Everett Community College
Findlay College
La Salle University
Le Moyne College
Marietta College
Mount Union College

Mundelein College
Northern Illinois University
Northern Kentucky University
Oakton Community College
Rice University
Southern Methodist University
University of Illinois at Chicago
University of Nevada
Weber State College
Western Oregon State College
William Jewell College

Undergraduate Area Program

California State University at Chico
California State University at
Fullerton
California State University at Hayward
California State University at Los Angeles
City College of The City University of
New York
Colgate University
George Washington University
Hawaii Pacific University
Kalamazoo College
Lake Forest College
Lehigh University

Northwestern University
Oakland University
Occidental College
Purdue University
Rhodes College
St. Cloud State University
Skidmore College
Southern Illinois University
State University of New York at
Binghamton
State University of New York College at
New Paltz
Syracuse University

Temple University
University of Cincinnati
University of Georgia
University of Missouri
University of Nebraska
University of New Mexico
University of Oklahoma
University of Puget Sound

University of Tennessee
University of Toledo
University of Wisconsin at Oshkosh
Washington State University
Western Michigan University
Whitman College
Wittenberg University

Full Undergraduate Program

Amherst College
Arizona State University
Bowling Green State University
Brigham Young University
Brown University
Bucknell University
Case Western Reserve University
Chaminade University of Honolulu
College of William and Mary
Columbia University
Connecticut College
Cornell University
De Pauw University
Duke University
Earlham College
Foothill College
Georgetown University
Harvard University
Illinois State University
Indiana University
Manhattanville College
Massachusetts Institute of Technology
Miami University
Middlebury College
Monterey Institute of International Studies
North Carolina State University
Oberlin College
Ohio State University
Old Dominion University
Portland State University
Princeton University
Rutgers State University
St. Olaf College
San Diego State University
San Jose State University
Smith College
Stanford University
State University of New York at Albany
State University of New York at Buffalo
Trinity College
University of Arizona

University of California at Berkeley
University of California at Davis
University of California at Irvine
University of California at Los Angeles
University of California at San Diego
University of California at Santa Barbara
University of Chicago
University of Colorado
University of Delaware
University of Florida
University of Hawaii at Hilo
University of Hawaii at Manoa
University of Illinois
University of Iowa
University of Kansas
University of Maryland
University of Massachusetts
University of Massachusetts at Boston
University of Michigan
University of Minnesota
University of New Hampshire
University of North Carolina
University of Oregon
University of Pennsylvania
University of Pittsburgh
University of Rochester
University of Southern California
University of Texas at Austin
University of The Pacific
University of Utah
University of Vermont
University of Washington
University of Wisconsin
Washington and Lee University
Washington University
Wellesley College
Wesleyan University
West Virginia University
Williams College
Yale University

Appendix C

GRADUATE PROGRAMS IN JAPANESE STUDIES

MA Programs

Arizona State University
Brigham Young University
Brown University
California State University at Chico
Chaminade University of Honolulu
George Washington University
Johns Hopkins University
Monterey Institute of International Studies
Old Dominion University

Portland State University
Rutgers State University
San Diego State University
University of Colorado
University of Massachusetts
University of Oklahoma
University of The Pacific
University of Virginia

Limited Graduate Programs

Georgetown University
State University of New York at Buffalo
University of Arizona
University of California at Davis
University of California at Irvine
University of California at San Diego
University of California at Santa Barbara
University of Iowa

University of Maryland
University of Minnesota
University of Oregon
University of Pennsylvania
University of Southern California
University of Texas at Austin
Washington University

Full Graduate Programs

Columbia University
Cornell University
Duke University
Harvard University
Indiana University
Ohio State University
Princeton University
Stanford University
University of California at Berkeley
University of California at Los Angeles
University of Chicago
University of Hawaii at Manoa
University of Illinois

University of Kansas
University of Michigan
University of Pittsburgh
University of Washington
University of Wisconsin
Yale University

Index

C

California • 8, 43, 206, 218, 219, 220, 221, 250, 254, 313, 314, 315, 317
Canada • xvii, xviii, 5, 19, 20, 21, 44, 167, 253, 259, 297, 302, 304
challenges for the 1990s • 281
China • 3, 7, 73, 74, 265, 291, 301
Claremont colleges • 219
Columbia University • 6, 8, 33, 43, 218, 219, 220, 221, 254, 313, 315, 317
Committee on East Asian Libraries • 249, 309, 310
communications • xx, 171, 263
comparative research • 158, 290
computers • xx, 171, 256, 257, 263, 293, 298, 300, 306, 311
conferences • 105, 106, 109, 115, 116, 162, 275, 276, 277, 295
Connecticut • 43, 315
consulting • 65, 103, 104, 134, 136, 270
consulting firms • 65
contemporary Japan • 40, 48, 66, 71, 72, 129, 155, 218, 295
Cornell University • 219, 220, 221, 254, 315, 317
corporations • 65, 108, 271, 305
courses • 129, 281, 287; area • 167, 169, 170, 171, 172, 174, 175, 179, 182, 186, 189, 193, 198, 202, 213, 236, 237; enrollment • 181, 184, 189, 213; exclusively on Japan • 41, 171, 172, 174, 175, 176, 177, 178, 179, 182, 183, 184, 189, 198, 202, 203, 209, 213, 237, 281, 289; graduate-level • 170, 171, 173, 180, 181, 182, 184, 207, 232, 234; Japanese language • 167, 168, 169, 185, 186, 187, 188, 189, 202, 213, 237, 281, 287, 289, 295, 304; language • 14, 94, 167, 168, 169, 179, 185, 186, 187, 188, 189, 197, 202, 213, 232, 237, 281, 287, 289, 295, 304; lower-division • 169, 170, 232; multinational • 171, 175, 176, 177, 178, 179, 183, 184, 189, 229, 287; undergraduate • 181, 183, 232, 237; upper-division • 170
CULCON • 4, 33, 44, 45, 48, 64, 170, 171, 172, 173, 180, 181, 185, 197, 198, 202, 204, 214, 216, 217, 219, 249

CULCON Report, 1977 • 33, 45, 48, 64, 170, 171, 172, 173, 180, 185, 197, 198, 202, 204, 217, 219, 249
Culter, Suzanne • xx, 5

D

data collection procedures • xvii, xix, xx, 13, 21, 35, 48, 50, 53, 54, 150, 214, 297, 312
databases, bibliographic • 163, 248, 258
Delaware • 43, 315
Diet Library • 252, 256, 258
differentiation • 9, 10, 13, 14, 15, 30, 31, 48, 50, 66, 69, 74, 128, 134, 136, 142, 146, 155, 156, 207, 248, 285, 286, 287, 294
Directory of Japan Specialists and Japanese Studies Institutions • 5, 14, 20, 51; 1989 edition • 5, 18, 20, 21, 22, 23, 24, 25, 27, 29, 31, 32, 33, 34, 35, 44, 51, 64, 75, 76, 77, 171, 195, 274, 298, 299, 300, 301, 302, 303, 304, 305, 306, 307, 310, 311, 312; 1995 edition • xviii, 19, 20, 21, 22, 23, 24, 25, 26, 27, 28, 29, 30, 31, 32, 33, 34, 35, 36, 38, 40, 45, 52, 64, 71, 75, 76, 77, 84, 152, 168, 195, 204, 214, 215, 218, 249, 250, 273, 301, 307, 308, 309, 311
disciplinary associations • 117
Dissertations Abstracts • 35
District of Columbia • 43
doctoral candidates • 13, 15, 25, 33, 34, 35, 36, 37, 38, 39, 40, 41, 42, 96, 195, 212, 213, 214, 216, 217, 218, 220, 221, 222, 223, 244, 246, 288, 295, 297, 298, 302, 305, 306, 307, 311, 312; completion rates • 36
doctoral dissertation topic • 33, 38, 39, 41, 100, 212; not on Japan • 145, 148; on Japan • 98, 99, 100
Doctoral Dissertations on Asia • 35, 214
Duke University • 219, 221, 254, 315, 317

E

East Asia • 39, 41, 63, 73, 170, 171, 176, 178, 196, 198, 207, 208, 209, 210, 211, 212, 213, 249, 270, 287, 309, 310

DATE DUE

Demco, Inc. 38-293